The Mormon Presence in Canada

The Mormon Presence
in Canada

EDITED BY

Brigham Y. Card

Herbert C. Northcott

John E. Foster

Howard Palmer

George K. Jarvis

THE UNIVERSITY OF ALBERTA PRESS

First published by
The University of Alberta Press
Athabasca Hall
Edmonton, Alberta
Canada T6G 2E8

Copyright © The University of Alberta Press 1990

ISBN 0-88864-212-1

Canadian Cataloging in Publication Data

The Mormon presence in Canada

Includes bibliographical references.
ISBN 0-88864-212-1

1. Mormons - Canada - History. I. Card, B. Y.
(Brigham Young), 1914-
FC106.M8M67 1990   289.3'71   C90-091079-8
F1035.M8M67 1990

This book has been printed on acid-free paper. ∞

Typesetting by Pièce de Résistance Ltée., Edmonton, Alberta, Canada

Printed by Gagné Printing Ltd., Louiseville, Quebec, Canada

CONTENTS

CONTRIBUTORS AND EDITORS

LEONARD J. ARRINGTON is senior research historian in the Charles Redd Center for Western Studies and in the Joseph Fielding Smith Institute for Church History, Brigham Young University, Provo, Utah. From 1972 to 1980 he was church historian and director of the Church History Division of the Church of Jesus Christ of Latter-day Saints, Salt Lake City, Utah.

MAUREEN URSENBACH BEECHER is professor of English and research associate of the Joseph Fielding Smith Institute for Church History, Brigham Young University, Provo, Utah.

RICHARD E. BENNETT is head of the Department of Archives and Special Collections, University of Manitoba, Winnipeg.

BRIGHAM Y. CARD is professor emeritus of sociology of education, Department of Educational Foundations, University of Alberta, Edmonton.

A. A. DEN OTTER is professor of history, Memorial University, St. John's, Newfoundland.

DAVID K. ELTON is professor of political science, University of Lethbridge, Alberta, and president of the Canada West Foundation Public Policy Institute, Calgary, Alberta.

JESSIE L. EMBRY is director of the Oral History Program of the Charles Redd Center for Western Studies, Brigham Young University, Provo, Utah.

JOHN E. FOSTER is professor of history, University of Alberta, Edmonton.

B. CARMON HARDY is professor of history, California State University, Fullerton.

GEORGE K. JARVIS is professor of sociology, University of Alberta, Edmonton.

DEAN R. LOUDER est professeur titulaire de géographie, Université Laval, Ste-Foy, Québec.

ARMAND L. MAUSS is professor of sociology, Washington State University, Pullman.

ROBERT J. MCCUE is professor of history, University of Victoria, British Columbia.

HERBERT C. NORTHCOTT is professor of sociology, University of Alberta, Edmonton.

BYRON C. PALMER is a consulting engineer with U.M.A. Engineering, Limited, Lethbridge, Alberta.

CRAIG J. PALMER was in 1987 a soil scientist with Alberta Department of the Environment at Lethbridge. Currently, he is a research specialist in soil pollution from acid rain, Oregon State University, Corvallis.

HOWARD PALMER is professor of history, University of Calgary, Alberta.

KEITH PARRY is professor of anthropology, University of Lethbridge, Alberta.

ANTHONY W. RASPORICH is professor of history and the dean of the Faculty of Social Sciences, University of Calgary, Alberta.

WILLIAM A. WILSON is professor and chairman of the Department of English, Brigham Young University, Provo, Utah.

PREFACE

THIS BOOK IS THE first multidisciplinary scholarly work on Mormons in Canada. It deals with a people whose presence in Canada spans over a century and a half. During this period, Canadian Mormons have been successively emigrant converts leaving for the United States; political refugee Mormons from Cache Valley, Utah; immigrant community builders and irrigationists from Utah and Idaho; and in recent times a distinctive, growing body of believers, extending from coast to coast, whose numbers have tripled in the last three decades. To describe and explain these people in their Canadian, North American and world contexts is the task initiated by the Canadian and American scholars who have contributed to this volume.

The beginning of this work can be traced to the centennial of the arrival of the first Mormon settlers—one of the founding peoples of Alberta—in the North-West Territories, Provisional District of Alberta, in 1887. During the planning of the 1987 centennial celebration, it became apparent that scholarship on Mormons in Canada was underdeveloped, and that no major work had been attempted in the recent decades of greatest Mormon growth. There was underdevelopment in relation to archival records, biographies, bibliographies, collections of books and periodicals in libraries, known networks of interested scholars, associations to promote scholarly study of Mormons, and financial resources for such studies. This was in marked contrast to the situation in the United States, where Mormon studies was a burgeoning field, having every kind of resource that Canadians lacked and a high rate of scholarly output. Nevertheless, an informal survey identified a number of scholars whose research and interests included Canadian Mormons. When Dr. Baha Abu-Laban, then Associate Vice-President of Research at the University of Alberta, was consulted about a seminar or conference on how to legitimate the study of Mormons in Canada, he challenged: "Why don't you hold a major national conference on Mormons in Canada and give it a title that means something, such as "The Mormon Presence in Canada?" He assured the Mormon and non-Mormon professors making the inquiry that the University would be interested in this kind of scholarly event.

This challenge resulted in both a major conference, "The Mormon Presence in Canada, 1830, 1887, 1987: A North American Ethno-religious People in Canadian Cultures," and the Mormon Folk Culture Festival arranged to complement the conference. Both were held in Edmonton, at the University of Alberta and at the auditorium of the Provincial Museum of Alberta, 6-9 May 1987. Eighty scholars from all parts of Canada and from the United States were presenters of papers, discussants or chairpersons for sessions in which historians, social scientists, two professional agriculturalists and a leading health expert probed the past and present of Mormons in Canada. Seventeen of the key papers, edited and revised, were selected for this volume by an editorial committee of sociologists and historians.

Putting the varied experiences of Canadian Mormons to the pages of a book is a complex endeavor, involving not only scholars but also many other indispensible persons and agencies. The result is a volume for scholars and interested nonacademics who wish to gain a better understanding of the Mormon experience in Canada. The volume's essays and unique assemblage of documentation will prove of interest to historians, social scientists and scholars in the humanities—particularly those in Canadian, American, ethnic, and religious studies. Scholars in Mormon studies will find in this work a further example of a field on its way to becoming more international and multicultural. It is hoped that the scholarship represented in this volume will add to the heritage of learning from which any group or people can examine their past, interpret their present, and anticipate a future.

ACKNOWLEDGMENTS

THE EDITORS TAKE final responsibility for the selection of papers and other writings in this volume. Appreciation is expressed to the authors who painstakingly revised their papers for publication.

The Mormon Presence in Canada Conference of 6-9 May 1987 was sponsored by the Faculty of Arts and the Faculty of Education, University of Alberta. These faculties not only contributed to the Committee entrusted to implement the Conference, but have also continued to be supportive in the production of this volume. The University of Alberta Press and Utah State University Press provided invaluable help in bringing this project to fruition.

The Conference was supported by the University of Alberta Conference Fund and other grants, and by aid from the Social Sciences and Humanities Research Council of Canada and from Multiculturalism Canada. In addition, corporate and private donations were contributed for the Conference and for this publication. This broad range of support is gratefully acknowledged. The Provincial Museum of Alberta, the Provincial Archives of Alberta, and Alberta Culture all provided suggestions and encouragement.

Thanks should be given also to the various archives whose services have been used by the editors and writers, and who have assisted in providing a number of the illustrations that have been used. We are indebted to the Provincial Archives of Alberta; the archives of the Glenbow Museum; the Church History Department Archives of the Church of Jesus Christ of Latter-day Saints; the Archives of the History Commission of the Reorganized Church of Jesus Christ of Latter-day Saints; the Cardston and District Historical Society; and the archives of the University of Alberta, Brigham Young University and Utah State University. Photographs are credited as they appear in the book.

Bringing out this volume has also required specialized services, among which are the cartography of Michael Fisher, and the editorial and word-processing skills of Laura Hargrave, Jane Macovichuk, Judy Mitchell and Shirley Stawnychy. David Evans did the copy editing and John Fisher provided logistical support. Appreciation is expressed to many others who have given their time, assistance and sustained support to this work.

Finally, a word of general appreciation is stated. This work represents the convergence of professional scholars and many nonprofessionals from the multifaith and multicultural segments of Canada and the United States. Their interest, valuable suggestions and assistance have helped transform this volume from a vision to a reality, to part of a literary and scholarly legacy that can be shared and, in the idiom of Mormon people, "added upon."

INTRODUCTION

To MOST CANADIANS the Mormon presence in Canada is relatively unimportant. Mormons in Canada are few in number, and, through much of their history have been tucked away in the southwestern corner of the Province of Alberta. In recent years, however, their growing numbers and their migration to all parts of the country invite attention to their unique history and their characteristics as a people. As one inspects more closely the Mormons in Canada, several underlying themes emerge. The strongest theme is recognition that "...every country or distinctive community has its own effective contribution to make to the broad science of society," as claimed by the late Robert M. MacIver in defining the scope of sociology.[1] From this viewpoint, the sociology and history of Canada, of the United States, and of the Mormons as a people, a continuing socio-religious movement, and an institutionalized church—remain incomplete without a study of Mormons in Canada.

Another important theme is migration, a theme common to the history of Canadians, Americans and Mormons. In the case of Mormons, this is cause for reflection and celebration, as they recall migration leading to the founding of Salt Lake City and other Great Basin communities in the American West, and of Mormon settlements in southwestern Alberta. Beginning in the 1830s, Mormon migrations from Canada anticipated and paralleled the movement of over a million-and-a-half Canadians to the United States in the nineteenth century. As that century drew to a close, and as American homestead land became scarce, the Mormon migration from northern Utah to Canada in 1887 was part of a vanguard for some two million people from the United States, who sought opportunities in

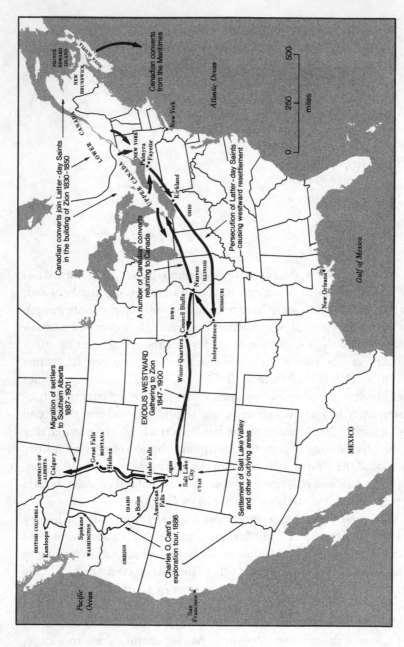

19th Century Movement of Mormon people from and to Canada

Canada up to 1931.[2] Half the chapters in this volume deal explicitly with Mormon migrations that were "integral" to North America as they involved crossing and recrossing the Canada-United States border.[3]

Canada's asymmetry and diversity within a North American context are also thematic in this volume, presumably influencing the Mormon experience in the United States and Canada and helping delineate the size, distribution and nature of the Canadian Mormon presence. Continentally, Canada's "northernness," which blended perceptually with the country's climate, geography, size of population, and lesser economic and political clout, presented a continuing and pervasive difference from the United States.[4] There was a divergence in the histories of the two countries that was inescapable: the revolutionary beginnings of the United States, and the Canadian beginnings of French settlement, conquest, colonial administration, Loyalist immigration, and nationhood out of political deadlock and a declining British imperialism. The two countries diverged in their experiences with native Americans, blacks, and ethnic peoples. The nature of a Mormon presence north of the border most probably reflects some less obvious cultural differences, such as (1) the greater impact of regions in Canadian life; (2) the role of the provinces in the national polity; (3) a stronger liberalism among all Canadian political parties in recent years than that found among American Republicans and Democrats; (4) a greater emphasis in Canada on equalitarianism expressed in redistributive programs and a universalized health-care system; and (5) a more protected environment for ethnic groups, expressed in the nineteenth century in settlement regulations and privileges associated with the "Dominion Land Policy" and, in modern times, as officially recognized multiculturalism. A most obvious cultural difference was Canada's constitutionally entrenched bilingualism, an anglophone and a francophone Canada.[5] The Canadian Mormon experience includes being exposed to these and other differences between the two countries. Ascertaining the extent to which such exposure occurred among Canada's Mormons in the past, and still takes place as part of present Mormon and Canadian life, is a challenging scholarly pursuit.

A fourth pervasive theme is curiosity about how Mormons, often perceived as similar in attributes and behavior, vary among themselves in Canada, between Canada and the United States, and between Canada and other lands. An understanding of the Canadian Mormon presence can scarcely exist without a knowledge of the commonalities and differences among Mormons in Canada and other places, in particular the United States.

One consequence of pursuing such themes is that a comparative approach becomes virtually imperative for studying Canada's Mormons. The comparative stance of scholarship in Canadian and religious studies can be transferred to the study of Canada's Mormons.

A consequence of being curious about Mormons and their differences in Canada or elsewhere is the scholarly necessity of understanding Mormon history and growth, including organizational and ideological developments. Fortunately, the course of Mormon history in its American setting has been and continues to be studied carefully. Two landmark studies appeared in the 1950s, Thomas F. O'Dea's *The Mormons*,[6] written from a sociology of religion perspective, and Leonard J. Arrington's *Great Basin Kingdom: An Economic History of the Latter-day Saints, 1830-1900*.[7] More recent works by historians include James B. Allen's and Glen M. Leonard's comprehensive *The Story of the Latter-day Saints*,[8] Leonard J. Arrington's and Davis Bitton's more thematic *The Mormon Experience: A History of the Latter-day Saints*,[9] and Jan Shipps's interpretive *Mormonism: The Story of a New Religious Tradition*.[10] The volume and scope of scholarly works on Mormons in the past four decades, a phenomenon in its own right, has become a useful and impressive resource for the study of Mormons in Canada and other lands. As a new entrant into the highly competitive and expansive world of scholarship, this emergent field is commonly referred to as "Mormon Studies."

As for Mormon phenomena, historically concentrated in the United States, only a bare description need be given here. Mormon phenomena can be characterized as complex, innovative, constantly in motion, often accompanied by stress and controversy and involved paradoxically in the main currents of social change. The focal phenomenon is the Church of Jesus Christ of Latter-day Saints, freely nicknamed "Mormon" almost from its inception in 1830—mainly because of its *Book of Mormon*.[11]

Its founder was Joseph Smith, a farm youth from upstate New York, whose religious experiences convinced him and others that he was to be the prophet of a restored primitive Christianity, with a mission to call America and the world to repentance, to lay the foundation for a literal new Zion in America, and to prepare for the imminent return of Jesus Christ as the Messiah and head of an earthly Kingdom of God. His successor prophet-leaders have come from several occupations: a glazier-carpenter; a former British-born Canadian Methodist preacher and the initiator of the 1887 Mormon migration to Canada; a miller; farmers; teachers; a historian; a municipal administrator; and a professional agriculturalist.[12] Members have been drawn from many walks of life and numerous countries. Leaders and members make up a lay ecclesiastical organization that has proven unusually durable and adaptable.

Mormon phenomena in Canada have tended to be comparatively small-scale and understudied. There was a beginning period, from 1830 to 1850, when approximately two thousand Mormon converts left eastern Canada to "gather" with the Saints trying to establish themselves first in the Midwest and then in the Great Basin of western America. From 1860 to 1886 there was an interlude with little Mormon presence, except as isolated families, migrant workers, a few travellers and considerable negative publicity about Mormons emanating from the United States. Section I, with its four chapters, deals with these beginnings.

An obvious, although minuscule Mormon presence, consisting of political refugees from the American crusade against Mormon polygamy, arrived in 1887 to settle on a limited area of southwestern Alberta. The story of their settlement, community building, irrigation development and population growth, which was concentrated in "Mormon Country" as their corner of Canada came to be known, is an essential prelude to understanding the Canadian reaction to the Mormons, to their relationships to other colonizing groups, and to their folklore. This story is told in Section II, making full use of the growing scholarly knowledge of Canadian history, social science and Mormon studies.

The most controversial aspect of the Mormon presence in the United States—and by reputation in Canada—was Mormon nineteenth-century plural marriage, technically polygyny but popularly named polygamy. Not surprisingly, a significant literature on this subject exists in the United States, but until 1985 there was virtually no scholarly work on this aspect of the Canadian Mormon presence. Further, whereas much is recorded of male roles in Mormon settlement, especially Mormon leaders, usually little mention is made of the role of females in the pioneering process. The Canadian Mormon adaptations of marriage patterns to the Canadian situation, in comparison with adaptations made in the United States and Mexico, are addressed in Section III, which also includes an account of the settlement process from the women's perspective.

As an immigrant people become accepted by, and accepting of, a host society, their presence is frequently noted and also assessed by their behavior in economic and political activities. This line of inquiry, an important component of Canadian ethnic studies, takes on added significance when Alberta's Mormons are regarded as one of the province's founding peoples. A first step towards examining Mormon economic and political behavior is taken in Section IV, where Mormon behavior in agriculture and politics, primarily in Alberta but also elsewhere in Canada, is examined.

If Alberta constitutes a Canadian Mormon core or heartland in any way analagous to Utah for the United States, then as out-migration occurs and as new converts join the faith, the vision of a Mormon presence must become national rather than regional. In both countries, the Mormons' national presence is in need of accurate assessment. This is initiated in Section V, where the Canadian Mormon family and the Canadian Mormon identity are examined.

One of the features of Mormon phenomena attracting scholarly attention is their peoplehood. Several American scholars have considered Mormons, especially the generations reared in the Great Basin area, as tending to be an indigenous North American ethnic people. Others have dissented from this view on various grounds, most recently because of the growing stature of the Mormon Church as a major American denomination domestically and as a significant body internationally. There have been ideological shifts away from nineteenth-century emphases on the meaning of Mormon peoplehood.[13] In Canada, since 1887, there has been little question that Mormons in southern Alberta were an ethno-religious people in their own eyes and in the eyes of their native Indian and anglophone neighbors. To what extent Canadian Mormons were and continue to be an ethno-religious people, or simply a religious people, is an intriguing line of inquiry, pursued sociologically and anthropologically in Section VI.

It is appropriate now to ask, What has been the scholarly response to Canada's Mormons, at least since the Alberta period of settlement? What knowledge base, apart from this work, is accessible to scholars? What patterns are discernible?

From 1887 to around 1931,[14] the knowledge response to Canada's Mormons by scholars and numerous others was primarily critical. The controversial literature emanating from the United States on Mormons was freely used and frequently applied uncritically to Canada's Mormons. This knowledge pattern is extensively examined for early British Columbia by Robert McCue in Chapter 3 and by Howard Palmer for anglophone Canada in Chapter 6.

A pattern of grounded-in-Canada empiricism began with the *Canadian Frontiers of Settlement Series*,[15] a major undertaking begun in the 1930s to record for posterity an authentic account of western Canadian settlement and development. This was published in a series of nine volumes, with Volume VII, attributed to C.A. Dawson, a McGill University sociologist,

containing a section specifically on Mormons in western Canada.[16] The
entire volume, published in 1936, was devoted to the group settlement of
ethnic peoples in the Canadian West, and Mormons were one of the five
groups studied. Dawson recruited a Mormon rural sociologist, Lowry
Nelson, from Utah to conduct an in-depth study of the Canadian Mormon
settlements. Nelson's study followed the 1931 historical account of Mormon
settlement by Donald W. Buchanan, a Lethbridge Rhodes scholar, appearing in the *Canadian Geographical Journal*.[17] Nelson's work was clearly a landmark event in the study of Canada's Mormons. His use of the Canadian
Census and other sources, combined with personal documents, including
diaries and letters, interviews and church documents, established a pattern
for empirical study that has been followed by John Lehr and Lynn Rosenvall, geographers; by Howard Palmer, ethnohistorian; and by Archie G.
Wilcox, Melvin S. Tagg, A. James Hudson, John R. Hicken and others in
their graduate research.[18]

The work of Nelson and subsequent scholars carried on a pattern of con-
centrating on southern Alberta Mormons. This was evident in the 1968
study, by American irrigation historian Lawrence B. Lee, of Mormon settlement and irrigation, and of the collaborative roles of the Canadian federal
government.[19] In the 1970s, anthropologist Keith Parry began studying the
relationships between southern Alberta Mormons and Blood Indians.[20]
Gisela Demharter, a West German American studies scholar, pursued a doctoral study of the socialization of Mormon daughters in southwestern Alberta
in the 1980s.[21] In short, southern Alberta's Mormons have been a scholarly
focus for a range of scholars for over fifty years.

Apart from Section V's two chapters, Canada's Mormons nationwide
have been studied only in the 1960s, when Melvin S. Tagg wrote his doctoral thesis at Brigham Young University, entitled "A History of the Church
of Jesus Christ of Latter-day Saints in Canada, 1830-1963." He later col-
laborated with Asael E. Palmer to bring out, in 1968, *A History of the
Mormon Church in Canada*,[22] which added a detailed history of each
Mormon organizational unit in Canada to a digest of Tagg's earlier study.

The cross-national possibilities for the study of Canada's Mormons have
remained but a glimmer, lighted by two researchers. In 1977, Université
Laval geographer Dean R. Louder presented a paper, unpublished, to the
American Association of Geographers on "Orthogenetic Cities: Quebec and
Salt Lake." Though not on Canada's Mormons, it illustrated an important
line of comparison between Utah Mormons and French Canada. A year later,
O. Kendall White Jr. linked Canada's Mormons with those in the United

States to support his thesis that the assimilation of Mormons in the United States and Canada was contingent on accommodating religious jurisdiction to the legitimacy of the nation-state.[23]

Although an inventory of Mormons in Canada as a subject for studies in religion has yet to be accomplished, available evidence suggests that such an inventory would be modest in size. In his 1948 work on relationships between religion and the development of Canada, S.D. Clark gave passing mention to the early Canadian Mormons who migrated southward.[24] In W.E. Mann's 1955 *Sect, Cult and Church in Alberta*, number six in the *Social Credit in Alberta Series* (edited by Clark), Mormons along with the Orthodox Church were excluded from the research design in order to include only "Protestant" churches.[25] (Connections between Alberta's Mormons and Social Credit are examined in the present volume's chapter on government in Section IV.) More recently, two sociologists, Harry H. Hiller[26] and Reginald W. Bibby,[27] have included Mormons tangentially in their studies of evangelical Protestantism continentally and of religiosity in Canada. Merlin B. Brinkerhoff and Marlene M. Mackie[28] have gone a step further by including Mormons in Alberta as one of the populations studied in their survey research on several religions. This rather bleak performance from religious research is mitigated somewhat by inclusion of Alberta's Mormons in some religious studies courses and of Mormons generally in one Canadian university course on "Mormon Society and Culture."[29]

There has been relatively little scholarly study of Canadian Mormons within American "Mormondom." Church historians B.H. Roberts[30] and Joseph Fielding Smith[31] described early missionary work in Canada, the founding of Mormon settlements and irrigation developments, and church growth, primarily in Alberta. Later Mormon historians, writing general histories of the church, tend to give passing mention to Alberta colonization. Under the editorship of Kate B. Carter of the Daughters of the Utah Pioneers, short articles and biographical sketches of Canadian Mormon pioneers appeared in collections published between 1929 and 1960.[32] The academic response to Canada's Mormons, though limited, included eight theses: six at Brigham Young University, one from Utah State University, and one from the University of California at Berkeley. Five of the writers were Canadians.[33] These scholars began using the rich historical records of the church in addition to other sources. Samuel Woolley Taylor, a freelance historian and novelist, wrote the story of his father, John W. Taylor, the church's resident apostle in western Canada during settlement years, in his 1951 work, *Family Kingdom*, published in New York for the book trade.

One chapter deals with his father "under the maple leaf."[34] In 1985, oral historian Jessie L. Embry of Brigham Young University wrote "Exiles for the Principle: LDS Polygamy in Canada," published in *Dialogue: A Journal of Mormon Thought*.[35] This was one of the first evidences of interest in Canadian Mormons by a scholar identified with Mormon studies in the United States.

This review of the knowledge based on Mormons in Canada, when combined with the contents of this volume, raises issues inviting further consideration. How long can a group of people *be* in Canada, how numerous must they *become*, what must they *do*, to attract the attention of scholars and the allocation of resources for their study? This is part of the age-old dilemma of the relationship between "being" and "knowing." Are there obstacles to the freedom of inquiry and expression in the study of Canada's Mormons, more or less than of other groups? To what extent are such obstacles the same as or different from those obtaining in American university or Mormon circles? What kinds of knowledge about Mormons in Canada serve the interests and purposes of different social groups? How have advances in certain branches of knowledge, for example, the social sciences in Canada, Canadian studies, religious studies, or Mormon studies in the United States, influenced the study of Mormons in Canada? What shifting social relationships in Canada and the United States have influenced the study of Mormons in Canada? What shifting social relationships in Canada and the United States have led to a concentration of studies on Alberta Mormon settlements and irrigation, at one time, and the effort to deal with Mormons as an ethno-religious people in Canadian cultures at another? These sociology-of-knowledge-like queries[36] relate to every theme mentioned in this introduction, especially the first theme of adding to the completeness of social knowledge and history with respect to Canada's Mormons. As a late twentieth-century response to the knowledge available on Canada's Mormon presence, this venture in scholarship must stand against the measure the future will apply—the level and quality of understanding and the scholarship that follows.

NOTES

1. Robert M. MacIver, "Sociology," *Encyclopedia of the Social Sciences*, Vol. 14 (New York: Macmillan, 1934), p. 246.
2. See Marcus Lee Hansen and John Bartlet Brebner, *The Mingling of the*

Canadian and American Peoples, Vol. I: Historical (New Haven: Yale University Press, 1940), pp. v, 2, 146, 183-4, 246, for migration totals, and 199-200, 229-30, 232 for mention of Mormon migration to Canada.

3. Maureen Ursenbach and Richard L. Jensen, "The Oft-crossed Border: Canadians in Utah," in Helen Papanikolas, ed., *Peoples of Utah* (Salt Lake City: Utah State Historical Society, 1976), pp. 279-300.

4. Richard Gwyn, *The 49th Paradox: Canadian North America* (Toronto: McClelland and Stewart, 1985); Pierre Berton, *Why We Act Like Canadians: A Personal Exploration of Our National Character* (Toronto: Penguin Books Canada/McClelland Stewart, 1987).

5. Seymour Martin Lipset, "Canada and the United States: The Cultural Dimension," in Charles F. Doran and John H. Sigler, eds. *Canada and the United States: Enduring Friendship, Persistent Stress* (Englewood Cliffs, New Jersey: Prentice-Hall, 1985), pp. 109-60.

6. Thomas F. O'Dea, *The Mormons* (Chicago: University of Chicago Press, 1957).

7. Leonard J. Arrington, *Great Basin Kingdom: An Economic History of the Latter-day Saints, 1830-1900* (Cambridge, Mass.: Harvard University Press, 1958, reissued as a Bison Book, Lincoln, Nebraska: University of Nebraska Press, 1966.)

8. James B. Allen and Glen M. Leonard, *The Story of the Latter-day Saints* (Salt Lake City: Deseret Book Company, 1976).

9. Leonard J. Arrington and Davis Bitton, *The Mormon Experience: A History of the Latter-day Saints* (New York: Vintage Books, Random House, 1980).

10. Jan Shipps, *Mormonism: The Story of a New Religious Tradition* (Urbana and Chicago: University of Illinois Press, 1985).

11. For origins see Richard L. Bushman, *Joseph Smith and the Beginnings of Mormonism* (Urbana and Chicago: University of Illinois Press, 1984). For an appraisal of the Mormon movement, see Klaus J. Hansen, *Mormonism and the American Experience* (Chicago: University of Chicago Press, 1981).

12. Emerson Roy West, *Profiles of the Presidents*, rev. edn. (Salt Lake City: Deseret Book Company, 1980).

13. Gordon Shepherd and Gary Shepherd, *A Kingdom Transformed: Themes in the Development of Mormonism* (Salt Lake City: University of Utah Press, 1985).

14. The ending of the critical pattern is taken to be 1931 when Father L. Le Jeune brought out his *Dictionnaire Général*, tome second (Ottawa: Université d'Ottawa, 1931), with its article "Mormons," pp. 321-22, based on the *American Encyclopedia*, New York, 1904, supplemented by Canadian Census data, in error for Ontario. In contrast it was W. Stewart Wallace, general editor, *The Encyclopedia of Canada* (Toronto: University Associates of Canada, 1936), whose Vol. IV, pp. 337-38, has an article, "Mormons," based on C.A. Dawson's *Group Settlement* (q.v.), also reflecting the Census overenumeration of Ontario Mormons. (Latter-day Saints or "Mormons" and the Reorganized Latter-day Saints, a separate group, were classified as "Mormon" by the Census from 1901 until 1981).

15. W.A. Mackintosh and W.L.G. Joerg, editors, *Canadian Frontiers of Settlement Series*, nine volumes (Toronto: Macmillan of Canada, various years, 1930s and 1940s.)

16. C.A. Dawson, *Group Settlement: Ethnic Communities in Western Canada*, Vol. VII, above series (Toronto: Macmillan of Canada, 1936).

17. Donald W. Buchanan, "The Mormons in Canada," *Canadian Geographical Journal*, Vol. 2, no. 4 (April 1931), pp. 255-70.

18. John Lehr, "Mormon Settlements in Southern Alberta" (unpublished master's thesis, University of Alberta, 1971); Howard Palmer, *Land of the Second Chance: A History of Ethnic Groups in Southern Alberta* (Lethbridge: *The Lethbridge Herald*, 1972), pp. 137-65; Archie G. Wilcox, "The Founding of the Mormon Community in Alberta" (unpublished master's thesis, University of Alberta, 1950); Melvin S. Tagg, "A History of the Church of Jesus Christ of Latter-day Saints, 1830-1963" (unpublished doctoral thesis, Brigham Young University, 1963); A. James Hudson, "Charles Ora Card: Pioneer and Colonizer" (unpublished master's thesis, Brigham Young University, 1961); John R. Hicken, "Events Leading to the Settlement of the Communities of Cardston, Magrath, Stirling and Raymond, Alberta" (unpublished master's thesis, Utah State University, 1968).

19. Lawrence B. Lee, "The Mormons come to Canada, 1887-1902," *Pacific Northwest Quarterly*, Vol. 59 (January, 1968), pp. 11-22.

20. Keith Parry, "To Raise These People up: An Examination of a Mormon Mission to an Indian Community as an Agent of Social Change," (unpublished doctoral dissertation, University of Rochester, 1972).

21. Gisela Demharter, "Socialization of girls among the Mormons in southern Alberta," *Journal of the Society for Canadian Studies* [*Zeitschrift der Gesellschaft für Kanada-Studien*], no. 2 (1985).

22. Melvin S. Tagg and Asael E. Palmer, *A History of the Mormon Church in Canada* (Lethbridge: Lethbridge Stake Historical Committee, 1968).

23. O. Kendall White, Jr, "Mormonism in America and Canada, accommodation to the nation-state," *Canadian Journal of Sociology*, Vol. 3, no. 2 (1978), pp. 161-81. As Sections II, III, and IV of the present volume show, the issue of nation-state accommodation was much more intense in the United States than in Canada.

24. S.D. Clark, *Church and Sect in Canada* (Toronto: University of Toronto Press, 1948).

25. W.E. Mann, *Sect, Cult and Church in Alberta* (Toronto: University of Toronto Press, 1955), p. 31.

26. Harry H. Hiller, "Continentalism and the third force in religion," *Canadian Journal of Sociology*, Vol. 3, no. 2 (1978), pp. 183-207.

27. Reginald W. Bibby, "The state of collective religiosity in Canada: an empirical analysis," *Canadian Review of Sociology and Anthropology*, Vol. 16 (1979), pp. 105-16.

28. Merlin B. Brinkerhoff and Marlene M. Mackie, "Religion and gender: A comparison of Canadian and American student attitudes," *Journal of Marriage and the Family*, Vol. 47, no. 2 (1985), pp. 415-29; idem. "Applicability of

social distance for religious research: an exploration," *Review of Religious Research*, Vol. 28, no. 7 (1986), pp. 151-61.

29. Examples, Religious Studies 385, "Religions in Western Canada," University of Alberta, 1988/1989 *Calendar*; Anthropology 3110/Religious Studies 3910, The University of Lethbridge, 1988-1989 *Calendar*. Some scholarship is also generated for the curriculum of LDS institutes and seminaries, which include a unit on Canadian Mormon history.

30. B.H. Roberts, *A Comprehensive History of The Church of Jesus Christ of Latter-day Saints, Century I*, 6 vols. (Provo, Utah: Brigham Young University Press, (1957, 1965).

31. Joseph Fielding Smith, *Essentials in Church History* (Salt Lake City: Deseret New Press, 1953).

32. Kate B. Carter, ed. and compiler, *Heart Throbs of the West*, 12 vols. (Salt Lake City: Daughters of the Utah Pioneers, 1939-51); idem., *Treasures of Pioneer History*, 6 vols. (1952-57); idem., *Our Pioneer Heritage*, 3 vols. (1958-60).

33. The Brigham Young University theses were: Wilbur Gordon Hackney, "A History of the Western Canadian Mission" (unpublished master's thesis, 1950); A. James Hudson, "Charles Ora Card, Pioneer and Colonizer" (unpublished master's thesis, 1961); Phyllip G. Redd, "A History of Formal Religious Instruction by the Church of Jesus Christ of Latter-day Saints in Alberta, 1890-1960" (unpublished master's thesis, 1961); Melvin S. Tagg, The Life of Edward J. Wood" (unpublished master's thesis, 1959); Melvin S. Tagg, "The History of the Church of Jesus Christ of Latter-day Saints in Canada, 1830-1963" (unpublished doctoral thesis, 1963); Richard E. Bennett, "A Study of the Church of Jesus Christ of Latter-day Saints in Upper-Canada, 1830-1850" (unpublished master's thesis, 1975).
   The Utah State University thesis was: John R. Hicken, "Events Leading to the Settlement of the Communities of Cardston, Magrath, Stirling and Raymond, Alberta" (unpublished master's thesis, 1968).
   The University of California at Berkeley thesis was: Samuel George Ellsworth, "A History of Mormon Missions in the United States and Canada, 1830-1860" (unpublished doctoral dissertation, 1951).

34. Samuel Woolley Taylor, *Family Kingdom* (New York: McGraw-Hill, 1951), Ch. 7.

35. Jessie L. Embry, "Exiles for the principle: LDS polygamy in Canada," *Dialogue: A Journal of Mormon Thought*, Vol. 18, no. 3 (Fall 1985), pp. 108-16.

36. Louis Wirth, "Preface," in Karl Mannheim, *Ideology and Utopia: An Introduction to the Sociology of Knowledge* (New York: Harcourt, Brace and Company, 1949), pp. xxvii-xxxi.

I | THE BEGINNINGS
1830-1886

THE BEGINNINGS OF the Mormon presence in Canada have several particular threads. The major area of focus, however, is southern Alberta where a distinct sociocultural community experienced an environment that was related to what the community had known but was different in many of its aspects. It was in this context that Mormon migrants would adapt particular practices to new circumstances, to emerge as a distinct and enduring community in the ethnic mosaic of the Canadian West.

Professor Leonard J. Arrington's essay offers the reader valuable insights into Mormon migration. He finds that many Mormon railway construction crews helped lay the roadbed for the Canadian Pacific Railway in many parts of the West before the advent of Mormon settlement. Professor Arrington sees these construction crews as a significant source of information for those Mormons contemplating the move north.

Professor Arrington's discussion of the nature of the Mormon frontier in the Great Basin area in comparison with the nature of other American frontiers offers insight into the nature of the cultural "baggage" that accompanied the Mormons northward and influenced their adaptive responses to their new home. While other articles in this volume offer related insights, it is equally obvious that much scholarship is necessary to illuminate this particular aspect of the Mormon story in southern Alberta.

Mormon experiences in what is today Canada outside of Alberta have attracted the attention of Dr. Richard E. Bennett and Professor Robert J. McCue. Bennett's "Plucking Not Planting..." article might seem to belong more properly to the early years of Mormonism, when as a religious movement it was initiating the individual and collective experiences that would see members emerge as a particular sociocultural community in the

Great Basin area. Yet Bennett's article cannot help but give rise to questions about the circumstances in British North America that led to the brief but brilliant success of Mormonism in the years immediately following its inception. For instance, What of the significant number of Canadian converts who returned to Canada and did not go west to Utah? As well, the reader might wonder about the factors that influenced circumstances in British North America in the 1830s and continued to be a part of the institutional climate that faced the Mormons in southern Alberta upon their arrival and in subsequent decades.

Professor McCue's exhaustive search of newspaper holdings in British Columbia examines usefully the relatively few expressions of Mormonism in a land that at one time had been heralded as a haven for the Latter-day Saints.

Professor A.A. den Otter sets the institutional environmental stage in southern Alberta that welcomed the Mormon migrants. In a most helpful descriptive narrative, Professor den Otter surveys the particular cultural elements already rooted in the soil of the Canadian West that would influence Mormon adaptation. Again, significant insight is offered when den Otter's essay is read in conjunction with those of Arrington and Bennett. The reader is led to compare den Otter's portrayal of the institutional basis of western Canada in the last quarter of the nineteenth century with Arrington's descriptions of the Mormons' Great Basin frontier as well as other American frontiers. Needless to say, the reader moves effortlessly to the question (as yet not answered) of what was the nature of the impact of den Otter's West on Arrington's Mormons.

The reader will also note the links between den Otter's West and Bennett's British North America in the 1830s; the scene of the first Mormon experiences in Canadian history. Perhaps the sense of two related cultural streams, separated for a half century, is appropriate. Perhaps, in the meeting of western Canadian institutions and Mormon migrants, old cultural acquaintances were "reintroducing" themselves. Whatever, the articles in this section on "Beginnings" serve to pose questions that are answered in part in subsequent sections.

1 Historical Roots of the Mormon Settlement in Southern Alberta

LEONARD J. ARRINGTON

IN THE SUMMER of 1886, when anti-Mormon persecutions were at their height in the United States, John Taylor, president of the Church of Jesus Christ of Latter-day Saints and former resident of Upper Canada, advised Charles O. Card, president of Cache Valley Stake in northern Utah and southern Idaho, to venture north of the 49th parallel and locate a suitable place for Latter-day Saint families to settle. Leaving with three companions in September 1886, Card explored the country south of Calgary to the international boundary, paying special attention to the region north of Lee Creek, a tributary of the St. Mary River, 14 miles north of the United States boundary. Satisfied that they had found a suitable location for settlement, they dedicated the land and returned to Utah where they reported to President Taylor. He instructed them to select forty families and lead them there the next spring.

Card's group left Logan in March 1887, further explored the region they had investigated the previous fall, and on April 26, selected a place for settlement, later named Cardston. Other settlers, seeking to avoid officers of the law who were searching for Mormon leaders in Utah, took immediate refuge in that remote settlement. They commenced plowing on May 2, held their first church meeting in a tent on Sunday, June 5, and enrolled their first Sunday School the next Sunday, June 12. A ward was organized in October 1888, other settlements were founded, and the Alberta Stake was organized in 1895. President Card pointed out that the Canadian federal government was lenient with these new colonists, as it had been, and would be, with certain other immigrants into the Canadian West—the Mennonites, Ukrainians and other national groups. And

3

Aerial view of Cardston, Alberta, c.1925. Note grid pattern, temple and tabernacle block, the public school, and CPR with grain elevators to the north on Blood Reserve. Courtesy of the Canadian Geographic Society.

because of Canadian tolerance and encouragement, Latter-day Saints eventually developed a flourishing community of industrious and loyal citizens.

There is another story of Mormon settlement in southern Alberta that has not been told. It is the story of groups of Latter-day Saint construction crews from northern Utah, particularly Cache and Weber valleys, who went to western Canada several years earlier than President Card and worked on the Canadian Pacific Railway. In 1880 the Canadian federal government, which had earlier obligated itself to build a transcontinental railway if British Columbia joined Confederation, turned the project over to a private syndicate and construction began at once, from Montreal to Vancouver.[1]

That Mormon crews were involved in making the roadbed was no happenstance.[2] Mormons had laid most of the roadbed for the Pacific Railroad in the United States, from Wyoming to California. After the joining of the rails at Promontory Summit in 1869, Mormon crews then proceeded to build several branch lines—one from the junction at Promontory to Ogden, another south from Ogden to Salt Lake City, and a third south from Salt Lake City to Juab in central Utah. They had also built a narrow-gauge line north from Ogden to Franklin in southern Idaho, and then on from Franklin to Garrison, Montana, where the Utah and Northern, as their railroad was called, joined up with the Northern Pacific, which extended from Duluth west to Portland, Oregon. All told, the Mormons built more than one thousand miles of roadbed, from southern Utah to Montana, and from Wyoming to California.

Not unexpectedly, as these assignments wound down, Mormon crews took contracts in the early 1880s to build the Denver and Rio Grande Western, the Northern Pacific, the Great Northern, the Oregon Short Line, and other railroads that stretched across the American West. Simultaneously, some Mormon crews took advantage of opportunities to work on the Canadian Pacific. Since almost nothing has been written on this subject, it is impossible to determine how many Mormons were involved in construction in the early 1880s, but from family histories and documents, two such gangs can be described, one from Cache Valley in northern Utah and southern Idaho, and one from Weber Valley, south of Cache Valley.[3]

Simeon Allen, of Hyrum, Utah, and his wife Boletta, a Norwegian immigrant, had been among the hundreds of Cache Valley settlers who had worked on the Utah Northern. When that work was finished in 1882, Simeon and his son Heber, then 17 years old, took a contract representing several gangs of Cache Valley laborers to work on the Northern Pacific in Hellgate Canyon, 28 miles east of Missoula, Montana. They returned to Cache Valley for the winter, and in 1883 went farther north into Canada, where Simeon took a contract to use two rock camps and 15 grading outfits from Cache Valley to grade part of the Canadian Pacific between Medicine Hat and Calgary.

Heber, now 19, remained in Canada for the winter, serving as a cowboy on the famous Cochrane Ranch, one of the large early-day cattle outfits established by the noted eastern Canadian, Senator Matthew H. Cochrane. Heber returned to Cache Valley the next year to help his father farm and to get some special training in bookkeeping, business communications, and other helpful subjects at Brigham Young College in Logan. When his father took a contract in 1886 to build 19 miles of railroad grade north of Helena, Montana, for the Great Northern Railroad, however, Heber went along as bookkeeper.

While Simeon and Heber and their associates were in their camp at Prickly Pear Canyon, south of Wolf Creek, Montana, in the fall of 1886, they were visited by Charles O. Card and his two Cache Valley companions as they were returning from their preliminary exploration of southern Alberta. Card and his companions held extensive conversations with Simeon and Heber. The latter and their comrades continued to work under Great Northern contracts in Montana and Washington state in 1887 and 1888. Heber had decided to return to Utah to teach school, but Simeon asked him, instead, to drive one of his teams, carrying his wife Rebecca and their five children.

Heber S. Allen, 1864-1944, c.1900.
Archives of the Church of Jesus Christ of
Latter-day Saints (hereafter LDS Archives),
P1700/3105.

Threatened with prosecution under the Edmunds Act, Simeon had decided to move his family to Cardston. When Heber and Rebecca and the children reached Cardston, in November 1888, Heber soon met Amy Leonard, daughter of Truman Leonard of Farmington, Utah, who had likewise taken part of his family to Cardston. Heber and Amy were married the following April, the first wedding in the new settlement.[4]

In Cardston, Heber became the schoolteacher and also engaged in farming. Meanwhile, Simeon homesteaded land near the new settlement of Mountain View and raised livestock, something he had done in Cache Valley. He and others established the Cardston Mercantile and Manufacturing Company, but later he returned to Utah, and Heber and his wife Amy were asked to manage the store. Heber later served as postmaster, built a roller flour mill, and in 1902 replaced Charles Card as president of the Alberta LDS Stake. When Taylor Stake was created the next year, he became its first president, before moving to Raymond, where he operated the Raymond Mercantile Company. He remained in Raymond as stake president for the next 32 years. Active in many business and civic enterprises, he died in 1944 at the age of 79. Amy reared a large family and likewise served in many leadership capacities in the LDS community.

A second group of settlers that worked on the Canadian Pacific were from Uinta, in Weber Valley, 25 miles north of Salt Lake City. They were three sons of Edmund Wattis and Mary Jane Corey, and four sons of George Corey and Mary Jane Spaulding. Like the Allens, the Wattises and Coreys had worked on the Pacific Railroad and opened the Corey Brothers Supply Store. They participated in the work on the Utah and Northern, as it was being graded from Ogden to Montana, took a major contract in 1881 to build the Oregon Short Line Railroad from Granger, Wyoming, to Huntington, Oregon, a distance of more than five hundred miles, and then took contracts to work on the construction of the Northern Pacific and Great Northern railroads and the Canadian Pacific Railway. Crews of up to five hundred were employed under the supervision of the four Corey brothers (George L., Charles J., Amos B. and Warren W.), their half-brother, J.E. Spaulding, and their nephews, Edmund O., William H. and Warren L. Wattis. A 1 January 1885 report in the *Salt Lake Tribune* describes their work at that time for the Canadian Pacific:

> They shipped their teams and tools to the northern terminus of the Utah and Northern, and drove some 700 miles northwest to the line of the road, since which they have pushed work with from 350 to 500 men with teams throughout the summer and are employing 200 men this winter.... Their work this winter is on a difficult tunnel, and four miles of heavy cuts, on a contract amounting to about $200,000. The tunnel is through hardpan, requiring to be timbered all the way, and is located on the Kicking Horse River, in British Columbia, fifteen miles west of the Columbia River.

The *Tribune* went on to say that the Coreys and Wattises had built more miles of railroad in the six preceding years than any other firm, Canadian or American, engaged in the business.

The Corey brothers, as mentioned earlier, were not alone. Dozens of other Mormon camps, with men from as far north as Weston, Idaho, to as far south as Willard, Utah, were engaged in filling such contracts. A contemporary non-Mormon observer suggested reasons for the Mormon success:

> They bid so close on grading jobs that no other contractor could compete with them, and they worked together like true brothers and sisters. [I] visited one of their grading camps and was amazed to see the order and cleanliness that was maintained under the most difficult conditions.... The men were particular to wash and to comb their hair before each meal.

The Mormon women did the cooking and waited on table. What was more, the grading was always completed within the time limits stipulated in the contract and was all done in a most satisfactory manner.[5]

Because of the modest conditions under which the workers had been reared, their costs of upkeep were not high. Many slept on the ground with some hay for a mattress on which they spread blankets. Tents were universal, with an occasional shack of crude lumber or sheet iron to house the blacksmith shop or some valuable equipment. Their recreation or amusement came primarily from a laborer who could play a mouth organ or a fiddle. Well supplied by their Ogden store, the company had the reputation of being a "good feeder."

The Coreys and Wattises continued to accept construction contracts in the 1890s, and with others organized the Utah Construction Company in 1900.[6] They built the Western Pacific Railroad line from Salt Lake City to Oroville, California; the American Falls, Deadwood, Guernsey, and Hetch-Hetchy dams; and they were the nucleus for the Six-Company consortium that built the Hoover Dam at Boulder, Nevada. They later joined other groups in building the Grand Coulee Dam and Bonneville system in Washington and Oregon. Utah Construction, more recently operating as Utah International, Inc., became one of the largest construction companies in the world.

These family histories suggest that several hundred Mormons had been in southern Saskatchewan, Alberta and British Columbia well before Charles O. Card and his fellow colonists settled there in 1887, and thus they had a knowledge of the country and its residents. There can be little doubt that they discussed the country with their relatives and neighbors in Cache and Weber valleys, and that this was one reason these people were so willing to move there. Wherever they settled, the Mormons did not colonize blindly. Colonizing families had followed construction crews of the Utah Northern Railroad north from Franklin, Idaho, to Montana; the Oregon Short Line as it moved northwest to Portland; and the Northern Pacific in Montana. In a similar manner, they went to southern Alberta where their sons and brothers had worked on the Canadian Pacific. That the initial settlement was made in 1887 by a small cadre seeking refuge for their families was, at least to some extent, coincidental. Settlement would surely have been made regardless of the anti-Mormon crusade. That the Latter-day Saints left a favorable impression with the Canadians they worked for helps to account for their favorable reception among many Canadian officials. The Canadians

did not prefer Mormons, but they did want industrious and loyal settlers—
farmers, craftsmen, stockmen and schoolteachers. And Latter-day Saints,
with their high birthrate and capacity for work, had plenty of young men
and women seeking land and water. Undeniably, they helped Alberta reach
provincial status, which was achieved about the time the Mormons completed their immigration in 1905.

Four patterns of social and economic organization developed in the
American West. We might refer to them as the miners' frontier, the cattle
frontier, the lumber frontier and the Mormon frontier.[7] Each represented
a different mode of adapting to the resources and environment of the West.
(Most Canadian historians believe the Canadian frontier differed from that
of the United States because of the greater degree of central government
control.)[8]

The mining west, that started in California in 1848 and continued on
to the cold Alaskan territory of the Yukon in the 1890s, has furnished, as
Robert Hine described it, "a kaleidoscope of the lonely prospector with mule
and pan, jerry-built stores along a muddy street, a mirrored saloon, a silent
poker game, dancing girls, outlaws, claim jumpers, the vigilance
committee—all supplanted finally by the smelter and the mill, the slag heap,
underground burrows, labor unions and Pinkerton detectives, [and] the company town."[9] Participating in the enterprise were Irishmen, Cornishmen,
Mexicans, Hawaiians and Chinese. There were also adventurous people
from the East, from the Southwest and Texas, and from farms and factories
in the Midwest. All had one primary motive, to get rich quickly and return
to their homes. None had any particular loyalty to the place they mined in,
or assumed any particular responsibility for what happened in the public
sector. Settlements developed accidentally around a store set somewhere.
There was no sense of planning, few wives and mothers, and widespread
suffering and disease. To establish and protect their claims they set up a
simple mining district government, with rules similar to those that they
remembered from experiences in Wales, Spanish America and Georgia.
Disputes were settled by do-it-yourself jurisprudence. After a decade or two
or three of these freewheeling arrangements, the small miners were
submerged by corporate structures that offered, if nothing else, stability and
outside capital.

The cattle frontier had existed in North Carolina and Georgia, but as
it moved on to the treeless, semiarid Great Plains states and provinces in
the 1860s, a tempting image developed—the Western cowboy. "Roughly
comparable to the lonely prospector with his mule and pan," as Robert Hine

points out, "was the lonely cowboy with his horse and lariat." He became an idealized person, so encased in clichés that neither truth nor parody could reduce the reverence or dim the delight that he generated within an admiring public.[10] But the industry that nurtured this hero, once openly competitive and ruggedly individualistic, witnessed the formation of local cattlemen's associations. These established range regulations and organized roundups for groups of owners over a wide district. Roundup committees came to exercise regimented control over movements of men and cattle. As frontier individualism gave way to economic necessity, a system of co-operation and control evolved that provided substantial stability. Local cattle associations formed county associations, and county associations joined together into territorial associations. Eventually, overstocking, fencing with barbed wire, wicked winters and protracted droughts, the introduction of expensive blooded stock too expensive for small operators to afford, and the invasion of large eastern and foreign investors brought an end to the frontier cattle kingdom. The cowboy, like the prospector before him, had become a wage earner in a large oligopolistic enterprise.

The lumber frontier went through a similar evolution. Beginning in California in the late years of the Gold Rush period, individual lumbermen stripped trees and then moved on northward to cut more. They soon moved into the Pacific Northwest and British Columbia, where, with eastern capital, they established networks of sawmills, acquired ships and forests, and set up pools to regulate and control production and distribution. Eventually, they adopted the self-sustaining yield concept, with the long-range planning policies that we see today.

In each of these frontiers, capital and organization replaced the devil-may-care individualism, wastefulness and fraud of the early years. The mining industry, supported by moneyed men, began to treat ores and brought water under high pressure. Foreign immigrants were attracted, and the beginnings of a class system appeared. There were ethnic distinctions, company towns, and strikes and lockouts. The cattle industry did something similar, with foreign stockholders taking control, while poor whites, blacks and Mexicans served as hired hands. The same thing happened in the lumber industry. Wandering Scandinavian immigrants were employed to cut timber, while older American families and corporate stockholders became the owners.

Was this to be the destiny of the American West? Class division, hierarchy, a replication of the past of European peoples? There were other patterns, and one of them was developed by the Mormons in the Great Basin and exported by groups of them as they settled parts of other western states and the province of Alberta.

For a generation, American settlement had remained poised on the Missouri River. The first tier beyond the Mississippi was being settled, but there was little settlement beyond the Missouri. A few jumped over to the Willamette Valley in Oregon and to California, but nobody conceived of settling in the dry arid region in-between. The Great Basin was a drastically different area, uninviting and inhospitable, with inadequate rainfall, few trees, rivers with water only during the spring runoff, and scant supply of edible wild animals. But in their frequent removals, from New York to Ohio to Missouri to Illinois to Nebraska, the Mormons had developed a co-operative pattern of work and economy that could successfully accommodate this new kind of wilderness. Their move west was a triumph of disciplined effort and mutual helpfulness. There was also group planning. Team captains were appointed, daily routines were specified, and rules and assigned tasks were agreed upon.

When the first settlers arrived in the Salt Lake Valley, they simply continued the pattern of co-operative organization that they had maintained during their trek across the Plains.[11] One group commenced to lay out a city of 135 ten-acre blocks, each of which was further divided into eight home lots apportioned by lottery. Other groups sought timber, began the building of a fort and log cabins, dug diversion canals, and planted and irrigated an initial plot of 35 acres of land. As the number of in-migrants increased, they divided into wards of nine square blocks each—enough to locate 72 families, with up to four hundred persons.

Each ward, whether in Salt Lake City or in an outlying colony, was in essence a little city, with its own officers. Subject to central direction on matters affecting the welfare of the whole group, each little ward or settlement, under the direction of the bishop, arranged for its own water, its own timber, its own livestock herds, and its own work projects. In seasons of inadequate food, due to failure of the water supply, infestation by grasshoppers or by early frost, each ward established a rationing system to assure that none would starve and that available supplies would be distributed as fairly as possible.

The larger investments necessary to build community life were planned and carried out by the central church. These included the making of through roads, the digging of highline canals from the mountain streams to service several wards, the construction of central meetinghouses or tabernacles, the erection of tanneries, gristmills and woollens factories, and the calling and provisioning of companies to colonize new settlements.

The basic institution for accomplishing all of these purposes was the ward or community tithinghouse, sometimes called the bishop's storehouse, which functioned as the community receiving and disbursing agency, general store, bank, telegraph office and welfare agency. Each family head was expected to contribute to the tithinghouse, which then distributed these receipts to widows and orphans, to the sick and disabled, and to those laboring on public works and central church enterprises. Most of the contributed livestock was sold to acquire the wherewithal to buy needed supplies and equipment in the Missouri River area for transporting immigrants to the Salt Lake Valley. The Department of Public Works planned the construction of larger buildings, the Perpetual Emigrating Company supervised the migration of converts from Europe and the East, and the Women's Relief Society was the key welfare and cultural agency.

A notable Mormon achievement was their development of institutions with respect to irrigation. The Wasatch Mountains, on the western side of which the Mormons had settled, catch forty to fifty inches of rain at the ten-thousand-foot level, whereas land forty miles to the west receives only five or six inches. The valleys below the Wasatch contained an alluvial soil that would grow good crops when properly watered.

There has been a fascination with how and why the Mormons stepped into irrigation. Although we now know that the Hohokam Indians of Arizona practiced irrigation agriculture for several hundred years before the Spanish ventured into the region in the sixteenth century, no people in the English-speaking world had adopted irrigation. Orson Pratt's record in his 1847 diary makes only a matter-of-fact mention of the Mormons' usage of irrigation. The Mormons had published references to irrigation in their newspapers. They recognized that water was the key to life. They had lots of manpower but no money, so the local bishops chose committees to organize the people. Each contributed labor in proportion to the land he expected to irrigate. The bishop usually served as watermaster or chose a trusted ward member to do so. Thus, they developed an irrigation system without any monetary debt and without engineering experience. Farming in an arid region was a new experience for English-speaking people, so they had to develop their own institutions.

The Mormons had settled the public domain. Federal land laws were not applied until 1869 when there were as many as eighty-six thousand people. They settled in small tracts apportioned in a community drawing. Water belonged to the community and the right to it came with the right to use land. Individual rights were safeguarded, but so was the community right.

They were a highly organized, old-fashioned people, accomplishing on a co-operative group basis what individuals working independently could not have done.

This system of co-operative economics could apply only as long as the Mormons' commonwealth was united and left alone. That was not to be their destiny. Rich mines were discovered and enclaves of non-Mormons with different values began to dot the region. The federal government, having subdued the South, now turned its attention to the Mormons, with their different social, political and economic practices. In a resulting "crusade," in which Mormon leaders were put in the penitentiary, church property was expropriated, and political control was placed in the hands of zealous Protestants, an uneasy stability arose. Thanks to the creation of the Bureau of Reclamation, the co-operative research and education programs of the Department of Agriculture, the Forest Service, and the Bureau of Land Management, the federal government stepped in as a force to provide some central planning and control similar to that previously exercised by the church. Nevertheless, the organized co-operation for which Mormons were famous survived on a somewhat limited basis. It was still evident during the Great Depression of the 1930s, World War II, and in such emergencies as floods, winds, earthquakes and other natural disasters. Fortunately, because of the strength of traditional Mormon institutions, the pattern of agriculture did not develop, as it seemed to do in California, into a concentration of wealth and power and the emergence of an oligarchy, with a permanent underclass of stoop-and-pick laborers having access neither to land nor to the water that enables it to produce.

The presence of Mormon work gangs throughout the northwest and western Canada in the late 1870s and early 1880s suggests that Utah was approaching the limit of population it could support under existing technology, institutions and policies. In every valley, there were signs that the continued flow of immigration and the natural increase in population had filled up the land. Young married couples were not able to find farms; older people found themselves underemployed. "I find," wrote one observer, "the settlements crowded up to their utmost capacity, land and water all appropriated, and our young people as they marry off have no place to settle near home.... The resources of the people are about exhausted, unless they go into manufacturing."[12] The church's program in these years reflected official recognition of the deterioration in the ratio of people to the land. Projects to increase the supply of irrigable land were sponsored by ward, stake and general church organizations. From Blackfoot, Idaho, in the north, to Mesa, Arizona, in the south; from Manassa, Colorado, in the east, to southern Nevada in the west; available patches of land were reclaimed from the desert and put in the way of raising grains, hay and vegetables. Not only new projects in the older valleys but also scores of church and semi-private colonizing missions were opening up new valleys for settlement. New settlements were founded in the Little Colorado and Salt River valleys in Arizona and New Mexico, in the San Luis Valley of southern Colorado, in the Upper Salt River Valley of western Wyoming, the Upper Snake River Valley in eastern Idaho, and the Goose Creek Valley in western Idaho. All told, at least a hundred new Mormon settlements, resembling—though in different ways—pioneer villages of the 1850s, were founded outside Utah during the four-year period 1876 to 1879. With the exception of the initial colonization of Utah 1847-1851, it was the greatest single colonization movement in Mormon history. Eventually, it spread to Sonora and Chihuahua, Mexico, and finally, in the late 1880s and 1890s, into southern Alberta.

Nearly all the settlements of the 1870s were founded in the same spirit and with the same type of organization and institutions as those founded in the 1850s and 1860s. Colonizing companies often moved as a group, with church direction; a characteristic village form of settlement prevailed; canals were built by co-operative labor; and the small holdings of farmland and village lots were parceled out in community drawings. Many of the settlements were given tithing and other assistance from the church. In the late 1880s and 1890s, however, with the expansion of farm acreage facilitated by federal land laws that provided homestead farms of at least 160 acres, with the development of dry farming, with the availability of capital for large land and water development projects, and with the extension of farm credit by newly organized banks, Mormon colonization was often on a semi-official or private basis. There was usually church encouragement and a certain amount of church direction and planning; there was often church financial support in the initial stages; and there was also a lively amount of private enterprise, involving families, neighborhoods, and Mormon capitalists. This pattern characterized the Canadian settlement, as it did those in Big Horn Basin, Wyoming; San Luis Valley, Colorado; White Pine County, Nevada; Millard County and Skull Valley, Utah; and Sonora and Chihuahua, Mexico.[13]

As with the pattern of the 1890s, then, the colonization of Alberta was partly done by officially called companies, and partly by families coming in small groups or on their own. Not untypical was the organization of the Alberta Land and Colonization Company, established in 1896 to promote the development of projects in southern Alberta. The Mormon Church held an important block of stock and assisted the company financially, so it was partly a church enterprise, but only partly.[14]

The "mixed" character of the colonies, partly official church and partly private, is illustrated not only in the Alberta Land and Colonization Company but also in the 1898 agreement between the Mormon Church and the Alberta Railway and Irrigation Company to provide labor and skills to build an irrigation system in the Cardston-Lethbridge area. Under the contract, the church agreed to establish two towns along the route, Magrath and Stirling. The church also encouraged Jesse Knight's arrangement with C.A. Magrath to settle Raymond and build a beet sugar factory. It was important to "build up the Kingdom," but it was also clear that here was cheap land and plenty of water from irrigation, something not available in Utah.

As for the migration, one can find instances in which persons and families were expressly called by local bishops, stake presidents, apostles, and even by the president of the church. But there are also many instances in which the families, as the result of encouragement from friends and relatives, decided, quite independently of church authority, to make the move. Particularly noticeable are the large number of brothers or brothers-in-law, or fathers and sons who settled in an area. This suggests, again, the welcome opportunity for cheap land and water that southern Alberta represented for these families, forced to migrate because of overcrowding in Utah and southern Idaho.

It is important to recognize that the Mormons went into Canada, or at least thought they went into Canada, as equals. Old Canadians, who had been confident that the Ukrainians, Icelanders and other ethnocultural groups would be subsidiary to the dominant Anglo-Protestant culture of the region, could not be sure that this would be true of the Mormons. And so there was, understandably, no more than a hesitant acceptance. While eastern and midwestern Americans opposed the Mormons because of their refusal to comply with dominant Protestant mores, Canadians, always fearful of American annexation, cultural if not political, saw these immigrants from south of the border as adding to the strength of the Americanizing influence.

Actually, of course, and as subsequent history demonstrated, Canadians need not have worried about the loyalty of the Mormons. They left the United States at a time when the American government was vigorously attacking the Mormons and their church. The president of the church when the first Alberta settlement was made, John Taylor, himself a British subject

and former resident of the colony of Upper Canada, had the highest regard
for British and Canadian laws, and encouraged the Latter-day Saints going
to Alberta to be loyal to Canadian institutions. That counsel was probably
not necessary; there were other Canadian attitudes that the Mormons had
long supported. The Mormons opposed, as did most Canadians, the
American frontier policy of trying to clear the aborigines from the land.
Mormon leaders had always sought to work with the Indians on a friendly
basis.[15] The horse, the gun, and the shootout might have been characteristic
of the Great Plains region of the United States, but not of the Mormon frontier or the Canadian frontier. There may have been something resembling
the cattle kingdom of the Great Plains in the two cultures, but there was little
vigilante activity and not as much class division. The Mormons could be
as comfortable supporting the North-West Mounted Police as they had been
supporting their own Nauvoo Legion militia in Utah; and their support of
organized co-operation was not substantially different from the western
Canadian support of the Saskatchewan Grain Growers' Association. So it
was easy for the Mormons to fit into the Canadian ambience, as it was easy
for Canadians, once they became acquainted with the Mormons, to accept
them, especially since they were mostly self-sufficient farmers attempting
a transition to a market economy featuring a more highly specialized and
intensive kind of agriculture than had been traditional in Utah.

In their establishment of the dozen or more small farming villages in
Alberta, the Mormons were struggling to preserve a pattern of community
living that had been advocated fifty years earlier by their founding prophet,
Joseph Smith, and that they had enjoyed as children in the farm villages of
pioneer Utah. It was a pattern that even today in many Alberta communities
differentiates Mormon occupancy from many western Canadian settlements.
Even in large urban centers, such as modern Calgary, Edmonton and Vancouver, Mormon wards, though not cohesive geographic units, exhibit many
characteristics of the earlier villages—the unity, mutual helpfulness and
social-mindedness for which Mormons have striven throughout their history.

NOTES
   1. Harold A. Innis, *A History of the Canadian Pacific Railway* (Toronto and
      Buffalo: University of Toronto Press [1923] 1971). James B. Hedges, *Building
      the Canadian West: The Land and Colonization Policies of the Canadian Pacific
      Railway* (New York: Russell and Russell, 1971).

2. Leonard J. Arrington, *Great Basin Kingdom: An Economic History of the Latter-day Saints, 1830-1900* (Cambridge, Mass: Harvard University Press, 1958), Chapters 8 and 9.
3. Leonard J. Arrington, "Grass Roots Entrepreneurship in the Frontier West: The Allens of Cache Valley and Wattises of Weber Valley," in Jessie L. Embry and Howard A. Christy, eds., *Community Development in the American West* (Provo, Utah: Charles Redd Center for Western Studies, 1985), pp. 183-220.
4. See the accounts of Simeon and Heber S. Allen in Jane E. Woolf Bates and Zina A. Woolf Hickman, *The Founding of Cardston and Vicinity: Pioneer Problems* (n.p., privately published by William L. Woolf, 1960).
5. *Salt Lake Tribune*, 1 January 1985.
6. Leonard J. Arrington, "Utah Construction Company," in *David Eccles: Pioneer Western Industrialist* (Logan, Utah: Utah State University Press, 1975), pp. 251-54.
7. Howard Lamar, ed., *The Reader's Encyclopedia of the American West* (New York: Crowell, 1977); Rodman W. Paul, *The Far West and the Great Plains in Transition, 1959-1900* (New York: Harper & Row, 1988); Patricia Limerick, *The Legacy of Conquest: The Unbroken Past of the American West* (New York; W.W. Norton, 1987); Robert V. Hine, *The American West: An Interpretive History* (Boston: Little, Brown and Company, 1973); Donald Worster, "New West, True West: Interpreting the Region's History," *Western Historical Quarterly*, 18 (April 1987), pp. 141-56; Arrington, *Great Basin Kingdom*.
8. The pattern in Canada, in some respects similar, in some respects different from the western United States, is described in W.T. Easterbrook and M.H. Watkins, eds., *Approaches to Canadian Economic History* (Toronto: McClelland and Stewart, Carleton Library edition, 1977); Henry C. Klassen, ed., *The Canadian West* (Calgary: The University of Calgary, 1977); Paul F. Sharp, *Whoop-up Country: The Canadian-American West* (Minneapolis: University of Minnesota Press, 1955); and David Breen, *The Canadian Prairie West and the Ranching Frontier* (Toronto: University of Toronto Press, 1983).
9. Hine, *The American West: An Interpretive History*, p. 113.
10. "The Cattle Frontier," in Robert V. Hine and Edwin R. Bingham, eds., *The Frontier Experience: Readings in the Trans-Mississippi West* (Belmont, Calif.: Wadsworth Publishing, 1963), p. 241.
11. Leonard J. Arrington, "Religion and Planning in the Great Basin, 1847-1900," in *Proceedings of the Thirty-Second Annual Conference of the Western Economic Association*, 1957, pp. 37-41, further elaborated in *Great Basin Kingdom*.
12. F.A. Hammond, *Deseret News* (Salt Lake City), 29 April 1885.
13. *Great Basin Kingdom*, pp. 383-84.
14. See Donald W. Buchanan, "The Mormons in Canada," *Canadian Geographical Journal*, 2 (April 1932), pp. 255-70; Kate B. Carter, ed., "The Mormons in Canada," in *Treasures of Pioneer History*, 2 (Salt Lake City: Daughters of Utah Pioneers, 1953), pp. 45-104; Joseph Austin Hammer,

"Mormon Trek to Canada," *Alberta Historical Review*, 7 (Spring, 1959), pp. 7-16; Lawrence B. Lee, "The Mormons Come to Canada, 1887-1902," *Pacific Northwest Quarterly*, 59 (January, 1968), pp. 11-22; John C. Lehr, "The Sequence of Mormon Settlement in Southern Alberta," *The Albertan Geographer*, 10 (1974), pp. 20-29; Lowry Nelson, "The Mormons," in C.A. Dawson, *Group Settlement: Ethnic Communities in Western Canada* (Toronto: The Macmillan Co., 1936), pp. 175-272; C. Frank Steele, "Latter-day Saint Settlement in Canada," *The Instructor* (Salt Lake City), January to December, 1948, serially in twelve issues; Melvin S. Tagg and Asael E. Palmer, *A History of the Mormon Church in Canada* (Lethbridge, Alberta: Lethbridge Stake Historical Committee, 1968); John R. Hicken, "Events leading to the Settlement of the Communities of Cardston, Magrath, Stirling and Raymond, Alberta," (master's thesis, Utah State University, 1968); Archie G. Wilcox, "Founding of the Mormon community in Alberta," (master's thesis, University of Alberta, 1950).

15. This needs to be understood with something less than complete generality. Although the Mormons made repeated attempts to obtain Indian approval before settling on "their" lands, there were always dissenters on both sides who did not agree, and there was scattered Indian opposition to Mormon settlement in central and southern Utah and southern Nevada near local tribes. The US government treaty of 1865 to remove the Ute Indians from central to eastern Utah was not initiated by Mormons; Brigham Young was only a reluctant observer.

2 "Plucking Not Planting"
Mormonism in Eastern Canada 1830-1850

RICHARD E. BENNETT

THE STORY OF Mormonism in Canada in the post-Confederation era is a well-known southern Alberta account of immigration, settlement and temple building. In eastern Canada, the lesser known story of pre-Confederation Mormonism is not the immigration of settlers and their subsequent experiences but the opposite, the emigration of old inhabitants, as new converts from Canada moved southward across the American border to join with the ever-westward-advancing Mormon Zion. The purpose of this study is to outline the dimensions of Mormon influence in eastern Canada from 1830 to 1850 and to consider briefly those factors that accounted for its rapid rise and fall—an almost meteoric flash across the mid-nineteenth-century skies of Canadian religious history.[1]

The origin of Mormonism, as it is called, is traceable to a young man in upstate New York. Joseph Smith, Jr. organized the Church of Jesus Christ of Latter-day Saints on 6 April 1830 in Fayette, Seneca Co., New York, barely one hundred miles from the Canadian border. The new faith was based on a strong personal belief in modern visions and revelations, the *Book of Mormon*, and the gathering of Zion prior to the impending millennial reign. Immediately following their conversion, many of the earliest converts became active missionaries in spreading the message of Cumorah. And before the year was out, Joseph's father, Joseph Smith, Sr., and his brother, Don Carlos, while preaching to relatives near the St. Lawrence River, touched "at several Canadian ports where [they] distributed a few copies of the *Book of Mormon*."[2]

If not "burned over" by the incredible scene of religious revivalism, camp meeting excitement, and experimentation that swept the land immediately to the south in the early nineteenth century, Upper Canada was at least receptive to religious innovations and change. The several scattered towns and villages of United Empire Loyalist origins were reeling under successive waves of Methodism, Presbyterianism, and other non-Anglican Protestant religious invasions. More than anyone else, the credit for making Upper Canada a more fertile soil for religious pluralism must go to the Methodists, with preachers such as William Losee who, like his later Mormon counterparts, had crossed the St. Lawrence River in 1790 to preach in the British colonies.[3] By the outbreak of the War of 1812, Losee and his Methodist colleagues had established their gospel with amazing success up and down the St. Lawrence Valley, into the eastern townships of Lower Canada and into many parts of Nova Scotia, New Brunswick and Prince Edward Island.[4] Relying on itinerant ministers, local preachers, camp meetings and a fiery evangelism, Methodists multiplied their numbers in Upper Canada from 165 in 1792 to more than 80,050 years later.[5]

The growth of Methodism challenged the so-called "Family Compact," the Anglican Tory elite that dominated colonial government and sought to "establish" the Church of England. By the time the first Mormon missionaries set foot on Upper Canadian soil, the battle lines were firmly drawn between Tory traditionalists, who favored the legal establishment of the Church of England, the granting of crown lands to support the established church, and the existing representative—but not responsible—structure of colonial government, and the Reformers, who sought a more responsible form of government, religious pluralism and local representation. The Canadian social and political climate of 1830 was, therefore, as unsettled and fluid politically as it was receptive religiously to change and experimentation.

Latter-day Saint missionary efforts in Canada between 1830 and 1850 evolved through three distinct stages, each of which was heavily influenced by developments within the church and colony. The first stage can be labelled the exploratory period; the second, the emphatic or concentrated years; and the third, the aftermath.

The earliest or exploratory stage, marking the first half of the decade of the 1830s, saw enthusiastic, new American converts visit their British Canadian relations. "Whether following an inward 'call' or appointed by the church to preach," wrote one keen observer of the time, "missionaries during these years followed the line of most profitable results and visited their friends and relatives.... As the church became more thoroughly organized...the number of appointed missions gradually increased."[6] These visits were motivated individually rather than the product of systematic organization. In the case of Phineas and Joseph Young, brothers of Brigham Young, the initial visit was a Methodist minister-turned-Mormon seeking after his preacher-brother in Canada and, along the way, preaching to all who would listen to him. "We soon reached Earnest Town where we commenced our labor," wrote Phineas. "I tarried some time with my brother [Joseph Young] trying to preach, but could think of little except the *Book of Mormon*...I then told him I could not preach and...I accordingly started in a few days."[7] Soon afterwards, in early 1832, Phineas and Brigham Young were back in the Kingston area specifically to convert their older brother. The trio was baptized in April of that year. Within a matter of months, all three were travelling back over their northern New York and Upper Canadian circuits, preaching their newfound faith to their old Reformed Methodist friends and congregations.

Joining the Youngs were Eliel Strong and Eleazer Miller who, though having baptized five in Earnestown in 1832, underscored the handicap of not receiving clear directions.

> We have labored under some disadvantage, not having instructions till within a few months past, respecting this great work, other than the *Articles*, *Book of Mormon* and the *Comforter*.... Hence we would call upon our Brethren in Zion, from whence the light is to flow, and to proceed to remember us....[8]

As a result of these missionary labors, approximately 150 people converted to Mormonism in the Frontenac region and at least four small branches (or congregations) were organized, including Kingston, Earnestown, Loughborough and West Loughborough.[9]

The preaching-to-relatives approach was also responsible for Mormonism's first inroads farther west in the Niagara peninsula region. Freeman Nickerson, who had been baptized in Dayton, New York, in April 1833, was so determined to convert his son and family living across the border that he cajoled and persuaded the first presidency of the church—Joseph Smith and Sidney Rigdon—to accompany him to Canada.[10] Subsequently, in October 1833, Freeman A. Nickerson and his wife were baptized by his father, as were several other family members, and branches were organized in the Mt. Pleasant, Brantford and Colborne areas.

Joseph Smith and Sidney Rigdon, themselves accompanied by Nickerson Sr., made the trip coming via Buffalo, Niagara, St. Catharines, and

Brantford, and Colborne, making a number of converts and organizing a branch of the Church at Mt. Pleasant, and Freeman Nickerson Jr., was ordained elder and made pastor of the Mt. Pleasant congregation.... Freeman Nickerson Jr. had so many converts he wrote to Joseph Smith for assistance a few months after he was ordained.[11]

From the Nickerson nucleus, new converts spread the work and soon established two more branches in Colborne and Brantford.

Gradually, these early visits gave way to a more systematic approach. By the spring of 1835 church government had matured to include a Council of Twelve Apostles, a presiding patriarch, and a First Council of Seventy.[12] In particular, the "Seventies" were to be missionaries and missionary directors. The results were an improved proselytizing effort with more careful and deliberate "callings" of missionaries to specified areas in the United States and British North America. With this refinement in church government came the second or "concentrated" stage in Mormon missionary efforts in the Canadas.

Between 1835 and 1839, at least 25 men were specifically called to leave America and come to the Canadas to preach in assigned areas. Their numbers quickly doubled when local convert companions were included in counts of missionaries.[13] Of these missionaries, five can be selected whose experiences are representative of the breadth and varying success of their efforts.

Peter Dustin, obviously following in the footsteps of his prophet-leader, Joseph Smith, left Kirtland, Ohio, 11 June 1835, not to visit relatives, but, as he said, "to fill a mission in the province of Upper Canada." Travelling by way of Buffalo, he proceeded on to Mt. Pleasant and from there to Malahide, where he soon established a branch of 35 members. Referring to his labors in crusading terms common among his colleagues, Dustin reported:

There, as in all other places, when the people or the meek began to embrace the truth, the enemy raged, and the meek rejoiced in the midst of all the slanderous reports. I stayed there about two months; one month baptizing and laboring publicly, and from house to house and the remainder of the time I spent in teaching them the pure daily walk.[14]

Lower Canada, with its overwhelming Catholic presence and French-speaking population, proved daunting to Mormon, as well as most Protestant evangelical efforts. Montreal and Quebec City were mere stopovers for missionaries on their way farther east to the Maritimes.[15] Some Latter-day Saint emissaries, however, penetrated the English-speaking, predominantly

Protestant southern townships. Hazen Aldrich and Winslow Farr preached through the region in the spring of 1836[16] and baptized the Joseph Fish, Hannah Leavitt and Franklin Chamberlain families in Stanstead County, where the first branch of the Latter-day Saints established in Lower Canada was organized in Hatley.[17] Within the year, 23 new converts, following the charge to gather to America, had sold their farms and were ready to migrate.[18] As Sarah Leavitt later recalled, "Grandfather had never belonged to any church but seemed to get the spirit of gathering, filled up an outfit, and with neighbors and relatives started for Zion. They left Hatley July 20, 1837," and in their wake they left only a remnant of believers behind.[19]

Farther east, Lyman E. Johnson was apparently the first missionary assigned to preach in New Brunswick. He visited Saint John in the spring of 1836.[20] Johnson, in company with John Heriot, travelled on to Sackville, near the Bay of Fundy, where they organized a branch of 18 members—the first in the Maritimes.[21]

Far and away the most successful Mormon missionary in British North America was John E. Page. Converted to Mormonism in August 1833, and manifesting a remarkable talent for preaching the *Book of Mormon*, Page received his first Canadian mission assignment in the fall of 1835.[22] His specific charge was to return to the Frontenac, Addington and Leeds counties area and resume the work that the Young brothers had begun three years before. Accompanied initially by William Harris, and later by James Blakesley, Page combed through the rocky townships of Loughborough, Bedford Mills, North Crosby, Elgin, as far north as Perth, and possibly extending to Bytown (Ottawa). After seven months of active proselytizing, he returned to Kirtland, leaving behind no less than 267 converts in newly established branches in Perth, Elgin, and North and South Crosby townships.[23]

Buoyed by Page's positive report, church leaders directed him to return the following spring, this time with his wife and two small children.[24] During his second missionary tour, Page realized even greater success, converting another four hundred souls and establishing branches in Bedford, Bathurst, North and East Bathurst, Leeds and Williamsburg. Clearly one of the most effective advocates of Mormonism, Page was called "Son of Thunder" because of his spellbinding and convincing style of preaching—a talent his converts remembered well.[25] Zadok Judd wrote:

The coming of the Mormon elders, John E. Page and James Blakesley...made quite a stir in the neighborhood. They preached a new

John Taylor, 1808-1887. Born in England, Methodist minister, converted to Mormon faith in Toronto, 1836, became a Church Apostle 1838 and President of the Church in 1880. P1300/4LDS Archives.

doctrine. My father went to their preaching and after hearing two or three sermons I heard him remark 'If the Methodists would preach as they do and prove all their points of doctrine like that, how I would like it.'[26]

Page's success might have benefited somewhat from the contrast between the depressed economic state of the settlers on the poor, rocky farmlands of Bathurst and Dundas districts and his persuasive remarks of a new land of promise on the American frontier.[27] By the time he returned to the United States in May 1838, Page captained a company of one to two hundred Canadian converts across the St. Lawrence, enroute to the Mormon settlements in western Missouri.[28]

In addition to Page, another convincing preacher assigned to Upper Canada at this time was Parley P. Pratt, a member of the recently organized Council of Twelve Apostles.[29] Pratt's two missions to Toronto in 1836 and 1837 are best remembered in Latter-day Saint history for his success among disaffected Primitive Methodists, particularly his conversion of the Englishman John Taylor, who later succeeded Brigham Young as the third president of the church. Scorned by Toronto's clergy and prevented from preaching in public or at pulpit, Pratt, in utter frustration, was about to return home when Isabella Walton, a friend of the Taylors', invited him into her house to hear his message. Soon afterwards, she, with her niece Ann Wanless and Sarah Kavanaugh were baptized in Toronto Bay.[30] From there, the message carried to her brother and sister, Isaac Russell and Frances Dawson, nine miles northwest of Toronto, in what was then called the Charleston settlement.

From this new base of operations, Pratt did well, converting such later well-known individuals in Mormon history as Theodore Turley, Samuel Mulliner, Joseph Fielding and his sisters Mary and Mercy, Isaac Russell, William and Wilson Law, and many more.[31] The work spread rapidly throughout the neighboring townships, enlarging the circuit of Pratt's labors to the point that he "had to travel continually from branch to branch and neighborhood to neighborhood."[32] During the summers of 1836 and 1837, Parley P. Pratt and Orson Hyde converted scores of people in Charleston, Markam, Scarborough, Boston Mills, Churchville and Toronto. It is difficult to determine precisely the Mormon impact on the people of these communities, but Fred Landon, a prominent southern Ontario historian, writes that, outside Toronto in the Yonge Street circuit, the Canadian Methodists, under Egerton Ryerson, "lost heavily to the Mormons, the[ir] membership declining from 951 to 578 in 1836."[33]

A thorough examination of the factors accounting for Pratt's success is beyond the scope of this essay, but three elements bear passing mention. Pratt and his companions were seasoned, skillful missionaries who taught forcefully and provided many of their listeners with the kinds of spiritual experiences one might expect from religious leaders. Wrote John Taylor,

> You ask about healing the sick. I have seen...scores of instances of it. The power of the Lord is indeed manifest in the church. When any are sick among us, we do not send for a doctor, but for the elders of the church, who, according to the admonitions of James, pray for the sick, and anoint them with oil in the name of the Lord; and the prayer of faith heals the sick and the Lord raises him up. They are not always healed but generally according to their faith.[34]

A second factor was the deteriorating political situation, which soon afterwards erupted into the Rebellions of 1837, pitting radical reformers against the ruling elite. William Lyon Mackenzie, the fiery leader of the reformers, befriended Pratt and offered him his journalistic support as well as his facilities for preaching.[35] Appearing in Mackenzie's popular, short-lived newspaper, *The Constitution*, while Pratt was preaching north of Toronto, was the following:

> Its miracles too are very well attested; the visit of the angel [Moroni] to Smith, its founder, is as positively stated, and fully believed, as any of the Angel visits mentioned in the Scripture...and all of its miracles being of a very similar kind to those recorded in the ancient records of our faith, they will probably possess a vigorous influence over the vastly swelling populations of the mighty west for many future centuries.[36]

If not religious allies, Mackenzie and Pratt were fast friends and obviously shared some of the same political views.[37] At the same time that Mackenzie and others were fleeing southward in 1837 to escape the reprisals of a victorious colonial compact, Pratt was leading his new converts in the same direction.

If political unrest was an aid to Pratt's preaching, so also was religious discord. The divisions then arising among Canadian Methodists, following Egerton Ryerson's decision to join the British Wesleyans, could not have come at a more propitious time. Many Methodists believed that Ryerson had compromised his reformist position in the name of religious unity to the point that his leadership was no longer acceptable. They began forming their own Methodist societies (including the Methodist Episcopal Church). It was in this climate of religious disruption that John Taylor and other discontents formed their own separate groups. They were open to preachers such as Pratt.

The third and final phase or twilight years of Mormon proselytizing efforts in pre-Confederation Canada coincided with the westward move of the church, first to Nauvoo, Illinois, and then later to the Great Basin in the Rocky Mountains. By 1840, the days of Mormonism's best preachers active in the Canadas—the Joseph Smiths, Sidney Rigdons, Parley P. Pratts and John E. Pages—were over. The church was looking overseas to Britain and Scandinavia and other more populated areas for much larger returns than Canada could provide. This period was characterized by the occasional family member returning to preach to relatives and friends, by significant if sporadic work in the Maritimes, and by a redoubling of efforts on the part of recent converts to sell out and immigrate to America.

Daniel Wood, an 1832 convert of Brigham Young in Sydenham, Upper Canada, is representative of the many who tried their hand with relatives who had previously rejected Mormonism or, if they had converted, refused to move south for economic or other reasons. After Daniel met his brother, James, at an outdoor Kingston market in the summer of 1845, the two travelled on to their father's home in Sydenham. "My father met me just outside the door and he took me by the hand and led me into his room and it was a long time before we could speak to each other and the tears flowed down our cheeks."[38] During his short ten-day visit, Wood preached as often as he could among his Reformed Methodist friends and relatives. "Not one of them raised an argument against me but they appeared to be astonished while I was preaching."[39]

George Lake, whose parents, James and Philomela Lake, had also been converted by Brigham Young, told of a similar experience when he returned later in the century (1870s) to preach among relatives. His experience with his uncle is indicative of the initially cool reception usually given these family emissaries.

> "Is Jim a Mormon yet?" meaning my Father. I answered, "Yes." Are you a Mormon? "Yes." "Where have you been?" To England on a mission." At this he loosened his bolts and all were invited into the house when he began a bitter herang [sic] against the Mormons. After he had belched forth the venom that long since accumulated in his heart I asked the liberty to reply which was granted...[I] gave an account of the restoration of the Gospel...which brought tears to the eyes of all present. At the close all was silent. The old gentleman stated that he had heard [sic] Brigham and Joseph Young and others of our leading men but never did he hear it as I explained it.[40]

Such receptions usually became warm, polite and kind, but rarely resulted in any conversions. The tide had gone out.[41]

The mid-1840s saw an acceleration of the church-wide trend for distant converts to sell out at any price and gather to Zion. In Lambton County, where Robert Borrowman had converted several families in the Watford-Alvinston area, the new converts readily accepted the counsel of John A. Smith (recently dispatched from Nauvoo in 1846) to head for the Rocky Mountains, as "there was no time to lose." "Property at that time was very low in price," Robert Gardner, Jr. remembered, and they sold their farm of one hundred acres "fifty of it cleared off and farmed, with a barn 60 feet long, 30 feet of it covered with walnut board and a good log house all for $500.00."[42] Enthusiasm for the migration was such that they willingly cut a new road through the forest for their wagons en route to Sarnia.[43] Similarly, in the Maritimes, the little success the Mormons had enjoyed was cut short by the rush to emigrate. Building on Lyman E. Johnson's efforts in New Brunswick eight years before, Jessie W. Crosby and his companions arrived in Fredericton in June 1844, and, in his words, "were the first Latter-day Saints that ever journeyed that way." Crosby's efforts eventually raised the ire of the province's crown-appointed lieutenant-governor.

> We repaired to Fredericton, appeared before his Excellency, the Governor; our names were recorded and our place of residence. Our documents underwent an investigation—the Governor was very inquisitive. I was somewhat surprised that the Governor should enter into a debate with us, but this he did, and it lasted about two hours. Many points of our doctrine were taken up; at last, finding himself hard run for arguments accused us of being unacquainted with the dead languages.... Lawyer Wilmot, the Governor's Chief Counselor, treated us kindly, and told us there was no law that could harm us.[44]

After converting a dozen people in Queensbury and another twenty in and about the capital, opponents soon forced them to leave. Farther south, four small branches had been organized the year before (1843) in Nova Scotia—Halifax, Preston, Onslow and Pope's Harbour—with a combined membership of roughly one hundred.[45] These congregations, plus the two in Charlottetown and Beddequi, Prince Edward Island, and the Miramachi branch of south New Brunswick, chartered a vessel in March 1846 "of about two hundred tons register" to leave Halifax for San Francisco the following September.[46] With their departure, Mormonism virtually vanished from Atlantic Canada for the next fifty years.

By the early 1840s, more than two thousand people had converted to Mormonism in British North America, constituting at least 38 branches from Lambton County, Upper Canada, to Prince Edward Island. And the popularity (or notoriety) of the new faith was relatively well documented in the press, as 22 different Upper Canadian newspapers ran at least 236 articles on the subject between 1830 and 1850. If the term "movement" is too strong an appellation for the Mormon experience in British North America at this time, it certainly constituted an "influence" of which most Canadians were aware.

The decline of the Latter-day Saint presence in what is today eastern Canada was as sharp and precipitous as was its sudden rise. Although there were upwards of two thousand converts in the 1830s and 1840s, by 1851,

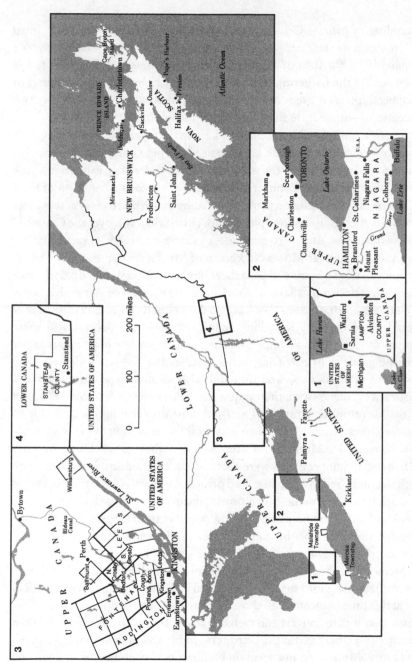

Figure 2.1: Mormon presence in Canada, 1830–1850

according to official Census tabulations, only 247 respondents claimed Mormonism as their religion. Ten years later, the figure was down to a minuscule 74.[47] Much of this decline can, of course, be attributed to the emphasis on the gathering and the plucking, rather than the planting, of membership. Yet even at its apex, Mormonism—with one or two exceptions—made little impact. Why was this so?

The first, and possibly foremost, factor in these years was Mormonism's organizational infancy. The advantage of the proximity of the Canadian mission field was offset by the small and diverse cadre of missionaries whose appeal was tied to kin connections and the absence of a tradition of local influence. As a new religion in the area, Mormonism had to gain acceptance. Unlike its Methodist counterparts, with circuit riders all over the Canadas, Mormonism was unable to generate a sufficient number of missionaries. One can almost hear Moses Nickerson of Mt. Pleasant pleading in 1833, "If you can send a couple of preachers out here...you would do us a kindness.... It is necessary that someone should be here,"[48] or Zerababel Snow declaring in exasperation, "We have no doubt but thousands in this country would come into the Kingdom...could faithful men proclaim in these regions."[49] And with so much of the local talent leaving or absent, or preaching in the British Isles, little wonder that the work slowed. The surprising thing is how well they did with so small and disorganized a missionary force. As well, there might have been a certain "latecomer" aspect to the Mormon penetration. The Methodist invasion had preceded it by thirty to forty years. Methodism was established among many who might have converted to Mormonism later. As it was, the overwhelming majority of Latter-day Saint converts were Methodists. Methodism, in the aftermath of the second Great Awakening, had preached a moral reform that had raged through English Canada. Mormonism, meanwhile, stressed more of a new theology and doctrine rather than a popular moral crusade. One must wonder how many of the common folk could grasp the theological differences that the Mormon preacher espoused.

Methodism, Anglicanism and certainly Catholicism had been able to weave themselves into the social, political and religious fabric of Canadian life at this time. Mormonism chose not to do so. The simple purpose of the missionary was to convert and then to gather. To be converted and then not sacrifice to gather, as did the Gardners, Judds and many others, was contradictory. Money was not spent on building local churches but in financing outfits for the American West. Though it is true that many made the move, many more refused to join—or, if they did join, they did so because of strong family connections and economic responsibilities. Those who stayed behind simply fell away.

If it can be argued that part of Mormonism's early success can be attributed to its acceptance by radical reformers such as William Lyon Mackenzie, it can be argued equally well that, among Loyalists and recent British immigrants prone to support British traditions, Mormonism smacked too much of "Yankeeism" at a time when folk memory could easily recall the events of the War of 1812. Some of Mormonism's earliest doctrines proclaimed that the American Revolution and Constitution were of "divine origin."[50] Wrote one Methodist preacher upon learning of such tenets,

> If this emanated from God, then it must be acknowledged 1. that the British colonies were in bondage; 2. that the end they proposed had the divine sanction; 3. that those who brought them to that end, were brought into existence for that purpose; and 4. that the republican government of the U.S. is of divine origin. But who will believe either [*sic*] propositions.[51]

Consequently, Mormonism made little headway among the Anglican and Loyalist populations. It is not coincidental that its decline began with the collapse of the Rebellions of 1837.

The full history of this significant chapter in both Mormon and Canadian history is a much larger story than what this essay has described. It is a story that has been overlooked by students in both areas of scholarship. Mormonism was an influence, albeit of varying proportions, in different regions of British North America during these years. In some areas, particularly along the Rideau Canal, its impact was substantial. Although its influence in relation to other churches might be evaluated as being small, Mormonism reached across a wide area of British North America. As well, Mormon historians must realize that the seeds of future and spectacular growth in the church in the British Isles were sown in the Canadian missionary work, as so many of the Toronto-area members in particular went on to play a pivotal role in the British proselytizing effort. Indeed, while it might be true that the church went on to make a real impact on the history and development of Alberta and the Canadian West later in the nineteenth century, a significant aspect of the heritage of early Mormonism can be traced to eastern Canada and the first attempts to preach in a new land among a new people.

NOTES

1. For a more extended study of the history of Mormonism in Upper Canada during these years, see the author's master's thesis, "A Study of the Church of Jesus Christ of Latter-day Saints in Upper Canada, 1830-1850" (Provo, Utah: Brigham Young University, 1975). See also Melvin S. Tagg, "A History of the Church of Jesus Christ of Latter-day Saints in Canada, 1830-1963" (doctoral dissertation, Brigham Young University, 1963), pp. 12-73.

2. Andrew Jenson, *Latter-day Saint Biographical Encyclopedia*, 4 vols. (Salt Lake City: Andrew Jenson History Company, 1901), Vol. 1, p. 187.

3. M.L. Scudder, *American Methodism* (Hartford, Conn: S.S. Scranton and Company, 1867), pp. 246-47.

4. Ibid., pp. 262-63.

5. J.A. Williams, "Methodism in Canada," *The Methodist Quarterly Review*, 49 (April 1867), p. 221.

6. Samuel George Ellsworth, "A History of Mormon Missions in the U.S. and Canada, 1830-1860" (doctoral dissertation, University of California, Berkeley, 1951), pp. 93-94.

7. "History of Brigham Young," *Millennial Star*, 25 (June 1863), p. 375.

8. Letter of Eliel Strong and Eleazer Miller to "Dear Brethren in Zion," 19 March 1833, and found in the *Evening and Morning Star*, Vol. 1, no. 12 (May 1833).

9. Journal History, 1 April 1833, Church Historical Department, the Church of Jesus Christ of Latter-day Saints, 50 East North Temple St., Salt Lake City, Utah. Hereafter referred to as Church Historical Dept.

10. Journal of Joseph Smith, Jr., 17-22 October 1833, Joseph Smith, Jr. Papers, Church Historical Dept.

11. "Tweedsmuir Histories," Ontario Public Archives, Toronto.

12. James B. Allen and Glen M. Leonard, *The Story of the Latter-day Saints* (Salt Lake City: Deseret Book Company, 1976), pp. 80-81. See also Joseph Smith, Jr., *History of the Church of Jesus Christ of Latter-day Saints*, 7 vols. (Salt Lake City: Deseret Book Company, 1948), 2, p. 203 and Doctrine and Covenants, Section 107.

13. See Bennett, "A Study of the Latter-day Saints in Upper Canada," pp. 93-95.

14. *The Latter-day Saints Messenger and Advocate*, 2 (October 1835), p. 207 for a letter from Peter Dustin to John Whitmer 21 October 1835.

15. Journal of Jessie Crosby, Church Historical Dept.

16. Melvin S. Tagg, "A Collection of Historical and Genealogical Items Concerning the Church of Jesus Christ of Latter-day Saints in Eastern Canada as copied from the collection of Thomas S. Monson and Mahala M. Waywell" (April 1963), p. 7. A copy of this compilation is in the hands of the author and on file in the Church Historical Dept.

17. Brigham H. Roberts, *The Comprehensive History of The Church of Jesus Christ of Latter-day Saints*, 6 vols. (Salt Lake City: Deseret News Press, 1930), 1, p. 394.

18. History of Sarah Studevant Leavitt, p. 7, Church Historical Dept. See also film #180.

19. Ibid.

20. "History of Lyman E. Johnson," *Millennial Star*, 27 (18 February 1865), p. 102.
21. Tagg, Collection of Historical and Genealogical Items, p. 6; and Journal of Marriner W. Merrill, Church Historical Dept.
22. "History of Brigham Young," *Millennial Star*, 27 (18 February 1865), p. 103.
23. *The Latter-day Saints Messenger and Advocate*, 3 (January 1837), p. 447.
24. "History of Brigham Young," *Millennial Star*, 27 (18 February 1865), p. 103.
25. Justin E. Page to Wilford Poulson, 22 April 1835, W. Poulson Papers, Special Collections, Harold B. Lee Library, Brigham Young University, Provo, Utah.
26. "Journal of Zadok Knapp Judd," n.d., Zadok Judd Papers, Church Historical Dept.
27. Dell H. and Deloris A. Hill, comp. *Daniel Currie Hill—Ancestry, History and Descendants* (Providence, Utah: Keith Watkins and Sons, n.d.), p. 8.
28. Canadian Mission Manuscript, 14 May 1838, Church Historical Dept. See also Journal History 14 May 1838.
29. Parley P. Pratt, ed., *Autobiography of Parley P. Pratt* (Salt Lake City: Deseret Book Company, 1980), pp. 130-31.
30. Mrs. Isabella Johnson, "Biographical Sketch of Isaac Russell," n.d., Isaac Russell Papers, Church Historical Dept.
31. Ibid.
32. Pratt, *Autobiography*, p. 153.
33. Fred Landon, *Western Ontario and the American Frontier* (Toronto: Ryerson Press, 1941), pp. 125-26.
34. Journal of Joseph Smith, 29 October 1833. Church Historical Dept.
35. Pratt, *Autobiography*, p. 179.
36. The *Constitution*, #9, 31 August 1836.
37. 1843-1857 newspaper clippings on Parley P. Pratt are found in the Mackenzie-Lindsey Papers, Ontario Archives, Toronto, Ontario. There are almost fifty clippings in the collection.
38. Journal of Daniel Wood, no specific date. Church Historical Dept.
39. Ibid.
40. "A Part of the Diary of George Lake," p.m., Papers of George Lake, Church Historical Dept.
41. One exception to this apparent failure of effort was Robert Borrowman who converted several members of his extended family in the Watford-Alvinston area of Lambton County, Upper Canada, in 1845.
42. "History of Robert Gardner, Jr., written by himself, January 7, 1884," p. 10. Church Historical Dept.
43. Report of William Nisbet to the Sarnia Historical Society, 5 December 1834, Ontario Archives.
44. The Journal of Jessie W. Crosby, pp. 17-19, Church Historical Dept. Cf., the author's "A Study of the Church of Jesus Christ of Latter-day Saints in Upper Canada, 1830-1850," with his later work: "*And Should We Die": Mormons at the Missouri, 1846-1852* (Norman: University of Oklahoma Press, 1987). See also Tagg, "A History of the Church of Jesus Christ of Latter-day Saints in Canada...," pp. 23, 43-46, 53-57, for instances of opposition.

45. Journal History, 18 September 1843 and 19 February 1844.
46. Letter of William A. Smith to Wilford Woodruff, Journal History, 2 March 1846.
47. *Census of the Canadas, 1851-1852*, Vol. 1 (Quebec: John Lovell Steam Printing Press, 1853, est.); and *Census of the Canadas* for 1861-62.
48. Moses Nickerson to Sidney Rigdon, 20 December 1833, as quoted in the *Evening and Morning Star*, 2, p. 269.
49. Latter-day Saints *Messenger and Advocate* (November 1834) 1, p. 45.
50. *Doctrine and Covenants of the Church of Jesus Christ of Latter-day Saints* (Salt Lake City: published by the church, 1981), Section 107, p. 80.
51. *The Christian Guardian*, 6 December 1837.

3 British Columbia and the Mormons in the Nineteenth Century

ROBERT J. McCUE

WHEN CHARLES ORA CARD established his "colony" of Latter-day Saints on Lee Creek in the spring of 1887, he was filled with joyful enthusiasm at the prospect of justice for all under the British flag. Initially there was no hostility, the newspaper editors apparently sizing up these American exiles to see if they fitted the Canadians' preconceived notions with respect to Mormons.

It took until 21 November 1888 for the editor of the *Victoria Daily Colonist* to make up his mind and he then pronounced Card and his followers to be "not desireable settlers." That he waited as long as he did to comment is a tribute to his sense of fair-play, when one considers the "Mormon" fare his paper had served up to his readers in the past. Much that he had printed was far from flattering, nevertheless he was prepared to "wait and see"; until the Mormon request to be allowed to bring more than one wife to Canada convinced him that Card and his company were no different than their fellows in Utah. This willingness to tolerate Mormons just as long as they did not practise polygamy should not be surprising as it is reminiscent of the official British government policy as outlined to James Douglas three decades earlier.

The relationship between Mormons, British Columbia and British Columbians in the four-and-one-half decades from 1845 to 1890 has two distinct aspects: Mormon interest in British Columbia as a place to settle, and British Columbian interest in Mormons as evidenced by the news items and editorials in local papers. These two aspects will be examined in turn.

The first mention of British Columbia as a possible center of Mormon colonization appears to have occurred in 1845 in a letter that Brigham

35

Young addressed to Latter-day Saints throughout the world, inviting them to gather in Nauvoo in preparation for moving westward in the spring of 1846. A postscript to this epistle observed, "There are said to be many good locations for settlement on the Pacific, especially Vancouver's Island, near the mouth of the Columbia."[1] Hubert Howe Bancroft, in his *History of Utah*,[2] cites the *Niles Register*[3] for the assertion that "There were many current reports in Illinois in 1845 that 'the Mormons had chosen Vancouver Island as their future home, the metropolis to be situated at Nootka.' "

Nootka of course is still no metropolis, Mormon or otherwise, and Brigham Young led the majority of the Latter-day Saints not to Vancouver Island but to the Great Basin of the Rocky Mountains in 1847. Meanwhile, Mormon interest in the Island had developed in another locale. The leaders of the Saints in Great Britain, knowing that the British government was actively considering the question of establishing colonies on Vancouver Island, petitioned Queen Victoria and the British Parliament. They asked for land on which to settle "nearly twenty thousand able and intelligent people."[4] As there were only some 15,000 Latter-day Saints in Britain at the time the difference was apparently to be made up with penurious non-Mormons who wished to emigrate.[5] This proposal was not favored, ostensibly because of the expense to the Crown in getting the immigrants to Vancouver Island and supplying them with land.[6] It became a dead issue in January 1849 when a charter was issued to the Hudson's Bay Company giving it exclusive rights to colonize Vancouver Island.[7]

But Mormon interest in the Island revived in 1857 with the possibility that the Mormons would be forced out of Utah by the "Mormon War" and the campaign of the United States government to force the abandonment of polygamy. Inquiries were directed by Mormon leaders to the British government relative to the availability of land in "British Territory on the North West Coast of America."[8] James Douglas, agent for the Hudson's Bay Company and governor of the Island, received detailed instruction from the British government on how to respond to any Mormon request to take up residence on the lands within his jurisdiction.

Should they apply...to occupy any portion of the North Western Territory...as a community or in scattered communities: you will remember that...Her Majesty's Government are [sic] not prepared at present to exercise the right reserved to them in the Company's license of forming a Colony in these parts. Least of all would they exercise that right in favour of refugees who have defied both the Authorities of their country and the usage of Christian and Civilized life.

No rights of occupation whatever are therefore to be granted to them.

If, however, Individuals or families...should peacefully apply for admission into Vancouver's Island the case is different. Much must be left to your discretion.... The acquisition of land for purposes of settlement under the ordinary rules...is not in the view of Her Majesty's Government to be refused, merely because the parties applying have been members of that territorial community against which the arms of the United States Government are now directed. But this can only take place on the supposition that such immigrants submit themselves entirely to the laws of England, as retained in the Colonial community over which you preside.

Polygamy is not tolerated by those laws; and if any attempt should be made to continue...that system, I rely on the good will of the Legislature and authorities to devise means by which such abuses may be effectually suppressed.[9]

It appears that Douglas had no need to implement these instructions as no group of Mormons ever requested his permission to settle within his jurisdiction.[10] The Mormon Church showed no further interest in British Columbia until 1886 when the Charles Ora Card party crossed the 49th parallel looking for a haven under the British flag.

The first documented arrival in British Columbia of Mormons to whom names can be attached was a Utah family which had made its way to Vancouver Island, not, evidently, in search of a haven from persecution but more likely in quest of wealth through prospecting for gold. William Francis Copley, his wife Maria and three small children arrived in Victoria from San Francisco in June 1875. The fact that the Copley's were Mormons seems to have passed either unknown or unnoticed by their contemporaries.[11]

It appears that the next Mormons to come to British Columbia arrived in 1886. Charles Ora Card and his companions would have been quite happy to settle in the southeastern portion of Canada's most westerly province, but they reported that the good land was all occupied, either as Indian reserves or as ranches.[12] They looked no farther west than Kamloops.

Although British Columbia did not become a Mormon haven, it did produce one convert to Mormonism in the nineteenth century. Anthony Maitland Stenhouse, son of a minor Scottish nobleman, arrived in Victoria on 22 March 1884.[13] After looking over available land on Vancouver Island, he settled in the Comox Valley, apparently intending to lead the life of a gentleman farmer. But that changed when he became an opposition candidate in the election of 1886 and won the right to represent Comox in the provincial parliament.[14] He played a very modest role in the legislature during the first session following his election, and then surprised everyone by announcing that he had been persuaded of the truthfulness of Mormonism, including polygamy, and intended to throw in his lot with that persecuted sect.[15] How he was converted remains a mystery. The Copleys are an unlikely source, and there were, of course, no Mormon missionaries in BC in 1886. It is known that Stenhouse carried on a correspondence with Wilford Woodruff, but the earliest of the extant six letters to Woodruff presupposes earlier correspondence, probably with John Taylor; however, no such letters have been found.[16] In fact, none of Stenhouse's correspondence, other than with Wilford Woodruff and some published letters in various newspapers, appears to have survived him. He did not remain in British Columbia after deciding to become a Mormon.

But what of British Columbian interest in and attitudes about Mormons? What image of Mormonism were British Columbians likely to possess as the Mormon settlement of Lee Creek struggled to establish itself?

In mid-1858 the residents of the far western portion of British North America began to be informed from local sources about the Mormons, as British Columbia's first newspaper, the *Victoria Gazette*, began publication on June 25, followed almost six months later by the *British Colonist* on December 8. Twice within the first couple of months of publication, the editor of the *Gazette* published extras (which he did not date), in both of which he devoted considerable space to the Mormons. It can be safely assumed that these reports gave British Columbia readers the distinct impression that the Mormons were a stubborn group. The arrival in Utah of Governor Alfred Cumming, Brigham Young's successor as governor of Utah Territory, was announced, and he reported that he had been respectfully received everywhere, but had been warned that if General Johnston's troops were to cross the mountains into the Great Salt Lake Valley, the torch would be applied to every house indiscriminately throughout the country.[17] But General Scott, in Washington, DC, indicated that General Johnston, in Utah with an army, disagreed with Governor Cumming's conclusions regarding the pacific intentions of the Mormons and considered them armed and dangerous. Not surprisingly, a later report from Salt Lake City indicated Mormon satisfaction with Governor Cumming, but "growing coldness between the Mormons and officers of the army."[18] (Any reference to Mormon interest in fleeing to Vancouver Island is conspicuously absent.)

Several examples from the mid-1880s served to show British Columbians that Mormons were not only stubborn but also violent.

Bishop West of Juab, Utah, spoke as follows on Sunday, March 9: It is time...that we ceased cowardly silence and humble submission.... It is time for us to fling their defiance and scurrilous domination back in their faces. The shade of the sainted martyr, Smith, calls aloud for vengeance. The time is at hand when the blood of our gentile persecutors shall be spilled on their own threshold to appease the anger of our prophet.... The thieving Murray [the governor] has...defied everyone but the devil, who is his sponsor. His head will be placed upon the walls of our city and his entrails scattered throughout the streets of Zion, that every gentile adventurer may behold....[19]

John Taylor, president of the Mormons, in a recent sermon said: "...forbearance might cease to be a virtue..." but he did not want blood to flow just yet. There would be a change before long.[20]

In the tabernacle yesterday Apostle Heber J. Grant said "Wo be unto the judge who sits on the bench of the Third District Court. We will not stand his abuse much longer...." The apostle warmly lauded those of the brethren who refused to submit to the law.... "Remember there is a limit, and this limit must soon be reached."[21]

More spectacular was an attack on the US district attorney "by three young Mormons who struck him in the face."[22] "Frank J. Cannon and Angus Cannon were held...in $1,000 bail each, for assault on US Attorney Dickson. S. Kenner was discharged."[23]

Rumors that the Mormons were arming to resist efforts to force cessation of polygamy also commanded attention,[24] as did mammoth Mormon meetings to protest anti-polygamy laws.[25] The prospect of having such neighbors, who in addition were accused of "throw[ing]...filth through the windows of lawyers and judges who took part in anti-polygamy trials"[26] must surely have seemed unattractive to British Columbia readers of the *Colonist*.

Another class of material that seems to have caught the eye of the editor regularly was friction between Mormon and "gentile" residents of Utah, material that conveys the impression that Mormons were unable to get along with their non-Mormon neighbors. For example, "both Mormon papers...call[ed] on their people to boycott the *Tribune*, the Gentile organ and...every business man who advertise [*sic*] in it."²⁷ Then the appointment by the federal government of Charles S. Zane, as chief justice of Utah inspired "a caucus of Mormon lawyers and their clients...to protest against the appointment.... The gentiles favor Zane, while the Mormons are satisfied with the nominal sentences pronounced upon their leaders by Chief Justice [Elliott] Sanford."²⁸ The impression had to be that the Mormons were a cantankerous lot.

But the conflict also had another side. Non-Mormons in Utah were not always easy to get along with either, and an unbiased reader of the *Colonist* might have concluded that the Mormons had been provoked. Consider these two incidents from 1884:

> Joseph Cook, addressing a mass-meeting at Salt Lake City, said; "Over the gate...of your False Prophet is represented a large eagle perched on a beehive, with his talons thrust deep into the hive. An excellent symbol of Mormonism—rapacity preying on industry! The priesthood preying on the people!"²⁹

This was followed only three weeks later by the report of an unpleasant welcome accorded an Irish immigrant convert on his arrival in Ogden and Salt Lake City by the non-Mormon Irish residents of those cities, "wearing green ribbons with a green flag draped in mourning [and] with a band wagon similarly trimmed...."³⁰

In 1885 considerable space was devoted to reporting a Fourth of July incident that intimated that Mormons were unpatriotic. Flags on public buildings and structures belonging to Mormons in Salt Lake City were flown at half-mast to mourn for "dead independence" (i.e., prosecution of polygamists) while non-Mormon residents expressed indignation at what they claimed was an insult to the flag.³¹

British Columbians might also have believed that Utah Mormons had no respect for the (non-Mormon) clergy. Mormon officials, it was said, were conspiring to "blacken the character of public men, and had begun the attack on 'Christian ministers'."³² A news story a year later seemingly confirmed this impression:

> An incendiary fire this morning burned the [Salt Lake City] Baptist mission school; insurance $8,000. It will be rebuilt immediately and the school will not be stopped.³³

Readers of the *Colonist* in 1887 had reason to think that the Mormon Church was about to collapse. It was reported that a US Marshall had taken "possession...of all books and property in the office of the President of the church."[34] It was speculated that Mormonism was at a crisis point, where it appeared that "failing energy and a readiness to give up the struggle" could be detected in Mormon ranks.[35] This idea would have been reinforced by the report of a "Victory for the Gentiles" in the Ogden, Utah, municipal elections of 1889: "The Gentiles carried the municipal elections today. It was their first victory and caused great rejoicing."[36]

Brigham Young and his family frequently seem to have been deemed good copy by Victoria editors, and literate British Columbians might have known quite a bit about them. Some of the published items, such as one copied from the Los Angeles *Star*, appealed to sensation seekers: "a letter from Salt Lake...states that one of Brigham Young's wives has lately given birth to a child with three eyes."[37] But years later there appeared this positive assessment of Brigham Young's children.

> As a physiological fact, of fifty-six children born to Brigham Young, not one was halt, lame, or blind, all being perfect in body and of sound mind and intellect;... The boys are a sound, healthy, industrious and intelligent group of men,...The girls are finely developed physically, quick and bright of intellect, highly spirited and often talented.[38]

Perhaps this favorable assessment in part resulted from the realization that members of the Young family were well received in many areas. For example, John W., "eldest son of Brigham Young," was reported to have "introduced Jos. D. Barclay, a member of parliament for Forfarshire, England... [and] president of the American pastoral company...."[39] Although the item does not indicate the locale or the audience to which the introduction was made, it had the effect of associating the name of a son of Brigham Young with prominent and respectable people.

An "informed" British Columbian in 1887 would also have "known" that by that time Brigham Young had fifteen hundred descendents[40] who were "fast going through" the more than $1,000,000 that he was reported to have left them.[41]

British Columbians would have known about the death of Brigham Young, "this remarkable administrator, prophet and despot." A rather lengthy biographical sketch told of his singular achievements but closed with this backhanded compliment:

He carved out a home for thousands in the heart of a howling wilderness; and divested of his many faults, indecencies, and hypocricies, Brigham Young will live in history as the author of much that was bad, mixed with a leaven of much that was good.[42]

The reading public of British Columbia was also informed about Mormon leadership changes and led to believe that change was not improvement. "John Taylor has been chosen president of the Twelve Apostles and acting president of the Mormon church,...Taylor was shot at the time Joseph Smith was killed, and is *a most bitter and bigotted fanatic*."[43] The subsequent death of this third president was announced with the terse statement that "John Taylor, president of the Mormon Church, died this afternoon."[44] More detailed notice was taken when the remains of the late president were transferred from a temporary grave to a

vault...built of large blocks of granite, girded together with steel bolts. The remains...were placed in the vault and a capstone weighing four and a half tons placed on it.[45]

The "succession question" created by Taylor's 1887 death was dealt with in a lengthy article that named Joseph F. Smith, George Q. Cannon and Wilford Woodruff as rivals for the vacant position and outlined the results hoped for by opponents of the Mormons:

The succession looks now very much as if it might be the rock on which all previous harmony is bound to split. The presidency is not likely to be settled for some time yet; and in any event disappointments are bound to come to the Mormon leaders.[46]

That is to say that the Mormons would in future likely get along among themselves no better than they were perceived to get along with the gentiles. The appointment of Woodruff was duly reported a year and a half later.[47]

Many British Columbians would have had their doubts about the authenticity of the *Book of Mormon* because of a story that practising Mormons have always denied:

David E. Whitmer,...still living in Missouri at the age of 80, was one of the three witnesses who in 1830 published a certificate declaring that they saw an angel come down with the golden book which Joseph Smith *pretended to interpret.* But when the witnesses were older they abjured Mormonism, and *declared their former testimony false.*[48]

British Columbians in the 1880s were relatively well informed of, and perhaps surprised at, the scope, problems and "threat" of Mormon missionary activity. "It will surprise many to know that the Mormon hierarchy had in the field last year more missionaries than the American Board [of Missions]."[49]

If one judges by the number of column inches devoted to it, the thing that residents of nineteenth-century British Columbia would most likely associate with Mormons was polygamy. An item quoting John T. Caine, "the Mormon delegate to Congress," gave some idea of why so many Mormon women were willing to enter into polygamy:

Marriage is with us a duty, and it is founded on the passage in the Scripture which says that a man must multiply and replenish the earth. The women of Utah look upon marriage as a religious duty and they marry in many cases more with a view to their condition in a future life than in this. According to our belief...the woman who does not marry does not attain her highest perfection on earth, and the old maid goes to heaven imperfectly prepared and unable there to stand on an equal plane with women who have been married.[50]

In addition, the *Colonist* supplied its readers with a considerable amount of information relating to the arrest and trial of polygamists. In the 22-month period between 21 March 1884 and 25 February 1886, it reported on the arrest of five "cohabitors" and the trial and sentencing of 16 others.[51]

Readers of the *Colonist* would have been justified in thinking that polygamy often generated tragedy:

A singular suicide occurred near Salt Lake this morning. Daniel Morris, age 84, a Mormon polygamist with three wives, after reading the governor's message, went to a shed adjoining the house and hanged himself.[52]

Isaac Langdon [of Salt Lake City], who lately took a second wife without the knowledge of the first, brought the former home a few days ago. The first wife was so shocked that she became temporarily insane. Her husband told her that she would soon get over it and went away with No. 2. The wife, in her frenzy, soon after rushed into the street and threw herself in front of a passing street car, which barely stopped in time to spare her life. Her dress was torn off and she received severe injuries, but was not seriously hurt.[53]

On the basis of Emma Smith Bidemon's vehement denial that her husband had ever practised it, readers of the *Colonist* would have concluded that polygamy was instituted in the Church of Jesus Christ of Latter-day Saints by Brigham Young. The *Colonist* borrowed from *Lippincott's Magazine* an account of a dramatic interview with the widow of the late prophet:

"No sir!...Joe Smith had but one wife and I was that one...Joe Smith knew very well that he couldn't have another wife, here or anywhere else. No, sir! Joe Smith had but one wife. He ruled the Mormons and I ruled him." As Mrs. Biddison [*sic*] spoke her eyes flashed, her nostrils expanded, and her whole form shook with passion. We were thoroughly satisfied that Mrs. Biddison had the ability to keep Joseph Smith...in the straight and narrow road of morality and decency.[54]

The editors of the *Colonist* had an eye for polygamy items that had a humorous touch, so that British Columbians, when not clucking their tongues in disgust at alleged Mormon immorality, must have at least smiled at some of the word pictures that were drawn:

We saw a week or two ago, walking down Main Street from the direction of the "President's Office," a man accompanied by four ladies. An air of slight perturbation in the party, mingled with evident expressions of satisfaction and happiness, led us to inquire who they were. Some one present informed us that they were a party that had been up to President Young's office to be married, and that the four ladies had just been united in indissoluble bonds to the man accompanying them. That, we suppose, might be termed marriage in gross.[55]

Then there was the case of Abram H. Cannon, on trial for unlawful cohabitation. "When asked if two women were his wives, and he had lived with them, he replied: 'They are, thank God! I have lived with them as charged.' Prompt conviction followed."[56]

But do the Mormons have a sense of humor? British Columbians might well have thought not on the basis of a story borrowed from the Salt Lake *Tribune*:

There is a "character" connected with one of the livery stables of this city who has on more than one occasion been the subject of anathemas from the *Deseret News*. His offence consists in driving tourists about the town to show them the sights of Zion, point out the double households, and in his own inimitable way tell the history of not a few of the chief polygamists....[57]

The impression was conveyed, even in stories intended to provoke a chuckle, that all Mormons were polygamous:

"Two girls and a merchant have disappeared from the town during the past three months, and have not been heard from since," says a dispatch from Clarington, Ohio. If the trio went together, Utah should be searched.[58]

John B. Wilkins, of St. Paul, *having the instincts of a Mormon*, married six wives within the year, and lived with them all, each having a separate establishment....[59]

The economics of polygamy held both a humorous and serious interest: "A Mormon editor has been arrested for supporting two wives. The arrest was undoubted[ly] justifiable. An editor with an income sufficient to support two wives must be engaged in some sort of crooked work."[60] On the serious side was a suggestion hardly to be expected, i.e., that there was nothing morally wrong with polygamy *per se*. Only when associated with religion was it objectionable:

Leaving the religious aspect of the case out of the question, *it would appear to be a good practical solution of the matrimonial question to permit men of means and polygamous tastes to marry as many wives as they choose to provide comfortable homes for!* Then the men who feel too poor to marry might remain single, as now, without cheating so many maidens...out of homes and husbands. In the multiplicity of doctrines for the settlement of the vexed questions of the day, a social science school may arise which will teach a system of this kind, not as a religion but as a philosophy or political economy. It would be a return, in one respect, to patriarchal days.[61]

And somewhere between the humorous and the practical is the suggestion "that the way to get the Mormons out of Utah is to populate the country with

Gentiles. But are the Gentiles as efficient populating agents as the Mormons?"[62]

British Columbians must have had some difficulty distinguishing fact from fiction when it came to stories about the Mormons. An example of an incredible tale comes from early 1887, apparently copied from an unnamed newspaper in the eastern United States. The story was that Brigham Young was not dead but living in Lincoln, Nebraska, and that he would soon make a public appearance claiming to be resurrected. Evidence presented to substantiate the story seems flimsy but interesting: (1) "The return of the prophet" has, for some time past, been taught by church leaders throughout Utah and Arizona. (2) Several months ago a St. Louis man claimed that Young was recognized in a London street. (3) Several prominent Salt Lake City Mormons were recently seen on the street in London. (4) "Important legislation is about to be enacted to the detriment of the Mormon church," and the veil of mystery with which the prophet's death has always been shrouded makes it almost certain that "he is risen."[63]

Regular readers of the *Colonist* were exposed to an interesting smattering of Utah statistics. For example, in 1885 there were said to be "twenty-eight baseball clubs and twenty brass bands in Salt Lake city" [sic],[64] and in 1887 that territory contained 400 Mormon bishops, 1,423 priests, 2,974 teachers and 6,854 deacons.[65]

Material that they would have read in 1888 probably made British Columbia residents distrustful of Mormon motives. When a bill to outlaw polygamy was introduced into the Utah legislature by a Mormon, it was said to be just "another move in the deliberate and desperate game that the Mormon leaders are playing to get their territory admitted as a state. If they could once accomplish their object, they would be free forever from Congressional control, and would thereafter manage their state to suit themselves."[66]

Mormons and Mormonism were usually so far away that British Columbians knew them only from hearsay. But when an occasional tourist group, such as the "Salt Lake Railway Party,"[67] visited Victoria, there was an opportunity to have personal contact with real, live Mormons. Visits by touring dramatic companies (but not from Utah) on occasion also offered a more intimate, although not necessarily accurate, perspective. A stage play,

"The Danites,"...was presented last evening by the McKee Rankin Company before a crowded house, and drew forth the highest enconiums. The scene of the play is laid in the Sierras, and the Danites are the destroying Angels of the Mormons...Sandy is a courageous and generous miner who takes an active part in punishing the Danites.[68]

When the play reappeared five years later, it attracted only a small audience.[69]

Great interest in Mormon colonization was aroused when news reached Victoria that Mormon colonists had taken up residence "at Lee's Creek, near Lethbridge," NWT.[70] Readers of the *Colonist* were informed regularly on the growth and success of Card's settlement, and the editor informed his readers that this colony "while part and parcel of the church of the Latter-day Saints...do[es] not practice polygamy."[71] Six months later, after the Lee Creek settlers had asked the Canadian federal government "to permit those of them who have already more than one wife to live with them," the editor was not so favorable:

They are not desirable settlers. At first they declared they had given up polygamy, and there were people simple enough to believe them. Now they are not so strong in their repudiation of their peculiar institution.... When they get stronger they will no doubt throw off the thin disguise they still retain and insist on practising polygamy according to the tenets of their religion. They will then be a separate community, and the tendency will be, as in the States, to make the distinction between Mormon and Gentile wider and wider as time progresses.... It will not be wise to aid in the introduction of such an element of discord and demoralization into the Canadian Northwest. If the Mormons settle in any part of the Dominion...no favors should be extended to them.[72]

Mormonism became of more local interest in British Columbia following the resignation of Mr. A. Maitland Stenhouse, MPP for Comox, from his seat in the legislature to facilitate his departure from the province and baptism into the Mormon Church. Stenhouse's resignation on 16 October 1887[73] was certainly not expected:

Mr. Maitland Stenhouse...yesterday tendered the resignation of his seat. It was somewhat of a surprise to the public when Mr. Stenhouse was declared the member for the northern island district,... But it will be a still greater surprise to know that Mr. Stenhouse has resigned his seat simply and solely for the purpose of becoming a member of the Mormon community in the great city by the Salt Lake.[74]

In the election campaign to fill the vacated seat, Stenhouse's motives were questioned,[75] and seven weeks after his resignation his political opponents were claiming that he had no intention of becoming a Mormon, of going to Salt Lake City, or of leaving British Columbia.[76] By mid-January 1888, it was confirmed that critics of Stenhouse were partly right. He would not go to Utah; he would go instead to join "the Mormon settlement in the Northwest."[77] The Mormon convert left Vancouver Island on the SS *Louise* on 21 April 1888[78] for the mainland, where he entrained for Lethbridge, proceeded immediately to Cardston, and was baptised into the Church of Jesus Christ of Latter-day Saints by Charles Ora Card, on 10 June 1888.[79] After his departure from British Columbia, references to him in the *Colonist* became less frequent, averaging once a month during the rest of 1888, a total of eight references in all of 1889, and only one reference in 1890. His baptism was of local interest,[80] as was his ordination into the Mormon priesthood.[81] Before the end of the year, rumor had it that "Apostle" Stenhouse had already married three wives,[82] but he apparently remained a bachelor to the end of his days.[83]

Mr. Stenhouse's spirited defence of polygamy and his claim that there was no law making it illegal in Canada[84] inspired the Parliament of Canada to pass an act imposing five years' imprisonment and a fine of $500 upon every person guilty of polygamy.[85]

So, as the Mormons settled in on Lee Creek, British Columbians had been told that Brigham Young, not Joseph Smith, was the father of polygamy, and that the same Brigham Young was not dead and would soon reappear claiming to be risen from the dead. They knew that there had been problems of unity among the Saints, and that some people, such as David Whitmer, a witness to the *Book of Mormon*, had become disaffected. Some had seen a play about the "Danites," which portrayed the Mormons as bloody murderers. They had also had personal contact with a few Mormon tourists, including a son of Brigham Young. The resulting opinion of British Columbians is probably well summed-up in two editorials published in a Victoria newspaper, one before, and the other shortly after, the "Manifesto" issued by Wilford Woodruff that abandoned polygamy as a practice of the Mormon Church.

The first editorial indicates rather clearly that the editor of the *Colonist* had a profound distrust of Mormons, particularly of those then emigrating from Utah to Canada:

> The laws of the Dominion as regards their peculiar institution are much the same as those of the United States. If they will not conform to the law of the United States in Utah, is it likely that they will be at all more law-abiding in Canada?... If the Mormons have made up their minds to

conform to the law of the land in which they live, why do they leave Utah, which has been their home for so many years?[86]

He feared that they would create an "*imperium in imperio*" in Canada, that like the Chinese they would not assimilate with the rest of the population, and because they were aggressive in proselytizing and prolific in natural increase they would be more objectionable than the Chinese. The Mormons were acknowledged to be "industrious and frugal, and if allowed to live as they desire will...become so numerous and so rich that they will set the laws of the country at defiance and give as much trouble in Canada as they do in the United States." The editor concluded, however, that it was "the business of the Government...to keep a strict watch over them,... If polygamy is put down and kept down...we venture to predict that their stay in Canada will not be long.[87]

The Manifesto that declared polygamy abandoned did little to reassure the editor:

Sudden conversions are always suspicious.... Until the other day the Mormons were polygamists.... A week or two ago we read of a large importation of young girls from Europe to reinforce the Mormon community. It was believed...that many of these girls were to be additions to the harems of hoary Mormons. But immediately following this news we read that the Mormons have repudiated or renounced polygamy.... Are the Mormons sincere...? The fact that the abandonment of polygamy will enfranchise all the Mormons, and cause the speedy admission of Utah into the Union as a state has, perhaps, something to do with the decision of President Woodruff.... The belief that, if polygamy were formally renounced property in their territory would immediately rise in value, may have something to do with the general acceptance of the repudiating proclamation. The Mormons are no doubt tired of fighting the United States government.... Many,...it is probable, have decided...that it would be best for them to appear to abandon their peculiar...institution, but it is not the nature of things that they can all have been made to see the error of their ways by the pressure that has been brought on them from the outside.... Convictions like those entertained by the Mormons with respect to polygamy are not got rid of in a day by means of a proclamation, real or sham.[88]

So, thirty years after James Douglas was instructed not to admit groups of Mormons into his colony, the situation remained much the same. Individual Mormons were unexceptional people, but groups of Mormons were likely to be polygamous, were not to be trusted, and should not be welcomed into the country. There is no reason to believe that the opinions of British Columbians in general differed to any significant extent from those of the editor of the *Colonist*.

As a prophet the editor had limited validity. Although some did indeed leave, forbidding polygamy in Canada did not make short the stay of the Mormons. Their base on Lee Creek became Cardston, and from that point their sons and daughters have established themselves in all parts of Canada. However, proposals for Mormon settlement in British Columbia did not materialize in the nineteenth century. British Columbian interest in Mormons subsided as polygamy became less of an issue, and the newpapers seldom mention them after 1890. The story of the virtually unnoticed growth of a Mormon community in British Columbia belongs to the next century.

NOTES

1. Melvin S. Tagg, "A History of the Church of Jesus Christ of Latter-day Saints in Canada, 1830-1963" (doctoral dissertation, Brigham Young University, 1963), p. 60, citing *Times and Seasons*, VI (1 Nov. 1845), p. 1019.

2. *The Works of Hubert Howe Bancroft*, Vol. 26 (San Francisco: The History Co., 1889), p. 238, footnote 6, as cited by Tagg, p. 60.

3. Ibid., Vol. 19, p. 134.

4. Tagg, op. cit., p. 62, citing the *Millennial Star*, IX (11 February 1847), p. 74.

5. Leigh Burpee Robinson, *Esquimalt: "Place of Shoaling Water"* (Victoria: Quality Press, 1947), p. 32; Tagg, op. cit., p. 61, citing the *Millennial Star*, VIII (October 1846), p. 142; J.B. Munro, "Mormon Colonization Scheme for Vancouver Island," *Washington Historical Quarterly*, XXV (1934), p. 278.

6. John Bowring to Thomas D. Brown, *Millennial Star*, IX (1 March 1847), pp. 74-75, as cited by Munro, op. cit.

7. Munro, op. cit.; Walter M. Sage, *Sir James Douglas and British Columbia* (Toronto: University of Toronto Press, 1930), p. 140; Robinson, op. cit., p. 32.

8. Labouchere to Douglas, Great Britain, Public Records Office, C0410/1, no. 4, 1 February 1858, p. 120.

9. Labouchere to Douglas, op. cit., pp. 120-23.

10. The earlier enquiries were apparently directed to the British government rather than to Governor Douglas.

11. For a more complete discussion of the development of a Mormon community in Vancouver Island, see Robert J. McCue, "The Church of Jesus Christ of Latter-day Saints and Vancouver Island: The Establishment and Growth of the Mormon community," *B.C. Studies*, 42 (Summer 1979), pp. 51-64.

12. Tagg, op. cit., p. 25.

13. *Daily British Colonist*, 23 March 1884, p. 3. Although this newspaper was

known from 1858-60 as the *British Colonist*, 1860-66 as the *Daily British Colonist and Victoria Chronicle*, and 1886 as the *Daily Colonist*, it will be referred to as the *Colonist*.

14. *Colonist*, 10 July 1886, p. 2.
15. Ibid., 16 October 1887, p. 4.
16. Stenhouse to Woodruff, 30 September, 23 October (2), 29 November, 9 December 1887; 7 August 1888, Salt Lake City: Historical Dept., the Church of Jesus Christ of Latter-day Saints.
17. *Victoria Gazette, Extra*, no date, but probably near the end of July, as there is a San Francisco dispatch dated 14 July included.
18. Ibid., 17 August 1858, p. 3.
19. *Colonist*, 21 March 1884, p. 2.
20. Ibid., 5 February 1885, p. 3.
21. Ibid., 10 October 1885, p. 2.
22. Ibid., 24 February 1886, p. 3.
23. Ibid., 25 February 1886, p. 2.
24. Ibid., 14 May 1885, p. 4; 6 December 1885, p. 2.
25. Ibid., 6 May 1885, p. 1.
26. Ibid., 15 September 1885, p. 4.
27. Ibid., 6 September 1884, p. 2.
28. Ibid., 26 March 1889, p. 1.
29. Ibid., 27 September 1884, p. 4.
30. Ibid., 30 September 1884, p. 3.
31. Ibid., 8 July 1885, p. 1; 11 July 1885, p. 2; 15 July 1885, p. 3.
32. Ibid., 25 December 1885, p. 1.
33. Ibid., 6 January 1887, p. 1.
34. Ibid., 25 November 1887, p. 1.
35. Ibid., 13 December 1887, p. 2.
36. Ibid., 12 February 1889, p. 1.
37. *Victoria Gazette*, 9 December 1858, p. 3.
38. *Colonist*, 25 April 1890, p. 3.
39. Ibid., 21 September 1887, p. 1.
40. Ibid., 17 April 1885, p. 1.
41. Ibid., 20 May 1886, p. 3.
42. Ibid., 31 August 1877, p. 2.
43. Ibid., 14 September 1877, p. 3, emphasis added.
44. Ibid., 27 July 1887, p. 1.
45. Ibid., 21 August 1887, p. 1.
46. Ibid., 22 October 1887, p. 3.
47. Ibid., 10 April 1889, p. 3.
48. Ibid., 5 April 1884, p. 4, emphasis added.
49. Ibid., 29 June 1884, p. 4.
50. Ibid., 7 October 1886, p. 2, citing the *Cleveland Leader*.
51. Ibid., 25 June 1885, p. 1; 27 September 1885, p. 2; 10 October 1885, p. 2; 28 May 1885, p. 3; 21 March 1884, p. 2; 9 October 1884, p. 3; 23 October 1884, p. 3; 26 October 1884, p. 2; 16 April 1885, p. 3; 25 February 1886, p. 2.

52. Ibid., 20 January 1884, p. 3.
53. Ibid., 17 June 1884, p. 1. How the good woman could receive severe injuries but not be seriously hurt begs explanation.
54. Ibid., 8 January 1885, p. 4.
55. Ibid., 22 December 1859, p. 1.
56. Ibid., 20 February 1886, p. 3.
57. Ibid., 29 May 1886, p. 3.
58. Ibid., 20 November 1884, p. 1.
59. Ibid., 18 February 1888, p. 2, emphasis added.
60. Ibid., 6 September 1885, p. 3.
61. Ibid., 18 February 1888, p. 2, emphasis added.
62. Ibid., 2 March 1884, p. 3.
63. Ibid., 3 February 1887, p. 1.
64. Ibid., 15 August 1885, p. 3.
65. Ibid., 5 November 1887, p. 1.
66. Ibid., 9 February 1888, p. 2.
67. Ibid., 24 April 1888, p. 4.
68. Ibid., 30 April 1885, p. 3.
69. Ibid., 7 November 1889, p. 4.
70. Ibid., 25 October 1887, p. 3.
71. Ibid., 20 May 1888, p. 2.
72. Ibid., 21 November 1888, p. 2.
73. Between 16 October 1887 and his departure from Canada, a period of 44 months, he figured in items in the *Colonist* 48 times, and in 32 of these Mormonism was also mentioned. There were 44 other references to Mormons and Mormonism that did not relate to Stenhouse.
74. *Colonist*, 16 October 1887, p. 4.
75. Ibid., 9 November 1887, p. 1; 12 November 1887, p. 2; 23 November 1887, p. 4; 30 November 1887, p. 2.
76. Ibid., 27 November 1887, pp. 2, 4; 29 November 1887, pp. 1, 2.
77. Ibid., 18 January 1888, p. 4; 21 January 1888, p. 4.
78. Ibid., 21 April 1888, p. 1.
79. "Record of Members, 1887-1890, Cardston Ward, Cache Stake," p. 39, Salt Lake City: Historical Dept, the Church of Jesus Christ of Latter-day Saints.
80. "Stenhouse Dipped," *Colonist*, 10 August 1888, p. 4.
81. Ibid., 27 October 1888, p. 4.
82. Ibid., 29 December 1888, p. 4.
83. D. Stenhouse to R. McCue, 3 October 1984.
84. *Vancouver Daily World*, 13 November 1889, p. 2.
85. "53 Vict. Chapter 37. An Act further to amend the Criminal Law." *Acts of the Parliament of the Dominion of Canada Relating to Criminal Law*, Ottawa: Queen's Printer, 1891, pp. 503-04.
86. *Colonist*, 8 December 1889, p. 2.
87. Ibid.
88. Ibid., 15 October 1890, p. 4.

4 A Congenial Environment
Southern Alberta on the Arrival of the Mormons

A. A. DEN OTTER

ON 2 MAY 1887, Charles Ora Card plowed the first furrow in the virgin soil of southern Alberta. Card and three companions had entered Canada several weeks earlier in the hope of finding a refuge from the religious persecution their community suffered in the United States. Mormon belief in the complete integration of secular and religious affairs and their practice of plural marriages had aroused bitter antagonism from more traditional believers. A polygamist, Card was stripped of his political offices and arrested, but he escaped and fled to Canada, where he believed British justice would tolerate a Mormon colony.[1]

In 1887, the southwestern Canadian prairies might have appeared empty to Card, apparently supporting only two, small urban centres, several large ranches, and virtually no homesteaders. Nevertheless, the region had historical connections with Great Britain. Its affinity for British traditions, conceived and nurtured in the tentative approaches of the Hudson's Bay Company, was reinforced when Canada acquired the territory in 1870. White newcomers, who immediately preceded the Mormons, founded on the southwestern fringe of the British North American plains a society that reincarnated in Canadian form British political and social institutions. They established in southern Alberta a small but cohesive community endowed with a strong sense of continuity and order, enhanced with a spirit of tolerance and justice, and leavened with a liberal commitment to economic progress and prosperity. Tightly bound to eastern Canada and Great Britain, southern Alberta proved to be a congenial environment for the Mormon settlers.

The cardinal feature of eastern Canadian traditions, which southern

53

Albertans established on the southwestern prairies, was an emphasis on order and regularity. W.L. Morton has called this the conservative principle, "the assertion that the chief political good is stability, the existence of order in the state and society..., an order arising from equilibrium reached among the elements of society by usage, tradition, and law."[2] Born in the Thomistic hierarchical structure of authoritarian New France, conservatism was firmly embedded in the Canadian mentality when refugees from the American Revolution fled northward and asserted British North America's loyalty to the empire. Both peoples, French and English, victims of lost causes, emphasized the value of language, custom, religion, law and community as the cement of society. Although the Loyalists believed in the principle of representative institutions, they held that political power must rest with an elite, those who are educated or who hold property, or as they put it, the respectable element in society. It was, in fact, the desire to preserve a faded eighteenth-century British society that colored colonial politics.

British North America's conservative ideal was modified by the rising ethos of liberalism, which blossomed during the late eighteenth century. Believing that every person was autonomous and rational, independent from anyone else, liberalism taught that government power had to be curbed, preferably by a constitution, whereas the church should be subservient to political or economic affairs. Rejecting the biblical concept of a provident God, liberalism envisioned nature as a dynamic, machinelike process, planned by God but allowed to run the course He had ordered according to great unchangeable laws. The awesome scientific discoveries and technological innovations of the eighteenth and nineteenth centuries demonstrated clearly that autonomous man could uncover these laws and then utilize them to control the process of nature. It was this deistic view of nature, confirmed by the achievements of the industrial revolution, that formed the foundation of a new economic theory, a view that held that deep-seated laws ruled the economy or marketplace. Despite the undulations of recurring business cycles, these laws propelled the marketplace consistently, regularly and inevitably to a better, more perfect world.[3]

As George Grant has noted, British North Americans readily adopted the economic and technological tenets of liberalism, accepting in the process contradictory social values.[4] On the one hand, the colonists valued tradition and order, on the other, they believed that they could utilize science and technology to fuel economic progress. If nineteenth-century Canadians were politically and religiously conservative, they were technologically and economically liberal. They accepted confidently the belief that technological and economic expansion was the primary avenue to national happiness.

Liberalism, then, gradually introduced profound changes in British North American society. After several decades of protest and armed rebellion, moderate liberal reformers used the principles of compromise and pragmatism to emasculate the forces of extreme conservatism, and by 1849 had wrested the right of responsible government from a disinterested imperial government. The Canadian invention of colonial responsible government, whereby the executive was answerable to the majority in the assembly, incorporated the democratic traditions of Anglo-America within the shell of British monarchical institutions. It allowed the will of the people to be expressed within British political structures.[5] Meanwhile, moderate reformers and conservatives formed leading majorities in the colonial legislatures and coped with British attempts to dismantle the economic structures of the empire. In their search for alternative trading partners, these moderate coalitions led British North America into economic and political union.

The ideal of economic progress and expansion, as the prerequisite to social well-being, became the common denominator that permitted the coalition of conservative and liberal politicians to implement the confederation of the British North American colonies in 1867. While complex factors of imperial and continental defense, and cultural and political considerations combined in the drive to the confederation of British North America, a crucial factor was the liberal principle of economic progress and expansion as the prerequisite of national welfare. To implement this view, the constitution retained the symbolic authority of the Crown and reaffirmed the legislative sovereignty of Parliament over the will of the people. The federal divisions of power and the checks on provincial legislatures clearly elevated the dominion government to predominant status in the union. Meanwhile, the new national government adopted an industrial strategy that became imperialist in nature. The promise of a Pacific railway lured British Columbia into the union, only a year after Canada had appropriated Rupert's Land from the Hudson's Bay Company. In the following decade, central Canadian industrialists used the Intercolonial Railway to absorb the production capacity of the Atlantic region and to reduce it to an exporter of natural resources.[6]

The acquisition of the Northwest was an integral part of Canada's economic development plans. Faced with a stagnant economy, rising land prices and falling crop prices, and the end of reciprocal free trade with the United States, Canadians focused their attention on the vast western territories. Spurred by the newfound confidence in the ability of science and technology to overcome obstacles of nature, Victorian Canadians began to reassess the economic value of a region traditionally assumed to be a hostile wilderness. Several scientific expeditions and studies declared the territories suitable for settlement, while railway technology provided the means of access. Even if Canada played its usual parsimonious, recalcitrant role in the negotiations, it nevertheless wanted the territories.[7]

Western annexation, therefore, was not based on lofty principles of liberty or justice but, as Vernon Fowke and W.L. Morton have shown, was carried out for imperialistic and commercial purposes.[8] Illustrative of eastern Canadian attitudes was their neglect of the indigenous peoples, a prime factor in the Red River insurrection. If, by the 1870s, Canadian politicians were comfortable with the liberal concepts of representative government and cultural self-determination, they were not ready to grant these rights voluntarily to newly acquired regions and native peoples. Moreover, because they assumed that the natural resources of the Northwest were to be exploited for the benefit of the nation as a whole, they retained control over all western resources in the central government, a fate no other region suffered. In the annexation of Rupert's Land, political centralization, economic exploitation and cultural homogeneity twisted economic liberalism into conservative mercantilism. The Northwest became the colony of a colony. If the liberal ideal of economic progress demanded expansion, the dominant conservative principle insisted that expansion include consolidation.

The integration of the Northwest into Canada was a relatively smooth procedure, because the histories of the two regions were interwoven. Centuries of fur trade, based on river transportation, created a northern, transatlantic economy and formed the basis of cultural communication between the Northwest and central Canada. Even the southwestern edge of the prairies, which lay on the periphery of the European fur trade, shared the British tradition. By the nineteenth century, Indian traders had tied the region into the fur empire of the Hudson's Bay Company. Although the local Blackfoot preferred to sell buffalo robes to American traders south of the international border during the winter months, they sold small furs and provisions to Hudson's Bay posts during the summer. Even if the Blackfoot moved freely across the international border, the economic and cultural integrity of the southwestern British North American prairies remained intact.[9]

The advance of white settlement onto the western Great Plains caused bitter conflicts. The gradual disappearance of buffalo from the northern prairies forced Indian hunters to move ever deeper into each other's traditional hunting grounds, increasing intertribal warfare. Conflict escalated until 1870 when a major battle, fought between Cree and Blackfoot on the bank of the Oldman River, cost the Cree hundreds of fatalities.[10]

The "last" Indian battle represented the native prairie dweller's desperate struggle for survival in a radically altered environment. By the early 1870s, the insatiable demand for buffalo robes, popular as sleigh blankets and bed throws, unleashed hundreds of traders, who scoured the great plains in search for the rapidly dwindling herds. Most of the free commerce originated in Fort Benton, a buffalo trade rendezvous founded in 1846. Its position at the head of navigation on the Missouri River made it the hub of transportation for northern Montana and a fleet of carts, wagons and stagecoaches spread across the territory. By the early 1870s, the collapse of the gold rush boom and the decimation of buffalo herds forced the town's traders to travel northwards deep into Canadian territory, sometimes reaching as far as Fort Edmonton. Although the Hudson's Bay Company was also involved in the buffalo trade, its stubborn reliance on archaic transportation techniques curbed its activities. Moreover, in 1870, the company surrendered its trade monopoly and political control over Rupert's Land to a parsimonious Canadian government. The company's retreat into the northern forests, coupled with Ottawa's reluctance to spend money on law enforcement in its new holdings, created an economic and political vacuum on the southwestern plains. The void was filled quickly by rapacious robe hunters, who were forced out of Montana territory by increasingly zealous US marshals, keen to stamp out the whisky trade. The result was a period of unrestricted free trade in this corner of western Canada.[11]

Although devastating the whisky trade lasted but a brief period. It began in earnest in December 1869, when two American traders, John J. Healy and Alfred B. Hamilton, escaped the pressure of American law enforcement and took advantage of the power vacuum in Canadian territory to build Fort Hamilton at the confluence of the St. Mary and Oldman rivers. The two traders spent the winter next to a favorite winter camp of the Bloods and swapped rotgut whisky for buffalo robes. In the spring, they burned the fort and loaded their carts for Fort Benton, where they netted $50,000 for one season's work.[12] Stories of their success spread like wildfire, and within a few years scores of small, temporary posts dotted the southwestern Canadian plains. Flitting across the border, often pursued by American marshals, the traders built strong forts, with descriptive names such as Robber's Roost, Stand-Off and Whiskey Gap. Here, they exploited the disease-weakened

Indians with adulterated alcohol. Of these posts, Fort Whoop-Up was the largest and most notorious. Built on the ruins of Fort Hamilton, near present-day Lethbridge, this solid, squared-log structure, guarded by two vintage cannons, protected the plunderers from their whisky-maddened victims.[13]

Repeated warnings from western residents eventually spurred the distant federal government to act. Particularly effective was Alexander Morris, the lieutenant-governor of Manitoba and the North-West Territories. Painting a vivid picture of potential Indian uprisings, particularly after the massacre of a score of Assiniboines in the Cypress Hills, he argued that the government could not afford the expensive wars fought on the US frontiers.[14] Morris's complaints were amplified by Colonel P. Robertson-Ross, the commander of the Canadian militia and the only government official to visit Whoop-Up country. In an official report, Robertson-Ross admitted that unescorted travel in the region was still possible, but hastened to add that it was but a matter of time before total anarchy made the far Northwest uninhabitable for white settlers. Serious unrest, he warned, would debilitate the settlement process.[15] Consequently, the fear of expensive Indian wars and retarded immigration forced Prime Minister John A. Macdonald to pass legislation early in 1873 permitting the establishment of a small, highly mobile, temporary police force in the west.[16]

Although the force nearly perished on its difficult march to Whoop-Up country, and had to be aided by Fort Benton merchants, it quickly established law and order in the region and incidentally asserted Canada's claims. There was little need for military action, as John McDougall, a Methodist missionary among the Stoneys, had prepared some of the Blackfoot with gifts and assurances that the police would end the disintegration of native society. More importantly, Indian leaders welcomed the North-West Mounted Police, because the force immediately curtailed the whisky trade. Its frequent patrols discouraged small-time traffickers obsessed with quick, high profits. Meanwhile, larger operators, with long-term interests in the region, altered their ways and welcomed the new regime, as it promised a stable business environment, free from costly Indian raids.[17] Several Fort Benton merchants continued to operate in Canadian territory, but their activities were subordinate to the authority of the mounted police.

The North-West Mounted Police (NWMP) were crucial in the establishment of government authority in western Canada, particularly in southern Alberta. Until the establishment of a territorial supreme court in 1886, the NWMP were the sole legal power in the Northwest; they were the peacemakers and law officers, the magistrates and jailers. With the backing

NWMP St. Mary River Detachment, near Cardston, 1902. The first building of logs with dirt roof was erected in 1886 and rebuilt in 1889. RCMP Photo Archives, Ottawa.

Sod-roof cabin of ranchers E. N. Barker and H. A. Donovan (ex-NWMP) on Lee Creek, southwestern Alberta, in 1887, adjoining land recommended by Barker to first Mormon settlers from Utah the same year. A5641 Provincial Archives of Alberta.

of the central government, they established a legal tyranny that worked because it lasted only a relatively short time and was administered by men with paternalistic attitudes toward Indians and lower-class whites. Rigidly enforcing relatively simple laws uniformly across the territories, the police suppressed the anarchistic self-expression so prevalent among the white population south of the border. Eventually, the role of the police extended beyond law enforcement, and they became mailmen, customs collectors, welfare officers and agricultural advisors; their uniforms came to symbolize the entire function of the dominion government. Founded in central Canada's image of respect for authority, the mounted police imposed upon the Northwest a British tradition of law and order at minimal cost.[18]

The success of the NWMP rested on much more than efficient operations and impartiality. The prime cause for the relatively peaceful history of the Canadian Northwest was the conservatism so prominent in Canada's historical development. The Ottawa bureaucrats and politicians, who created the force, belonged to the mid-Victorian generation of conservative politicians who thought they had learned an important lesson from the American experience: although never fully articulated, they held the belief that the United States lost control not over the Indians but over the whites. American concern with abstract thoughts of social contract and inalienable rights, so they argued, caused them to decentralize law enforcement and allow too much liberty among white settlers.[19] Therefore, Canadian politicians preferred to build on their Loyalist heritage and colonial tradition to perpetuate British ideals of paternalism and centralization. Order and continuity became the cardinal features of southern Alberta society.

The belief in political consolidation and the desire for economic progress impelled the Canadian government to come to terms with the original inhabitants of the plains. Apart from the object of integrating them peacefully into the new agricultural society at minimal cost, the government had no coherent policy, resisting calls for treaties until the Indians threatened violence. Finally, a mutual desire for peaceful accommodation formed the foundation of a series of Indian treaties signed in the 1870s. Haunted by the prospect of starvation on prairies destitute of buffalo and frightened by the spectre of bloody wars as in the United States, the Indians pressed the government to assist and protect them.[20] The central government shared the wish to prevent bloodshed and it negotiated a series of treaties by which the natives surrendered their land in return for reserves, annuities, agricultural implements, food, and other goods. While they might not have been entirely clear on the meaning of land surrender, the Indians understood that the pressure of white civilization had radically altered their way of life; they wanted protection against annihilation. The federal government, for its part, anxious to develop the prairies, sought to control the Indians and forestall potential and costly Indian wars.[21]

Treaty 7, signed on 22 September 1877, included the Blackfoot of southern Alberta. As procedures were well established by then, the negotiations were typical and took less than a week. In retrospect, Treaty 7 Indians apparently did not think of the treaty as primarily a total, irrevocable surrender of their title to all wildlife, surface and mineral rights, but rather as a sharing of the land for agricultural use.[22] They were the first to insist that the location of reserves be defined in the treaty. The theme, that without a treaty white settlers would use violence to take the land, dominated the discussions and created the strong sense that the Queen as protector of the Indians would prevent war in the future. As other prairie Indians before them, the Blackfoot viewed the negotiations as a peace treaty.[23]

The federal government, intent on controlling western resources, was also slow to grant political rights to prairie settlers. Canadian politicians followed the American example of slow evolution from territory to statehood, and favored reluctant concessions in response to western agitation. Five years after the nation acquired Rupert's Land, a Liberal administration passed the North-West Territories Act, a hastily prepared piece of legislation devoid of a real understanding of western conditions. Even though the territories received their own lieutenant-governor, assisted by a council that could gradually become elective as population warranted, Ottawa relinquished no political control; it curtailed the duties of the territorial government, combined its executive and legislative functions, and granted it annual parliamentary appropriations instead of significant taxing powers, administered by the Department of the Interior. Despite the gradual increase in elected representation, the lieutenant-governor retained most of the political power and assumed virtually all executive functions. By 1887, the Northwest was the only region in Canada that did not enjoy the rights of responsible government. And, until that year, it was not permitted to elect members to the House of Commons and obtain representation in the Senate.[24]

The dominion government's reluctance to grant westerners the same measure of political self-determination enjoyed by other Canadians generated considerable political unrest. Nurtured by economic depression, falling grain prices, repeated crop failures, high freight rates, lagging immigration and unresponsive federal administrators, alienation festered, leading a number of white settlers to join with the Metis in the initial stages of the agitation that expressed itself eventually as rebellion in 1885. According to the Regina *Journal*:

> The North-West is being settled by a liberty loving people, educated in self-government, who will be satisfied with nothing short of an administration responsible to the people in the fullest sense of the word. And if a makeshift is given, it will invite agitation and lead to an early struggle for the rights and privileges enjoyed by the Provinces.[25]

Canada's handling of the human resources of the territories, then, was haphazard and conservative, marred by dated imperialistic aims. The young nation annexed the Northwest for economic reasons at some cost, and it determined to exploit the region's natural wealth for the good of the entire country. Economic centralization obviously demanded stringent political controls; consequently, the Conservative government's administration of human affairs was authoritarian and often improvised, a policy no longer in tune with the political realities of the late nineteenth century.

If conservatism dominated the central government's human resources policy, liberalism motivated its natural resources agenda. In contrast to its haphazard political program, Canada's western economic development policy was coherent and liberal, executed with modern scientific precision. Starting from the premise that the revenues from the sale or lease of western lands would pay for the cost of administering and developing the Northwest, the government followed a clearly defined settlement strategy. In April 1871, surveyors began dividing the entire plains into squares of half a mile by half a mile, containing 160 acres, called quarter sections. In 1872, the Dominion Lands Act, copied from the United States in spirit if not in detail, provided for the sale of quarter sections of crown land to genuine settlers at virtually no cost. The uniformity and simplicity of the survey and homestead policies reflected the nineteenth-century bureaucratic mind driven by clear objectives and pragmatic principles, able to plan land development from the start. Moreover, the speed of the survey and the generosity of the homestead act demonstrated the important place of western lands in the government's national policies.[26]

Since Canada had to compete for settlers, it advertised its lands extensively. The Department of Agriculture published thousands of pamphlets, brochures and maps in Great Britain and continental Europe. Canada also paid bonuses to immigration agents and subsidized travel to Canada. Perhaps the most important initiative was group settlement, in which the government set aside parcels of land for ethnic groups such as the Swiss, Icelanders, Germans, Scots, expatriate French Canadians in the United States, as well as religious groups such as the Mennonites. The government also attempted to induce large-scale immigration by granting licenses to several colonization companies. None of the schemes were successful in luring massive numbers of settlers to the Northwest, however, and its population remained relatively small.[27] Nevertheless, the group settlement policy, considered to be an effective instrument for adaptation and survival on the plains, prepared the way for the large-scale migration of Mormons into southern Alberta in the late 1880s and 1890s.

The capstone of Canada's western economic development policies was the Canadian Pacific Railway. Providing relatively easy and economical access to the Northwest, the railway represented the triumph of liberalism's exuberant confidence in technology and science as tools for taming the vagaries of nature. Even though the completion of the railway did not immediately erase western Canada's perceived disadvantages among prospective emigrants, and thus failed to stimulate a massive influx of settlers, the CPR made western lands accessible. For the first time in its history, the territories possessed a technically efficient means of shipping bulk products. The railway made the export of wheat and the import of manufactured goods economically feasible; it made the settlement of the plains practical. With the completion of the CPR in 1885, the resources of the Northwest were ready for exploitation.

In Canada, railway technology, the facilitator of economic growth and expansion, required considerable state intervention. Part of this came in the form of direct subsidies, loan guarantees and land grants. Other aid took the form of monopolistic practices, discriminatory freight rates and protective tariffs. Anxious to protect the CPR from American railroads, the Conservatives handed the company a monopoly of all western freight, prohibiting the construction of competing branch lines to the border. They also allowed the railway to set rates that favored central Canadian wholesalers over Winnipeg merchants.[28] And, perhaps most importantly, the government instituted the National Policy, a protective tariff that effectively declared that Canadian consumers belonged to Canadian industries.[29] These conservative measures of consolidation and continuity ensured that east-west trade would flow through Canadian channels and repay the costly investment central Canadians had made in the Pacific railway and western development.

Undoubtedly, the government's economic policy, clearly enunciated and ably executed, stimulated the development of the Northwest as quickly as was possible under the circumstances. Motivated by the liberal premise of economic growth as the prerequisite for national progress and welfare, spurred by the confident faith in the ability of technology and science to tame the inhospitable forces of nature on the vast plains, the Canadian government set out to build a transcontinental nation. But, the conservative principle of consolidation and centralization remained predominant in the central government's thinking. Its insistence that the process of development be controlled politically from the centre, its casual and parsimonious attitude toward the natives, and its discriminatory concessions to the CPR and eastern Canadian manufacturers and merchants primed the alienation of the inhabitants of the plains, an estrangement that erupted violently among Indian and Metis people in the Saskatchewan rebellion of 1885 and simmered ominously among the white newcomers.

Neither the natives nor newcomers of southern Alberta participated in the 1885 rebellion. The Indians remained peaceful because of historic distrust of the Cree and Metis, the heavy concentration of mounted police in the area, and the uncertainty of a future without Treaty 7. As for the white population, its economic and political ties were clearly with the Conservatives, the political party that pursued a western development program most aggressively and dispensed patronage concessions most generously. Forming the region's new elite, the newcomers provided the economic, social and political continuity with central Canadian power structures.[30] These ties, lacking in the northern territories, kept southern Alberta securely in the Canadian fold.

Southern Alberta's strong identification with British-American institutions, established by the Hudson's Bay Company and reinforced by the NWMP, was strengthened by the emergence of a vigorous ranching community in the early 1880s. The federal government, which evaluated the semiarid southwest as suitable only for grazing, developed a generous leasing policy to attract large ranching companies. In marked contrast to the American frontier, Canadian administrators instituted a leasing policy that, no matter how generous, clearly indicated that land title remained with the Crown. Several large corporations took advantage of the grazing leases and monopolized most of the extensive grasslands. By 1887, for example, four companies controlled nearly 900,000 acres or 42% of the leased grasslands and a compact block of almost 10,000,000 acres extended northward from the international border to the Bow River. Although the most desirable locations were in the outer foothills, ranching also spilled onto the plains.[31] The new industry adopted many American techniques, but capital and management came from central Canada and Great Britain. The ranching industry of western Canada, therefore, had intimate connections with eastern Canada's commercial elite as well as the Conservative Party. Forming the leading edge of the metropolitan advance, the ranching community ensured that the cultural associations of the southwestern prairies were with central Canada. Since the ranchers mingled socially with the NWMP officers, the two groups formed a tightly knit regional establishment whose values dominated southwestern society.[32] The intimate connection between ranch and police communities, and their mutual link to the federal administration, imparted to the southwestern part of the prairies a distinct conservative tone.

For several decades, the conservative triangle withstood all challenges to its supremacy. In the mid-1880s, settlers arriving in southern Alberta discovered that most arable land was leased to ranchers. While many newcomers left the region, some determined to challenge the hegemony. They formed the Alberta Settlers' Rights Association but their appeals to Ottawa elicited no more than rigorous enforcement of leasing regulations and orders to the NWMP to remove squatters from legitimate leases. Tension remained high, especially in the Bow River valley, but also in the south where the Cochrane Ranch regularly used the NWMP to evict squatters.[33] In 1886, the ranchers petitioned the minister of the Interior for a system of stock water reserves to end the problem of squatters. This policy, implemented by the government late in 1886, simply forbade settlers to fence land adjacent to lakes, ponds and rivers. If the policy made sense to ranchers, because farmers could render useless thousands of square miles of surrounding grasslands by fencing a stream or pond, the water reserves were devastating for squatters, as they could not cultivate arid tablelands away from a stable water supply.[34]

When Charles Ora Card led his Mormon followers to southern Alberta in 1887, he quickly discovered that available land was not as abundant as he had thought. Added to grazing leases and stock watering reserves were lands set aside for railway building subsidies, schools and the Hudson's Bay Company, leaving little for agricultural settlement. "The next day we commenced our explorations for the most suitable site on which to locate," Card recalled. "But to my astonishment, the most desireable lands between the Belly River and Ft. Mcleod [*sic*] were covered by stock leases, and we could not settle on them without perplexity from the lease holder."[35] This surprising scarcity of freehold land led Card into a unique relationship with Sir Alexander

Tilloch Galt, whose extensive coal-mining and railway operations in southern Alberta had benefited from the government's generous prairie lands policy.

Galt serves as an excellent example of a conservative politician, imbued with the liberal ethic of economic progress and expansion. His endeavors in western Canada, managed by his son Elliott, also illustrate clearly the means by which the central Canadian business community, aided by a supportive government, expanded westward and welded the Northwest firmly into its economy, politics and culture. Moreover, his influence furnishes yet another explanation for the conservative tenor of southern Alberta.

Galt became interested in coal mining in southern Alberta. In 1881, he founded the North Western Coal and Navigation Company to operate a colliery at Lethbridge, then known as Coal Banks. Backed by several London businessmen, including publishing magnate W.H. Smith and his lieutenant, William Lethbridge, the colliery began production in 1882. Most coal was used locally, but some was shipped to Fort Macleod and Fort Benton. Experimental shipments of coal by steamboat and barge downriver to the Canadian Pacific Railway main line at Medicine Hat failed, and in 1885 Galt constructed a narrow gauge railway from Lethbridge to Dunmore, near Medicine Hat.

The NWC&N Co. benefited handsomely from the dominion government's eagerness to breathe life into its stagnating development policy. By 1883, the buoyant spirit, engendered by the start of CPR construction, had dissipated in the onset of a general depression. The CPR, the keystone of the government's national policies, was close to collapse; the happy vision of a settled Northwest threatened to become a nightmare of failure. More than ever before, the government felt compelled to grant generous concessions to lure investment capital to the prairies. Deeply committed to developing the seemingly unlimited western soil resource, it willingly granted the cheapest incentive available to the nation—arable land. Consequently, Parliament granted the Canadian Pacific Railway a large land subsidy for building the transcontinental railway and permitted other colonization railways to purchase land at minimal cost. Galt, a close friend of Prime Minister Macdonald and other prominent Conservatives, took advantage of the government's eagerness to develop the Northwest and persuaded it to extend the CPR principle of free land grants to the NWC&N Co., even though it was a narrow gauge, resource development road rather than a colonization railway. The government granted the company 420,480 acres of land for building 109.5 miles of narrow-gauge railway.[36] Five years later, after the Galts had built a railway to the United States border, they earned an additional 413,516 acres of land as well as another 280,320 acres for promising to widen the Lethbridge-Dunmore section.[37] Taking advantage of his friendship with leading Conservative politicians, Galt exploited to the fullest the government's obsession to develop the western plains as quickly as possible.

The arrival of the Mormons in southern Alberta in the spring of 1887 was welcome news to the region's businessmen, particularly the Galts. Located in a semiarid environment, the NWC&N Co. experienced difficulty selling its land grants. As company officials intended to sell the lands for grazing purposes, they successfully requested the government to grant the subsidy in alternate townships rather than the prescribed sections.[38] Sales to ranchers were sluggish because the ranching boom in the United States attracted most of the foreign capital, and domestic investors preferred to take up the government's generous grazing leases. By the end of 1887, the company had realized only $30,012 for 22,587 acres of land.[39] Little wonder that the company's land agent, C.A. Magrath, greeted the arrival of Charles Ora Card and his followers at Lee Creek with considerable enthusiasm.

The colonization plans of the church were particularly suited to the needs of the Galt companies. Since the Mormons were accustomed to living in small hamlets and going out each day to work in the surrounding fields, Card petitioned the Canadian government for the right to buy an entire township of land.[40] The entry of the Mormons into western Canada, however, had aroused a vociferous storm of protest outside southern Alberta, and the federal government, buffeted by bitter petitions against the "polygamous" Mormons, was afraid to grant special favors to the group. As a result, federal officials told Card to settle his people according to homestead regulations.[41] Rebuffed by the government, Card sought the aid of Charles Magrath. The two had met during Card's frequent trips to Lethbridge for supplies and land negotiations, and they had since become close friends. Magrath worked out an arrangement whereby the NWC&N Co. would choose as part of its land grant that township in which Cardston was located and subsequently sell it to the Mormons.[42] But the cabinet was so sensitive to the Mormon issue that it refused to grant the NWC&N Co. the required township. Nevertheless, in 1889, the church purchased 9,690 acres from the company elsewhere at $1.25 an acre.[43] It was the first installment in a long and fruitful relationship which would see the church purchase extensive properties from the Galts and introduce irrigation to much of southern Alberta.

Lethbridge Mainstreet c. 1890, with Indian travois and democrat buggy in foreground. P4009 Pollard Collection, Provincial Archives of Alberta.

As a large business, the NWC&N Co. was a powerful force in the southwest corner of the prairies. The coal mines had spawned a small town of a few thousand inhabitants, while the railway had made Lethbridge the transportation and distribution centre of the region. The young men— company executives, businessmen, professionals and police officers—who built the town shared Galt's conservative politics and progressive economics. They strove to suppress the unruliness that was so often a part of frontier mining towns and endeavored to establish instead the idealized features of central Canadian institutions. Although socially conservative, town leaders made economic progress an integral part of community building, envisioning a large and prosperous industrial city on the banks of the Belly River. They worked hard to realize that dream and believed that the Conservative Party, which embodied the ideals of economic expansion and industrialization as well as western development, was the best political instrument to achieve their objective. Like the ranchers on the surrounding prairies, the townsmen imbedded firmly in the southwestern mentality the conservative sentiments of English Canada and an abiding loyalty to the Conservative Party. Lethbridge, therefore, was deeply and fundamentally conservative.[44]

In March 1887, southern Alberta fought its first federal election, a campaign that quickly revealed how deeply conservatism was ingrained in its mentality. The Conservative candidate, D.W. Davis, a store manager in Macleod, handily defeated an Independent from Edmonton and a Liberal from Calgary. Extremely significant in the election was the concentration of Alberta's population in the south, virtually disenfranchising the northern part of the constituency. Moreover, the two relatively large urban centers of Macleod and Lethbridge almost unanimously supported the southern, Conservative candidate, effectively ensuring his election.[45] Dominated by the two southern towns, the election was a ringing endorsement of the Conservative nation-building platform.

The *Lethbridge News* defended its support of the government candidate by noting that his party had brought the Northwest into Confederation, recognized its potential, built the CPR, created a good land policy, vigorously prosecuted the survey, and promised Lethbridge a courthouse.[46] The *Macleod Gazette* echoed its counterpart, and observed:

> The Conservative party is in fact identified with the entire development of the Northwest, and there can be no choice among true Nor'Westers between the policy of that party toward the Northwest, and that of the Grits, which begrudges the expenditure of money in the Territories and openly sympathizes with the rebellion of 1885.[47]

The *Gazette's* editor, commenting on the rivalry between northern and southern Alberta, added that the south would never support Edmonton's independent candidate who could be elected only "by the votes of hundreds of ignorant and superstitious half-breeds in the north."[48]

The *Gazette's* barely concealed contempt for the northern mixed bloods mirrored the prevailing attitude to race relations in the Northwest. Generally, the Indians and mixed bloods were considered a block to the economic development of the territories, to be removed from valuable or strategic areas to isolated reserves where they could be taught the new, white way of life.[49] The two southern Alberta newspapers agreed that the local Indians should be settled on reserves near the Red Deer River in central Alberta; or, as the *Lethbridge News* explained, they should be scattered so "that their civilization would sooner be effected, as we feel that so long as the tribal system is maintained the Indians will cling to their old habits."[50] The interest of the district, the paper continued, demanded "that the Bloods and Peigans should be removed to some remote and scarcely settled district where they will have less opportunity for killing and stealing cattle and retarding the development of the country than they have in the district where they are located." Moreover, the paper asserted, native children should be placed in boarding schools far from the reserve, thus to be more quickly integrated into the newcomers' society.[51]

The conservative newspaper voice in southern Alberta was not unanimous on all issues, and late in 1887 a rancorous split appeared. Incensed by repeated CPR vetos of NWC&N Co. plans for a railway to Montana, The *Macleod Gazette* complained that the heavily subsidized CPR monopoly, with its exorbitant freight rates, was choking western economic growth. According to the *Gazette*, not only must the monopoly be abolished but also the tariff must be altered to permit free trade with the United States. Free trade and competitive railways would benefit the cattle industry of southern Alberta as well as the NWC&N Co., which could compete with American coal unhindered by high tariffs and monopolistic freight rates.[52] Only months after supporting a Conservative candidate, Macleod's newspaper adopted the Liberal's commercial union concept, a policy gaining favor in the Northwest but unpopular in industrializing central Canada.

The *Lethbridge News* chided the *Gazette* for its flirtation with commercial union and remained loyal to the Conservative protectionist stand on the free trade issue. Lethbridge was Alexander Galt's town, and Galt was a strong defender of the National Policy. While the newspaper conceded that the CPR monopoly and high American tariffs shut Galt's coal out of the Montana market, it voiced the opinion that commercial union was not the panacea for the economic ills of western Canada. Closer economic ties, the Lethbridge editor asserted, would eventually destroy the British imperial connection; it would make Canada an economic adjunct of its much larger neighbor. "With commercial union in force, and unrestricted railway connections with the United States," the paper warned, "it is certain that our Northwest merchants would purchase a large if not the largest portion of their stock from St. Paul, Chicago, and other American wholesale cities."[53] Placed in emotional and patriotic terms, the *News*'s imperialistic sentiments made removal of tariffs between Canada and the United States unacceptable. From a more pragmatic and economic perspective, however, the weekly viewed a rail connection with Montana as essential to the vitality of the NWC&N Co. and Lethbridge. In typically Canadian fashion, the newspaper reconciled the conservative and liberal concepts: the tariff structure must remain intact, but the Montana railway should be exempt from the railway monopoly clause. In this very special way, Lethbridge could remain within the national economic context of traditional imperial systems and the Galt railway would not disrupt the east-west pattern of Canada's economic nationalism.[54] Thus, with some special pleading, the Lethbridge paper confirmed the basic conservative principle, reaffirming its adherence to British-Canadian ideals and institutions.

The liberal economics of expansion and progress absorbed into the conservative politics of continuity and consolidation allowed the *Lethbridge News* to welcome the Mormons to southern Alberta. Undoubtedly, the details of the religious beliefs of the Mormons must have appeared peculiar to the readers of the paper, but they respected their basically conservative lifestyle and ambitious work ethic. Within years, the religious community built a thriving agricultural settlement, transforming the expansive grasslands into valuable agricultural properties, vigorously stimulating the economic development of the region. When the *Lethbridge News* defended the Mormons against attack from central Canadian newspapers, it observed that the Mormons:

>...appear to be all steady, industrious men, and are for the most men with sufficient means to make farming a success. They appear to belong to the most desirable class of settlers and their immigration deserves to be encouraged rather than discouraged.[55]

The ready acceptance of the Mormons into southern Alberta society was inspired by more than their potential for economic success. As L.G. Thomas has noted, the spirit of biculturalism in Canada, even if still extremely weak in 1887, unfurled a protective umbrella for various ethnic and minority groups, including Icelanders, Hutterites, Doukhobors and, of course, Mormons.[56] To some extent, even the privileged ranchers and the police were minorities in the Northwest, anxious to maintain the cultural shield that fostered a social and ethnic mosaic in western Canada. Combining liberal principles of economics and religious tolerance, The *Macleod Gazette* argued that "Canada needs all the settlers it can get, and as long as they [the Mormons] are law-abiding, she cannot afford to interfere in any way with their religious belief."[57] Thus, opposition to the Mormons, at times shrill in the northern and eastern parts of the territories, hardly arose in southern Alberta and was never strong enough to hamper the vigorous growth of the settlement.

NOTES

1. A. James Hudson, *Charles Ora Card: Pioneer and Colonizer* (Cardston, Alberta: by the author, 1963); Melvin S. Tagg, "A History of the Church of Jesus Christ of Latter-day Saints in Canada, 1830-1963" (doctoral dissertation, Brigham Young University, 1963).

2. W.L. Morton, "The Conservative Principle in Confederation," *Queen's Quarterly*, 81 (Winter, 1965), pp. 528-46.

3. Anthony Arblaster, *The Rise and Decline of Western Liberalism* (Oxford: Blackwell, 1984); Bob Goudzwaard, *Capitalism and Progress: A Diagnosis of Western Society* (Toronto: Wedge Publishing Foundation, 1979); John Douglas Hall, "Man and Nature in the Modern West: A Revolution of Images," in *Man and Nature on the Prairies*, ed., Richard Allen (Regina: Canadian Plains and Research Center, 1976).

4. George Grant, *Technology and Empire: Perspectives on North America* (Toronto: House of Anansi, 1969).

5. Arthur R.M. Lower, *This Most Famous Stream: The Liberal Democratic Way of Life* (Toronto: The Ryerson Press, 1954), pp. 149-50.

6. D.G. Creighton, "Economic Nationalism and Confederation," Canadian Historical Association, *Report*, 1942; T.W. Acheson, "The National Policy and the industrialization of the Maritimes, 1880-1910." *Acadensis* 1 (Spring 1972), pp. 3-28.

7. Henry Youle Hind, *Narrative of the Canadian Red River Exploring Expedition of 1857 and the Assiniboine and Saskatchewan Exploring Expedition of 1858* (Edmonton: Hurtig Publishers, 1971, original ed., 1860); Irene M. Spry, *The Palliser Expedition: An Account of John Palliser's Exploring Expedition, 1857-1860* (Toronto: Macmillan Company, 1973); G.S. Dunbar, "Isotherms and Politics: Perception of the Northwest in the 1850s," in *Prairie Perspectives 2*, eds., Anthony Rasporich and Henry C. Klassen (Toronto: Holt, Rinehart and Winston, 1973).

8. W.L. Morton, "Clio in Canada: The interpretation of Canadian history," *University of Toronto Quarterly*, 15 (April 1946), pp. 227-34; Vernon C. Fowke, *The National Policy and the Wheat Economy* (Toronto: University of Toronto Press, 1957).

9. Harold A. Innis, *The Fur Trade in Canada: An Introduction to Canadian Economic History*, Canadian University Paperbacks (Toronto: University of Toronto Press, 1967, original ed., 1930); John C. Ewers, *The Blackfoot: Raiders of the Northwestern Plains* (Norman: University of Oklahoma Press, 1958); and Oscar Lewis, *The Effect of White Contact Upon Blackfoot Culture with Special Reference to the Fur Trade* (New York: J.J. Augustine Publishers, 1942).

10. A. Johnston, *The Battle at Belly River: Stories of the Last Great Indian Battle* (Lethbridge: Historical Society of Alberta, 1966).

11. Glenbow Alberta Institute [GAI], Hardisty Papers, L'Heureux to Christie, dated 1871; William Francis Butler, *Great Lone Land: A Tale of Adventure in the North-West of America* (Edmonton: Hurtig Publishers, 1960), pp. 213-14, 379-80; Paul F. Sharp, *Whoop-Up Country: The Canadian-*

American West, 1865-1885 (Minneapolis: University of Minnesota Press, 1955), pp. 36-50.

12. *Daily Herald* (Helena), 15 June 1870.
13. Gerald Berry, *The Whoop-Up Trail: Early Days in Alberta-Montana* (Edmonton: Applied Arts Products Ltd.), pp. 39-40.
14. For example, see National Archives of Canada [NAC], Macdonald Papers, Vol. 252, Morris to Macdonald, 16 November 1872; 17 January 1873.
15. Canada, Parliament, *Sessional Papers*, 5, no. 9, 1873; P. Robertson-Ross, "Reconnaissance of the North West Provinces and Indian Territories of the Dominion of Canada."
16. NAC, Macdonald Papers, Vol. 574, Macdonald to Cartier, 16 June 1871; Canada, *Statutes*, 36 Victoria, Chapter 35, 1873.
17. Montana Historical Society [MHS], Power Papers, Letterbook 178-1, Power to Field, 18 August 1869.
18. R.C. Macleod, *The North-West Mounted Police and Law Enforcement, 1873-1905* (Toronto: University of Toronto Press, 1976), pp. 33-37.
19. John Jennings, "The Plains Indians and the Law," in *Men in Scarlet*, ed., Hugh A. Dempsey (Calgary: Historical Society of Alberta/McClelland and Stewart West, 1975).
20. Scollen to Morris, 8 September 1876, cited in Alexander Morris, *The Treaties of Canada with the Indians of Manitoba and the North-West Territories* (Toronto: Willing & Williamson, 1880), pp. 247-49; John L. Tobias, "Canada's subjugation of the Plains Cree, 1879-1885," *Canadian Historical Review*, 64 (December 1983), pp. 519-48.
21. John Leonard Taylor, "Canada's Northwest Indian Policy in the 1870s: Traditional Promises and Necessary Innovations," in *The Spirit of the Alberta Indian Treaties*, ed., Richard Price (Montreal: Institute for Research on Public Policy, 1979).
22. Morris, *Treaties of Canada*, pp. 245-75; Hugh Dempsey, *Crowfoot: Chief of the Blackfoot* (Edmonton: Hurtig Publishers, 1976), pp. 94-107.
23. John Leonard Taylor, "Two Views on the Meaning of Treaties Six and Seven," in *The Spirit of the Alberta Indian Treaties*, ed., Richard Price (Montreal: Institute for Research on Public Policy, 1979).
24. Lewis Herbert Thomas, *The Struggle for Responsible Government in the North-West Territories, 1870-97* (Toronto: University of Toronto Press, 1956).
25. *Regina Journal*, 10 November 1887.
26. Gerald Friesen, *The Canadian Prairies: A History* (Toronto: University of Toronto Press, 1984), pp. 181-86.
27. C.A. Dawson, *Group Settlement: Ethnic Communities in Western Canada*, Vol. 7 of Canadian Frontiers of Settlement, eds., W.A. Mackintosh and W.L.G. Joerg (Toronto: Macmillan Company, 1936); André Lalonde, "Settlement in the North-West Territories by Colonization Companies, 1881-1891" (doctoral dissertation, Université Laval, 1969).
28. Harold A. Innis, *A History of the Canadian Pacific Railway* (Toronto: University of Toronto Press, 1971), pp. 176-79.

29. Ben Forster, *Conjunction of Interests: Business, Politics, and Tariffs, 1825-1879* (Toronto: University of Toronto Press, 1986), pp. 178-80.
30. Lewis G. Thomas in Patrick A. Dunae, ed., *Ranchers' Legacy: Alberta Essays by Lewis G. Thomas* (Edmonton: University of Alberta Press, 1986).
31. Simon Evans, "Spatial Aspects of the Cattle Kingdom: The First Decade, 1882-1892," in *Frontier Calgary, 1875-1914*, eds., A.W. Rasporich and Henry Klassen (Calgary: University of Calgary/McClelland and Stewart West, 1975), pp. 42-46.
32. David H. Breen, *The Canadian Prairie West and the Ranching Frontier, 1874-1924* (Toronto: University of Toronto Press, 1983). See also D.H. Breen, "The Mounted Police and the Ranching Frontier," in *Men in Scarlet*, ed., Hugh A. Dempsey (Calgary: Historical Society of Alberta/McClelland and Stewart West, 1975).
33. David H. Breen, "The Canadian prairie West and the 'harmonious' settlement interpretation," *Agricultural History*, 67 (January 1973), pp. 63-75.
34. A.A. den Otter, "Adapting the environment: Ranching, irrigation, and dry land farming in southern Alberta," *Great Plains Quarterly*, 6 (Summer 1986), pp. 171-89.
35. Charles Ora Card, Diary, cited in Dawson, *Group Settlement*, p. 198.
36. Canada, House of Commons, *Debates*, 27 March and 10 and 11 June 1885.
37. Canada, Order in Council, 17 January 1885.
38. Ibid., 19 October 1885; NAC, Department of the Interior Records, Vol. 291, file 62709-2, Burgess to Wilson, 25 February 1886; Canada, *Statutes of Canada*, 49 Victoria, chapter 12, 2 June 1886.
39. NAC, Canadian Transport Commission, Vol. 853.
40. Hudson, *Charles Card*.
41. University of Alberta Archives, Pearce Papers, box 42, 14-b-11, no. 2275, Ferguson to Magrath, 3 June 1889; Pearce to Magrath, 20 November 1888.
42. Ibid., Magrath to Pearce, 15 November 1888.
43. Ibid., Card to Pearce, 6 August 1889.
44. Andy A. den Otter, *Civilizing the West: the Galts and the Development of Western Canada* (Edmonton: University of Alberta Press, 1982), pp. 161-98.
45. The total Alberta vote was 1,049 Conservative, 781 Independent and 232 Liberal. *Lethbridge News*, 30 March 1887.
46. Ibid., 9 March 1887.
47. *The Macleod Gazette*, 22 February 1887.
48. Ibid., 22 March 1887.
49. Tobias, "Subjugation of the Crees."
50. *Lethbridge News*, 11 May 1887; *The Macleod Gazette*, 26 April 1887.
51. *Lethbridge News*, 20 July 1887.
52. *The Macleod Gazette*, 8 February, 3 and 17 May, 14 June, 25 October, 8 November and 20 December 1887.
53. *Lethbridge News*, 29 December 1887.
54. Ibid., 5 January and 7 December 1887.
55. Ibid., 17 August 1887.
56. Dunae, *Ranchers' Legacy*, pp. 61-80.
57. *The Macleod Gazette*, 27 September 1887.

II | THE ALBERTA SETTLEMENTS
1887-1925

MORMON SETTLERS FROM the United States sought refuge in
Canada in 1887, and thereby began a permanent Mormon presence. Mormons were among many different groups that came to Canada seeking
refuge from political or religious persecution in the United States. These
included the Loyalists, refugee slaves, Huttcrites (during World War I) and
thousands of American war resisters (during the Vietnam War of the 1960s
and early 1970s). The Mormons settled in a Canadian West that was ready
for them, following their unique experience in colonizing the arid Great
Basin area of the American West.

The coming of the Mormons, known for the vigor of their restorationist,
communitarian and millenarian religious beliefs and practices, which
included a controlled experiment with plural marriage, provoked a negative
public reaction that persisted well into the 1920s. The Mormon colonists
were soon successful; however, their reputation in the United States as
an immoral and aberrant sect followed them. They became the focus of
the zeal of Canadian reformers who were seeking to build Canada and
the West in their own image.

An analysis of the development of Mormon settlements in the Canadian
West between 1885 and 1925 opens up a panoramic view on the concerns, norms, values and behaviors of Canadian and American societies.
Brigham Y. Card sets the founding of the Mormon settlements in their
North American context of geography and history, as he deals with the
personal, problematic and dynamic aspects of the founding of Cardston
and other Mormon settlements. He is concerned with the ways in which
these settlements acquired and maintained particularistic and distinctive
qualities. Howard Palmer follows the public reaction, locally, regionally

and nationally to the coming of the Mormons. He suggests reasons for the prolonged opposition against Canadian Mormons amongst those who continued to agitate. Anthony W. Rasporich focuses on Mormons as an ethno-religious and millenarian people and their relationship to other such peoples in the Canadian West, with special attention to the effective combination of the sacred and secular in Mormon community-building in Canada. William A. Wilson examines folk expressions of humor, pathos, struggle and faith that helped sustain Mormon pioneer settlers in southwestern Alberta and continue to influence Canadian Mormon identity. These four essays attempt to bridge the gap between the extensive scholarly work done on Mormons in the United States and the small amount of scholarship done on Mormons in Canada while at the same time making use of new source materials and conceptual frameworks.

5 Charles Ora Card and the Founding of the Mormon Settlements in Southwestern Alberta, North-West Territories

BRIGHAM Y. CARD

THE MORMON PRESENCE in Canada East during the nineteenth century was tentative, transitory and diminishing.[1] This experience is poignantly symbolized by Monument 109, marking "The Nauvoo Road" leading southward out of Upper Canada, which was erected by the Utah Pioneer Trails and Landmarks Association in 1946 near Alvinston, Ontario.[2] By contrast, a different Mormon presence was created in western Canada between 1887 and 1903. Within a short 16 years, the Canadian cultural and geographical landscape came to have a new people, immigrant Mormons from the Great Basin of the Interior West of the United States. They founded visually, institutionally and culturally distinctive communities. Cardston,[3] Magrath, Stirling and Raymond,[4] unique place-names,[5] demarked "Mormon Country," a new term[6] for Canadians. The log home of the principal leader in Canadian settlement, Charles Ora Card, stands on its original location one century later, on Cardston's Main Street. It has its own marker and bronze plaque as an Alberta Historical Site.[7] Both the pioneer home and the marker are literally in the shadow of an even more impressive monument, the Cardston "Alberta Temple," built of granite and dedicated as a sacred Mormon edifice in 1923.[8] The pioneer log house and landmark temple symbolize home, durability and permanence. What is the "inside" story behind this cross-continental change in the locus and nature of the Mormon presence in Canada? What large-scale sociohistorical forces combined with smaller-scale contingencies, processes and biographies to generate in so short a period a "Mormon Country" in western Canada?

Charles Ora Card, 1839-1906, founder of
Cardston. NA 1759-1 Glenbow Archives.

Zina Young Card, 1850-1931, wife of
C.O. Card, and "Aunt Zina" to many
in the settlement. Courtesy Marie C.
Burnham, Edmonton.

Though the Alberta Mormon settlement story has been told a number
of times, and with different perspectives and emphases, this retelling
by a third-generation "Mormon country" descendant will vary from the
earlier accounts in several ways.[9] It begins with reference to large-scale
sociohistorical forces that converged in the late nineteenth century to
precipitate migration northward from Utah to Canada. It tells the "inside"
story, with reference to Utah's unique Cache Valley from which the
first voluntary refugees came north to become Canadian colonists.

The central theme of this retelling is that a dynamic combination of many
factors, motivational, leadership and situational, led to the genesis of a
distinctive western Canadian Mormon country and people.[10] The Canadian
Mormon settlements were more than an extension of the American Mormon
settlement corridor and village patterns into Canada.[11] They were more than
a reproduction of Utah Mormon culture in Alberta.[12] They were more than
an inevitable assimilation and accommodation to the American and Canadian nation-states as argued by O. Kendall White.[13] There was a quality of

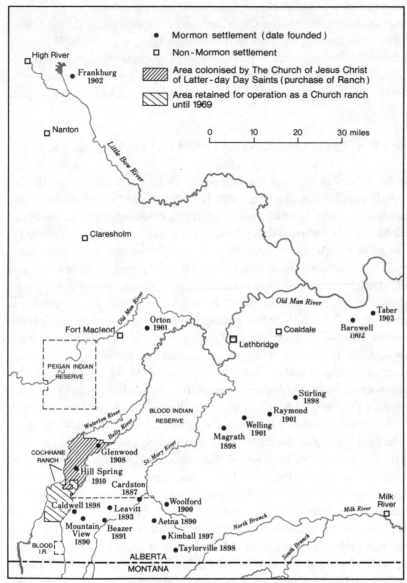

Figure 5.1: Mormon settlements in Southwestern Alberta

of apartness to the Canadian settlements that kept them from full integration into the dominant anglophone Canadian culture[14] or into the subcultural strata of ethnoreligious peoples celebrated in much western Canadiana.[15] Turning the theme into a question, it is asked: Is there a residual uniqueness, particularism or distinctiveness to this small corner of Canada with its Mormons that resists reductionist modes of explanation and understanding?[16]

THE CONTINENTAL CONTEXT OF TWO SMALL AREAS

The geographical settings for beginning this settlement story are two relatively small areas. To the south is Cache Valley, a 600-square-mile area approximately 12 miles wide and 60 long, extending from northeastern Utah into southeastern Idaho.[17] In western Canada, "Mormon Country," at the peak of settlement, was an area of 3500 square miles, extending 50 miles north from the international boundary and 70 miles east and west, though not a perfect rectangle because of an eastward extension and the "peninsula" of the Blood Indian reserve that partly divides it midway.[18] Both areas shared a common heritage in many respects, simply by being part of the landlocked Interior West of the continent. They were isolated from nineteenth-century centres of growth on waterways and in rain belts. Further, both were stigmatized so far as settlement was concerned by aridity and continental climate, symbolized as "The Great American Desert" or, in Canada, "The Palliser Triangle." Each small area was thus affected by large-scale continental sociohistorical forces.

The first force was the quest for independence from European control and the concomitant struggle for full nationhood on two subcontinents. The United States chose the route of revolutionary severance of British political ties, while retaining much of their British heritage and commercial linkages.[19] Canada, under British tutelage and control, combined French and British peoples on a route of peaceful and gradual separation from Great Britain.[20] In the sacralizing ideology of the Mormons from 1830 onward, the founding of the United States was inspired, British and European origins were providential, Native Americans were part of a dispersed Israel, and the whole of America, north and south, was a "choice land," a Zion, with a global, time-transcending role to play in the salvation of mankind.[21] Migration from Cache Valley to the Canadian West in 1887 linked the United States, "The First New Nation," with the new "Dominion" within this ideological framework of a special mission for the Americas.

The second sociohistorical force was the drive by the two fledgling nations toward economic domain and national sovereignty from sea to sea across the North American continent. In the United States, the requisite mix for this drive, of people, technology, trade, and political leadership emerged faster than in Canada.[22] The junction for east-west overland communication and transportation in the American West proved to be the Great Basin, where the religiously motivated Mormon commonwealth, bent on self-sufficiency, had been started in 1847. With the coming of telegraph and railway, national sovereignty in both countries was visibly and technologically confirmed. In the United States, transcontinental telegraph service was established in 1861. The first transcontinental railroad was finished in 1869. In both instances, the junction took place in Utah, with Mormon leadership and labor providing the critically important help needed to complete these projects. In Canada, a boldly conceived and heavily subsidized Canadian Pacific Railway crossed the continent in 1885, bringing both telegraph and rail services continent wide to the northern dominion.[23] Great Basin Mormons were among the builders of the CPR.[24]

An important spin-off from the quest for national sovereignty through railways was the development of branch lines in both the Great Basin and western Canada, which met in Montana in 1890. The Mormons cooperatively built and financed the Utah Northern, which reached Logan in Cache Valley in 1873. Under private companies after 1877, it reached Butte, Montana, in 1881.[25] In western Canada, Sir Alexander Galt and his son Elliott led in the development of a branch line from Dunmore on the CPR main line to the Lethbridge coal mines in 1885. This line was linked to Great Falls, Montana, in 1890. The drive for national sovereignty had equipped the Interior West with railway technology. Still lacking, especially in western Canada, were people and something to trade.[26]

A third continental force rarely considered in most accounts of settlement is southerly tropism, the strong attraction southward observable in both countries and among Mormon people.[27] On a macro-scale, southerly tropism in the early development of the United States was expressed in patterns of territorial expansion, migration and ideologically expressed aspirations, including the "Monroe Doctrine."[28] In Canada, southerly tropism was most continually and obviously expressed by the voluntary movement of people to the United States.[29] From 1859 to 1901, emigration from Canada, most of it southward, exceeded immigration, as native-born Canadians joined with stopover immigrants on their way to the United States.[30]

Among Mormons, southerly tropism was reflected in the choice of the

Great Basin for settlement rather than northerly alternatives, including Vancouver Island.[31] It was manifested even more clearly in the creation of settlements southward rather than northward from Salt Lake City during the first three decades of settlement after 1847. Cache Valley settlement, despite nearness to Salt Lake City, was delayed until 1859-60. In the mid-1880s, it was expressed through intense interest in Mexico as a place of refuge for politically harassed Mormons in the Great Basin.[32]

Southerly tropism as a continental phenomenon pervades the developmental history of the two countries and the Mormon settlements in western Canada. As a force, it was a blend of climatic determinism and perceptual behaviorism among humans who needed strong incentives to make a northern clime a home when a more southerly one was an alternative.

The fourth continent-wide force was the colonialization of the Interior West by dominant central and eastern regions, containing burgeoning metropolises in search of hinterlands. In the western United States, the predominant pattern was "laissez-faire" settlement of receding frontiers, helped on occasion by military intervention, a period of apprenticeship and adjustment as a federal territory, and then statehood, usually with national political strings attached.[33] The Canadian pattern, expressed as National Policy, was to create a territory ready for settlement, and then fill it with settlers. Later, Ottawa would grant provincehood in such a way that the effective powers of the older central provinces would remain largely unfettered. The component regions of the dominion were not to be equal.[34] Further, from its earliest beginnings, western Canadian settlement included settlement by groups of ethnoreligiously homogeneous peoples, as well as by individuals seeking personal or family opportunities.[35] The colonializing of the Canadian West was muted in the 1880s by visions of prosperity and progress engendered by the National Policy and its promoters.[36]

A different settlement pattern occurred in the Great Basin when the Mormons arrived in 1847, abruptly becoming a salient element in a westward expanding American frontier. The intent was to create an institutionally complete commonwealth based on principles of co-operation and self-sufficiency. The entire enterprise, infused with religious devotion and value commitment, was to be practically expressed.[37] It soon became apparent that Mormon aspirations and accomplishments did not fit into the evolving agenda of Manifest Destiny and economic expansion in the United States. Colonialization began early, with the reduction of Mormon territorial claims from one large State of Deseret to a much smaller Territory of Utah. A later phase of colonialization took place in the 1880s under the guise of

a national crusade to end Mormon polygamy.[38] A draconian effort was made
to bring the Mormon commonwealth into mainstream dominant American
culture. The openly expressed intent was to exploit without hindrance the
mineral, land, water and human resources of the Great Basin, occupied by
a Mormon majority, with their diversified, relatively self-sufficient and
egalitarian society.[39] The coalescing power interests of a federal government,
big business and organized Protestantism, based in the East, used drastic
federal laws to put down a minor form of marriage, which had become a
politically popular target for northern states' politicians and their lobbies.[40]
With legislation aimed at the Mormon Church ownership of property and
control of assets, it was clear that the objective was to reduce the power of
the church as a viable institution in American society.[41] The colonializing
mode of developing the Interior West was to have no rival.

In the 1880s the consequences of the enforcement of the Edmunds Act
of 1882 and the Edmunds-Tucker Act of 1887 became apparent in Mormon
communities generally and for Mormon leaders particularly.[42] Federally
appointed officers took over federal, state and many local governing functions. Federal marshals scoured the Great Basin area seeking men to arrest
for "unlawful co-habitation," a misdemeanor subject to fine and imprisonment. Businesses, farms, families and church organizations became
destabilized as husbands and sometimes wives became fugitives. The men
were imprisoned and local governments were weakened. Non-Mormons
were installed in local federal positions. Thousands of men and women were
excluded from electoral privileges. The "underground" ways of life of many
families caused much distress for people used to full religious and civic
freedom. Mormons became the focus of a national crusade. Their plural
marriages were seen as a threat to family life and their regional dominance
was viewed as a threat to national sovereignty. The colonialization process,
under the guise of an anti-Mormon crusade, reached an apex of conflict
during the 1880s.

CACHE VALLEY TO WESTERN CANADA

The migration northward to Canada from Cache Valley was the product
of these times and circumstances, and a series of decisions taken by key persons, especially C.O. Card and church President John Taylor. The attitudes
were expressed eloquently by the *Utah Journal*, published at Logan, the
major Cache Valley community.[43] Its masthead read, "The highest possible

liberty to man and woman." Its first edition editorial, on 1 August 1882, pledged the paper "to avoid all objectionable material..., contend for the rights of man and oppose all those who encroach on the liberties of the people..., sustain all in the practice of their civil, religious and political rights..., and contend for the just and constitutional rights of the 'Peoples Party in Utah'." The editorial ended with a commitment. "While recognizing the power of Congress to enact proscriptive, un-American and even infamous laws for the government of territorial citizens, we shall urge the people of Utah to contest, by every lawful means, its right to do so." There was strong resistance to what was perceived as oppression.

The events precipitating migration northward took place four years later. On the afternoon of 26 July 1886, in Salt Lake City the following special dispatch from Logan, Cache County, was published in the late afternoon edition of the *Deseret News*.[44]

CHARLES ORA CARD ARRESTED
President C.O. Card was arrested this morning, about 9:30 by Deputy Marshall Garr. His house was searched and several members of his family subpoenaed. Will leave for Ogden on the two o'clock train.

For faithful Mormons, the news would be saddening. Another respected leader was on his way to jail. His loved ones would be deprived of their father and husband. The projects he was striving to supervise, while a fugitive-in-hiding, would languish. For their gentile opponents, a growing minority in Salt Lake City and Logan, there would be rejoicing that another ranking churchman from the Cache Stake would now get his just reward. Non-Mormons could now hope for increased opportunities to influence affairs in Cache County according to their own interests. For Mormon men already in jail under federal anti-polygamy laws, there would be the expectation of the company of one more brother, another unfairly treated person at the hands of an unjust oppressor. Card was the seventh Cache county leader to be arrested. More would soon follow.[45]

Paradoxically, the expectation relating to Card would not be fulfilled. As the train carrying Card to jail left the Logan Station, he asked permission from Marshal Exum to get a drink of water at the end of the car.[46] Instead of returning, he simply jumped from the moving train, appropriated a saddled horse tied to a rail, and galloped through Logan streets toward the bushes along the Logan River, where he would hide until dark. When Marshal Exum discovered his prisoner had fled, he asked the non-Mormon conductor to stop the train. The conductor refused. After nightfall, Card found refuge with friends. His escape was the precipitating incident starting a chain of events and decisions that would lead him to Canada.

Migration northward, however, was not a simple response to the federal intent to colonialize the Interior West by attacking Mormon polygamy. The precipitating incident expressed one man's decision to be free and take the consequences for seeking freedom and justice to which he felt entitled as a respected citizen, church leader, and faithful, dedicated father and husband.[47] For Card, the push out of Cache Valley had started. But where? With a wagon packed, he was prepared to leave for Mexico.

By 1 September 1886, Card finally made contact with the president of the church, John Taylor, also in hiding, to seek advice. Card's Cache Valley associate, Moses Thatcher, a member of the church's Quorum of Twelve Apostles, was in Mexico trying to establish colonies for Mormons seeking refuge from the federal "raid." The two had exchanged letters.[48] Card was well briefed on what was required to travel to the Mexican settlement sites. He fully expected Taylor to approve his plans for this migration. Instead, the venerable president, born in England and a former Methodist preacher in Upper Canada at the time of his conversion to the Mormon faith, advised Card to go to British Columbia to find a site for a Mormon settlement. In Canada, Taylor affirmed, he would find British justice.[49] In this decision, southerly tropism was reversed as the British Northwest became a refuge offering freedom and justice.

Card responded promptly.[50] He interviewed several men, selecting two to accompany him to explore for a site. On 10 September 1886, Apostle Francis M. Lyman, under authorization from Taylor, "set apart," by prayer and the imposition of the hands, both Card and one of the men selected, James W. Hendricks, an experienced Cache Valley pioneer. Later Card, under authorization, "set apart" the second man, Isaac Zundell of Idaho, who had extensive experience working with Indians.[51]

Leaving Logan the night of 14 September 1886, Card and Hendricks had a rendezvous three days later with Zundell near American Falls, Idaho. Here they boarded the train to Spokane, Washington, travelling under assumed names. From Spokane, they travelled by packhorse north into Canada. As they stepped across the border into British Columbia, Card threw his hat in the air and shouted, "In Columbia we are free."[52] On the shore of Lake Osoyoos, the three held a church service on Sunday 3 October 1886. Card recounted in his diary:[53]

Our prayer is constantly, "Father, direct us by revelation that we might find the right place." Up to this time we have not had a cross word in our trio but have night and morning invoked the blessing of God upon us in seeking a haven of rest for the persecuted and imprisoned. We not only remember ourselves, but our dear ones at home that pray for us and all the faithful that the cause of Christ may triumph....

In the remainder of the entry, Card recorded his blessing for the Indian family on whose land they were camped, and his prophecy concerning the opening of "the door of the gospel" to the seed of Joseph, the Lamanites in "these parts." He also observed "This was the first meeting under the authority of the Melchizedek Priesthood in the District of British Columbia in the latter days."

The exploring trio found the British Columbia mountain valleys unable to sustain agricultural colonists. Most of the limited land was already tied up in long-term leases to a few ranchers. In an unexpected encounter, they heard from a Montana mountaineer of the buffalo plains south of Calgary. They promptly sold their gear, took a train to Calgary, bought a team and buckboard, and headed south over the prairies. Between the Kootenai (Waterton) and Belly rivers near present-day Stand Off they found the country for which they were searching.

The "pulls" of the area were listed in Card's 22 October 1886 diary entry. There was good land and water, moderate winters, timber somewhat distant, and coal thirty miles away at Lethbridge, which was the terminus of a narrow-gauge railway. This area was also in the heart of Indian country, and thus an advantageous place for a mission. The Indians were raising successful crops of wheat and oats and seemed "intelligent." Two days later, Sunday 24 October, Card and Zundell knelt in prayer on the Kootenai River, dedicating the "land to the Lord for the benefit of Israel, both Red and White." The following morning the trio left for their return to Utah, passing by Lee Creek where it joined the St. Mary River. They had found the land they wanted to settle.[54]

Upon returning to Utah, many details occupied Charles Card's attention over the succeeding months.[55] President Taylor released him from the exploration mission and asked him to seek out colonists to go north the next spring—1887. While still in hiding, he recruited forty families who were approved by Taylor for the settlement mission in Canada. As the planned departure date of 25 March 1887 drew near, however, Card learned that fewer than ten were willing to stand by their promise to accompany him.

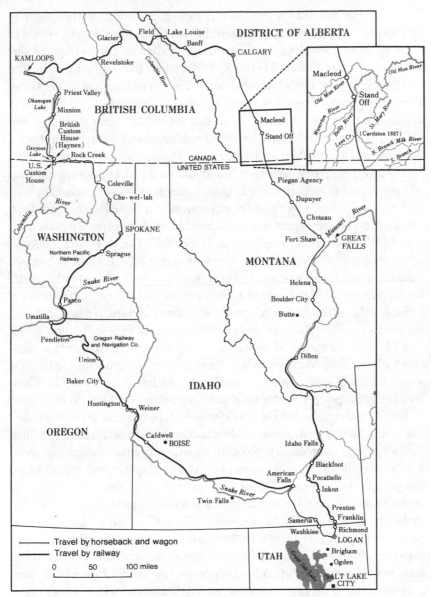

Figure 5.2: Charles O. Card's exploration tour, 1886

The others had decided "to stay and run their chances" with the law, or "felt they were too poor."[56] As for himself, he was resolved to depart, even if it must be alone. Word had reached Cache Valley of the passage of the Edmunds-Tucker Act on 19 February 1887, which to Card "meant plunder and persecution of the whole church."[57] Federal officers now intensified efforts to capture polygamists. Barely escaping arrest again, Card left Logan in disguise the night of March 23 to entrain at McCammon, Idaho, for Helena, Montana. At Helena, he would rendezvous with three men chosen to help select a Canadian settlement site.

The selection party arrived at Stand Off on April 16, during a severe storm.[58] Upon finding that the land that they favored for settlement was under lease or owned by ranchers and unavailable, Card wrote from Fort Macleod to Taylor, suggesting that the church supply funds to purchase land near the Blood Indian Reserve "to gain a foothold." Two days later, on April 25, however, while exploring Lee Creek, they met E.N. Barker, an English rancher, who with his partner, Herbert Donovan, had a cabin on the creek. Barker informed the Utah men of an expired lease on land a mile downstream from his cabin and adjacent to the Blood Reserve. The next day, Card and his companions voted unanimously to select this land for a settlement. Word was left with the mounted police on the St. Mary River to direct settlers coming from Utah to the site. Card then travelled to Lethbridge, where he wrote Taylor of their achievement. As well, he inquired about Canadian laws and regulations from the dominion land officer and the customs officer.

When Card returned to Lee Creek on May 1, he found that the first party from Utah had arrived, Andrew Allen and his son Warner from Coveville, Cache County. Immediately, plowing began and grain and vegetable seeds were sowed. In all, ten acres were planted. On May 3, Card and his three companions headed south, Card to meet his family coming by team, the others to return to their railroad building activities in Montana, and later to their home in Rexburg, Idaho. Near Helena, Card joined his wife Zina, two-year-old son Joseph, and sixteen-year-old stepson, Sterling Williams (by Zina's first marriage). They travelled by wagon with the Woolfs and other families from Cache Valley. When they crossed the border 1 June 1887, they gave three cheers for their new land, added their own rocks to a rock cairn on the border to mark the occasion, and proceeded on to Lee Creek, arriving 3 June 1887.

The next day, Sunday, the little group of 41 souls, except for two young men looking for lost horses, met in a tent for a church service. Card, as leader of the colony and as stake president of Cache Stake, presided, using a box

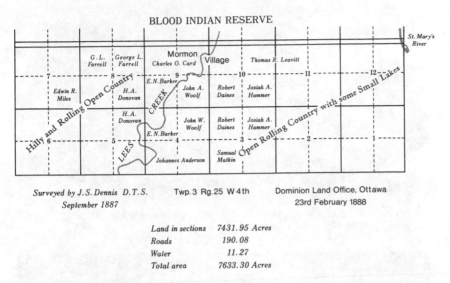

Figure 5.3: Cardston Settlement, 1888

the women had covered with a red chenille tablecloth for the pulpit. In his diary he wrote:

> In this meeting, Elders Robert Daines, G.L. Farrell, A.L. Allen, John A. Woolfe [*sic*], J.E. Layne and self expressed our pleasure of having a peaceful place to meet, also our satisfaction with our locations. All seemed pleased with our first meeting, although we had to crowd into a 14x16 tent to worship the Lord our God…and partake the Holy Sacrament for the renewal of our covenants and refreshing of our spirits.[59]

Jane Woolf (Bates), a 14-year-old girl who attended this meeting, later wrote:

> All the men spoke and expressed their satisfaction for the hand-dealing of the Lord toward them for preserving them in their journey to this land. Here they could do His will in establishing a colony of Latter-day Saints, as had the pioneers in Utah under the leadership of Brigham Young in 1847, just forty years earlier. All present were from Cache Stake of which Brother Card was president. The Lee's Creek colony was now to be a branch of the Cache Stake.[60]

Pioneer home of Charles and Zina Card, built 1887, photographed in 1889, Cardston, Alberta. NA 124-1 Glenbow Archives.

Second home of Charles and Zina Card, built 1900, Cardston, Alberta. Photo by B. Y. Card, 1940.

THE CARDSTON SETTLEMENT

Settlement began with much enthusiasm. On 12 June 1887, the second Sunday after the arrival of the colonists, a Sunday School organization was formed. On this occasion, Jonathan E. Layne, called to be the superintendent, prophesied that a temple would one day be built in the new land, a prophecy later repeated by Apostle John W. Taylor.[61] During much of the early growth of the settlement, Taylor served in essence as a resident apostle. Sixty-eight persons stayed through the first winter.[62] As the population grew, the church organization expanded and matured. The Cardston Ward of Cache Stake was organized in 1888, and then other wards were organized in surrounding hamlets of Mormons. By 1891, there were 359 Mormons in Cardston and vicinity. By October 1894, the number was 674.[63] The Alberta Stake was created in 1895, with Card as president. Though a small stake, consisting of three wards and a few outlying branches in the Cardston district, its formation was an expression of confidence in the future of the Mormon settlement in Canada.

The material side of life was not neglected but blended into a pattern of religious and practical living.[64] In 1887, in addition to the construction of log homes, a blacksmith shop and a butcher shop were opened, a townsite surveyed, and a mail service to Macleod started. The next year, Card opened a general store, which was expanded later to become the Cardston Company Limited, a multipurpose joint stock venture. A stage coach began service to Lethbridge, a shoemaker opened shop, and the district rancher, who was also a dentist, moved to the town where he also served as customs officer. A co-operative irrigation project was started, with the canal water also operating a grist-mill. In the next few years, the settlement had a hotel, a cheese factory, an improved flour mill, a postmaster and mail contractor, a brickmaker, a livery stable, a limekiln, a telephone line to Lethbridge, and a steel bridge over the river on the road to Lethbridge. By 1895, there was also a bank. The development of services included in the first year the dispatch of a local woman to Utah for training in midwifery. A school was held in the fall of 1887 in local log homes, and later in a log school and meeting-house. Dominion days were regularly celebrated, starting with 1 July 1887, bringing together Mormons and non-Mormons of the district. The Mormons were busy recreating another Cache Valley, but with "the mantle of the country" draping "itself around the shoulders of the people."[65]

Always assisted by capable counselors and associates, Card proved to be a practical leader, able to delegate work and authority, and able to blend

Mormon and non-Mormon personnel and resources for mutual benefit. As events would demonstrate, he was able to enlist local and outside persons of talent and vision to bring about many developments in the southwest corner of Alberta.[66] After reviewing one of his talks to the local priesthood in 1890, historian Wilcox later called attention to the "simple, genuine and complete way of life" of the settlers, under "a benign, almost patriarchal leadership," in which Card was the "nerve center" in the life of the colony.[67]

An important influence on the Cardston settlement was the trip to Ottawa of apostles John W. Taylor and Francis M. Lyman, of Salt Lake City, and Card, in November 1888.[68] The purpose was to seek certain benefits for the new settlement and to test the possibility of bringing the plural families of the settlers to the colony. The appeal to the Canadian government was limited to seeking relief for families in distress because of persecution in the United States, with the assurance that this appeal was not intended to be a way of introducing plural marriage into Canada. In their attempt to lobby the Canadian government, the Ottawa delegation learned two cardinal features concerning their settlement in Canada. First, most of the benefits they sought were already provided in legislation or in existing government regulations. Second, Mormons with one wife in Canada would be welcome as settlers, along with their possessions, but plural wives or the practice of polygamy would not be tolerated. The rule was clear. The Canadian government would treat the Mormon settlers with equity under Canadian law, but they could expect no special privileges. The government clinched the point a year later by passing a Criminal Code amendment, specifically making the practice or advocacy of polygamy or "spiritual wifery" an indictable offense.

A critical turning point in the history of the Mormon settlement in Canada took place in Logan, Utah, 2 and 3 August 1890.[69] On the advice of his first counselor in the Cache Stake presidency, Card had gone to Utah in July to surrender to US marshals, expecting to gain his liberty after a nominal penalty. He was released on bail, and he walked the streets of his home city for the first time in four years as a free man. He now saw his return from Canada as permanent and expected to carry on his life and responsibilities in Cache Valley as stake president. Instead, when he visited the office of President Woodruff he was advised that he had already been called to remain in Canada, and that letter was on its way. This call was confirmed at the August 2 and 3 Cache Stake Conference when Woodruff released him from all Utah responsibilities, calling him to remain indefinitely in Canada as head of what was termed the "Canadian Mission."

Always loyal to his presiding brethren, he returned north and immediately took out Canadian citizenship.

He did return to Utah in December 1890, however, to stand trial on four charges of cohabitation and polygamy, levied by his ex-wife, Sarah Jane Bird-neau.[70] When Sarah Jane's weak testimony was refuted during the trial, much to the discomfiture of the coterie who had been urging her on, Card was acquitted. He was now a volunteer colonist, and no longer an exile. He had a mission to develop the Canadian settlement.

IRRIGATION AND NEW COMMUNITIES

In the next few years, there was a coalescence of vision, prophecy, trial and error organization, and experience that led the way to major new developments. Upon returning from Utah at the close of 1890, Card opened a land office to assist settlers in securing land.[71] Experience with irrigation in Utah, and with small irrigation systems in the Cardston area, motivated Card, but more particularly Apostle Taylor, to promote larger-scale irrigation and development. The key to this development was the utilization of the large landholdings of the Galts.[72] Card and Taylor speculatively bought 711,000 acres between 1891 and 1895, with low yearly interim rent and a low guaranteed purchase price, with the contract specifying that irrigation must be provided as a necessary condition for the sale. To help this development, Elliott Galt formed the Alberta Irrigation Company in 1893 to serve as a broker among the purchasers, the Galts, and the government. The response of potential settlers in Utah was cool, despite the efforts of the Alberta Land and Colonization Company, formed in Utah in January 1895. The alternate townships held by the Galts were seen as a serious obstacle, especially when the federal government delayed making the arrangements necessary to treat the land as a single block in preparation for irrigation development. The Card-Taylor speculation fell through when the time limit for the fulfillment of their contract ran out. One new town, Pot Hole, later to be named Magrath, was planned in 1894 but not built. The lessons learned from the failure were not lost on Elliott Galt and C.A. Magrath, his project manager, or on federal officials. In 1896, a consolidated block of land was finally granted.

As the attractive farmsteads of the Cardston area demonstrated the agricultural potential of the area between Cardston and Lethbridge, the Alberta Irrigation Company decided to try once more to build a major

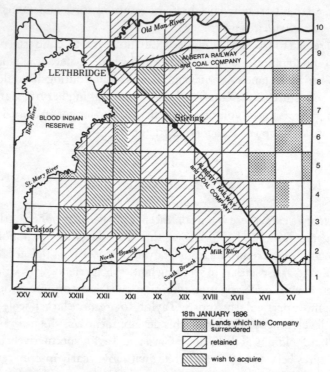

18th JANUARY 1896

Lands which the Company
surrendered

retained

wish to acquire

Figure 5.4: The Galt land grants (1) of alternate townships that contributed to the unsuc-
cessful 1893 Alberta Irrigation Company irrigation development promoted privately through
John W. Taylor and C. O. Card; (2) the consolidation approved in 1896 that led to the
successful Canal building by the Galt interests with the Mormon church as contractors,
1898-1900 (Proposed land grants, Privy Council, 1896)

irrigation canal.[73] Card, Taylor and the Mormons at Cardston encouraged
the project. The Alberta Irrigation Company enlisted the support of the
Mormon Church through a meeting of church officials, C.A. Magrath and
Card in Utah. A revised development plan was approved. The church would
be the contractor to build the canal, not as a speculative venture, but as a
way of providing profitable work for those in need of assistance and
helping a number of potential settlers acquire their own land in Canada.
Workers were to be compensated half in cash and half in land. On 7 October
1897, the church announced that Card "was authorized to invite settlers
to locate on lands in Canada." On 14 April 1898, the final contract was
signed. It stipulated that the fifty-mile canal from Kimball, on the St.
Mary River, to Stirling was to be completed by 31 December 1899,
with the settlement of a minimum of 250 people on each of two townsites

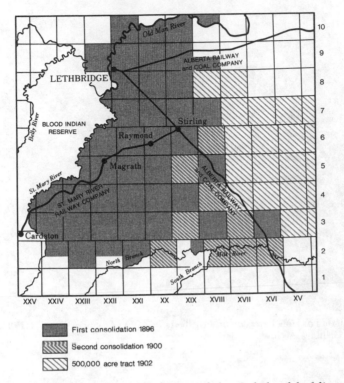

Figure 5.5: The further consolidation of the Galt land holdings that permitted extension of irrigation beyond original fifty mile-long Canal.

that would be at the centers of the two, large blocks of land to be irrigated.

Much had to be done if the Mormons in Canada and Utah were to avail themselves of this settlement opportunity. The church presidency appointed Card to supervise their contract work in Canada and to see that it was carried out properly. In February 1899, supervision of canal construction was turned over to M.D. Hammond, an irrigation specialist from Cache Valley who worked closely with the company engineer, G.G. Anderson of Denver, Colorado. This freed Card to devote greater effort to recruiting canal workers and settlers. Card, Taylor and H.C. Jacobs, called to assist in recruitment, covered Utah promoting the project. In the initial phases of the project, it was Cardston district men more than Utahans who provided the needed workers. When the church became concerned about the lack of Utah volunteers, it began to call men, with their teams, on missions to Alberta, some for canal building, others to immigrate and become settlers. These were

Deep cut on Pot Hole Diversion of the Alberta Irrigation Company Canal, c.1900. NA 922-16 Glenbow Archives.

Canal flume of Alberta Irrigation Company over Pot Hole Creek between Magrath and Stirling, c.1900. NA 922-12 Glenbow Archives.

serious mission calls, beginning with a letter from a presiding church official, and ending with a formal release. In this way, hundreds of men and teams were recruited for canal building and settlement.

On 14 November 1899, Sir Clifford Sifton, minister of the Interior, opened officially the main 50-mile canal that brought water to Magrath, with 424 settlers, and Stirling, with 349 settlers.[74] By July 1900, another 65 miles of branch canals were built, taking water into Lethbridge and south of Stirling. The whole project was opened officially at Lethbridge in September of the same year by Governor General Lord Minto.[75] With the church contract filled on time, and settlers on the land, Card advised the first presidency of the church that the "colonies were stable and could stand alone."[76]

The successful settlement of Magrath and Stirling through large-scale irrigation stimulated the development of the town of Raymond, which would have, however, a somewhat different beginning.[77] Early in the 1890s, Taylor had advocated the planting of sugar beets as a crop for the land he foresaw coming under irrigation. With the completion of the canal in 1899, and acting on the Taylor suggestion, Magrath passed out sugar beet seed on a trial basis to Magrath farmers. Tests at the Lehi Sugar Factory in Utah confirmed that a high quality of beet could be grown in Alberta. Meanwhile, Magrath tried to interest the wealthy Utah entrepreneur Jesse Knight, and his sons Ray and William, in southern Alberta land. Magrath was surprised when Jesse purchased 30,000 acres in January 1901, on the basis of the information on a map and the report of his sons. In the spring of 1901, Jesse Knight came to southern Alberta to see the land he had purchased, called the Bar K2 Ranch. (In time, it would become one of the best known and most successful ranches in southern Alberta.) Two days after his arrival, he startled Magrath once more by offering to erect, with his own capital, a sugar beet factory between Magrath and Stirling. He placed a $50,000 deposit with the Alberta Irrigation Company to confirm his offer. The contract was negotiated and signed on 16 August 1901. Though the land was unbroken prairie, he envisioned a prosperous settlement. Even before the contract was signed, he had purchased 3,000 acres from the company, which were to be ploughed and ready for "cultivation and settlers" by the following spring. The sugar factory was "to be ready for operation in the autumn of 1902" and "...operated for a minimun of twelve years." There were two other aspects of the "deal." Knight was to be allowed to purchase 226,000 acres of company land near the townsite, which was to be named Raymond, after his eldest son. Also, the town was to have a special charter, which would

Temple and Tabernacle, Temple Block, Cardston, 1927. ND 277-11 Glenbow Archives.

"prohibit any liquor licenses, gambling halls, or houses of prostitution."[78] If Knight was to introduce sugar beet culture and manufacture, and create thereby a new community, he wanted the social environment to be the best his own religious experience and convictions as a Mormon could help encourage. With this unusual start, about 150 Mormons, mostly from the three Alberta settlements, "...gathered around an old buffalo skull," on the open prairie, and dedicated the spot as the townsite of Raymond, "...asking God's blessing on the land and the people who would inhabit it."[79]

The development of the Knight vision of a sugar beet factory and a supporting community took place as planned. Some eighty teams began breaking land in 1901.[80] The town of Raymond was laid out on a grand scale by Taylor, complete with Paris-like radial boulevards. Workmen and settlers, attracted by jobs and land, and also pushed out of Utah by declining opportunities for new farmers, "streamed" to the area. Within six months, there were four hundred inhabitants. The settlement, with church and public buildings, businesses and schools, went from hamlet to village to town in just over two years. Between 1903 and 1906, it was Alberta's largest Mormon town, with over 1500 residents, outdistancing Cardston with its 1001, Magrath with 884, and Stirling with 438.[81] The Mormon settlements were now in place, complete with necessary institutions, irrigation projects, and a major local industry to supplement agriculture.

CONCLUSION

It can been seen once more how different the Mormon experience in the Canadian East in the three decades after 1830 was from that in the Canadian West from 1887 to 1903. Early Canadian Mormons migrated southward to join the main body of Saints readying for a journey to a new Zion in the West, the Great Basin as it later turned out. They had given their allegiance to a new faith, a minority sect, an unpopular movement competing for members in the Canadas and the Atlantic colonies. Their Canadian presence receded with their departure. In the Great Basin area, those who got that far were melded into a people who formed their own majority culture, their unique commonwealth and religiously integrated Zion that became a new homeland. When the political condition of this homeland became undesirable, and for some intolerable, a different kind of Mormon migrated to a different kind of country in the Canadian West. He was the settler, the agricultural colonist, sure of his religion, of the worth of his experience and heritage in the West, and of his ability to become a productive member of Canadian society. In 1887, the Mormons re-entered Canadian history, out of phase with the sects who survived in Canada and had themselves been transformed as religions clambering for a place in Canada's cities and countryside.[82] The new Mormon presence would be harder to classify and reduce to stereotypes than the earlier one. They had become a Canadian Mormon people living in a small, but unique, Canadian Mormon country.[83]

NOTES

1. Richard E. Bennett, " 'Plucking Not Planting': Mormonism in Eastern Canada 1830-1850," this volume.

2. Octave W. Ursenbach, "The Nauvoo Road," in The Canadian Mission, The Church of Jesus Christ of Latter-day Saints, *The Great Canadian Mission: A Jubilee History* (Brampton, Ontario: n.d., ca 1969), pp. 112-15.

3. See C.O. Card, Diary, Monday, 5 November 1889 as transcribed by Clarice Card Godfrey in Charles Ora Card, *The Journal of Charles Ora Card, September 14, 1886 to July 7, 1903*, compiled by Donald G. Godfrey and Melva R. Whitbeck (n.p., published privately by Donald G. Godfrey, 1981); hereafter cited as "*Card Journal*: Godfrey," to distinguish it from reference to the original, cited as "Card Diary," and from the 1871-1885 transcription of diaries by Brigham Young University Archives, not publicly available, cited here as "Card Diary: BYU Archives."

4. See Ernest G. Mardon, *Community Names of Alberta* (Lethbridge: The University of Lethbridge, 1973).

5. According to the *Britannica World Atlas* (1968), there was only one Cardston and one Magrath worldwide; three Stirlings, one in Alberta, one in Australia, and one in Great Britain; and four Raymonds, one in Alberta, the others in the USA.

6. "Mormon Country" is a folk term originating in the United States, where it applied to the Great Basin Mormon settlements. See Wallace Stegner, *Mormon Country* (New York: Duell, Sloan and Pearce, 1942). Lowry Nelson, a Utah sociologist studying Alberta Mormon settlements in 1930, used it frequently in his report, published as part of C.A. Dawson's *Group Settlement: Ethnic Communities in Western Canada*, Volume VII, *Canadian Frontiers of Settlement Series*, W.A. Mackintosh and W.L. Joerg, editors (Toronto: Macmillan Company, 1936), pp. 178-95. It was used earlier in southern Alberta as a folk term, see *The Lethbridge Herald*, 22 July 1915, p.1.

7. See Jane Eliza Woolf Bates and Zina Alberta Woolf Hickman, *Founding of Cardston and Vicinity: Pioneer Problems* (n.p., published privately by William L. Woolf, 1960), p. 16.

8. See V.A. Wood, *The Alberta Temple: Centre and Symbol of Faith* (Calgary: Detselig Enterprises, 1989).

9. The first basic research on Canadian Mormon settlements was by Lowry Nelson, in Dawson, *Group Settlement*, pp. 173-272, and republished with condensation in Nelson, *The Mormon Village* (Salt Lake City: University of Utah Press, 1952), pp. 213-71. Nelson's authorship of pages noted in Dawson was confirmed in an interview with Nelson by B.Y. Card, 29 July 1986.

Five theses extended Nelson's contribution between 1950 and 1971: Archie G. Wilcox, "The Founding of the Mormon Community in Alberta" (master's thesis, University of Alberta, 1950), A. James Hudson, "Charles Ora Card: Pioneer and Colonizer" (master's thesis, Brigham Young University, 1961, published privately by the author in 1963); Melvin S. Tagg, "A History of the Church of Jesus Christ of Latter-day Saints, 1830-1963" (doctoral dissertation, Brigham Young University, 1963, and published privately by the author that same year); John R. Hicken, "Events Leading to the Settlement of the Communities of Cardston, Magrath, Stirling and Raymond, Alberta" (master's thesis, Utah State University, 1968); John Lehr, "Mormon Settlements in Southern Alberta" (master's thesis, University of Alberta, 1971).

Lawrence B. Lee, an American historian specializing in the history of irrigation, in "The Mormons come to Canada, 1887-1902," *Pacific Northwest Quarterly*, 59 (January 1968), pp. 11-22, shows the interplay of the Mormon Church, Canadian government and Galt interests in the settlement process. Howard Palmer, *Land of the Second Chance: A History of Ethnic Groups in Southern Alberta* (Lethbridge: *The Lethbridge Herald*, 1972), continues the Mormons-as-ethnics theme of Dawson.

There are also important local histories. Those consulted were Bates and Hickman, *Founding of Cardston and Vicinity*; Keith Shaw (ed.), *Chief Mountain Country: A History of Cardston and District* (Cardston and District Historical Society, 1978) and Beryl Bectell (ed.), ibid., Volume II (1987).

Other sources dealing with Mormon settlement in Canada have been used. An early landmark publication was N.W. Macleod, *Picturesque Cardston and Environments: A Story of Colonization and Progress in Southern Alberta, 1886-1900* (Cardston: N.W. Macleod, Publisher, 1900), combining text and photographs. A similar format was used by Lethbridge Oxford scholar, Donald W. Buchanan, "The Mormons in Canada," *Canadian Geographical Journal*, Vol. 2, no. 4 (April 1931), pp. 255-70, who also tells the Mormon settlement story with an emphasis on irrigation. An effort to link early Mormon settlement with Mormons in contemporary Canada was made by Cardston-born freelance writer Robert Cleland Christie, "When the Saints came marching north," *Maclean's Magazine* (3 April 1965), pp. 20-21, 30, 32-33. Regular and special editions of *The Lethbridge Herald*, a daily paper, notably the Cardston Golden Jubilee edition, 25 June 1937, provide useful journalistic accounts of the Mormon settlements in southern Alberta, which supplement the more limited writing in the archival copies of local Mormon community newspapers.

10. Three theoretical sources are involved in this theme. Randall Collins, *Sociology Since Midcentury: Essays in Theory Cumulation* (New York: Academic Press, 1981), pp. 261-93, on "The microfoundations of macrosociology," with special reference to Table 1, "Time and Space Levels of Sociological Analysis," p. 263. Allan Pred, "Place as historically contingent process: structuration and the time-geography of becoming places," *Annals of the Association of American Geographers*, 74, no. 2, 1984, pp. 279-97, also stresses micro- and macro-level interaction of biography formation, structural processes and power transformations in the becoming of place. The importance of the inner perspective of a participant observer, who can draw on personal identity and a "reflective phenomenology" based on experience in a group, is the concern of Severyn T. Bruyn, *The Human Perspective in Sociology: The Method of Participation* (Englewood Cliffs, New Jersey: Prentice-Hall, 1966), especially pp. 168-74. All three perspectives are combined in coming to this statement of theme.

11. The tendency to see Canadian Mormon settlements as American Mormon

extensions into Canada is found in Leonard J. Arrington, *Great Basin Kingdom, An Economic History of the Latter-day Saints, 1830-1900* (Lincoln, Nebraska: University of Nebraska Press, 1958, 1966), pp. 354-55 and 382-84; Dawson, *Group Settlement*, pp. 221-27 and 251-72; Nelson, *The Mormon Village.*

12. L.A. Rosenvall, "The transfer of Mormon culture to Alberta," *The American Review of Canadian Studies*, XII, no. 2 (Summer 1982), pp. 51-63. See also D.W. Meinig, "The Mormon culture region: Strategies and patterns in the geography of the American West, 1874-1964," *Annals of the Association of American Geographers*, LV (1965), pp. 191-221, especially his Figure 7. Cultural reproduction or "extension of the work" of the church into western Canada has been common in the writings of church historians based in Utah, for example, B.H. Roberts, *A Comprehensive History of The Church of Jesus Christ of Latter-day Saints: Century I* (Provo, Utah: Brigham Young University Press, 1965), Vol. VI, pp. 274-76. Mormon settlements in Alberta as a persisting colony based on the Mormon colony model are described briefly by Thomas G. Alexander, *Mormonism in Transition: A History of the Latter-day Saints, 1890-1930* (Urbana, Illinois: University of Illinois Press, 1986), pp. 201 and 204.

13. O. Kendall White, Jr, "Mormonism in America and Canada: Accommodation to the nation-state," *Canadian Journal of Sociology*, 3, no. 2 (1978), pp. 161-81.

14. John Blue, *Alberta Past and Present: Historical and Biographical* (Chicago: Pioneer Historical Publishing Co., 1924), 3 Volumes. See Howard Palmer, "Polygamy and progress: Reaction to Mormons in Canada: 1887-1923" (this volume), for others who chose to see Mormons as integrated Canadians.

15. Southern Alberta Mormon settlements were placed at midpoint in a series of five cases of ethnic groups representing progression from highly segregated ethno-religious communities to the most individualistic, least segregated peoples, by Dawson, *Group Settlement*, p. xx, all of whom he foresaw transformed into heterogeneous groups in their secularizing Canadian context, i.e., a loss of distinctiveness. Earle Waugh, "The Almighty Has Not Got This Far Yet: Religious Models in Alberta's and Saskatchewan's History," in Howard Palmer and Donald Smith (eds.) *The New Provinces: Alberta and Saskatchewan, 1905-1980* (Vancouver: Tantalus Research Limited, 1973), pp. 199-215, sees Alberta Mormons blending into western Canadian society through their millennial eschatology interacting strongly with the sociopolitical realm during the rise of Social Credit in Alberta in the 1930s.

16. Two scholars have produced empirical evidence of Mormon country's distinctiveness as a continuing quality. Lehr, "Mormon Settlements in Southern Alberta," pp. 94-113, delineates Alberta Mormon country geographically. Keith Parry, "Blood Indians and 'Mormon' Public Schools: A Case Study of Ethnicity and Integrated Education," in Richard A. Carlton, Louise A. Colley and Neil J. MacKinnon, *Education, Change and Society: A Sociology of Canadian Education* (Toronto: Gage Educational Publishing Limited, 1977), pp. 225-38, sees two culturally distinct groups, Blood Indian and Mormon, in

the Indian reserve-Mormon community context. See also Parry, in this volume.

17. For two cartographic depictions of Cache Valley see Joel E. Ricks and Everett L. Cooley (eds.), *The History of a Valley: Cache Valley, Utah-Idaho* (Logan, Utah: Cache Valley Centennial Commission, 1956), for maps of settlements and irrigation development; and A.J. Simmonds, *The Gentile Comes to Cache Valley* (Logan, Utah: Utah State University Press, 1976), for a map of "Gentile Cache Valley, 1867-1976."

18. For maps of Alberta Mormon country, see Dawson, *Group Settlement*, pp. 179, 181 and 254. For visual limits of Mormon country, see Lehr, "Mormon Settlements in Southern Alberta," p. 8.

19. Seymour Martin Lipset, *The First New Nation: The United States in Historical and Cultural Perspective* (New York: Basic Books, 1963).

20. Arthur R.M. Lower, *Colony to Nation: A History of Canada* (Toronto: Longmans, Green & Company, 1946).

21. The original Mormon source for the ideology of America is Joseph Smith, Jr. (Translator), *The Book of Mormon*, first published at Palmyra, New York, 1830. For an American Mormon elaboration of the ideology, see Mark E. Petersen, *The Great Prologue* (Salt Lake City: Deseret Book Company, 1975). For a Canadian Mormon development of the ideology, with special reference to Canada, see Larry D. Hurd, *The Divine Development of Canadian Confederation* (Calgary: Hurd Canadian Developments, 1978). For an anthropological tracing of the key Mormon concept of Zion, see Steven L. Olsen, "Zion: The structure of a theological revolution," *Sunstone*, 6 (6) (November-December 1981), pp. 21-26.

22. See Harry T. Williams, Richard N. Current and Frank Freidel, *A History of the United States [Since 1865]*, second edition (New York: Alfred A. Knopf, 1965); Leonard Arrington, *Great Basin Kingdom*, pp. 257-92; for Mormons and telegraphs, ibid., pp. 199-201 and 228-31.

23. See H.A. Innis, "Canadian Pacific Railway," in *Encyclopedia Canadiana* (Ottawa: The Canadiana Company Ltd., 1958), Vol. 2, pp. 202-07.

24. Arrington, in this volume.

25. Arrington, *Great Basin Kingdom*, pp. 283-89 and Arrington's more detailed account for Cache Valley, "Railroad Building and Cooperatives," in Ricks and Cooley, *The History of a Valley*, pp. 170-86.

26. A.A. den Otter, *Civilizing the West: The Galts and the Development of Western Canada* (Edmonton: The University of Alberta Press, 1982), pp. 101-14; C.A. Magrath, *The Galts and How Alberta Grew Up* (Lethbridge: Lethbridge Herald Printing, 1936; recopied by The Archives, Sir Alexander Galt Museum, Lethbridge), pp. 13 and 33-34.

27. "Southerly tropism" is a term selected to replace the terms "north-south linkages" or "ties," which have no connotation of a dominant directional pull. North-south linkages are referred to by Garth Stephenson, "Canadian regionalism in continental perspective," *Journal of Canadian Studies*, 15 (1980), pp. 16-28; Harry Hiller, *Canadian Society: A Macro-Analysis* (Scarborough, Ontario: Prentice-Hall, 1986), pp. 115-16 and 119; B. Kaye and D.W. Moodie, "Geographical Perspectives on the Canadian Plains," in Richard

Allen (ed.), *A Region of the Mind: Interpreting the Canadian Plains* (Regina: Canadian Plains Research Center, 1973), p. 22, with reference to the fur trade era only. See also Marcus Lee Hansen and John Bartlet Brebner, *The Mingling of Canadian and American Peoples* (New Haven, Connecticut: Yale University Press, 1940), chs. VI and IX.

28. These points are made by Norman K. Risjord in his article, "The rise of the American nation, 1783-1850," *Encyclopedia Britannica* (1968), Vol. 22, pp. 629 and 633-635.

29. See W.L. Morton, *The Kingdom of Canada: A General History from Earliest Times* (Toronto: McClelland and Stewart, 1963), pp. 209-346, especially pp. 318-19.

30. N. Keyfitz, "The Changing Canadian Population," in S.D. Clark (ed.), *Urbanism and the Changing Canadian Society* (Toronto: University of Toronto Press, 1961), pp. 6-11; Lower, *Colony to Nation*, pp. 404-07.

31. See McCue, in this volume, for Mormon interest in British Columbia for settlement purposes. The best writing on Mormon southerly tropism is Richard H. Jackson, "Mormon perception and settlement," *Annals of the Association of American Geographers*, 68, no. 3 (September 1978), pp. 317-34. The southerly tropism theme is carried forward to the present era by Peter Wiley and Robert Gottlieb, *Empires in the Sun: The Rise of the New American West* (New York: G.P. Putnam's Sons, 1982), pp. iv-xix.

32. James M. Allen and Glen B. Leonard, *The Story of the Latter-day Saints* (Salt Lake City: Deseret Book Company, 1976), pp. 386-87.

33. On the colonialization of the American West, see John Walton Caughey, *The American West: Frontier & Region* (Los Angeles: The Ward Ritchie Press, 1969), pp. 16-27; Carl F. Kraenzel, "Great Plains Regionalism Reconsidered," in B.Y. Card (ed.), *Perspectives on Regions and Regionalism and Other Papers* (Edmonton: University of Alberta Printing Services, 1969), pp. 77-90; Linton R. Hayes, *Energy, Economic Growth and Regionalism in the West* (Albuquerque: University of New Mexico Press, 1980), pp. 51-57; Bernard de Voto, "The West: A plundered province," *Harper's Magazine*, Vol. 1, 969 (August, 1934), pp. 355-64.

     On the colonialization of the Great Basin, see Leonard J. Arrington and Thomas G. Alexander, *A Dependent Commonwealth: Utah's Economy from Statehood to the Great Depression* (Provo: Brigham Young University Press, 1974), especially the Introduction by Dean May, pp. ix-xv; Mark P. Leone, *The Roots of Mormonism* (Cambridge, Mass: Harvard University Press, 1979), pp.26-27 and 148-66.

34. C. Cecil Lingard, "The Division of the North-west Territories," in D.K. Elton (ed.), *One Prairie Province? A Question for Canada* (Lethbridge: The University of Lethbridge and *The Lethbridge Herald*, 1972), pp. 445-51.

35. Lower, *Colony to Nation*, pp. 418-26; Dawson, *Group Settlement*, map p. iii and entire volume.

36. See, for example, den Otter, *Civilizing the West*, pp. 116-17, and muting of colonialization in western United States, Caughey, *The American West*, p. 24.

37. Lowell L. Bennion, *Max Weber's Methodology* (Paris: Les Presses Modernes,

1933), pp. 128-35, for interplay between economic and religious factors in Mormon "civilization"; Arrington, *Great Basin Kingdom*, Part II and Part III; Leonard J. Arrington, Feramorz Y. Fox and Dean L. May, *Building the City of God: Community and Cooperation Among the Mormons* (Salt Lake City: Deseret Book Company, 1976).

38. Klaus Hansen, "The metamorphosis of the Kingdom of God: Toward a reinterpretation of Mormon history," *Dialogue*, 1, no. 3 (Autumn 1966), pp. 73-6, especially the quotation by Senator Frederick T. Dubois of Idaho; Thomas F. O'Dea, *The Mormons* (Chicago: University of Chicago Press, 1957), pp. 114-18. See Leonard J. Arrington and Davis Bitton, *The Mormon Experience: A History of the Latter-day Saints* (New York: Vintage Books, 1980), pp. 182-83.

39. Leonard Arrington, *Great Basin Kingdom*, pp. 353-79, for economic aspects of colonialization during "the Raid." The self-sufficiency and equalitarianism that characterized Cache Valley society are reflected in Arrington, Fox and May, *Building the City of God*, pp. 223-24.

40. The coalescence of power in relation to Utah is mentioned by Arrington, *Great Basin Kingdom*, p. 356; by Howard W. Lamar, "Statehood for Utah: A Different Path," in Marvin S. Hill and James B. Allen (eds.) *Mormonism and American Culture* (New York: Harper & Row, 1972), pp. 134-35; in relation to Cache Valley by Simmonds, *The Gentile Comes to Cache Valley*, pp. 55-65, who describes the operation of the "draconian Edmunds-Tucker Act," pp. 59-60. For the emergence of the power coalition in the country generally, see Risjord, "The rise of the American nation 1783-1850," *Encyclopedia Britannica*, 1968, pp. 620-37. There is evidence that statistically polygamy was minor in Utah in the 1880s. See Lowell "Ben" Bennion, "The incidence of Mormon polygamy in 1880: Dixie versus Davis Stake," *Journal of Mormon History*, Vol. 11 (1984), pp. 27-42. According to S. George Ellsworth, "Political Developments," in Ricks and Cooley (eds.) *The History of a Valley*, p. 111, there were approximately 160 polygamous families out of 2,367 families in Cache County, or 7% in 1880.

41. For the Mormon view that the "real struggle was political," see Roberts, *A Comprehensive History of the Church*, Vol. VI, pp. 133-48.

42. For disrupting effects of federal law enforcement, see Allen and Leonard, *The Story of the Latter-day Saints*, pp. 394-400; Arrington, *Great Basin Kingdom*, pp. 359-60; Arrington and Bitton, *The Mormon Experience*, pp. 180-83.

43. *Utah Journal* microfilm, Utah State University Archives. For its representativeness of the Logan Mormon community, see Gunnar Rasmussen, "Journalism," in Ricks and Cooley, *The History of a Valley*, pp. 397-99. For accounts of the political situation in Cache Valley, see S. George Ellsworth, "Political Developments," ibid., pp. 109-21, and A.J. Simmonds, *The Gentile Comes to Cache Valley*.

44. Hudson, *Charles Ora Card*, p. 77.

45. Unpublished compilation of Cache County arrests by Lowell C. Bennion, from his ongoing research into the incidence of polygamy, and his unpublished paper, "Patterns of relocation in response to polygamy raids," presented at

the Annual Meeting of the Mormon Historical Association Meeting in Salt Lake City, 1-4 May 1986. See also William Mulder, *Homeward to Zion: The Mormon Migration from Scandinavia* (Minneapolis: University of Minnesota Press, 1957), p. 241.

46. Hudson, *Charles Ora Card*, pp. 75-83; C.O. Card Diary, detailed account by himself of the arrest and escape on 26 July 1886, in the archives of the Church History Dept, the Church of Jesus Christ of Latter-day Saints (hereafter cited as LDS Archives), Zina Card Brown Collection.

47. Hudson, *Charles Ora Card*, pp. 82-83.

48. Letters to C.O. Card from Moses Thatcher from Mexico, 9 September and 9 December 1886, photocopy from Zina Y. Card Collection, Brigham Young University Archives.

49. Hudson, *Charles Ora Card*, pp. 83-84; Bates and Hickman, *Founding of Cardston*, p. 1.

50. The exploration narrative is based on *Card Journal*: Godfrey, supplemented by Hudson, *Charles Ora Card*, pp. 85-96, and Tagg, *A History of the Church in Canada*, pp. 91-97, map p. 94.

51. Hudson, *Charles Ora Card*, pp. 83-84.

52. *Card Journal*: Godfrey, 29 September 1886.

53. Ibid., 3 October 1886.

54. Ibid., 24 October 1886.

55. Hudson, *Charles Ora Card*, pp. 97-102.

56. *Card Journal*: Godfrey, 4 March 1887.

57. Ibid.

58. The site selection and immigrant arrival narrative is from *Card Journal*: Godfrey; and Hudson, *Charles Ora Card*, pp. 102-15.

59. *Card Journal*: Godfrey, 5 June 1887.

60. Bates and Hickman, *Founding of Cardston*, pp. 22-23.

61. Ibid., pp. 66-67.

62. Ibid., p. 56.

63. Ibid., p. 66, for account of Cardston Ward, pp. 133-34 of the Stake, and p. 121 for population in 1894. The 1891 population was tabulated by B.Y. Card from the Canada Census, 1891, Alberta District 197, Lethbridge, pp. 90-107. Hicken, "Events in the Settlements…," pp. 55-56, uncritically accepts John Blue's *Alberta Past and Present* p. 212 figure of 1000 Mormons in Cardston in 1891, which is much too large for that year. It would be correct for 1906, when Canada Census reported a Cardston population of 1001.

64. For development of the Cardston settlement, see Shaw, *Chief Mountain Country*, Vol. I, p. 131, for the dentist; Bectell, ibid., Vol. II, pp. 1-4, for chronology of developments.

65. Bates and Hickman, *Founding of Cardston*, pp. 65-66 and 111.

66. C.A. Magrath, *The Galts and How Alberta Grew Up*, p. 15, on the capabilities of Mormon pioneer leaders and their wives.

67. Wilcox, "The Founding of the Mormon Community in Alberta," p. 100.

68. Card Diary, original for 10 November 1888 and Godfrey transcription for other days. See Bates and Hickman, *Founding of Cardston*, pp. 70-74, dealing

with the practicalities of the Ottawa visit; Nelson, in Dawson, *Group Settlement*, pp. 203-04, with political adjustment aspects of the visit; Wilcox, "The Founding of the Mormon Community in Alberta," pp. 93-96 and 120-133, for a full account of the visit and Mormon response to criticism afterward; B. Carmon Hardy, in this volume, for the legal issues relating to polygamy in Canada from the visit; Howard Palmer, in this volume for the public response to the visit.

69. *Card Journal*: Godfrey; Bates and Hickman, *Founding of Cardston*, p. 89.

70. *Card Journal*: Godfrey, entries for 13 to 27 December 1890.

71. Hudson, *Charles Ora Card*, p. 132.

72. Hicken, "Events Leading to the Settlement...," pp. 60-67, for a relatively complete account of the Card and Taylor land speculation.

73. Ibid., pp. 67-69, for canal building and the settlement of Magrath and Stirling; den Otter, *Civilizing the West,* pp. 212-27.

74. Ibid., p. 78.

75. den Otter, *Civilizing the West*, p. 226.

76. Hicken, "Events Leading to Settlement...," p. 78.

77. See Ibid., pp. 81-107, for a full account of the settlement of Raymond. A proposal for a settlement, such as Raymond became, was made by C.A. Magrath to the Church First Presidency 30 January 1900. See *Card Journal*: Godfrey, noted by Tagg, *History of the Church*, p. 193. Magrath wanted Mormons along the whole canal.

78. Hicken, "Events Leading to Settlement...," p. 98.

79. Ibid., p. 95. *Card Journal*: Godfrey records the dedication of the Knight Ranch, 4 August 1901, by Patriarch H.L. Hinman of Cardston, of the sugar factory site 11 August 1901, by Patriarch J.A. Woolf of Cardston; and the townsite of Raymond the same day by President Card.

80. The team number is the estimate of C.A. Magrath; see Hicken, "Events Leading to Settlement...," p. 100.

81. Ibid., p. 99.

82. See S.D. Clark, *Church and Sect in Canada* (Toronto: University of Toronto Press, 1948), pp. 234-435, for the development of religious groups in Canada from 1832 to 1948, and pp. 308 and 357-58, for the minor importance of Mormons. See also I. Hexham, R.F. Currie and J.B. Townsend, "New Religious Movements," *The Canadian Encyclopedia* (Edmonton: Hurtig Publishers, 1985), pp. 1241-43, where Methodists and Mormons are mentioned as once suspect movements now acceptable because of positive contributions.

83. See Brigham Y. Card, "The Mormon Settlements in Canada, 1886 to 1925—North American Perspectives," (unpublished paper, 1989), for examination of continental sociohistorical forces and the Canadian settlements.

6 Polygamy and Progress

The Reaction to Mormons in Canada,
1887-1923

HOWARD PALMER

WHEN THE MORMONS first came to western Canada in 1887 to escape anti-polygamy laws in the United States, their arrival touched off a debate that lasted for thirty years. The desirability of Mormon immigration was frequently and intensely debated. Within three years of their arrival, two local weeklies, the *Macleod Gazette* and the *Lethbridge News*, carried over fifty different articles, letters and editorials on Mormons. In February 1890, the Dominion Parliament debated the desirability of Mormons, as it moved to outlaw polygamy. Even the *New York Times* and the *Chicago Evening Journal* carried articles on Mormon settlement in southern Alberta.[1] The central Canadian press followed developments in Utah and carried stories and editorials on the Mormon settlements in southern Alberta. Several books and articles dealing with immigration at the national level also discussed Mormons. This essay pays special attention to changing opinion as expressed in local newspapers in southern Alberta, since they most directly affected changing Mormon-non-Mormon relations.

From 1890 to World War I, Canadian Protestant clergymen crusaded against the Mormons. The Presbyterian Church established a special committee to look into the "Mormon question," and a Home Mission in southern Alberta to convert Mormons, and issued a flood of pamphlets about the evils of Mormonism. Given the small numbers of Mormons, and the lack of evidence for either polygamy or church domination of political life in Canada, it is tempting to account for the distorted image of Mormons—as portrayed by the Protestant churches—by examining their own self-image and the internal anxieties of these churches.

Debates over immigration require a nation to define itself. Thus, the debate on Mormon immigration reveals ideas of Canadian identity and the Canadian West in the late nineteenth and early twentieth centuries. In addition to touching issues concerning the nature of marriage, the family and religious tolerance, the debate also reflected attitudes toward the United States. Before Mormons even arrived, nineteenth-century Canadian nationalists cited their religion, along with slavery and Indian wars, as examples of the social evils spawned by American republicanism, confirming the nationalists' belief in Canada's superiority.[2]

The intensity of the debate over Mormons changed over time. To understand the evolution of attitudes, one must consider Canada's immigration, religious, intellectual and social history from the late 1890s to the early 1920s.[3] We need to understand general patterns of ethnic relations and also the context of the social and intellectual history of the progressive era.

MORMONS AND THE SETTLEMENT OF THE CANADIAN WEST

Probably the most important factor in the acceptance of Mormons was the favorable attitude of federal politicians and government officials. In his article, "The Mormons come to Canada, 1887-1902," Lawrence Lee contrasts this favorable government attitude with popular prejudice, and notes that "under the Canadian system of territorial administration, it was far easier for agents of the Ottawa government to defy popular prejudices in achieving national purposes in the West than was true south of the border."[4] Under the National Policy, the federal government vigorously promoted immigration into western Canada to establish a market for eastern manufactured goods and secure the West for Canada. At first, the federal government concentrated on securing British immigrants, but during the 1870s and 1880s it encouraged the settlement of a variety of ethnic and religious groups: in the 1870s, Icelanders and Mennonites; in the 1880s, Americans, Russian Jews, Hungarians, Scots and Germans.[5] Mormons were not the first persecuted religious minority seeking asylum, and the federal government had already shown it was willing to have a pluralistic West to achieve its goals.

When the Mormons arrived in 1887, there were new elements of southern Alberta society that welcomed experienced farmers. The Mormons might show conclusively that the region could support a farming population.

In Lethbridge, the Galt interests, which dominated the local economy and also had strong ties with the Conservatives, became convinced that irrigation and colonization of their land grants was the key to economic survival.[6] C.A. Magrath was land commissioner for the Galts' North Western Coal and Navigation Company. As a company official and as a Lethbridge community leader, he saw the potential of Mormon colonists as customers and, because of their experience with irrigation, as agricultural pioneers.

When the Mormons arrived, they encountered a federal Conservative government anxious to attract immigrants, but with strong allies in ranching and mining in southern Alberta. These allies held contrary opinions on immigration. The business interests of Lethbridge and Macleod eyed the newcomers as potential additions to their hinterlands. By 1887, Lethbridge had outstripped Macleod as the economic center of southwestern Alberta and, with a population of about 1,000, had great hopes for the future.[7]

The Mormons also encountered a dominant British group, from Britain and central Canada, who were overwhelmingly Protestant. Anglicans, Presbyterians and Methodists dominated the social, economic and political life of Macleod and Lethbridge.[8] Though there was rivalry between Protestant clergymen,[9] the main religious cleavage in the population was Protestant-Catholic.

Mormons arrived when social institutions in southern Alberta were new, fragile and evolving. A public debate had already begun in Lethbridge in 1885 over central and eastern European and Chinese immigrants. British Canadian Protestants were torn between the pressing need to populate the prairies and their reservations about securing immigrants who were culturally different.[10]

INITIAL REACTION TO THE MORMONS

Canadian attitudes toward Mormons had already been shaped by the prolonged conflict between the American government and the Mormons. Though secretly introduced by Joseph Smith in Illinois during the 1840s, polygamy was not acknowledged publicly until 1852, eight years after the murder of Joseph Smith and five years after the Mormons' arrival in Utah. During the 1880s, the American government passed increasingly harsh anti-polygamy laws. The Edmunds Act in 1882 imposed heavy fines on polygamists, declared the children of polygamist unions to be illegitimate, and eventually sent 1,300 polygamists to jail; while the Edmunds-Tucker Act of 1887 dissolved the church as a corporate entity and placed the church's assets in the hands of receivers.[11] This conflict received press coverage in Canada through newspapers and American magazines. In the late nineteenth century, Canadians were widely exposed to American magazines, and the more than thirty anti-Mormon articles that appeared each year during the 1880s in the American magazines influenced Canadian attitudes.[12] The Methodists' national newspaper in Canada, *The Christian Guardian*, carried seven anti-Mormon articles in 1885 and eleven in 1886, the two years before the Mormons came to western Canada. In addition, the fifty anti-Mormon novels that appeared in the US in the late nineteenth century had some impact on Canadian readers who avidly read American "westerns."

Popular attitudes may have been hostile when the Mormons arrived because of these influences, yet the Mormons who arrived with C.O. Card in the spring and summer of 1887 were welcomed by federal government officials. In December 1887, the collector of customs at Fort Macleod told the press that the Mormons "make first class settlers and are industrious, zealous and well behaved."[13] The first visit made by an official of the Department of the Interior, J.S. Dennis, the inspector of surveys, was in the spring of 1888. Overall, he was favorably impressed:

Any person visiting the colony cannot help being struck with the wonderful progress made by them during the short time they have been in the country. And I may say that I have never seen any new settlement where so much has been accomplished in the same length of time. I am satisfied that they are an exceedingly industrious and intelligent people who thoroughly understand prairie farming.[14]

Dennis also struck a cautionary note. He warned against their settlement in large numbers because they were fugitives from justice; they believed in polygamy; and had a tendency to become intolerant when they became a majority.

Dennis's superiors in the Department of the Interior had fewer reservations about the Mormons. William Pearce was the senior officer of the Department of the Interior in the West responsible for the federal government's land, timber, mineral and water resources policies. Pearce was known unofficially as "the Czar of the West" because of his influence. He was convinced that much of the southwest was unsuitable for farming unless irrigated. In 1881, when he had visited Utah, he had been impressed by the success of irrigation. As a result, when controversy concerning the Mormons arose, he defended them.[15] Pearce saw irrigation as essential to the opening of the semiarid region of the southern prairies and launched his own private irrigation schemes. He relied on Card for practical advice on irrigation practices.[16]

The favorable attitudes of officials contrasted sharply with the hostile reaction in several western newspapers, including the *Edmonton Bulletin*, the *Saskatchewan Herald* and the *Calgary Herald*. The Mormons were cast in the roles of defiers of the state because of their resistance to American law. The *Bulletin* conceded that the Mormons were "sober, industrious and thrifty," but Frank Oliver, the Ontario-born editor of the paper, who would later play a prominent role in both territorial and national politics, adamantly opposed their entry because of their belief in polygamy and their defiance of American law.

[They] belong to a sect in comparison with whose belief that of the Mahometan of Soudan or of the Thugs of India is light and liberty. Their polygamy to which such strong objections are raised is one of the milder manifestations of their principles. In so much as their numbers are increased by so much is the welfare of society and the safety of the state endangered. Mormonism is as essentially a treason as a religion.[17]

According to Oliver, they were a "conspiracy against society" and were "quite as nasty as the Chinamen and more dangerous than the Nihilists." As the "scum of creation, the cancer of civilization," they were an "utter abomination which no effort should be spared to rid the nation of."[18] After he became minister of the Interior (1905 to 1911), however, during the peak years of immigration to the Canadian West, he defended the Mormons publicly.

The Macleod and Lethbridge newspapers, nearer the Cardston settlement, were more favorable. One suspects that their defense of the Mormons— virtually the only positive press the Mormons received—was part of the ongoing commercial rivalry between the two towns. The first southern Alberta press reaction to the Mormons appeared in the *Lethbridge News* in August, 1887 in an article reprinted from the *Montreal Star* that argued that the immigration of Mormons should be discouraged and that "any attempt to establish polygamy in the Canadian NorthWest must be met with the utmost severity by the Dominion Government."[19] Both the *News* and the *Gazette* condemned this attitude, the *Gazette* arguing that the accusations were "most unfair" to the Mormon settlers.

They are generally acknowledged to be a class which make the most desirable settlers and we have no hesitation in giving them and as many more as come, a hearty welcome. These settlers have come here prepared to obey the laws of Canada to the letter, and there will be plenty of time to warn the government against them when they show the least inclination to break them.[20]

The *Lethbridge News* noted that only a few Mormons had ever practised polygamy, and that the Mormons had no desire to continue polygamy in Alberta. In any case, the *News* argued, it was almost inconceivable that the Mormons could grow large enough to affect the laws of the territories. Mormons were, according to the *News*, "intelligent, industrious and frugal; indeed in these respects, they are not excelled by any class of settlers." If the Chinese and Jews could be allowed in, could there be any reason to object to Mormons?[21] In March 1888, the *Macleod Gazette* apologized to the Mormons after twice publishing a syndicated column entitled "Domestic Barbarities of the Polygamous System." The newspaper gave front-page coverage to a lengthy letter from C.O. Card that pointed out the misrepresentations. The editor stated that he was "genuinely ashamed of being a party to the circulation of such bigoted nonsense."[22]

Despite Card's reassurances that they were not practising polygamy, outside fears began to build in late 1888. These fears were aroused by Cardston's postmaster, A.M. Stenhouse, a Mormon convert, who defended polygamy publicly.[23] After coming to southern Alberta, he argued in western papers that, since Canada had no law that prohibited plural marriage, polygamy should be accepted. Although, as Carmon Hardy shows elsewhere in this volume, his legal facts were wrong, his arguments influenced public opinion. He defended polygamy on the grounds that it would perpetuate the "fittest," since women could choose from among the "best" men.[24] These arguments further alienated Mormons' opponents.[25] The church-owned *Deseret News* gave reassurances that Stenhouse spoke neither for the church nor the settlement where he resided. They reassured no one.[26]

Fears about polygamy were further aroused in late 1888 when Canadian Mormon leaders travelled to Ottawa to request the federal government to allow them to bring their plural families to Canada. Despite evidence of hostility towards them, the Mormon leaders believed that the government might be willing to grant them concessions. On 16 November 1888, however, the cabinet met and flatly refused the request to allow them to bring in plural wives.[27]

The delegation's requests brought an avalanche of press criticism. The *Lethbridge News* published an editorial—"Mormons or Canadians?," which demanded the Mormons assimilate to "make the Canadian Dominion a country in which the whole people are blended together harmoniously and not an ill-assorted patchwork." The *News* argued that the Mormons' request to bring their plural wives to Canada "revealed [them] before the public in the hideous aspect of polygamists and apparently proud of what Canadians consider their shame."[28] The *Gazette*, however, continued to defend them, arguing that since they were not practising polygamy, they should not be interfered with.[29] The editor of the *Gazette* argued for an open-door policy, as long as the Mormons obeyed the law.[30]

Throughout 1889, government officials kept a vigilant eye on the Mormons. Mackenzie Bowell, the minister of Customs, visited Cardston in the fall of 1889. When he returned to Ottawa, his praise of the Mormons was so effusive that the press conjectured jocularly over whether "the fascinating influences which surrounded him at Lee's Creek will not prove sufficiently strong as to induce him to resign his seat in parliament and join the Saints...."[31]

The North-West Mounted Police also kept a close watch on the Mormons. Although early contacts between the NWMP and the Mormons had been positive, NWMP officer Sam Steele reported to the commissioner of the NWMP in December 1889 that "the Mormons are believed by almost all of the people in the district to be practising polygamy in secret," and argued that "the majority of the settlers look upon the Mormons with distrust and contempt, a feeling which will have the result that no people of any other sect will settle in the vicinity...." Steele went on to say that "the intelligence of the Mormon is far below the average intelligence of the settlers of any country...," and that they were "as perfect slaves to the Church and Elders as it is possible for any community of people to be." At the same time, Steele reported that "the Mormons are a very industrious people and have made a better show towards success than any settlement in the district." He concluded that laws against polygamy needed to "be made as stringent as they are in the United States."[32] Deputy Minister of the Interior A.M. Burgess, in submitting Steele's report to Dewdney, the minister of the Interior, dismissed the report as "flimsy and unsatisfactory" and contradictory. Burgess reassured Dewdney that "the circumstances under which they have settled in our country are entirely different from those under which they settled in Utah," that upon their arrival in the Northwest the laws were already in place, and that "if they are found to be guilty of infringing this law [marriage] they are liable to the pains and penalties upon conviction." Burgess reminded Dewdney of the economic potential of Mormon settlement because of their irrigation experience. Faced with the NWMP accusations, Card wrote to assure Burgess that "the alleged crimes to which you refer, of polygamy and cohabitation are not practiced either in or out of Cardston..." and asked "that you will give our people a chance to prove their innocence."[33]

Despite these private reassurances, the press campaign against the Mormons continued to grow, and the government soon strengthened the provisions in the Criminal Code against polygamy.[34] Thus, by the early 1890s, virtually all the arguments that had been used against the Mormons in the United States in the late nineteenth century were circulating in western Canada. The fears about the Mormons as a deviant, immoral sect were rationalized by the most powerful appeals to the sanctity of marriage and the family. The growing public concern about Mormon polygamy undoubtedly reflected wider concerns about threats to the stability of marriage and sexual mores. This social movement, according to J.G. Snell, hoped to

> [strengthen] marriage and the family through an attack on marital and sexual misconduct....The movement to defend marriage and sexual morality originated as a response among the increasingly assertive middle class to the social and economic turmoil and disruption of the late nineteenth and early twentieth centuries, when so much of what was valued in society seemed to be threatened.[35]

In response to the public clamor against the Mormons, in February 1890, the government introduced into the House of Commons amendments to the Criminal Code that included "a more effectual provision for the suppression of polygamy."[36] During the debate, Sir John Thompson, the minister of justice, explained that the bill prohibited polygamy and made violation of the law punishable by five years in prison and a fine of $500.[37] The debate over the bill focused mostly on the Liberal Opposition's charges that the Conservatives had "induced" the Mormons to come to Canada. The bill was passed on 2 May 1890, however, and received royal assent on May 16.[38]

While the bill allayed fears temporarily that the Mormons might introduce polygamy, the issue periodically resurfaced. The continued influx of Mormons caused concern, and although there were only 359 Mormons in southern Alberta by 1891, fears grew that they were trying to take over the region. These fears were heightened by the application in July 1890 to the lieutenant-governor of the North-West Territories for incorporation of the Cardston Company as a joint stock company to establish gristmills and sawmills and begin irrigation projects. Macleod residents held a public meeting to protest;

they saw the application as evidence of Mormon boldness and growing power. The protesters drew up a petition that recapitulated the history of the opposition to Mormons in the US and objected that the charter would enable the Mormons to acquire large blocks of land. It cited the US government attempts to destroy the economic power of Utah Mormons and warned that Mormon economic power would lead to control over civil affairs.

> We believe that these people are not advantageous settlers for any country and will be a detriment to this country, and that they should not be encouraged in any way by Government act, or allowed to form themselves into a...more corporative [sic], corporate, political and religious unit than they are now.[39]

Protesters also held public meetings in Pincher Creek and Lethbridge, and 93 signed the petition. The Alberta press, with the exception of the *Macleod Gazette*, supported the petition. The *Calgary Herald* urged politicians to investigate polygamy among the Mormons:

> Through the supineness of our public men we are preparing trouble for our country, for as surely as the United States had the most serious difficulties to encounter in dealing with the most infamous conspiracy of modern times against morals and loyalty to a nation, so surely we will in Canada...be obliged to deal with the same dangerous element...we hope the Protestants of Alberta will be found joining hands [with the Roman Catholics] in an Anti-Mormon Movement which will arrest the Mormon scheme of over-running and taking possession of southern Alberta.[40]

The issue also attracted attention in the eastern press. In response to a negative editorial in the Ottawa *Free Press*, C.O. Card explained the need for co-operation to develop new projects, and asked "why such a furore over this small matter?"[41]

A committee of the territorial assembly examined the petitions, and passing the buck, concluded that the lieutenant-governor should decide the issue. The lieutenant-governor referred the matter to Ottawa, and it was not until Card enlisted the support of Elliott Galt to intercede with federal authorities that the Mormons were able to obtain the charter.[42]

The press and politicians could do little under the existing legislation to prevent the Cardston Company or stop Mormon immigration. More importantly, the issue soon subsided further since the controversy coincided with the Manifesto in October 1890 by the president of the Mormon Church, Wilford Woodruff (following a US Supreme Court ruling that upheld the legality of anti-polygamy laws) that polygamy would no longer be practised.[43] While the concern about polygamy took three more decades to die, the issue began to fade. Although there were doubts expressed in the national press about the sincerity of the Manifesto and warnings that the Mormons would have to be watched closely, the Manifesto effectively ended the fears about a large-scale migration of Mormons coming to escape anti-polygamy laws.[44] From 1891 to 1897, there were only eight articles about the Mormons in the *Lethbridge News* and three in the *Macleod Gazette*, and most of these were positive.[45] In 1893, Mayor Bentley of Lethbridge told the press on a visit to central Canada that polygamy was "unknown" in the Mormon settlements in southern Alberta, and that "I must say that a more intelligent, industrious, law abiding lot of people I never saw. They are all conspicuously honest."[46]

REACTION TO THE SECOND WAVE OF MORMON IMMIGRATION: 1898-1914

Like the majority of the American farmers who came to western Canada, Mormon farmers in Utah and Idaho at the turn of the century had utilized available land and were seeking new economic opportunities. Of the over one-half million farmers and their families from the American Midwest and West who arrived between 1898 and 1914, approximately 8,500 were Mormons. From the perspective of the prairies as a whole, Mormons were lost in the much larger number of American immigrants. By 1911, the 9,793 Mormons in Alberta made up 2.6% of the population of 375,000 in the province and 10.8% of the population in the census division in southern Alberta, where they were most highly concentrated.[47]

Most of the Mormons came to work on an irrigation system that was built through the co-operation of the Mormon Church, a local land colonization company and the federal government. As early as the late 1880s, the Mormons' success in irrigating aroused hope that a government-financed irrigation project might be started. C.A. Magrath negotiated the sale of 10,000 acres of land to the Mormons in 1889. In December 1891, Card and John W. Taylor signed a contract to buy over 720,000 acres of land, build several villages, bring in settlers, and provide labor for the construction of an irrigation canal. Despite Magrath's strong efforts to push the project ahead, neither he nor Taylor were able to get the backing of British investors or get the federal government to consolidate land grants into a single block, which was necessary for the irrigation project. Because of the combination of economics and lingering anti-Mormon prejudice, the project could not proceed, and in 1895 the contract was cancelled.[48]

The project, however, had the strong support of William Pearce who convinced his superiors—despite fears that talk of irrigation would scare off potential immigrants—that irrigation was essential to developing southern Alberta. The federal government's support of irrigation was embodied in the Northwest Irrigation Act in 1894. After 1896, under Liberal Minister of the Interior, Clifford Sifton, interest in the irrigation project revived.[49]

With the blessing of the federal government, negotiations proceeded between C.A. Magrath (representing the Galt interests) and the Mormon Church. In July 1898 they came to an agreement to build an irrigation system and bring Mormons to settle the land. Elliott Galt, president of the Canadian North-West Irrigation Company, outlined the advantages of the Mormons to Sifton. "They are accustomed to the use of irrigated lands...in point of industry, thrift and other qualifications...they, as pioneer settlers cannot be excelled."[50] The Galt interests nonetheless were worried about anti-Mormon sentiment and avoided the word Mormon in public discussion of the project, speaking euphemistically of "Utah gentlemen" and "Utah friends."[51]

During the summer of 1898, settlers from Utah and surrounding states arrived to work on the irrigation project and established the towns of Magrath and Stirling. Officials of the Department of the Interior reported on the rapid progress and industriousness of the settlers.[52] Local immigration officials in both Alberta and the United States reassured their superiors that polygamy was a dead issue.[53]

A new surge of Mormon settlement began between 1901 and 1903 with the building of a sugar factory in Raymond.[54] In 1906, Mormon families began settling on lands that the church had bought from the Cochrane Ranch, establishing three villages and forming the United Irrigation District. Mormons also moved into other farming areas in southwestern Alberta, and into Lethbridge.

The contributions Mormons made to irrigation helped allay hostility. The Lethbridge News in an editorial in 1899, gave its impressions of new Mormon farmers. Roles were reversed, and the paper wanted reassurance from the Mormons that southern Alberta was a land of opportunity.

We have reason to believe that there is a possibility of Southern Alberta becoming a place similar to that of Utah, both in population and importance.

They [the Mormons] have great faith in the system of irrigation and are confident that it is only a matter of short time until this will be the most fruitful and prosperous part of the North-West....Thus far we have found the Mormons to be an industrious and progressive people, well qualified to convert barren soil into one of fruitfulness....[55]

An indication of the national significance of the project came in September 1900 when Governor General Lord Minto, along with Elliott Galt, president of the Canadian North-West Irrigation Company, and J.S. Dennis, the deputy commissioner of Public Works of the North-West Territories, inspected the irrigation system. Minto visited the towns of Stirling and Magrath and met George Q. Cannon and Joseph F. Smith, both members of the First Presidency.[56] The federal government and the company publicized the project across North America and Europe.[57]

The Mormons' financial dealings with business and government leaders enhanced their prestige. Mormons now had political and economic allies at the centers of Canadian power. Canadian Pacific Railway officials watched the irrigation project closely, since the resultant railway traffic was potentially an important feeder to the CPR, and the CPR helped finance the project. Vice-president Thomas Shaughnessy told Galt that the Mormons were "the most efficient colonizing instruments on the continent."[58] William Van Horne, president of the company, told the press Mormons were "a most desirable acquisition to the population...they have accomplished wonders in Utah, and their system of government, from a material standpoint, is worthy of all praise."[59] C.A. Magrath, now Member of Parliament for the area, vigorously defended them in his book, *Canada's Growth and Problems Affecting It* (1910). He contrasted the Mormons favorably with central and eastern European immigrants.[60]

Alberta's newspapers, which previously had been largely anti-Mormon, carried several favorable booster-oriented articles on Mormon settlement.[61] In addition, the influx of eastern Europeans and Asians also drew attention away from the Mormons. The *Lethbridge News*, *Macleod Gazette*, and *Calgary Herald* attacked the new immigrants from central and eastern Europe while at the same time defending the Mormons.[62] Anti-Mormon sentiment expressed by partisan newspapers would have also hurt party fortunes in Mormon areas.

Liberals and Conservatives vied for Mormons' support. They tried to secure Mormon candidates in predominantly Mormon areas and labelled one another as anti-Mormon. When in the 1900 federal election, the *Cardston*

Record charged that Conservative Senator James Lougheed, had libeled the Mormons, the Conservative *Calgary Herald*, heatedly denied the charge.[63] During the 1905 provincial election, Cardston Conservatives circulated a statement made by Prime Minister Laurier during the 1905 autonomy debates (when Alberta had become a province) alleging that "The Galicians are certainly Christians, but the Mormons are not."[64] Local Liberals asked Laurier for an explanation. Laurier, who had visited Salt Lake City in 1904, explained that he meant that the Mormons were not Catholics or Protestants, and continued, that Mormons were "excellent citizens and their conduct is unimpeachable."[65] This allayed resentment, since Mormons themselves claimed not to be Protestants. Liberal and Mormon candidate John W. Woolf was elected with the largest Liberal majority in southern Alberta.

Both Conservatives and Liberals in Alberta defended them against the hostile accusations of the Protestant clergy. In 1907, when the United States senatorial investigation concerning the seating of Senator and Mormon apostle Reed Smoot was reaching a climax, Edmonton Member of Parliament Frank Oliver now defended these "sober, orderly, law abiding and progressive" citizens against the attacks of Presbyterian clergymen:

> The region now occupied by Mormons was unoccupied until they came. So far as we can see, it would have remained unoccupied for an interminable period had it not been for their knowledge of like conditions in the United States.... They have given an object lesson in agriculture in the southwestern corner of the prairies which has increased the value of the whole semi-arid region....[66]

THE MORMON "MENACE": THE PROTESTANT CHURCHES AND THE ANTI-MORMON CRUSADE

Despite Mormon denials,[67] rumors that polygamy was still being practised excited Protestant ministers and women's organizations in western Canada and Ontario from the 1890s until World War I. Protestant reformers also saw alleged Mormon authoritarianism and theocratic political beliefs as antithetical to Protestantism and democracy. Significantly, the concern that Mormons posed a threat to sexual morality and democracy were exact parallels of the two main tenets of anti-Catholic thought in Victorian Canada.[68]

From the early 1890s to World War I, Mormonism loomed as an important issue among Canadian Protestants, particularly in the largest denominations—Presbyterian and Methodist. Clergymen kept the anti-Mormon sentiment alive for another twenty years, even though it was dying among politicians and journalists. These two denominations had led the anti-Mormon crusade in the United States, and their Canadian counterparts now took up the campaign. Their national religious papers repeatedly denounced the Mormons. Between 1885 and 1902, in a sampling of eight years of the Methodists' national newspaper, the *Christian Guardian* ran 41 negative articles on the Mormons. From 1910 to 1913, there were 13 hostile articles. Approximately half dealt with Mormons in the United States or Mormon theology, and the remainder with Canadian Mormons.

Both denominations published several pamphlets denouncing Mormonism, and Presbyterians established a "Home Mission" in the Mormon towns to win converts. Between 1904 and 1914, the "Mormon question" became an almost annual topic at provincial and national Presbyterian meetings. An anti-Mormon committee submitted annual reports to the Presbyterian General Assembly. The views of the two churches on this issue are important, since the majority of Alberta's business and political leaders belonged to one of them.[69] Individual Presbyterians or Methodists did not necessarily follow their church's official line, but churchgoers were, nonetheless, exposed to anti-Mormon propaganda.

The anti-Mormon crusade in Canada was a spin-off of larger anti-Mormon movements in the United States and Great Britain. The campaign peaked during the debate surrounding the seating of Senator Smoot, 1904-07 (when it became public that polygamy had not totally died out among Mormons) and during the intense anti-Mormon movement in Britain 1910-14.[70] By early 1911, magazine articles and books attacking the Mormons on the subject of new polygamy cases in the United States led to both the decision of the Mormon leaders to excommunicate Apostle John W. Taylor for promoting plural marriage,[71] and to an upsurge of anti-Mormon sentiment in Canada.

Canadian anti-Mormon literature echoed all the anti-Mormon themes from the United States and Britain. The anti-Mormon campaign, however, was not as strong in Canada. Mormons were a smaller minority in Canada. The anti-Mormon campaign in Canada remained at the rhetorical level; there was no violence or even threats of violence as in Great Britain or parts of the United States.

The anti-Mormon crusade in Canada was in part linked to the Social Gospel movement that developed as part of an effort in mainline Protestantism to root out social evils and establish Canada as a Christian society.[72]

Protestant clergymen saw Mormonism as a social evil, to be stamped out along with liquor, prostitution and the violation of the Sabbath.

The "Home Mission" efforts to immigrant groups in western Canada, included efforts to save the Mormons. Both Presbyterians and Methodists worried about the social and moral impact of massive immigration, and they felt a special duty to "Canadianize" and "Christianize" the new immigrants.[73] To counter these allegedly undesirable social influences, the two churches established "home missions" among the Ukrainians, Chinese and Mormons. The Methodists concentrated on the Ukrainians, the Presbyterians took on the Mormons, and both groups worked among the Chinese.[74] The Presbyterians began missionary work among the Mormons in the mid-1890s in Cardston and later in Raymond in 1903.[75]

This work was of particular interest to the women's home missionary societies of the Presbyterian and Methodist churches. By 1917, they enlisted one out of every three women churchgoers.[76] They distributed at least two pamphlets on Mormons, in 1912 and 1923.[77] In all likelihood, it was through the women's missionary societies that the Woman's Christian Temperance Union and the Canadian Council of Women became interested in the Mormon issue; they warned the federal government of the persistence of polygamy and demanded a governmental investigation. The 1905 annual convention of the WCTU pictured Mormon missionaries swarming over Saskatchewan and Manitoba persuading young, innocent girls to go to southern Alberta to live in polygamous relationships.[78] Despite all the resolutions and pamphleteering, little missionary work was actually done. Mormons were uninterested, and pastoral work among non-Mormon settlers took up most of the time of those assigned to the missions.[79]

As in the United States and Europe, the anti-Mormon campaign focused on the twin dangers of polygamy and alleged anti-democratic designs of the church hierarchy.[80] The Presbyterian Board of Home Missions pamphlet in 1912 claimed that the Mormons' "avowed purpose is to secure the balance of power in Parliament and thus control the laws of the land to such an extent as to legalize polygamy."[81]

The essence of the anti-Mormon view was summed up in a resolution passed by the national Presbyterian annual assembly in 1911.[82] It condemned the Mormons and claimed that Mormon leaders demanded "absolute obedience...not only in their religious, but also in their material, and political relationship." The Mormons' alleged "controlled vote" was one of the most dangerous aspects of their faith.

This resolution touched off a storm of controversy in the local newspapers in southern Alberta. The *Lethbridge Herald* condemned the Presbyterian resolution as unsubstantiated, and pointed to the contradiction of clergymen bemoaning "race suicide" because of declining birth and marriage rates among whites, while at the same time attacking the Mormons because they encouraged marriage and large families.[83]

The anti-Mormon campaign was nationwide. For example, in November 1912, a committee of Protestant clergymen in Montreal met to "investigate and combat the Mormon peril." Members of the committee claimed that Mormon missionaries met incoming boats, and then would "approach young immigrant women...and make specious promises to decoy them away" in order to entice them to enter polygamy.[84]

One influential and widely read anti-Mormon statement that reiterated the dangers of polygamy and church hierarchy appeared in J.S. Woodsworth's book on the "immigration question," *Strangers Within Our Gates* (1909). Woodsworth, the Methodist director of the All People's Mission in Winnipeg, which promoted immigrant assimilation programs,[85] argued that Mormons were a "serious menace to our Western civilization" because of their alleged controlled vote. Woodsworth warned "of greater importance to our country than material development are freedom and morality and true religion and to these the system of Mormonism is antagonistic."[86]

The Presbyterian position on Mormons was embodied in a lengthy anti-Mormon pamphlet published by Presbyterian clergyman H.W. Toombs, in 1917. He maintained that the appeal of Mormonism could only be explained by the opportunities that it offered to those with economic, political and "lustful" ambitions, since Mormonism was a commercial and social institution before it was a religious institution.[87]

While the Protestant anti-Mormon campaign was extensive, it had no impact on Canadian public policy towards the Mormons. The campaign does reveal, however, a good deal about intellectual and social anxieties in mainline Protestantism.

WORLD WAR I AND CHANGING ATTITUDES

Although anti-Mormon propaganda continued in the Protestant churches and the WCTU into the 1920s, it began to lose momentum during World War I. The mission to the Mormons faltered, as the Protestant churches focused their attention on the war effort and faced growing social and intellectual challenges.

Cardston Troop in "C" Squadron, 13th Regiment of Mounted Rifles, Canadian Overseas Expeditionary Force, Calgary, 1915, two-thirds of whom were Mormon. NA 147-35 Glenbow Archives.

The outbreak of World War I saw a rapid increase in nativism towards a number of different immigrant minorities. Concern about Germans and immigrants from the Austro-Hungarian Empire drew attention away from the Mormons.

Before the war, Mormon leaders were aware of concerns about their loyalty. As early as 1887, they had enthusiastically celebrated Dominion Day on July 1 and had subsequently continued the practice. In 1909, a recruiter from Ottawa had come to the Mormon communities.[88] When a recruiting meeting in Cardston had to be cancelled, the *Macleod Advocate* jumped to the conclusion that Mormon leaders opposed recruitment. These leaders claimed that they had been misrepresented. Both E.J. Wood, the president of the Alberta Stake, and Bishop Josiah Hammer declared their support for military training.[89] Wood asked several young men to volunteer for an officer-training course, and they in turn soon recruited 67 young men for the militia.

With the outbreak of war, Mormon leaders urged Mormon men to enlist. Large, enthusiastic meetings in the Mormon towns preceded the establishment of patriotic funds.[90] In 1915, the Cardston militia was taken into the regular army, by which time over two hundred men from the Cardston area had been recruited.[91]

Nonetheless, some opponents raised doubts about their loyalty and aroused fears about Mormon proselytizing. In October 1916, the superintendent of the mounted police in Macleod forwarded an article from the official church publication, *The Improvement Era,* to the commissioner of the mounted police, contending that one article was "not conducive to the loyality [sic] of a large number of citizens who live under the protection of our laws and Empire...."[92] The article, "Mormonism Makes for Good Citizenship," was a conference address by church leader Charles Nibley. It stated that Mormom beliefs were that God would be King of America and that, therefore, Mormons must be good citizens.[93] The commissioner forwarded the article to Ernest Chambers, Canada's chief press censor. On the basis of the article, Chambers concluded that "this publication is pro-German in its sentiments and should be prohibited from circulation." Chambers advised the deputy postmaster general that the references to the war were "decidedly biased in favour of the enemy and calculated to cause disaffection among recently arrived settlers in Canada...."[94] This absurd judgment reflected the spirit of wartime hysteria that led to the suppression of many ethnic newspapers and of International Bible Students' (later called Jehovah's Witnesses) literature during the war.[95] Ultimate authority, however, rested with the deputy postmaster general who rejected Chambers' advice.[96]

At the national level, the WCTU kept up its campaign against the Mormons. Their concern focused on Mormon missionary work. In August 1913 a Canadian conference of the Mormons' Eastern States Mission had been established with its headquarters in Toronto, and by 1917 there were 14 missionaries in Ontario and Quebec.[97] An article in the WCTU magazine, *Canadian White Ribbon Tidings,* in July 1918 warned of the "house to house canvass that is going on," and argued that the Mormons were responsible for conditions in Germany "and have the support of the German Government."[98] In fact, Mormon missionaries had been expelled from Germany in December 1910.[99] In response to WCTU pressure, Department of Justice officials inquired of Toronto's police about Mormon activity, but they were "unable to obtain any information of Mormon propaganda" and the matter ended there.[100] This campaign to have the Mormon missionaries either watched or banned in Canada had little impetus, and federal authorities simply ignored it. Government inaction is not surprising, however, given Canada's religious pluralism, the pressing concerns of wartime, and the small number of either Mormons or Mormon missionaries.

At the local level, there were isolated incidents, as Mormons expanded their missionary activity into other new cities. In July 1917, police in Guelph, Ontario, arrested two missionaries, though they were not prosecuted. In July 1919, the mayor of Saint John, New Brunswick, warned missionaries that if they preached on the street, their meetings might be broken up by police.[101] In southern Alberta, Presbyterian Home Mission Superintendent J.T. Ferguson sparked a flurry of controversy when he again warned in February 1918 that Mormonism was a "menace to Canadianism."[102]

The gradual removal of the "Mormon question" from public debate stemmed from the growing economic, social and political integration of Mormons. This growing integration was highlighted by the arrival in southern Alberta in 1918 of the Hutterites from North Dakota who purchased a large tract of land in southern Alberta and established eight colonies. Opposition to the Hutterites from newspapers, patriotic organizations, politicians, and church groups was immediate.[103] The presence in the middle of the Mormon bloc settlement of the pacifist, German-speaking, Hutterites who lived in colonies and wore distinctive clothing, highlighted the fact that Mormons were English-speaking, of predominantly British origin, and politically and economically integrated into western Canadian society. The presence of the Hutterites solidified the perception of Mormons as a founding group in the region.

Another development that indirectly helped their acceptability was the temperance movement. The temperance campaign, which culminated in Alberta's decision to go dry in 1915, highlighted values that Mormons shared with the Protestant majority.[104] The 80% in the Cardston constituency who voted dry affirmed the compatibility of Mormon values and patriotism with the reform-minded Protestant majority.[105] As the prohibition and farm protest movements attempted to achieve their reform goals, they had to reach out to new groups. The WCTU did not embrace Mormon support, and their publications still warned of the dangers of Mormonism,[106] but the abstemious Mormons could not serve as the arch-demon for the prohibitionists. The political radicalism of immigrant labor in 1918-19 in the Alberta coal mines and the consequent public hysteria about "dangerous foreigners" also contrasted sharply with the more conventional political behavior of Mormons.[107]

Indirectly, the lack of public attention given the Mormons in the late teens and early 1920s strongly suggests growing indifference, if not acceptance.

Press discussion in Lethbridge of the Mormons was limited to coverage of the temple opening in 1923. The positive press coverage of the temple opening suggests a growing acceptance of the permanence of the Mormon presence.[108] Another sign of Mormon acceptability was their treatment in the three-volume book, *Alberta Past and Present*, published in 1924. John Blue, the Alberta provincial librarian, included 54 Mormons (7.5%) in the 719 biographies of prominent Albertans. Though those included had to pay a $75 fee for the privilege, the book nonetheless brought an equality of space and significance to hundreds of Alberta males, whatever their religion. Accounts of the lives of Mormon ranchers, farmers, businessmen and professionals concluded with praise.[109] There was no mention of polygamy, though an observant reader would have noted that many of the men came from polygamous families. Past prejudices were subsumed under the egalitarianism of business success, community boosterism, and the Protestant work ethic.

ATTITUDES TOWARD CANADIAN MORMONS IN COMPARATIVE CONTEXT

One critical element in understanding both the positive and negative responses to Canadian Mormons is the all-pervasive belief in social progress in the late nineteenth and early twentieth centuries. The social beliefs of the progressive era were central both to Mormons' friends and foes. The main assumption of their opponents was that alleged Mormon beliefs in polygamy and subservience to the church hierarchy were backward and unprogressive and threatened the family and political democracy. Thus, the campaign against Mormonism was linked to the Social Gospel, which advocated a new social order and saw various immigrant groups as a threat to progressive British Canadian Protestant values.

At the same time, many influential political and business leaders defended the Mormons. Rather than being backward, they saw Mormons as technological innovators in agriculture. Thus, the progressive rhetoric of western settlement could lead to either hostility or acceptance of the Mormons. The prevailing economic and political forces, and the changing social and ethnic composition of Alberta, ultimately encouraged their acceptance.

How did the opposition to the Mormons compare to the nativism experienced by other religious and ethnic minorities? The opposition to Jews, central and eastern Europeans, Mennonites, Hutterites, Doukhobors, Blacks, Chinese, Japanese and East Indians led to restrictive immigration measures.

Mormons were never barred from entering Canada and no legislation, except for the legislation outlawing polygamy, was passed that limited their civil rights. Mormons had ceased to be a public issue by the early 1920s. It would be several more decades, however, before racial or pacifist religious minorities found a similar measure of tolerance.

Despite the intense opposition that initially greeted the Mormons, their acceptance came relatively quickly. Unlike the central and eastern Europeans, who when they first arrived did not speak English and were often poor and illiterate, the Mormons were educated, middle class and predominantly of British and Scandinavian background. The Mormons did not face the charges of being educationally deficient, intemperate, politically radical or "racially" inferior.

Although nativist hostility toward Mormons was minor compare to some other immigrant groups, nonetheless, for a period of thirty years, Mormons faced significant prejudice. The anti-Mormon movement was clearly an off-shoot of the anti-Mormon movement in the United States, and depended on arguments garnered from American anti-Mormon sources. One striking aspect of the Canadian anti-Mormon movement is how little touch it had with Canadian Mormons.

The Mormons as presented in the literature of the Protestant clergy and women's organizations were caricatures. Charges that Mormons were prac-tising polygamy in secret were misleading and wildly exaggerated. A rearguard attempt was made by a few Mormon leaders to keep polygamy alive in southern Alberta, but it was limited to a handful of people, and plural wives did not live in Canada. Mormon sexual morality was in fact puritanical, with strong moral prescriptions against adultery and premarital sex. The percep-tion of the clergy that Mormon missionaries were recruiting young women to live in polygamous relationships was simply false. The charges of church political domination in Canada were likewise false. There was no united Mormon vote.[110]

Why did the Protestant churches become so agitated? Clearly, it was not because of the success of Mormon missionaries. From 1900 to the early 1920s, there were cumulatively only approximately two hundred missionaries scat-tered across the whole country, and they had relatively little success.

The causes of the anti-Mormon movement in Canada seem strikingly similar to those in the United States in the second quarter of the nineteenth century. David Brion Davis and Malcolm Thorp argue that during a period of rapid social change when traditional values were called into question, Americans and Britons were hostile to any group that seemed to threaten established ways. American nativists turned on Mormons and other groups such as the Catholics "because it gave them a sense of identity they otherwise lacked."[111] In the late nineteenth and early twentieth centuries, Canada was undergoing massive social and economic change with urbanization, industrialization, growing labor unrest, the settlement of the West, secularization, and changing family and male-female relationships. English-French, Protestant-Catholic and regional tensions were also profound and recurring.

Thus the hostility to the Mormons could serve many functions. The opposition to Mormonism from clergymen and women's organizations was part of a larger movement to defend marriage and sexual morality.[112] The perception of the Mormon threat could further strengthen moral crusaders who hoped to preserve traditional values that seemed threatened because of social change and conflict.

In the hostility of the Protestant clergy to the Mormons, one also senses their need for a visible and relatively powerless target that could help unify the churches when so many other divisive forces threatened them. Anti-Mormon sentiment may have served some of the same functions that anti-Catholic sentiment had earlier served at a time when anti-Catholic sentiment was on the wane in the mainline Protestant churches. The anti-Mormon campaign began to gain steam just after the turn of the century when the Presbyterian missions to the French-Catholics went into a steep decline.[113] Presbyterians debating the danger of Mormonism at their annual general assembly in 1911 argued that "Mormonism was more of a menace than Roman Catholicism, because the Mormon priest had a greater hold on the people."

The years from 1890-1914 were marked by a growing debate and growing confusion about the role of clergymen, of Protestantism and of the church in general in an increasingly plural, secular, and industrial society. The churches were concerned about growing religious indifference and in their own diminishing moral authority. This confusion was also reflected in the struggle between conservative and liberals within the major Protestant churches, and in the growing debate in the two largest Protestant churches over whether or not either Methodism and Presbyterianism should remain as separate denominations or join together in a new one.[114] Given this range of troubling and divisive issues, could not all right-thinking people agree on the evils of Mormonism?

Mormon theology unquestionably differed from mainline Protestantism, yet the intensity of the anti-Mormon campaign cannot simply be explained as a recognition of fundamental theological differences. Protestant clergymen needed a place to draw the line, a place where the frustrations over the internal divisions in Protestantism and over growing signs of secularization could be buried. The Mormon question was by no means the foremost question on the minds of Protestant leaders, yet it served a useful unifying function.

Despite the range and intensity of anti-Mormon sentiment within Canadian Protestant circles, from an international perspective, the Mormons who came to Canada in the late nineteenth and early twentieth centuries encountered less hostility than did Mormons anywhere in the world outside of the western Great Basin. They did not face the open violence encountered by Mormons in the American south and in Britain, nor were they expelled in large numbers as they were from Mexico. Mormon missionaries were not outlawed as they were in several European countries.[115] This acceptance, from a comparative perspective, can be attributed to the sparseness of population in the Canadian West, and to the pluralism of the western population. Ultimately, the perception of Mormons as progressive farmers, who could open an unpopulated and semiarid region, overcame most doubts and enabled them to find their place during the boomtime of western settlement.

NOTES

1. *New York Times*, 11 December 1887; *Chicago Evening Journal*, 15 February 1896.

2. Carl Berger, *Sense of Power* (Toronto: University of Toronto Press, 1970), chapter 6.

3. One must address also the far-reaching and fundamental changes that occurred within Mormon culture during this period. For an overview of the major changes in Mormonism during this time period, see Thomas Alexander, *Mormonism in Transition: A History of the Latter-day Saints, 1890-1930* (Urbana: University of Illinois Press, 1986).

4. Lawrence Lee, "The Mormons come to Canada, 1887-1902," *Pacific Northwest Quarterly*, Vol. 59 (January 1968), p.12.

5. Norman MacDonald, *Canada: Immigration and Colonization* (Toronto: Macmillan, 1966), Chapter 11.

6. A.A. den Otter, *Civilizing the West: The Galts and the Development of Western Canada* (Edmonton: University of Alberta Press, 1982), chapter 6.

7. den Otter, Ibid., chapter 7.

8. Ibid., pp.166 and 168-70.

9. James Nix, "John Maclean's Mission to the Blood Indians, 1880-1889" (unpublished master's thesis, McGill University, 1977), pp. 104-220.

10. On attitudes towards immigration in Alberta, see H. Palmer, "Responses to

Foreign Immigration: Nativism and Ethnic Tolerance in Alberta, 1880-1920" (unpublished master's thesis, University of Alberta, 1971), chapter 1.

11. Leonard Arrington and Davis Bitton, *The Mormon Experience* (New York: Alfred A. Knopf, 1979), chapter 9.

12. For a quantitative study of anti-Mormon attitudes in American periodicals, see Jan Shipps, "From Satyr to Saint: American Attitudes toward the Mormons, 1860-1960." Paper presented to 1973 annual meeting of Organization of American Historians. On the impact of American periodicals in Canada in the late nineteenth and early twentieth centuries, see Samuel Moffett, *The Americanization of Canada* (Toronto: University of Toronto Press, 1972), chapter 9. (The Moffett study was originally written in 1907.)

13. *Lethbridge News* [LN] 22 December 1887.

14. LN, 29 March 1888.

15. *Edmonton Bulletin* [EB], 31 March 1888; Department of the Interior, Sessional Papers, 1890, #17, p.13; E.A. Mitchener, "William Pearce and federal government activity in the West, 1874-1904," *Canadian Public Administration*, Vol. 10 (June 1967), pp. 235-43.

16. University of Alberta Archives, Pearce Papers, C.O. Card file.

17. EB, 3 September 1887.

18. EB, 8 October 1887; 31 March 1888.

19. LN, 10 August 1887.

20. *Macleod Gazette* [MG], 16 August 1887; LN, 17 August 1887.

21. LN, 17 August 1887, 21 September 1887, 31 May 1888.

22. MG, 21 March 1888.

23. *Canadian Parliamentary Guide*, 1887, p. 351. For more on Stenhouse, see paper by Robert McCue, "British Columbia and the Mormons in the Nineteenth Century," in this volume.

24. *Saskatchewan Herald*, 11 December 1889, 26 February 1890, 24 July 1890; MG, 10 January 1889; LN, 12 December 1888, 26 December 1888.

25. *Calgary Herald* [CH], 18 December 1889.

26. *Deseret News*, 26 August 1889.

27. Charles O. Card, *The Journal of Charles Ora Card, September 14, 1886 to July 7, 1902*, compiled by Donald Godfrey and Melva Witbeck (n.p., published privately, 1981), 10 and 14 November 1888. For a Mormon account of the trip, see *Deseret News*, 15 November 1888.

28. LN, 14 November 1888, 12 December 1888.

29. MG, 20 December 1888, 6 June 1889, 31 October 31, 1889.

30. Ibid., 31 October 1889.

31. LN, 23 and 30 October 1889.

32. National Archives of Canada, R.G. 18, Vol. 41, Steele to Commissioner, NWMP, Regina, 4 December 1889; Ibid., A.M. Burgess to Dewdney, 16 December 1889.

33. Ibid., Card to Burgess, 22 February 1890. See also the denial by the church's official newspaper, *Deseret News*, 26 August 1889.

34. EB, 21 December 1889.

35. J.G. Snell, "The white life for two: The defence of marriage and sexual morality

in Canada, 1890-1914," *Social History/Histoire Sociale*, Vol. XVI, No. 31 (May 1983) pp. 117 and 129.

36. *Debates, House of Commons*, 30:342, 1890.

37. A similar bill, which had been introduced in February in the Senate by Senator Macdonald from British Columbia, was withdrawn.

38. *Debates, House of Commons*, 10 April 1890, c. 3172-3180.

39. LN, 20 August 1890; North-West Territories, Sessional Papers, Petition and counter-petition re Incorporation of Cardston Company Limited.

40. CH, 6 August 1890; LN, 23 July, 13 August, 10 September 1890; *Medicine Hat Times*, 24 August 1890; EB, 30 August 1890.

41. Quoted in *Deseret Weekly*, August-September 1890, pp. 449-50.

42. Melvin S. Tagg, "A History of the Church of Jesus Christ of Latter-day Saints in Canada," (doctoral dissertation, Brigham Young University, 1963), pp. 161-63; Glenbow Archives, Journals of the Legislative Assembly of the NWT, 31 October, 4 and 28 November 1890.

43. LN, 15 October 1890.

44. *Christian Guardian* [CG], 22 October 1890. See also CG, 30 July, 6 August, 15 October, 31 December 1890. The *Toronto Mail*, 8 October 1890, ed., "Mormonism and Polygamy." See also *Toronto World*, 7 October 1890; *Toronto Empire*, 7 October 1890; *Toronto News*, 7 October 1890.

45. LN, 27 March 1891, 7 December 1892, 11 January 1893, 13 April 1893, 6 July 1893, 13 July 1893, 30 October 1895; MG, 23 April 1891, 5 January 1893, 24 March 1893. See especially letter in MG, 23 April 1891.

46. Quoted in LN, 23 July 1893.

47. Census of Canada, 1911 Table II, "Religions of the People."

48. A.A. den Otter, *Civilizing the West*, chapter 8; J.B. Hedges, *Building the Canadian West* (New York: Macmillan, 1939), p. 171; J.R. Hicken, "Events Leading to the Settlement of the Communities of Cardston, Magrath, Stirling and Raymond, Alberta" (unpublished master's thesis, Utah State University, 1968), pp. 60-65; Sam Porter and Charles Raley, "A Brief History of the Development of Irrigation in the Lethbridge District" (Lethbridge Public Library, 1925), pp. 15-18. These accounts differ in the details of the contract.

49. den Otter, *Civilizing the West*, chapter 9.

50. Glenbow Archives, Northwest Coal and Navigation Co. Papers Box 2, file 22, Galt to Sifton, 15 December 1897.

51. den Otter, *Civilizing the West*, pp. 222-23; Glenbow Archives, W.L. Jacobson, "History of Irrigation in Western Canada: Biographical Sketch of Charles Ora Card," pp. 10-11.

52. NAC, RG 76, Vol. 195 file 76054, C.W. Speers to Frank Pedley, 1 March 1899.

53. Ibid., W.J. White to Frank Pedley, 21 May 1899.

54. LN, 25 July 1901.

55. LN, 28 December 1899.

56. LN, 20 September 1900; Paul Stevens and J.T. Saywell, eds., *Lord Minto's Canadian Papers*, Vol. 1 (Toronto: Champlain Society, 1981), p. 406.

57. Glenbow Archives, Northwest Coal and Navigation Co. Papers, "Outline: The Alberta Irrigation Company," pp. 6-7.

58. Quoted in den Otter, *Civilizing the West*, p. 223; Hedges, *Building the Canadian West*, p. 173; CH, 1 June 1899.

59. *Montreal Star*, 22 May 1899.

60. C.A. Magrath, *Canada's Growth and Problems Affecting It* (Ottawa: Mortimer Press, 1910), pp. 120-23.

61. CH, 5, 12 and 19 January 1905; LH, 26 July 1906, 16 August 1906.

62. On attitudes toward central and eastern Europeans during this time period, see H. Palmer, *Patterns of Prejudice* (Toronto: McClelland & Stewart, 1982), pp. 27-31. See MG, 24 March 1899, for an example of the juxtaposition of the favorable attitude toward Mormons with the unfavorable attitude toward Doukhobors.

63. CH, 6 December 1900.

64. *Debates, House of Commons*, 1905, c. 8519.

65. NAC, Laurier Papers, Woolf to Laurier, 5 October 1905; Laurier to Woolf, 10 October 1905.

66. *Canadian Annual Review*, 1907, p. 296; LH, 21 February 1907.

67. John R. Hicken, "Events Leading to the Settlement of the Communities of Cardston, Magrath, Stirling and Raymond, Alberta" (unpublished master's thesis, Utah State University, 1968), pp. 37-46.

68. J.R. Miller, "Anti-Catholic thought in Victorian Canada," *Canadian Historical Review* (December 1985), pp. 482-84 and 492-93.

69. For example, two-thirds of the cabinet ministers in the Liberal government, which was in power in Alberta from 1905 to 1921, were Presbyterians or Methodists. In 1924, 43% of the 719 people listed in a "Who's Who" of Alberta were Presbyterians or Methodists. John Blue, *Alberta Past and Present* (Chicago: Pioneer Historical Publishing, 1924).

70. Alexander, *Mormonism in Transition*, chapter 2; Malcolm Thorp, " 'The Mormon Peril': The crusade against the Saints in Britain, 1910-1914," *Journal of Mormon History*, 2 (1975), pp. 69-88.

71. Alexander, *Mormonism in Transition*, p. 70.

72. Richard Allen, *The Social Passion: Religion and Social Reform in Canada, 1914-1928* (Toronto: University of Toronto Press, 1971).

73. Marilyn Barber, "Nationalism, Nativism and the Social Gospel: The Protestant Church Response to Foreign Immigrants in Western Canada, 1897-1914," in Richard Allen, ed., *The Social Gospel in Canada* (Ottawa: National Museums of Canada, 1975); J.W. Grant, *The Church in the Canadian Era* (Toronto: McGraw-Hill Ryerson, 1972), pp. 94-98; John Moir, *Enduring Witness: A History of the Presbyterian Church in Canada* (Toronto: Presybterian Publications, 1978), pp. 164-69; N.K. Clifford, "His Dominion: a vision in crisis," *Studies in Religion*, Vol. 2, No. 4 (1973), pp. 314-26.

74. Palmer, *Patterns of Prejudice*, pp. 40-42.

75. LN, 30 March 1893; Minute Books, Calgary Presbytery, 8 and 30 September 1896, p. 47 (Edmonton: St. Stephen's Theological Library).

76. Michael Owen, "Women with a mission," *Horizon Canada*, Vol. 9, No. 103 (1985), pp. 2462-67.

77. United Church Archives, "The Latter-day Saints or Mormonism," Woman's

Home Missionary Society, 1912; "Mormonism," Women's Missionary Society, 1923.

78. LN, 15 November 1905; *Raymond Leader*, 9 November 1911; James Snell, "The Defence of Marriage and Sexual Morality," p. 128.

79. *Proceedings*, Presbyterian General Assembly, 1913, p. 50; 1914, p. 46; 1915, p. 49.

80. Richard Cowan, "Mormonism in National Periodicals," (unpublished doctoral dissertation Stanford University, 1961).

81. Glenbow Library, W.D. Reid, "Mission Work in Alberta," Board of Home Missions, 1912.

82. CH, 13 June 1911.

83. LH, 14 June 1911.

84. CG, 12 November 1913.

85. George Emery, "The Methodist Church and the 'European Foreigners' of Winni-
peg: The All People's Mission, 1889-1914," *H.S.S.M. Transactions*, Series III, 28 (1971-72), pp. 85-100.

86. J.S. Woodsworth, *Strangers Within Our Gates* (Toronto: Missionary Society of the Methodist Church, 1909).

87. W.H. Toombs, *Mormonism* (Toronto: n.p., 1917), p. 38.

88. Eugene Campbell and Richard Poll, *Hugh B. Brown: His Life and Thought* (Salt Lake City: Bookcraft, 1975), pp. 52-53.

89. LN, 22 June, 29 June, 10 July 1906; LH, 5 July 1906.

90. LH, 4 January, 28 October, 9 November 1915, 24 November 1916.

91. Campbell and Poll, Ibid., CH, 6 July 1915; *Cardston Globe*, 15 July 1915.

92. PAC, RG 6E, Vol. 553, Supt. Commanding Division D. to Commissioner, RNWMP, 2 October 1916.

93. *Improvement Era*, Vol. XIX No. 8, June 1916, pp.741-43. Before the Americans entered the war in April 1917, the leaders of the Mormon Church supported President Wilson's peace policy, and one church leader published an article supporting the right of conscientious objection. Alexander, *Mormonism in Transition*, pp. 46 and 49.

94. NAC, RG 6E, Vol. 553, Chambers to Coulter, 31 October 1916.

95. For more background on the role of the press censor and the suppression of ethnic newspapers, see W. Entz, "The suppression of the German language press in September 1918," *Canadian Ethnic Studies*, Vol. VIII, No. 2 (1976), pp. 56-70; M. James Penton, *Jehovah's Witnesses in Canada* (Toronto: Macmillan, 1976).

96. NAC, RG 6E, Vol. 553, Coulter to Chambers, 3 November 1916.

97. LDS Archives, *Liahona* (publication of the Eastern States Mission), 3 August 1913, 11 February 1917.

98. *The Canadian White Ribbon Tidings*, 15 July 1918.

99. Alexander, *Mormonism in Transition*, p. 228.

100. NAC, Department of Justice, RG 13, A2, Vol. 229, file 2600.

101. LDS Archives, *Liahona*, 13 July 1917; Manuscript History of the Canadian Mission, 20 July 1919.

102. LH, 11 February 1918.
103. CA, 26 September 1918; Palmer, "Nativism and Ethnic Tolerance in Alberta,"
pp. 255-56.
104. R.I. McLean, "A 'Most Effectual Remedy': Temperance and Prohibition in
Alberta, 1875-1915" (unpublished master's thesis, University of Calgary,
1969), pp. 150-51.
105. *Cardston Globe*, 22 July 1915.
106. *The Canadian White Ribbon Tidings*, February 1922, p. 30; March 1922,
p. 55; June 1925, p. 127.
107. For a brief discussion of anti-radical nativism at the end of the war in Alberta,
see Palmer, *Patterns of Prejudice*, pp. 53-56.
108. LH, 22 and 27-31 August 1923.
109. Blue, *Alberta Past and Present*.
110. Howard Palmer, "Mormon political behavior in Alberta," *Tangents*, 1 (1969),
pp. 85-112. For background on post-Manifesto polygamy, see work cited in
footnotes 67 and 70; D. Michael Quinn, "LDS Church authority and new
plural marriages, 1890-1904," *Dialogue*, Vol. 18, no.1 (Spring 1985), pp.
9-105; and article by Jessie Embry in this volume.
111. David Brion Davis, "Some Themes of Counter-Subversion: An Analysis of
Anti-Masonic, Anti-Catholic, Anti-Mormon Literature," *Mississippi Valley
Historical Review*, XLVII (1960), pp. 205-24; Malcolm Thorp, "The Mormon Peril," p. 70.
112. J.G. Snell, "Defence of Marriage," p. 129.
113. John Moir, *Enduring Witness*.
114. For an excellent discussion of the broad range of issues facing Presbyterian
and Methodist clergymen between 1890 and 1914, see David Marshall, "The
Clerical Response to Secularization: Canadian Methodists and Presbyterians,
1880-1940" (unpublished doctoral dissertation, University of Toronto, 1986).
115. Alexander, *Mormonism in Transition*, chapters 10 and 11.

7 Early Mormon Settlement in Western Canada

A Comparative Communitarian Perspective

ANTHONY W. RASPORICH

THE HUNDREDTH ANNIVERSARY of Mormon settlement in Alberta has historical resonances with another Canadian anniversary—the bicentennial of Loyalist settlement recently celebrated in Ontario. The analogy is perhaps not an inapt one, for the Loyalists were the first of the "un-American" Americans.[1] Fleeing persecution from the American revolutionary wars, this first founding remnant of Toryism in Upper Canada provided the dominant ideological underpinning of English Canadian nationalism, just as another American heresy was in the making in northern New York state. Ironically, both Mormonism and the tentative arm of the central Canadian state would meet again a half-century later in the North-West Territories of Canada. Somewhat symbolically, Card and his small Mormon band were a living re-enactment of the first Loyalist experience, as un-Americans fleeing political and religious persecution. Now, on behalf of his flock, Card sought asylum and sanction for polygamy from John A. Macdonald. But what awaited them?

A common context that should be given to this discussion is the Edenic version of the Canadian West that was expressed in the speeches and writings of central Canadian expansionists. This Edenic vision became blurred with the entry of the snake into the garden (i.e., John A. Macdonald, the CPR, and the quelling of the Riel rebellions of 1870 and 1885), and the subsequent "pacification" of the West for settlement.[2] The opening of western Canada to settlement had of course by the 1870s already begun to attract a broad variety of group settlers into the Canadian West. Among these highly variegated groups were a large variety of communitarian settlements of an ethnic, religious and utopian character.[3]

One of the prominent themes of religious settlement on the prairies has been put forward by B.J. Smillie. As he points out, "Many of the groups who immigrated to the Canadian West identified themselves as a pilgrim people not with an earthly, but a heavenly destination." With considerable effect Smillie cites an old hymn by Isaac Watts: "We're marching to Zion/Beautiful, beautiful Zion, we're marching upward to Zion, the beautiful City of God."[4] Several ethnic and religious groups are then described to demonstrate his general argument, some obvious ones, such as the Hutterites, Mennonites, Doukhobors and Jews, and others less so, such as the Germans, Ukrainians, Anglicans and Protestants. A curious omission from this largely Saskatchewan-based selection were the Mormons of Alberta, doubly unfortunate because it also overlooks the strong New Jerusalem, Zionist theme that persists in Mormon theology.[5]

It is this fusion of the ethnic communitarian and utopian ideological elements with the millennialist sectarian outlook that imparts a unique quality to western settlements on the Canadian prairies. A useful index to the survival skills, both social and ideological, of utopian and communitarian groups in America has been provided by Rosabeth Moss Kanter. She studied commitment mechanisms among utopian and sectarian groups, whereby they establish a collective identity versus the *outside* in order to regulate the community in an effective way. She argues further that utopian communities have a common set of values that include the millennialist ideal of human perfectibility, order, brotherhood, the unity of mind and body, and group coherence. The commitment mechanisms for ensuring these ideals vary but are most often instrumental (cost and reward), and affective or moral (emotional or religious acceptance of social norms and beliefs), since community success or failure depends on the effectiveness of the group in maximizing personal commitments.[6] Further commitment mechanisms might involve mortification, renunciation and transcendence, as well as physical isolation, abstinence, vegetarianism, polygamy, labor in common, common investment in property and goods, charismatic leadership and deference.[7]

The first of these religious-sectarian utopias in the Canadian West was established by the Mennonites in Manitoba in 1874, where they hoped to build a new society based upon the New Testament.[8] In the religious realm, their quest had been a centuries long pursuit of the earthly realization of the Kingdom of God on earth, but it had secular aspects as well, in that the Mennonites sought after, and received from the Canadian government, large land tracts, religious freedom, military exemptions and control over their

Hutterite Colony at Stand Off, Alberta, in 1920, located on the tract of land selected in 1886 by C.O. Card and party as a preferred site for a Mormon settlement, NA 2635-52 Glenbow Archives

own schools.[9] Once established, the traditional commitment mechanisms, both instrumental and moral, were practised with varying degrees of success in the East and West reserves. Attitudes toward leadership, communal government, common property and modernity fluctuated both spatially and through time.[10] Similarly, other differences emerged over the questions of transcendence (i.e., "in the world, but not of the world") and the means of establishing the Kingdom of God on a higher spiritual plane.[11] Factionalism between progressive and conservative elements in each of the several colonies was characteristic of a host of groups: Klein Gemeinde, Holdemann, Bruderthaler, Bergthaler, Sommerfelder and Old Colony Mennonites. Yet, cultural persistence and survival were the norm to World War I, despite schismatic factionalism and pressures from the external community on schooling and military service—"diversity within a corporate personality."[12]

Perhaps even more dramatically, the historical ethos of the Hutterian Brethren underlined the hardening effects of nationalist orthodoxy and persecution, as this group suffered double displacement—from Russia to South Dakota and then to Canada during World War I. Indeed, the fluctuation of group ideology on such key issues as the community of goods, family and property has been a historically dialectical relationship related to the relative degree of the persecution of the group.[13] Equally, there have been significant differences among colonies on issues of modernization.[14] The colonies established from 1880 to 1920 were able to impose the regimen of the community of goods and works as instrumental commitments, and a common Anabaptist religious ideology on their membership.[15]

The Doukhobors were yet a more notorious sect, thrown into the Canadian West by Russian nationalism and conscription in the late nineteenth century. While its sectarian roots ran deep into seventeenth-century dissent against orthodoxy, the "Spirit Wrestlers" evolved a unique set of religious practices and beliefs with strong utopian and millenarian tendencies.[16] Further adaptation of their religious ideology occurred during Peter Verigin's leadership in exile, including proscriptions against alcohol and tobacco, and then, under Tolstoy's influence, the ideal of common property.[17] Further support and influence came from English Tolstoyans, such as J.C. Kenworthy, who were already experimenting with utopian colonies of Christian Brotherhood, and led to Verigin's adoption of the name, the Brotherhood Church. Upon immigration to Canada, the Doukhobors had established, near Kamsack in the North-West Territories, the short-lived Doukhobor Trading Company and co-operative industries.[18]

In the process of settlement, the factionalism that plagued communitarian groups appeared in groups from orthodox independents and radicals such as the conservative Christian Community of Universal Brotherhood, the Independents and the *Svobodniki* or Sons of Freedom chiliasts who paraded in the nude to Yorkton in 1903. Equally, other challenges to the messianic leadership of Peter "The Lordly" Verigin emerged from the radical zealots who questioned his "Christness," and the Independents who rejected the principle of communal property.[19] With the establishment of the second community in British Columbia after 1907, yet another "utopian" phase replaced the earlier millenarian one—Verigin's role as leader was diminished somewhat, communal architecture adopted a nineteenth-century Icarian or Fourierist phalansterian style, and experimentation occurred with a moneyless economy.[20] Tensions between and within the prairie and BC communities persisted, and relations with the state in both jurisdictions worsened, but clearly this peculiar millenarian and utopian sect had rooted firmly in Canada by the eve of World War I.

The case of the Mormons as a combined utopian-millennialist religious sect in American history was made by Lowry Nelson, who argued that Mormonism was a sectarian offshoot of millenarianism in western New York, holding much in common with the emergence of Millerism and other sects in the "Burned-over District" of upstate New York.[21] Nelson argued further that Mormonism fused American nationalism of that era uniquely with economic communism and millennialism. In describing the first, he noted that the gathering at Zion in America imparted a Hebraic sense of "God's Chosen People" to the Mormons; indeed, it is interesting to compare this nationalistic source of identity to S.F. Wise's exploration of the Hebraic roots of Loyalism, i.e., "God's Peculiar Peoples," as a source of Canadian nationalism.[22] The further element of economic communism is explained further by Nelson as expressed in the social system of early experiments in the law of consecration and the "United Order" in which land and economic surplus reverts to the group, and in the spatial organization of land in the Plat of Zion as the millennial space for the "gathering of Israel."

The eclectic or fusionist aspects of Mormon thought were explored further by Nelson in his discussion of the possible utopian influences of Robert Owen and Charles Fourier via Albert Brisbane on Mormonism in the 1840s. This theme has been picked up and elaborated on again by Michael Barkun, who argues that the utopians were in fact much better prepared for the economic disasters of the 1840s than their more theologically hidebound millennialist brethren such as the Millerites.[23] More specific to the Mormons, a recent book by Gordon and Gary Shepherd, *A Kingdom Transformed*, argues—in their application of R.M. Kanter's work—that Mormonism had much in common with the utopians in their views on human perfectibility, centralized authority, order and group adherence, to name but a few of their commonly held assumptions.[24] Thus, it might well be that further hybridization with utopian-progressivism strengthened further the complex and eclectic weave of the millennialism, economic communism and nationalism that gave Mormonism the considerable resilience that sustained it throughout various westward migrations. As Thomas O'Dea has argued, nineteenth-century Mormonism was characterized by "a creative eclecticism which although it failed to achieve logical consistency, nevertheless possessed a cohesiveness of tendency and congruity of fundamental principle that rendered it a unified point of view."[25]

This essay is less concerned with the migration of Mormonism in western America than with its impulse northwards to Canada after the introduction of the anti-polygamy laws. In ideological terms, the extra-legal activities of the community's founder, Charles Ora Card, fleeing from "the land of persecution" in the United States northwards to Canada, bear repetition since they cast light on the millennialist perceptions held of "the northern refuge":

Bro. Samuel Smith of Brigham City, told me he was present in a Priesthood Meeting in the basement of the Temple meeting in Nauvoo in the year 1843, and heard the prophet Joseph Smith state that England or the nation of Great Britain would be the last to go to pieces. She would be instrumental in aiding to crush other nations, even this nation of the United States, and she would only be overthrown by the ten tribes from the north. She would never persecute the Saints as a nation. She would gather up great treasures of gold and yet we should seek refuge in her dominion.[26]

Later diary entries, during the first year of settlement, reflected on the transition to a new political dispensation, structurally not unlike that of the United Empire Loyalists one hundred years earlier. On New Year's Day 1887, Charles Ora Card reflected on the historical ironies that had befallen Americans, like himself, now in exile:

> I welcome another year although my fate seems to be an exile driven or compelled for freedom's sake to seek a foreign land. It seems strange to think that my grandsires fought to establish religious liberty and in that great struggle that stained our fair land with a deluge of blood to free us from the rule of a Tyrant King that now, it seems their grandchildren should be obliged to gather into the domains of that government that is ruled by the Queen.[27]

Further disquisitions on the whiggish verities of British liberty and the role of the Crown were evident in a petition to Governor General Lord Stanley, during his visit in mid-October 1889.[28] Thus, the governor general as the "personal and living bond" between the Crown and its new subjects rapidly became the ideological currency of this un-American fragment of republicanism as much as it had for the Loyalists in exile, or the nineteenth-century French Canadians.[29]

The theme of community-building became the predominant concern of Card and the Mormons in their early settlement at Lee Creek. This communitarian pioneering phase, dominated by the patriarchal leadership of Card, manifested all the prerequisites laid out by Kanter's criteria for group survival, namely, effective commitment mechanisms of an instrumental nature. In the first instance of instrumental commitments, the elements of sacrifice and investment in the community were well developed in successful utopian communities. And it is clear, given the nature of the Mormon exile and trek northward, that the sense of separation from the larger American community was acute enough to induce some colonists to return permanently to Utah. The strong sense of exile among the surviving remnant was made much of as an element of destiny as well, for Card recorded, "Truly I feel that we have a faithful band of exiles here who are bound to make a mark on this land that will weigh on the credit side for the Saints."[30] The Card diaries also abound in puritanical references during the 1890s to the dangers of "round dancing," of pool tables and whiskey, Sunday baseball and "kissing abroad—do that at home."[31] In addition to personal sacrifice and abstinence, there was the larger investment of time, money and work towards the larger interest of the community, *via* tithing, communal building, agricultural labor, investment in joint-stock companies and other co-operative ventures.

No better blending of the pragmatic and spiritual aspects of community-building has been expressed than the balanced counsel Card gave to the priesthood meeting at the end of May 1890:

I spoke to them upon the necessity of unity among us in all things temporal and spiritual. Advised co-operation in our business operations. Advised the brethren to herd our stock and save our grain. Advised the brethren to take the Oath of Allegiance to the Canadian Government. Also to pay their tithes and offerings. Referred to the propriety of buying a sawmill that we may obtain building material more convenient and cheaper. We should seek to market our butter and other produce under management that would secure best market price. Advised them to buy their merchandise in bulk and divide it among themselves. We should seek to breed from the best horses and cattle. Advised the brethren in gathering the things of this world to not set their hearts upon them and think more of the gift than the giver and constantly nurture the good spirit and live by the light of revelation....[32]

Thus, the rapid establishment by 1890 of a co-operative store, a co-operative sawmill, and a joint-stock company in the form of the Cardston Company were all evident applications of the "instrumental" or cost-commitments to economic co-operation in Cardston. So also were other later innovations, which followed between 1890 and 1895, such as the communal dairy and cheese factory, a co-operative flour mill, a butcher shop, a coal mine, an implements store and several other artisan and retail establishments. The degree of economic commitment in this pioneering phase of scarcity was so intense that Card signed his name to paper scrip that circulated in the community, and when prosperity returned in 1895, the Cardston Company paid a 40% dividend, half in cash and half in goods.[33]

The second order of nineteenth-century utopian commitment mechanisms discussed by Kanter were the "affective" bonds developed through the processes of "renunciation" and "communion."[34] By the process of renunciation, individuals are absorbed into a collective whole or group solidarity, perhaps by new sexual norms ranging from celibacy to free love or plural marriage, or socially through communal education of children. These communal bonds were particularly well developed in this Canadian Mormon fragment because of early commitment to plural marriage by Card, A.M. Stenhouse, and the Utah leaders such as John W. Taylor and Francis Lyman.[35] With their failure to persuade John A. Macdonald personally to allow plural marriage in 1888, and the passage of legislation in Canada specifically prohibiting polygamy in April 1890, the practice fell into official disrepute. Given the further severity of public reaction in Alberta in 1890, and Card's own legal problems relating to polygamy in Utah, he diminished references to the practice in his diaries and strongly denounced its existence in a letter to the minister of the Interior in 1890 (also 1894).[36] But it is also clear that his communal familial vision still persisted in his wistful lament in 1891 that his families were so far removed and his hope that "Sometime that in the future to have a gathering dispensation when I may be able to call around me my loved ones and instruct them in the Gospel principles."[37] It has also been maintained by John Hicken that few plural marriages took place in Alberta to 1904, although there were polygamists who had a wife in each country.[38]

The second element of affective commitment through communion with the larger whole, through the process of shared experiences in work, education and in public assemblies and celebrations, was highly developed in both American Mormonism and in its Alberta offshoot. That national celebratory rituals were quickly adapted from the American to Canadian experience was readily apparent in the enthusiastic transference of July 4 celebrations to July 1 in 1887.

The unique spatial arrangement of American Mormon communities was yet another aspect of the transfer of Mormon culture to Alberta, as geographers such as Lynn Rosenvall and John Lehr have observed so ably, following upon the earlier pioneering work of Lowry Nelson on *The Mormon Village*. The Plat of Zion evolved from the attempt "to establish in Missouri a Utopia," and this grid pattern of farm villages was carried forward to Utah and Idaho, and then to Canada.[39] In Alberta, the New

England type of farm village was adopted because of "the social and religious advantages of community living."[40] First, the grid pattern offered order, replication and uniformity; second, it encouraged equal distribution of property; and, third, it was the easiest to effect with crude survey instruments. While this grid pattern was certainly true of the first settlements in the founding period of the early 1890s, it was also apparent later in the decade that settlement variations had begun to emerge. This was particularly the case with the founding of Raymond by Apostle John W. Taylor, who introduced the radial street pattern.[41] But whatever the spatial adaptations to the Plat of Zion, the essential social and religious assumptions remained intact, that is the total integration of the individual in a compact, concentrated social order.

Yet another salient element in renunciatory values held dear by utopian-communitarian groups, such as the Hutterians' notion of the "Outside," is that of insulation against the external world. That was accomplished partly by spatial separation, but segregation and isolation were particularly strong themes in hostile Mormon-gentile economic relations during the 1880s in Utah.[42] The sense that emerges from the record of the early Cardston years is that the tensions raised by polygamy and economic competition fostered a good deal of the same kind of hostile nativism in Canada as it had south of the border.[43] But in the period after polygamy was disallowed, Mormon isolation from the larger Canadian community diminished, much as it did in the United States.

The third major element of maintaining utopian group commitment was achieved through the means of social control through mortification, among them such elements as public confessions, mutual criticism and other deindividualizing techniques. Techniques of sectarian control among other western Christian sects ranged from "shunning" and expulsion, in the Anabaptist colonies, to similar means of ostracism and expulsion from Anglo-Canadian utopias from HAMONA in western Manitoba to E.A. Partridge's harsh puritan commonwealth of COALSAMAO.[44] The Shepherds, in their study of Utah Mormonism, detail several later reinforcement mechanisms, such as disfellowshipment and excommunication as forms of group sanction, as well as other means of spiritual differentiation and status conferment, and deindividualization as a sectarian social control.

The degree to which these sanctions were apparent in the early Alberta experiment is difficult to determine since both factionalism and doctrinal disputes were apparently on the wane in the late nineteenth century, and certainly would have been less evident in the orthodoxy of a small conservative fragment. There are embedded here and there, however, evidences of Card's abilities as a firm leader in the face of opposition, either from dissidents who challenged his leadership or from others who left.[45] By exercises of collective leadership and reinforcement, the Mormon colony was spared the excesses of factionalism that wrecked many other ethnic and sectarian settlements in western Canada prior to World War I.

Social control might also be attained through transcendence of the individual within the larger community, whereby the self is given meaning and purpose beyond everyday experience through the mechanism of "institutionalized awe." The community might prescribe a systematic program for everyday life, providing for conversion to group mores, and create and maintain historical myths and traditions that sustain group morale, such as, for example, the "miracle of the gulls" that attended Brigham Young's entry in the valley of Great Salt Lake.[46]

Perhaps it is in this area of positive communal transcendence rather than the negative aspect of social control that the Card diaries are richest rhetorically. A powerful sense of providential optimism suffuses the Card diaries from their inception to conclusion, with many references to divine interventions that saved the colony. In the first year of its existence, he staved off a challenge from a few defectors to Montana when he "predicted to the Saints, that if they would remain, the Lord would open the way." And He did, with the appearance of two wealthy women, the Amussen sisters, whose wealth enabled the men to plant their crops and fence their fields.[47]

The elements themselves were subjected to the power of community prayer, as in 1896 when a two-month drought was snapped after a fast-meeting praying for rain. Conversely, the summer flood of 1902 did not diminish the old partriarch's faith as he prayed for good crops and alternative sources of income in its wake. Lamenting community property losses of over $100,000, Card observed laconically, "A surplus of water is a cruel matter."[48] In this respect, the challenge of and Mormon response to ecological disasters, such as floods and consequent destruction of irrigation dams, was a repetition of preadaptive cultural responses to life in the Great Plains. The Mormon *expectation* was that community-rebuilding would have to occur on a regular basis, or that crops would have to be replanted and the process of regeneration begun. As Mark Leone has ably put it in the American context,

> All communities invested materially, thus guaranteeing their own future by rebuilding an economic base that would one day reciprocate in

concrete, predictable ways…reciprocity was guaranteed and balance for the whole set of communities resulted. In addition, a portion of the earth was permanently "redeemed."[49]

The power of communal transcendence was apparent in a wide range of communal activities designed for the larger social good, ranging from the Women's Relief Society for the poor, to industrial bureaus to relieve unemployment.[50] More than this, the overriding importance of community versus individual objectives emerges time and again from Card's written reflections on the progress of his flock.[51]

The early Mormon settlements in Alberta represent perhaps communitarian ideals in their purest state. For after the infusion of the second and third waves of settlers in 1898 and 1902,[52] the Mormon communities altered both spatially and structurally, as they experienced the absorbing forces of capitalist institutions and waves of migration to the surrounding region. Thus, both within the Mormon communities themselves and without, there were subtle changes, such as the change in motivations from political to economic ones.[53]

While these changes might not have altered substantially the nature of Mormonism as a belief system, certain social characteristics from the primitive community of the Cardston core in the 1890s were altered profoundly in the twentieth century. The initial impulse to membership in the colony declined in the 1890s and finally ended with the fully binding ban on polygamy throughout the world in 1904.[54] While many of the commitment mechanisms to sustain membership were firmly in place, and would be developed and improved upon with the increasing metropolitan ties with Salt Lake City, the frontier phase of the first community had passed in this "northern refuge" of Mormon believers.

With the completion of the frontier phase in southern Alberta, a part of Mormonism had reintegrated their ethnic communitarian and utopian ideological elements in a new context. In recreating the old on a new frontier they laid the basis for new experiences. To the north were others with whom they were inevitably linked. The bonds of commerce and government were already becoming apparent. But, perhaps, as well, there were strands however ill-defined, which spanned the years to an earlier frontier when Loyalist refugees would establish their better world on the foundation of their shared traditions.

NOTES

1. Louis Hartz, *The Founding of New Societies* (New York: Harcourt, Brace & World, 1964).

2. Doug Owram, *The Promise of Eden: The Canadian Expansionist Movement and the Idea of the West, 1856-1900* (Toronto: University of Toronto Press, 1980).

3. A.W. Rasporich, "Utopian Ideals and Community Settlements in Western Canada, 1880-1914," in H.C. Klassen, ed., *The Canadian West* (Calgary: Comprint, 1976), pp. 37-62.

4. Benjamin J. Smillie, *Visions of the New Jerusalem: Religious Settlement on the Prairies* (Edmonton: NeWest Press, 1963), p. 7.

5. See W.D. Davis, "Israel, the Mormons and the Land," in T.G. Madsen, ed., *Reflections on Mormonism: Judaeo-Christian Parallels* (Provo: Brigham Young, Publishers Press, 1980), pp. 79-97.

6. See R.M. Kanter, *Commitment and Community: Communes and Utopias in Sociological Perspective* (Cambridge: Harvard University Press, 1972).

7. See Barbara Goodwin and Keith Taylor, *The Politics of Utopia: A Study in Theory and Practice* (London: Hutchison, 1982), pp. 191-95.

8. E.K. Francis, *In Search of Utopia: The Mennonites in Manitoba* (Altona: D.W. Friesen and Sons, 1955).

9. T.D. Regehr, "Mennonites and the New Jerusalem in Western Canada," in B. Smillie, ed., *Visions of the New Jerusalem*, pp. 100-21.

10. Francis, *In Search of Utopia*, pp. 44-45.

11. Regehr, "Mennonites and the New Jerusalem," pp. 115-17.

12. Frank Epp, *Mennonites in Canada*, 1920-40 (Toronto: Macmillan, 1982), pp. 29-35. See also the first issue of *Journal of Mennonite Studies*, vol.1 (1983).

13. Karl Peter, "The Instability of Community of Goods in the Social History of the Hutterites," in A.W. Rasporich, ed., *Western Canada: Past and Present* (Toronto: University of Calgary/McClelland and Stewart West, 1975), pp. 98-119.

14. Ibid., essay by John Bennett, "Change and Transition in Hutterian Society," pp. 120-32.

15. John Hostetler, *Communitarian Societies* (New York: Holt, Rinehart and Winston, 1974), pp. 34-46; Hostetler, *Hutterite Society* (Baltimore: Johns Hopkins University Press, 1974), pp. 255-96; Victor Peters, *All Things Common: The Hutterian Way of Life* (Minneapolis: University of Minnesota Press, 1965), pp. 75-171; V.C. Serl, "Stability and Change in Hutterite Society," (doctoral dissertation, Oregon, 1964), pp. 96-131.

16. George Woodcock and Ivan Avakumovic, *The Doukhobors* (Toronto: McClelland and Stewart, 1977), p. 25.

17. Ibid., pp. 191-92.

18. Koozma Tarasoff, "The Western Settlement of Canadian Doukhobors," in B. Smillie, *Visions of the New Jerusalem*, p. 126. See also L.A. Sulerzhitsky, *To America with the Doukhobors* (Regina: Canadian Plains Research Center, University of Regina, 1982), pp. 108-15.

19. Woodcock and Avakumovic, *The Doukhobors*, pp. 196-8.

20. Ibid., pp. 234-40.

21. Lowry Nelson, "The Settlement of Mormons in Alberta," chapter X, of C.A. Dawson, ed., *Group Settlement: Ethnic Communities in Western Canada*, in W.A. Mackintosh & W.L. Joerg, eds., *Canadian Frontiers of Settlement*, VII (Toronto: Macmillan, 1936), p. 176. See also Nelson, *The Mormon Village* (Salt Lake City: University of Utah Press, 1952).

22. S.F. Wise, "God's Peculiar Peoples," in W.L. Morton, ed., *The Shield of Achilles: Aspects of Canada in the Victorian Age* (Toronto: McClelland and Stewart, 1968), pp. 36-59.

23. Michael Barkun, *The Crucible of the Millennium: The Burned-Over District of New York in the 1840's* (New York: Syracuse University Press, 1986), pp. 137-38.

24. Gordon Shepherd & Gary Shepherd, *A Kingdom Transformed: Themes in the Development of Mormonism* (Salt Lake City: University of Utah Press, 1984), pp. 103-47.

25. T.F. O'Dea, *The Mormons* (Chicago: University of Chicago Press, 1957), p. 125.

26. Charles Ora Card, *The Journal of Charles Ora Card, 1886-1903*, compiled by Donald G. Godfrey and Melva R. Whitbeck (n.p., published privately by D.G. Godfrey, 1981), 21 January 1887, p. 21. Hereafter as Card *Journal*.

27. Card *Journal*, 1 January 1887, p. 29.

28. Ibid., pp. 70-71.

29. See J. Monet, "The Personal and Living Bond," in W.L. Morton, ed., *The Shield of Achilles*.

30. Cited in Lowry Nelson, *The Mormon Village*, p. 227, fn. 5.

31. Card *Journal, passim*, pp. 151-52, 161, 198, 214, 230, 271.

32. Ibid., 31 May 1890, p. 89.

33. See, for example, Jane Eliza Woolf Bates & Zina A. Woolf Hickman, *Founding of Cardston & Vicinity* (n.p., published privately by William L. Woolf, 1960), pp. 85-94. See also Melvin S. Tagg and Asael E. Palmer, *A History of the Mormon Church in Canada* (Lethbridge: Lethbridge Stake Historical Committee, 1968), pp. 55-58.

34. See Shepherd & Shepherd, *A Kingdom Transformed*, pp. 109-16.

35. See, for example, John Hicken, "Events Leading to the Settlement of the Communities of Cardston, McGrath, Stirling and Raymond, Alberta" (unpublished master's thesis, Utah State University, 1968), pp. 37-52.

36. See, for example, C.O. Card to A.M. Burgess, Minister of the Interior, 22 February 1890, printed in A. Wilcox, "The Founding of the Mormon Community in Alberta" (unpublished master's thesis, University of Alberta, 1950), pp. 94-95. See also Brian Champion, "Mormon polygamy: Parliamentary comments," *Alberta History*, Vol. 35, no. 2 (Spring 1987), pp. 10-18.

37. Card *Journal*, 23 May 1891.

38. John Hicken, "Events Leading to the Settlement of Cardston...," pp. 40-46. See also Jessie Embry, "Two legal wives: Mormon polygamy in Canada, the United States, and Mexico," in this volume.

39. Lowry Nelson, "The Mormon Settlement Process," in C.A. Dawson, *Group Settlement*, VII, p. 226.
40. L. Rosenvall, "The transfer of Mormon culture to Alberta," *American Review of Canadian Studies*, XII, no. 2 (Summer 1982), pp. 57-58.
41. J. Lehr, "Mormon settlement morphology in southern Alberta," *Albertan Geographer*, 9 (1972), p. 10.
42. See Carlana Bartlett, "Early Mormon Settlement in Alberta" (honors thesis, Lakehead University, 1973).
43. See Howard Palmer in this volume.
44. See A.W. Rasporich, "Utopian Ideals and Community Settlements," pp. 42-44.
45. See A. Wilcox, "The Founding of Cardston," p. 80.
46. Shepherd & Shepherd, *A Kingdom Transformed*, p. 128.
47. Card *Journal*, April 1888, p. 44.
48. Ibid., 5 July 1902, p. 319.
49. Mark Leone, "The Economic Basis for the Evolution of Mormon Religion," in Irving Zaretsky & Mark Leone, *Religious Movements in Contemporary America* (Princeton: Princeton University Press, 1974), p. 734. See also Lowry Nelson, "Weather Crisis and Community Prayer," in *The Mormon Village*, pp. 270-71.
50. See, for example, Bates and Hickman, *Founding of Cardston and Vicinity*, pp. 170-77, 190-92.
51. Card *Journal*, 25 August 1895, p. 162.
52. J.A. Lehr, "Mormon Settlements in Southern Alberta" (unpublished master's thesis, University of Alberta, 1971), pp. 44-47.
53. Lowry Nelson, "Mormon Settlement Process," p. 213.
54. Hicken, "Events Leading to the Settlement of Cardston...," p. 112.

8 Mormon Folklore and History
Implications for Canadian Research

WILLIAM A. WILSON

FOR SEVERAL DECADES, the study of Mormon folklore has helped illuminate the Mormon experience in the United States.[1] But to my knowledge, no comparable work has been carried out in Canada. In what follows, therefore, I shall argue that a marriage of folklore study and Canadian Mormon historical research could do much to help us better understand the Mormon experience in Canada. I shall try to demonstrate that while folklore study and historical research often follow almost identical paths, folklore study can at times throw light on the past, and especially on its impact on our lives, that we cannot obtain in other ways. Though I shall refer to the few items on file at the Brigham Young University Folklore Archive, my focus will be primarily on method rather than on subject matter, in the hope that those who study, or will study, the history of Canadian Mormons will find in this essay some additional help for the work in which they are engaged.

First, a definition. What is folklore? It is that part of our cultural heritage that we pass from person to person and from generation to generation in face-to-face interactions with each other; it is that part of our heritage that we share with others, not through the written word or through formal instruction, but through the processes of oral transmission or customary example—that is, through hearing a story and then repeating it to someone else or by watching someone make a quilt or participate in a Christmas ritual and then imitating what we have observed.

The materials of folklore fall roughly into three broad categories: first, verbal lore, things that we make with words (stories, songs, proverbs, rhymes, riddles); second, material lore, things that we make with our hands

A verbal folklore site: Group of Magrath Mormons 'picknicking,' c.1901. NA 131-1 Glenbow Archives.

Customary folklore site: The Raymond Opera House, built by popular share ownership, 1908-09, with spring dance floor, spacious stage and basketball court. Courtesy Mary Heggie, Raymond.

Customary folklore mobile site: Cardston's first band in bandwagon, 1898. NA 143-4
Glenbow Archives.

Material folklore: Original Christmas cards of Edward J. Wood and family, designed by
himself with photographic work by John F. Atterton, Cardston photographer, the card
for 1932. Courtesy Dr. V. A. Wood, Cardston.

(houses, barns, fences, tools, toys, foods, and things stitched, woven, whittled, quilted, and braided); and, third, customary lore, things we make with our actions (dances, games, work processes, rituals, and community and family celebrations). I stress the word "make" in describing these folklore forms because the categories are dynamic rather than static; each telling of a well-known supernatural legend, each quilting of a familiar log-cabin pattern, each performance of a family birthday game is in every instance a new act of creation that speaks to us from both the past and the present—a point I will return to later. The materials of folklore can be studied from a number of theoretical perspectives—comparative, artistic, psychological, sociological and historical. My concern here is primarily with the historical, with the attempt to use folklore as a means of getting at our past and especially at our perceptions of it.

In the attempt to uncover the past, the efforts of the folklorist and the historian often parallel each other closely. For example, in a recent article on early twentieth-century farming customs in the mountain West, I described harvesting practices as follows:

> In August the grain would ripen and the harvest would begin. In some instances, the grain would be cut with a binder, a machine that cut the grain stocks, tied them into bundles and left them in the field, where they were bunched into shocks, heads leaning together, butts out. The bundles would later be pitched onto a wagon, brought to the farmyard and stacked. More commonly, the wheat was cut by a header, a machine which cut the grain stocks and dumped them loose into a specially built wagon called a header box. These wagons were then driven into the farmyard where, again, the wheat was pitched and stacked. When the wheat had all been cut and stacked, a threshing machine was brought onto the farm. The grain stocks were pitched into the machine, which separated the grain kernels from the grain stocks and heads. The stocks were stacked again as straw to be used later for bedding for cattle or for filling mattresses and ticks. The grain was sewed in sacks and stored in the granary.[2]

In their community history, *The Founding of Cardston and Vicinity*, Jane Eliza Woolf Bates and Zina Alberta Woolf Hickman describe harvest practices of the first Mormon settlers in Canada:

> When ripened, the grain was cut, some with sickle and some with cradle. The threshing was done by flail or by horses tramping it out. The flail

was an implement consisting of a wooden bar—the swingle—hinged or tied to a handle. When the wind was right the swingle was used by the strong arm of a man for beating the grain as it was lifted up by another, with a shovel, who gently tossed it to the wind, which blew almost continuously. When the wheat fell to the canvass on the ground, the wind blew the chaff away. Women often helped to gather the grain in milk pans with which the children supplied them. How they all worked while the wind lasted! For threshing with a horse, a big work mare was used, often with a colt following. A man stood in the center turning the grain over with a pitchfork. A child rode the animal around and around, trampling out the grain. The straw was pitched aside in a little stack and fresh grain replaced. So it went on until all the threshing was done. All the grain was winnowed over canvas by the wind.[3]

My description of mountain West harvesting was published in a folklore journal, the Bates and Hickman description in an historical work; but either description could have been published in either place because the aims were the same—to depict customary harvest practices of the past. Indeed, the rich descriptions in the Bates and Hickman book of material and customary practices—building techniques and designs, house decoration, quilting bees, Christmas parties, recreations and weddings—demonstrate that local and community histories can provide excellent data for folkloristic analysis. Listen, for example, to this description of making Christmas gifts:

At appointed times they met at Aunt Zina's to make Christmas stockings of mosquito netting elaborately finished by needle with red or green yarn. There was corn to be popped and strung for tree-trimming as well as colored-paper chains. There were old hand-knitted socks to be unravelled and wound into firm round balls for the boys. Each ball was marked like the sections of an orange, and stitched with fine chain stitching in varied colors of brown, yellow, and red. Well dressed rag dolls were made for the small girls. Pretty work bags, aprons or fancy pin-cushions were made for the teen-agers. The men, who had already turned out homemade furniture lent a hand at making doll beds and cradles, small tables and stools.... Socks were knit for husbands and sons. O. LeGrand Robinson officiated as a well disguised Santa Claus.[4]

In other endeavors, the efforts of folklorist and historian do not parallel each other quite so closely. This is particularly true in the study of what we call oral history, stories people tell about the past. I say "call" oral history because, while I am realist enough to know I cannot change established usage, in this paper at least I would like to broaden the definition of that term. Folklorists had been collecting and studying oral history for at least a hundred years before Allan Nevins set up the oral history program at Columbia University in the 1930s[5] and thus set the course many historians in subsequent years were to follow with increasing enthusiasm. If what these scholars study is oral history, what, then, have folklorists been studying all these years? Well, perhaps they have been studying another kind of oral history.

To avoid confusion, I would suggest the use of the terms "personal history" and "folk history"—both of them oral. Personal history comprises accounts of historical events collected from people who observed or participated in the events they describe. Folk history, on the other hand, is based not on individual memory but on the collective memory of a particular group of people, that is, the folk. It is simply a view of the past that circulates within a community by word of mouth. It comprises accounts of earlier events, collected from people who learned the stories from others and who did not themselves observe or participate in the events they describe.

In the main, personal history has been the domain of the historian; folk history the domain of the folklorist. That remains true today, though folklorists have in recent years been paying more and more attention to personal experience narratives. Because they have looked at these narratives comparatively—that is, they have looked elsewhere for analogues or parallels to the stories and for parallel functions in different stories—and because they are interested as much in the *process* of story telling as they are in the events recounted, folklorists have gained at least two major insights that should influence the ways in which we interpret the narratives that individuals tell about their past.

First, what we know from looking at a lot of different stories is that people shape the telling of *actual* events according to the narrative patterns available to them. My mother wondered aloud not long ago why so many recently returned Mormon missionaries, who had had such a variety of different experiences, all seemed to give the same return home address when they reported their completed missions to their local congregations. What she had perceived is that the return-home address is a traditional form into which the missionary must fit his personal experiences, dropping and embellishing, and perhaps even adding, details to fit the demands of the form. What is true of Mormon missionaries is true of the rest of us as well. As we attempt to pass on knowledge of certain recurring human situations through the spoken word—immigration to a new homeland, courtship, the loss of family fortune, the death of a loved one, and so on—we tend to develop structured narrative patterns, or molds, that give shape and meaning to the stories we tell about these experiences. As a result, narratives recounting any of these events might, like the missionary stories, all tend to sound alike.

As we study the history of Mormons in Canada, therefore, we ought to work carefully through the personal histories already recorded, identify those recurrent situations in the Canadian Mormon experience around which recurrent narrative patterns have developed—the migration, the establishment of homesteads, struggles with polygamy, struggles with the natural environment, struggles over irrigation waters, and so on—and then show how available narrative structures might have shaped people's perception of the past as well as the telling of individual stories about that past, causing narrators of their own experiences at times to sacrifice historical accuracy to the demands of narrative form.

A second insight we gain from studying personal histories from a folkloristic perspective is a clearer understanding that the narratives one tells about his or her past are almost always projections of the narrator's own personality and needs in the present moment. Those Canadian Mormons who have told or will tell their stories to recorders of personal history will have shaped their stories of the past to reflect the world they want to remember and to meet their own personal needs.[6] We should certainly not pass these stories by in our attempts to reconstruct the history of the Mormons in Canada—they provide an extremely valuable resource—but we should use them with greater caution than is sometimes the case, remembering that many of them will tell us more about the narrators than about the events described.

If folklorists have shown increasing interest in personal history, most historians have remained singularly uninterested in folk history—primarily because folk narratives, unlike personal narratives, are not firsthand accounts and because they are constantly changed as they are passed from person to person. These narratives, therefore, are often thought to contain little reliable data, even though they might originally have been based on actual historical happenings. This view has caused many scholars to ignore material that would have enriched their research and provided them with data not always available from other sources. It is to be hoped that those studying Mormons in Canada will not make the same error.

It is difficult to discuss Canadian Mormon folk narratives and the contributions they could make to the study of Canadian church history because so few of the stories have been collected. The thin trickle of Canadian material that has made its way into the BYU Folklore Archive suggests that at least three kinds of narratives have been told in Canada.

Stories belonging to the first group of narratives have primarily to do with the natural environment Mormons encountered when they migrated to Canada. On the surface, at least, these stories were probably never intended to be taken too seriously, as the following examples should illustrate:

The land in Alberta is so flat that you can see for forty miles if you stand on a sardine can.

They say that in Southern Alberta the wells are so deep and the water is so hard that an iron magnet is needed to draw it to the surface.

Often in winter the freeze would come so fast that whole herds of cattle would freeze solid and remain that way until they thawed out in the spring and came home.

Some say that the springs are so cold the farmers have to plow the ground using sharp-shod horses to keep from slipping on the ice.

One time it got so hot where I lived that a man saw a dog chasing a coyote and they were both walking.

In summer the wind blew so hard and the dust was so thick that sometimes you could see gophers digging their burrows fifteen feet in the air.

I remember when the wind blew so hard that a man who fenced his property in Alberta one night woke up to find it one mile into Saskatchewan the next morning.

Once when the wind quit blowing the telephone poles all fell down.

A man came home late and flung his saddle across the fence post. A chinook came during the night and the next morning he couldn't find his saddle. Finally he spotted it on top of a telephone pole.

Almost every year this same phenomenon occurs in Cardston. One side of Main Street will be 20 degrees below zero, while the other side of the street is 40 degrees above zero. It is easy to tell which side of the street had the Chinook.[7]

The second cycle of stories, only slightly more serious, tells of strange things that have occurred in LDS Canadian wards. For example:

There was this old farmer in Magrath, and he had lost his cow. He decided to ask the bishop to announce it in church and ask if anyone saw it to let him know. They used to do things like that all the time up in those little farm towns; but anyway, the farmer was hard of hearing and didn't hear the bishop announce about this cow, and a little later in the meeting the bishop stood up to tell about a woman who was going to sing, and in the middle of the introduction this old half-deaf man stood up and said, "If it'll help, she's got a big black spot on her back and a frozen teat."[8]

Another example:

There was this woman in our ward—her name is Hope—in Raymond, and she used to be a good singer. Well, she was pregnant (about 8 months worth), and I remember one time she was leading the singing, and we were singing "We Thank Thee, Oh God, for a Prophet"; and you remember the words, where it says, "There is hope smiling brightly before us, for we know that deliverance is nigh." Boy, did the congregation fall apart.[9]

Should people from Magrath or Raymond feel that these stories impugn the character of their wards, they might take comfort from the following story, collected in Arizona and sworn to have taken place in a local ward there:

Old man Hawkins lost a cow. He was really concerned about getting her back, so he asked his son, Bishop Hawkins, to announce his loss at church that day so that anyone seeing his cow might let him know of its whereabouts. His son promised to make the announcement. Sacrament meeting began and the bishop made the announcements, including the one about the lost cow, and then the service commenced. Now the old man was nearly totally deaf, and so he didn't hear the announcements. He fidgeted through the opening song, the prayer, and the sacrament, thinking that his son had forgotten to tell about his cow. After the sacrament, the bishop arose to announce a special musical number, a solo by Gloria Hawkins—his daughter. As the bishop sat down, the accompanist began the introduction, and the soloist arose, unseen by the old man, who decided that his son had just made the announcement about the lost cow. Thinking he would help matters by furnishing a good description of the cow, the old man arose and loudly declared, "She's got one horn knocked off and all the hair scraped off her belly but, ahhh, she's a fine one," then sat down. The congregation sought to contain their laughter while the stunned soloist sat down in tears.[10]

And the pregnant chorister, Hope, has appeared before wards from Canada to Mexico. Maybe she once did live in Raymond, but if so, she has since then been one of the best traveled and most frequently pregnant women in the church.

The third group of stories deals with much more serious subjects. As one would expect, the temple in Cardston has inspired a number of these narratives, just as have temples everywhere throughout the church. For example:

One day President E.J. Wood [first president of the temple] was doing temple work. He was assisting at the veil, and while laboring, he was confronted by Apostle Melvin J. Ballard. President Wood had not been informed that Brother Ballard was visiting the temple. The two brethren went off to the side for a while and talked, and when finished, Brother Ballard disappeared behind the veil. All this took place about three o'clock in the afternoon on July 30. When President Wood arose the next morning, he was handed a telegram telling him that Apostle Ballard had died the day before at three o'clock.[11]

The saints in Canada seem also to have circulated a substantial number of stories about the Three Nephites, those ancient *Book of Mormon* disciples of Christ who were granted the privilege of remaining on earth until the Savior's second coming and who help the Saints in times of distress.[12] The following stories are typical:

[My grandfather, from Hillspring,] had been called to administer to a sick person just across the gully, across the deep canyon. And he and his oldest boy started out in the buggy. And as they started out the fog came in, and they couldn't see where they were going at all. In fact, my grandfather had stopped, and he was debating whether to come back when three men appeared and came right up to them and helped them right across the gully, kept them on the trail, through the canyon, through the mountain pass and to the other side. And as he turned to thank them, they were gone, completely gone.[13]

Mrs. Card lived in Southern Alberta when she was a small girl. She had to walk quite a ways to go home. And one night she was very frightened, and it was dark, and so she stopped in a grocery store and was gonna call her mother and tell her to come and get her and pick her up. And nobody answered the phone. And she had to go home, so she says that right there in the phone booth she just kind of said a little prayer that somebody'd help, you know, guide her home, and so she went outside, and as she walked out the door, a man walked in front of her. And he was a stranger in town, except she just felt really easy about it, very much at ease. And so she followed him, and he walked the exact route that she went home, so she just followed him all the way.[14]

In other stories, the Nephites comfort a woman who has just had a baby, heal a sick child, prepare the Indians for the gospel, and rescue missionaries from an assortment of disasters.[15]

In addition to these narratives, there must surely exist in the memories of Canadian Mormons numerous stories that also develop those themes noted earlier—migration, settlement, struggles with the environment, struggles with polygamy—stories that reveal the joys, sorrows, hopes and anxieties of the church members in Canada. But for the most part, they have not been collected. Let us hope that a new generation of scholars will remedy that situation.

It is certainly true that because they are constantly changing, such stories are not usually reliable indicators of "what really happened" in the past, but it is equally true that they will give us a good picture of how people feel or have felt about what really happened. We turn to the stories, therefore, not to discover the ledger book truths of particular events but to fathom the truths of the human heart and mind. The stories mirror a group's beliefs and embody its values and world view, and they capture those thoughts and feelings that move people to action—thoughts and feelings that, like the actions they inspire, are also historical facts.

The narratives capture what is of central concern to a group, for the simple reason that people tell stories about those things that interest them most or are most important to them. Because folk narratives are oral, depending on the spoken word for their survival, and because those that fail broadly to appeal to members of a particular social group will simply not continue to be told, they serve as a kind of barometer for the main concerns, values, attitudes and stresses of the group. Consider again the stories I have just related.

The tall tales about the forces of nature are, on second glance, really not so tall after all. Those who have endured the scorching heat, the chilling cold, and the winds and storms of the prairies know that the stories exaggerate reality only slightly. The Bates and Hickman book I referred to above gives dramatic and frightening accounts of Alberta winters, with their chilling temperatures and life-threatening blizzards, winters only a little less severe than those depicted in the tall tales. In describing chinook winds, Bates and Hickman quote the diary of Johnathan Layne:

> Chinook wind began. Thermometer fourteen below when it started. Forty-five above twelve hours after it started. Snow eight inches deep was all gone in two days.... Doors open all day and flies buzzing around as in summer.... On the 26th [three days after the wind began] the boys played baseball in their shirt sleeves.[16]

From a description like that, it is not really far to the following folk narratives about chinooks:

> Whenever a chinook sprang up and caught the people off guard, they would have to quickly change their back sleigh runners to wheels and gallup their horses to keep even the front runners ahead of the melting snow.[17]
>
> A man took his wife to the doctor. When he left home the reins were frozen stiff; by the time they got to town the sleigh was on dry ground, and when they got back the dog had died of thirst.[18]

The great value of these stories to the people who tell them is that by exaggerating reality they mitigate it, providing tellers and audiences alike the means to endure through laughter the threatening forces of nature that constantly surround them.

The stories, of course, are not just Canadian narratives but are actually part of that rich body of humor—songs, tales and anecdotes—that speak eloquently of the resilience of the human spirit and of the toughness of people who can laugh at circumstances that by all rights should undo them. That Canadian Mormons have carried on this proud tradition is, in my judgment, a historical fact worth knowing.

The stories about the lost cow and the pregnant chorister belong to that large store of humorous anecdotes that Mormons tell about the circumstances of their social and ecclesiastical lives.[19] Again, it seems worth knowing that church members in Canada are part of this humane tradition and that, no matter how serious life might have been, or might still be, they have shared with fellow Mormons elsewhere the saving grace of being able to laugh not only at the external forces that threaten them but also at themselves.

The stories of President Wood and the temple and of the Three Nephites surely are only a weak echo from the rich vein of religious lore shared and circulated by Mormons in Canada. The BYU Folklore Archive contains volumes of these kinds of stories, collected primarily in the United States. There is no reason to believe that the stories do not exist in Canada as well. These narratives, ranging broadly over almost all Mormon precepts and practices, help us grasp something of the faith of those who tell and believe them—a faith in a God who loves His children and who, if they remain obedient, will fight their battles and keep them from harm. The intensity of faith revealed by these stories is also a fact worth knowing in any attempt to understand the motivating forces in the lives of Canadian Mormons.

Another reason why these stories provide such an excellent measure of public sentiment is that they are constantly changing, constantly being recreated—the very circumstance that causes some scholars to look at them askance. What is important for us to observe is that the changes do not occur randomly but are dictated by cultural determinants. Every group of people will have what I have called a *value center*,[20] a common core of shared beliefs. It is this value center that determines the changes that occur in narratives. Whether a story is based on an actual event, is a migratory tale borrowed from another group, or is simply a product of fancy, the story will be changed as it is passed from person to person, usually unconsciously, to conform to the group's value center, to express the people's interests and to meet their needs.

As already noted, individuals relating their personal histories will often recreate the past in terms meaningful to them in the present. With folk history, the same process occurs, but this time it is the larger group that makes the changes, as stories circulate among them in response to group needs and beliefs.

The way this process works is illustrated well by the experience of a young man who served a Mormon proselytizing mission in Canada. While on his mission, he and his companion had a frightening experience, which he interpreted as an encounter with an evil spirit. He recorded the experience in his journal and related it to a few close friends. Three years later, now a member of a Brigham Young University folklore class, he decided to do a class project on the folklore of his mission field and began collecting stories from recently returned missionaries. Much to his surprise, he collected versions of his own experience from informants who did not know that he was the missionary in the story. He was startled to discover that in some accounts he and his companion, who had done nothing wrong, had in the repeated telling of the story been converted into rule-breaking missionaries who, because of their misconduct, had become subject to the power of evil. In just three years, then, the story had moved far afield from the actual experience on which it was based.[21]

As important as the original account of this experience might be in any effort to understand missionary life, the orally circulating versions are still more important because they contain beliefs that the missionary storytellers, influenced by their value center, have infused into the story—in this instance the belief that disobedient missionaries subject themselves to the power of Satan. The changes made in the story reflect and reinforce the belief, and turn the story into a cautionary tale that can serve to warn other missionaries of what might happen to them if they too stray from the path of righteousness. And the changes made in the story provide the scholar with a valuable insight into the workings of the missionary mind.

What is true of this missionary story will be true of folk historical narratives in general; they will be changed as they are told and retold. And because they will be changed, the stories, as historians correctly point out and as I have suggested, will not provide reliable data about what actually happened in the past. But they will give an excellent view of what the people think happened. And since people are moved to action not by actual reality but by their perception of it, not by what really took place but by what they think took place, then studying folk historical narratives, the people's history, should be an important endeavor.

This is particularly true with volatile issues such as polygamy. One could read through Bates's and Hickman's history of Cardston and never get the slightest hint that the Mormon Church had ever practised polygamy, or that many of the first Mormon settlers in Canada were polygamists—indeed, had come to Canada because they were polygamists. Because of the reluctance to talk about polygamy in print or in official circles, what many Canadian Mormons know about polygamy today they probably know from their folk history, from the stories that have been passed down in their families and communities. And these stories, like the missionary-and-the-evil-spirit account, will often have been changed to express the attitudes and values of the narrators. Consider the following polygamy story, collected in Utah but surely similar to stories known in Canada as well:

> Mother used to tell this story about a prominent family who lived in Ephraim. The first wife of this fella had quite a few children. She was heavy set and not too attractive. Later her husband married a younger,

more attractive girl. Now their house was set up in such a way that to get to the kitchen you had to go through the bedroom. One day the first wife had to pass through the bedroom, and she was carrying some slop for the pigs. As she passed by the bed, her husband threw back the covers, gave his second wife a nice swat and said to the first wife, "See, Mary Jane, what a nice shape she has." Well, it made the first wife so mad that she threw the pig slop on both of them.[22]

In stories like this, and there are a lot of them, the first wife usually appears in a favorable light, the second wife as an interloper, and the husband as a callous individual with little regard for his first wife's feelings; the first wife, in contrast to what often happened, usually emerges victorious. Almost all these stories are told by women. What they reflect and reinforce are not the historical realities of polygamy but rather the perceptions and feelings of contemporary Mormon women (or at least some contemporary Mormon women) towards that peculiar institution. Many of these women identify with the first wife in the stories, applaud her way of handling a problem they themselves would not want to live with, and take comfort that even "back then" the demands of poetic justice were sometimes met. Once again, it is the oral narrative, altered to reflect present-day perceptions, that helps us understand the feelings of contemporary Mormon women about polygamy and sometimes, as a result, about the church.

What does the folklore of Canadian Mormons reveal about their perceptions of polygamy and its role in the Mormon settlements? No one can say for sure. Once again, we have insufficient data. Therefore, the first tasks for Canadian Mormon scholars interested in folklore and research in Canadian Mormon social life and history should be to collect, systematize and archive the materials on which solid studies can be based. They should pick up their tape recorders and head to the field (even though that field might be no farther than the person sitting across the room), pick up their cameras and document their family and community events and their objects of material culture,[23] and read with new eyes the journals and records of their ancestors.

Once they have gathered and carefully analyzed the data, these researchers can then come to a better understanding of what it was like to be a Canadian Mormon and what it is like to be one today; they can understand more fully which values have motivated Canadian Mormons in both the past and the present; they can understand better the coping mechanisms that made, and still make, life possible in the face of extreme hardship; and they can gain a little better feeling for a faith that can move not only mountains but also can settle and subdue the northern prairies. Folklore might not give us a complete picture of the Canadian Mormon experience, but we will certainly not get an accurate picture without it.

NOTES

1. The standard work for Mormon folklore remains Austin E. and Alta S. Fife, *Saints of Sage and Saddle: Folklore Among the Mormons* (Bloomington: Indiana University Press, 1956). For more recent surveys, see William A. Wilson, "The paradox of Mormon folklore," *Brigham Young University Studies*, 17 (1976), pp. 40-58, and "Mormon Folklore," in *Handbook of American Folklore*, ed., Richard M. Dorson (Bloomington: Indiana University Press, 1983), pp. 155-61. See also William A. Wilson, "A bibliography of studies in Mormon folklore," *Utah Historical Quarterly*, 44 (1976), pp. 389-94.

2. William A. Wilson, "We did everything together: Farming customs of the mountainwest," *Northwest Folklore*, 4 (1985), pp. 24-25.

3. Jane Eliza Woolf Bates and Zina Alberta Woolf Hickman, *Founding of Cardston and Vicinity* (privately printed by William L. Woolf, 1960), pp. 23-24.

4. Ibid., p. 52.

5. See Allan Nevins, *The Gateway to History* (Boston, 1938).

6. See Rowland W. Rider, *Sixshooters and Sagebrush: Cowboy Stories of the Southwest*, compiled by Deirdre Paulsen (Provo, Utah: Brigham Young University Press, 1979), and the conceptualization expressed by William A. Wilson, "Foreword," in ibid., pp. x-xii.

7. The first nine of these items were collected by Gail LeBaron in 1965; the tenth item was collected by Debra Steed in 1971. The items are in the Tall Tale Collection, 5.4.0 and 5.5.0, Brigham Young University Folklore Archive.

8. Collected by Jerilyn Wakefield, "On the Lighter Side of the Mormons," 1969, Item 7, Focused MS #430, Brigham Young University Folklore Archive.

9. Ibid., Item 9.

10. Collected by Dixie Pearce, "Pearce Family Folklore," 1980, Item 7, Focused MS #87, Brigham Young University Folklore Archive. The names of characters in this story have been changed.

11. Collected by Delena F. Ford, n.d., Mormon Religious Legend Collection, #1.1.2.6.20.1, Brigham Young University Folklore Archive.

12. See Hector Lee, *The Three Nephites: The Substance and Significance of the Legend in Folklore*, University of New Mexico Publications in Language and Literature, no. 2 (Albuquerque: University of New Mexico Press, 1949).

13. Collected by C. Janean McPolin, 1969, Three Nephites Collection, #1.3.0.0.91, Brigham Young University Folklore Archive.

14. Collected by Anita Abbott, 1970, Three Nephites Collection, #1.3.1.1.20, Brigham Young University Folklore Archive.

15. Three Nephites Collection, #1.3.2.1.2.1, #1.3.2.1.98, #1.3.4.2.34, #1.3.2.2.5, #1.3.4.2.25, #1.3.1.1.22, #1.3.5.3.4, #1.3.1.28, Brigham Young University Folklore Archive.

16. Bates and Hickman, p. 53.

17. Collected by Gail LeBaron, 1965, Tall Tale Collection, #5.5.0.16.2.

18. Ibid., #5.5.0.18.1.

19. See William A. Wilson, "The seriousness of Mormon humor," *Sunstone*, 10, no. 1 (1985), pp. 6-13.

20. William A. Wilson, "Folklore and history: Fact amid the legends," *Utah Historical Quarterly*, 41 (1973), pp. 48-49.

21. Gregory Vernon, "Missionary Stories," 1968, Focused MS #427, Brigham Young University Folklore Archive.

22. Collected by Peggy Hansen, "Polygamy Stories," 1971, Item 24, Focused MS Collection #253.

23. The beginning collector might find useful William A. Wilson, "Documenting Folklore," in *Folk Groups and Folk Genres: An Introduction*, ed., Elliott Oring (Logan: Utah State University Press, 1986), pp. 225-54. More detailed directions can be found in Edward D. Ives, *The Tape-Recorded Interview: A Manual for Fieldworkers in Folklore and Oral History* (Knoxville: The University of Tennessee Press, 1980), and Bruce Jackson, *Fieldwork* (Urbana and Chicago: University of Illinois Press, 1987).

III | THE MORMON FAMILY IN HISTORICAL PERSPECTIVE

THE MORMON FAMILY was almost an unknown phenomenon in Canadian society, except for its association with polygamy by the press even before the Mormon settlers arrived and more intensively thereafter (as McCue and H. Palmer show in their essays). Yet despite the publicity, there is no known study of the Canadian Mormon family until 1948. In that year, Enid Charles, in her study of changing family size in Canada (based on the 1941 Census) wrote, "A first glance at Mormon families proved so interesting that the scope of the investigation was extended outside limits previously laid down."[1] She classified Mormons as a "local culture type," along with Mennonites, Doukhobors, Indians and Eskimos, Chinese and Japanese, Jews and Greek Orthodox. In her limited treatment of these groups, Canadian Mormon women, nearly all born in the United States and all English speaking, stood out for the consistency of their high fertility. Whatever their place of residence—rural, town or city, or their level of education—all Alberta Mormon women 45 to 54 years of age had, on average, families of five or six children.

While the families of numerous other peoples in Canada have been studied,[2] the Canadian Mormon family remains insufficiently studied.[3] Some scholars continue to perpetuate nineteenth-century stereotypes that are being challenged by scholarship in the United States.[4]

In the 1880s, when the Mormon experiment with plural marriage was rapidly winding down due to pressures both inside and outside the church, Canada and Mexico were havens for Mormons seeking refuge. While some research has been done on the Mormon family in Mexico,[5] there was no published work, until 1985, on the Canadian Mormon family associating it with the larger North American picture.[6]

To round out this scholarship, we need to study the Canadian and Mexican experiences with Mormon polygamy in a comparative way. Jessie Embry, using oral history and documentary sources, compares Mormon polygamy in Canada, the United States and Mexico, concluding that the "impact of law and culture" shaped the lives of Mormon people more than their Utah experience with polygamy. Hardy, after making a detailed comparison of the legal antecedents in Mexico and Canada of legislation relating to bigamy and polygamy, traces the Mormon experience with these laws in the two countries. These two essays make a unique contribution to our knowledge of Mormon marriage and families in the final years of Mormon polygamy. In Canada, Mormon conformity to Canadian laws had from the beginning of settlement led to monogamous living. One consequence of legal pressure by Canadian and American authorities was the emergence of an adaptive arrangement for plural families to finish their family-life cycle by existing as "legal" entities, with one family in Canada, and another in the United States.

In the previous section, considerable attention was given to the Mormon role of leadership in colonizing the Canadian West, especially the leadership of pioneer males. The third essay in this section deals exclusively with women's roles in the settlement process. Mormon women were major contributors to the creation of a distinctive Mormon ethnoreligious culture in southwestern Alberta. In this account of the everyday life and concerns of pioneer Mormon women in Canada, one sees their patterns of adaptation to making new homes on the Canadian prairies, while at the same time catching a glimpse of the inner motivations of these women displaced from their Utah homeland.

NOTES
1. Enid Charles, *The Changing Size of the Family in Canada, Census Monograph No. 1, Eighth Census of Canada, 1941* (Ottawa: Edmond Cloutier, King's Printer, 1948), pp. 59 and 63-92, quotation on p. 90.
2. K. Ishwaran, ed., *The Canadian Family* (Toronto: Gage, 1983).
3. Two doctoral studies have been done on the Mormon family by scholars working in Canada. Helen Colbert, an American scholar, using Mormon archival materials in the United States for data, wrote, "Natural Fertility among Monogamous and Polygamous Families: A Historical Demographic Study" (doctoral dissertation, University of Alberta, 1979). The only study relating to contemporary Mormon families is by Gisela Demharter, a specialist in

Mormon history and culture in the American Studies program of the University of Munich, West Germany, who has written a research report, "Socialization of girls among Mormons in southern Alberta," *Journal of the Society for Canadian Studies* [*Zeitschrift der Gesellshaft für Kanada-Studien*], no. 2 (1985). Her doctoral dissertation, of the same title, was completed in 1987.

4. A striking example is a nineteenth-century cartoon, "Brigham Young's Mormon family goes to church," in K. Ishwaran, "The Family," in Michael Rosenberg, William B. Shaffir et al., eds., *An Introduction to Sociology* (Toronto: Methuen, 1983), pp. 236-37. Mormon marriage and family patterns in the United States have been studied intensively by many Mormon and non-Mormon scholars working from a variety of disciplinary perspectives. Among these are Kimball Young, *Isn't One Wife Enough?* (New York: Henry Holt, 1954); Stanley B. Ivins, "Notes on Mormon Polygamy," in Marvin S. Hill and James B. Allen, eds., *Mormonism and American Culture* (New York: Harper & Row, 1972), pp. 101-11; Leonard J. Arrington and Davis Bitton, "Marriage and Family Patterns," in *The Mormon Experience: A History of the Latter-day Saints* (New York: Random House, 1980), pp. 185-205; Klaus J. Hansen, "Changing Perspectives on Sexuality and Marriage," in *Mormonism and the American Experience* (Chicago: University of Chicago Press, 1981), pp. 147-78; Thomas G. Alexander, "Recurrent encounters with plural marriage," in *Mormonism in Transition: A History of the Latter-day Saints, 1890-1930* (Urbana: University of Illinois Press, 1986), pp. 60-73; Jessie Embry, *Mormon Polygamous Families: Life in the Principle* (Salt Lake City: University of Utah Press, 1987); and Richard S. van Wagoner, *Mormon Polygamy: A History* (Salt Lake City: Signature Books, 1986).

Three recent works represent anthropology, Freudian social history, and sociology, each using a comparative approach to examine Mormon marriage and family in relation to other nineteenth-century innovative groups concerned with creating distinctive societies within the United States: Lawrence Foster, *Religion and Sexuality: Three American Communal Experiments of the Nineteenth Century* (New York: Oxford University Press, 1981); Louis J. Kern, *An Ordered Love: Sex Roles and Sexuality in Victorian Utopias — The Shakers, the Mormons, and the Oneida Community* (Chapel Hill: University of North Carolina Press, 1981); William M. Kephart, *Extraordinary Groups: The Sociology of Unconventional Life-Styles*, 2nd edition (New York: St. Martin's Press, 1982).

5. Nelle Spilsbury Hatch and B. Carmon Hardy, *Stalwarts South of the Border* (Anaheim, California: Shumway Family History Publishing Co., 1985); F. Lamond Tullis, *Mormons in Mexico: The Dynamics of Faith and Culture* (Logan, Utah: Utah State University Press, 1987), pp. 51-59 and 92-104.

6. Jessie L. Embry, "Exiles for the principle: LDS polygamy in Canada," *Dialogue: A Journal of Mormon Thought*, 18 (Fall 1985), pp. 108-16.

9 "Two Legal Wives"

Mormon Polygamy In Canada, the United States and Mexico

JESSIE L. EMBRY

LIKE THE CHRISTIAN SAINTS after the death of Christ, the members of the Church of Jesus Christ of Latter-day Saints felt that they were "persecuted for righteousness's sake." One of their unique practices that led to this "persecution" was polygamy. As George Q. Cannon explained to the Saints in Canada, "Can you see that the work of God has been retarded by the persecution we have received? 800 of us have been victims of unjust laws. The rising generation have had embedded in them the truth of the persecution."[1] To avoid these "unjust laws," during the 1880s Mormons went on what they called "the underground" in Utah, moved outside the Utah territory to states where the federal laws against polygamy did not directly apply or to territories where the federal marshals assigned to Utah did not have jurisdiction, and sought refuge in Canada and Mexico.

On the surface, the underground in states and territories such as Arizona, Wyoming, Nevada and Idaho, and the settlements in Mexico and Canada, had certain similarities—polygamous families moved outside of Utah and then out of the United States to avoid being arrested by federal marshals. There were also marked differences, especially in how polygamy was practised and in the cultural impact. This essay will compare and contrast the Mormon settlements in the United States, Canada and Mexico.

When Orson Pratt preached the first public defense—and hence acknowledgement of polygamy—in 1852, he confirmed rumors that had followed the Mormons since Kirtland, Ohio. Although Joseph Smith did not record the revelation on plural marriage—now Section 132 of the

170

Doctrine and Covenants—until 1843, he married his first plural wife apparently as early as 1835. Although many nonmembers accused the Mormons of practising polygamy, the public announcement triggered even more negative reaction. Four years after the public announcement, the Republican platform called for the elimination of "the twin relics of barbarism"—slavery and polygamy.

Opponents of plural marriage petitioned Congress to pass laws, and, in 1862, the Morrill Act, introduced by Justin S. Morrill, a representative from Vermont, among other things, prohibited plural marriage in the territories. Although President Lincoln signed the bill, the nation was in the midst of the Civil War and he reportedly said, "You tell Brigham Young if he will leave me alone, I'll leave him alone."[2] After the Civil War, other bills were introduced, including the Cullom Bill (1870), which did not pass, and the Poland Act (1874). Despite these laws against polygamy, the Mormons continued to practise polygamy because they felt it was a religious practice protected by the First Amendment. George Reynolds, Brigham Young's private secretary, became a test case; in 1879 in *Reynolds* v. *United States* the Supreme Court ruled the Morrill Act constitutional. According to the court, "Laws are made for the government of actions, and while they cannot interfere with mere religious belief and opinion, they may with practice."[3]

Three United States presidents, Rutherford B. Hayes, James A. Garfield and Chester A. Arthur, spoke against the "barbarous system" of polygamy, and petitions against the practice flooded Congress during 1881-82. In response, Congress passed the Edmunds Act in 1882, actually a series of amendments to the Morrill Act. Because the Edmunds Act was not successful in controlling polygamy, in 1887 Congress passed what one historian has called the "hodge-podge Edmunds-Tucker Bill." The Cullom-Struble Bill, with even stricter measures, was debated in 1889, but the church helped to prevent its passage by promising to do away with polygamy.[4]

These pressures, despite the increased hardship, expense and suffering they cost, did not compel the abolition of polygamy. John Taylor and Wilford Woodruff, Brigham Young's successors, made public announcements affirming the continual practice of plural marriage. When the Edmunds Act provided for US marshals to arrest polygamists, church leaders as well as many of the members of the church went into hiding—on the "underground" as it was called—either to avoid arrest or to avoid testifying.

At first, polygamists hid in or near their homes. Edwin Nelson Austin, a surveyor and engineer in Liberty, Idaho, built a false room in the attic of the family home that was "just high enough for a man to stand in. He had a false partition put in that was just like the outer wall as near as he could make it."[5] When persecution intensified, sometimes one of the wives or the husband would move to another state or territory. Truman Call said that his father, John Holbrook, settled in Wyoming in 1889 because "they were polygamists. They came to Afton because the Wyoming governor said he wanted some good citizens in this end of the state. There were a lot of polygamists that came to Afton, Star Valley, about that time."[6] When Christopher Layton, a polygamous husband moved to Arizona in the 1880s, he remembered:

> Finally my wives and children agreed that, although they disliked very much to do without my presence, yet they would rather know that I was at liberty than to have me dodging the hounds of the laws, and under these conditions I accepted a call to preside over, and make a home for, Saints in Southern Arizona.[7]

Fear of arrest, however, did not end out of Utah. Edwin Austin lived in the Bear Lake, Idaho, area and still had to hide to avoid arrest. Convicted Mormon men in Arizona were imprisoned in territorial prisons or were sent to the federal penitentiary in Detroit.[8] In response to these arrests, in 1884, John Taylor, then church president, wrote to the stake presidents in Arizona, "Our counsel has been and is to obtain a place of refuge under a foreign government to which our people can flee when menaced in this land. [It is] better for parts of families to remove and go where they can live in peace than to be hauled to jail."[9] In 1885, John Taylor, his counselors, and some other members of the church explored the Mexican states of Sonora and Chihuahua for a settlement site.

At first, the sudden arrival of large numbers of Americans in Mexico alarmed Mexican officials who feared another Texas. On 9 April 1885, shortly after the Mormons began arriving in Chihuahua, the acting governor ordered them to leave within 15 days. When the Mormon leaders were unable to persuade him that they should be allowed to stay, two apostles, Moses Thatcher and Erastus Snow, met with officials in Mexico City and succeeded in persuading them to reverse the order. According to Helaman Pratt, the Mormon leaders talked with Secretary of Public Works Carlos Pacheco about polygamy, and he told them that they could bring their plural families to Mexico but asked that they do so quietly. Although there is no evidence that President Porfirio Diaz approved of the Mormons practising polygamy in Mexico, he must have known of their family practices. The

Mormons did not advertise the fact to the Mexican government, and, in fact, George Q. Cannon, a counselor in the church's First Presidency, might have told Anthony W. Ivins, a new stake president to the Mormon colonies in Mexico, to tell Diaz that the Mormons were not practising polygamy. Nevertheless, the Mormons in Colonia Juarez, Colonia Dublan, Colonia Diaz and the mountain colonies lived openly with their plural families.[10]

Therefore, although polygamy was against the law in Mexico, Diaz did not pass statutes criminalizing the practice as the United States had done. Instead, he encouraged the Mormons to settle in the country. According to B. Carmon Hardy, a historian of Mormon polygamy in Mexico, Diaz

> took a far more lackadaisical view of laws relating to sexual relations than law enforcement officers...in the United States.... [He was] quite willing to subordinate whatever reservations [he] felt about the Mormon domestic manners to the more important goal of allowing industrious settlers to colonize vacant lands along the border.[11]

In 1886, Charles Card, then stake president in Cache Valley, planned to move to Mexico; however, John Taylor advised him to go to Canada because, as Taylor explained, "I have always found justice under the British flag."[12] The Mormons received a more reserved welcome in Canada than they did in Mexico. When the Mormons first arrived in Alberta, they were not sure if the Canadian federal government would allow them to bring their plural families, so at first husbands came with only one wife. The federal government informed the Mormon leaders that the Saints would be allowed to settle only if they agreed to live monogamously in Canada.

To ensure that the Mormons obeyed the law, the federal government took steps in 1890 to strengthen their Criminal Code. The new code specifically prohibited "what among the persons commonly called Mormons is known as spiritual or plural marriage," and made cohabitation a misdemeanor punishable by five years in prison—the former penalty had been two. Although it was easier to prove cohabitation than bigamy, the bigamy law was also stiffened:

> Every one who, being married, marries any other person during the life of the former husband or wife, whether the second marriage takes place in Canada or elsewhere, and every male person who, in Canada, simultaneously, or on the same day, marries more than one woman, is guilty of felony and liable to seven years' imprisonment."[13]

Original 1887 Mormon pioneers of Cardston, c.1900. First row: younger children of pioneers. Second row, l-r: J. W. Woolf, J. A. Hammer, S. Matkin, J. A. Woolf, C. O. Card, H. L. Hinman, J. Anderson, L. Hinman. Third Row, l-r: unknown, Mrs. R. Ibey, Mrs. J. A. Hammer, Mrs. S. Williams, Mrs. S. Matkin, Mrs. J. A. Woolf, Mrs. C. O. Card, Mrs. S. B. Daines, Mrs. J. Anderson, Mrs. O. E. Bates, O. E. Bates. Fourth row: older children of the pioneers. NA 114-15 Glenbow Archives.

Sir John Thompson from Nova Scotia, later a prime minister of Canada, argued that the law was necessary. "I think it will be much more prudent that legislation should be adopted at once in anticipation of the offence if there is any probability of its introduction rather than we should wait until it has become established in Canada." Without further debate on this section, the law was passed after its third reading.[14]

The official responses in the United States, Canada and Mexico are, not surprisingly, directly correlated to the number of new marriages performed in the three countries. Plural marriages ended officially in the Mormon Church just three years after the Mormons settled Canada, although authorized plural marriages continued to be contracted secretly for the next 14 years. Wilford Woodruff, then president of the church, issued the Manifesto in 1890, which stated he would encourage members to enter no new marriages "contrary to the laws of the land." Many church leaders saw this press release, later canonized, as an attempt to relieve some of the

The widows of Charles Ora Card in 1923 in Cardston for dedication of the Temple, with descendants, kin and old-timer friends: Zina P. Young, Sarah J. Painter, and Lavinia C. Rigby. Montage and photo courtesy Marie C. Burnham, Edmonton.

pressures caused by the US laws, but not as an attempt to terminate authoritatively all new plural marriages. LDS General Authorities and specially appointed local leaders continued to perform polygamous marriages in Canada and Mexico, and even in the United States. Church leaders such as Stake President Anthony W. Ivins in Mexico and church apostles Matthias Cowley and John W. Taylor and others continued to perform plural marriages, which were accepted by the church until 1904, when Joseph F. Smith issued what historians have called the Second Manifesto, which stated that those continuing to marry plural wives or to perform those marriages would be disciplined by the church. Cowley was disfellowshipped and Taylor was excommunicated for the marriages they performed after the Second Manifesto.

Since Mexico did not take a firm stand against polygamy, more new marriages were performed there between 1890 and 1904. For example, a limited sample taken from family group sheets of families who were interviewed as part of the LDS Polygamy Oral History Project shows that of 85 polygamous marriages of Mormons living in Canada and 133 plural marriages of families residing in the United States, only 12% and 11% respectively were performed after 1890. Usually only one wife lived in Canada, and one in the United States, especially in the Canadian marriages. A plural husband therefore claimed one legal wife in the United States and one in Canada. In Mexico, however, one-half of the 76 polygamous marriages were performed after that date.[15]

The different emphasis on enforcing laws against polygamy also made a difference in the family arrangements in Canada, Mexico and the United States. The underground period forced some families in the United States to be separated temporarily. Although United States President Benjamin Harrison granted amnesty and pardon for polygamists who had not cohabited with their wives since 1 November 1890, and President Grover Cleveland broadened the amnesty proclamation, most church leaders and members continued their polygamous relationships and lived in some fear of being "vigorously prosecuted" by the law.[16]

Joseph F. Smith expressed the feelings of many church members when he testified before the Senate Committee on Privileges and Elections in 1904. The Committee, in addition to determining whether Reed Smoot, an apostle and monogamist, should be allowed to be seated in the Senate, also examined the structure of the Mormon Church and the practice of polygamy. When asked if he had obeyed the law and not lived with his plural wives, Joseph F. Smith replied that he preferred

> to meet the consequences of the law rather than abandon my children and their mothers; and I have cohabited with my wives—not openly, that is not in a manner that I thought would be offensive to my neighbors— but I have acknowledged them; I have visited them.... Since the admission of the state there has been a sentiment existing and prevalent in Utah that these old marriages would be in a measure condoned. They were not looked upon as offensive, as really violative of law; they were, in other words, regarded as existing fact, and if they saw any wrong in it they simply winked at it.[17]

Because of continued cohabitation, the underground did not end with the Manifesto. Georgina Bolette Critchlow Bickmore moved to Star Valley, Wyoming, with her mother, a second wife, during the 1890s. She remembered Afton, Wyoming, as still being "mostly made up of polygamous families" on the underground.[18] Those married after the Manifesto also took steps to avoid public knowledge of the marriages, although they still cohabited. Arthur Hart, for example, married his second wife, Vady Henderson, in 1903 in Preston, Idaho. Matthias Cowley, an apostle and Arthur's friend, performed the marriages. For the first few years of marriage, Vady lived in Farmington, Utah; but shortly after her first child was born, she moved back to Preston, where she lived with Ada, the first wife, long enough that the community recognized that Ada accepted Vady as a co-wife. Then Arthur provided separate homes for both wives. He visited each home regularly, changing residences every night. Children's needs and economic reasons, rather than pressure against polygamy, later changed the living arrangements. During the 1920s, Vady moved to Logan, Utah, so the children could attend the Utah State Agricultural College. During World War II, she moved again to Ogden to work in war-related industries;[19] however, Arthur did keep a low profile to avoid public attention. His son, Mark, explained that his father was asked to be the judge of the Fifth Judicial District in Idaho twice. "He could have taken the job and doubled his salary by taking it. Because of the fact that he was living in polygamy and other families were not..., it was sort of a delicate situation. So the Church leaders, including President Heber J. Grant, told him not to accept anything out of town." He was the prosecuting attorney in Preston, Idaho, for years.[20]

Other attempts were made to avoid public attention to these post-Manifesto marriages. In 1911, a committee of apostles, chaired by Francis M. Lyman, investigated plural marriages performed between 1890 and 1904. The committee determined that men in the United States who had married after 1890 should not be called to church positions where they would have to be sustained by the church membership.[21] Karl Skousen explained:

> My father was never given a position in the Church other than high priest group leader in the time that he lived in Arizona [after he left Mexico in 1912] as far as I know, even though he had been a member of the bishopric in Mexico. I suppose the Church wanted to keep him in the background. I think this was wise.[22]

In Mexico, polygamy was practised more openly. It continued to play a more important role in the Mormon colonies in Mexico after 1890 than it did in most US communities. Polygamy was the reason for going to a foreign country with a different language and culture; it, along with the other religious beliefs of the Mormon Church, held the people together. According to one contemporary nineteenth-century account, the practice of polygamy in the colonies was "almost universal" and "close to 100 percent of the people then living in Juarez Stake were so attached to this order that it was the very woof and warp of their domestic life and also the theme and central idea of community worship."[23]

In contrast, Latter-day Saints in Canada lived a de facto monogamy. Husbands usually lived with one wife in Canada, leaving their other wife or wives in the United States. Winnifred Newton Thomas's father brought her mother, the second wife, to Canada and left his first wife in Utah. She explained, "The ones [the plural husbands] that were here were okay because they only had one wife here. Then if they went down there [to the United States, usually Utah] and had a fling, that was up to them. They had two legal wives in two different countries."[24] Nearly half (43%) of the husbands lived with their second wives in Canada. Twenty percent brought their first wife, and 18% lived with a third wife in Canada. To date, only three men can be proved to have brought more than one wife to Canada: John Lye Gibb, Franklin Dewey Leavitt and Thomas Rowell Leavitt. Their wives lived in different communities. A grandson of John Lye Gibb told me that Gibb took his first wife, Sarah Phillips Smith, to Canada. His second wife, Hannah Simmons, followed on her own. Sarah lived in Magrath and Hannah lived in Stirling. As William L. Woolf, who grew up in Alberta, explained, "The Canadian government['s]…agreement was generally adhered to." Interviewed in 1972, he remembered "four to six" men who lived with more than one wife in Alberta.[25] Some husbands visited their wives in the United States at the time of the LDS General Conference in April and October. Others never returned to see the wives they left behind.

The comparative stability of life in Canada compared with the United States contrasted with the disruption caused by the revolution in Mexico. These differences have led to some discussions of whether the Canadian or Mexican settlements were more successful. A history of Cardston reported:

> As perspective clears our vision, we begin to see the greatness of our pioneer fathers, the sincerity of their lives, the depth of their colorful existence and the strength acquired through unity. We see the foresight of President John Taylor in advising settlement in Canada and justification for his faith in British justice. This is particularly true when we compare the treatment of the Saints in Canada with that of those who settled in Old Mexico where they were first granted special governmental favors and later driven from their homes. We see confidence and community strength inspired by Church leadership.[26]

Lawrence Lee, who studied the Mormons in Canada, pointed out, "While there were parallels between Mexican and Canadian organization, there were also notable contrasts. Without attempting a comparison, one can sum up the situation by saying that colonization in Mexico proved to be a qualified failure, while Canadian colonization was successful beyond expectations."[27] Even as early as 1890, John W. Taylor, according to the Cardston minutes, "Compared our situation with those in Mexico. Said we are much more comfortable. Wished the people to be satisfied here."[28]

Those in Mexico, however, were equally positive about their own experience. Ellice Marie Bentley LaBaron, who lived in Mexico and then moved to Canada, said:

> I was shocked when I came to Canada and heard some of the recriminations against polygamy. I believe that a different kind of people came to Canada. The ones that came up here as pioneers mostly brought their young wives and left their old wives in Utah. The children of those older wives felt like their mothers had been deserted. Nothing like that happened in Mexico. Mostly all the families went to Mexico together.[29]

Grant Ivins said, "If ever polygamy had an opportunity to function in a modern western community it had that opportunity in the Mormon colonies in Mexico." He went on to explain why.

> Fortified by deep religious conviction, centered around the doctrine of celestial marriage, members of the communities experienced relatively little marital conflict, no more than occurs in the average monogamous family. To those who took part in the practice, polygamy was definitely successful in Mexico.[30]

Many differences between the Mormon settlements in Mexico and those in Canada and the United States were not related to polygamy but to the more important elements of culture and government. In all countries, the Mormons made efforts to build bridges with their neighbors. One way was celebrating national holidays. Latter-day Saints throughout the intermountain West observed the Fourth of July with parades, patriotic speeches, dances and ball games. Zina Patterson Dunford remembered that in Bloomington, Idaho, a brass band played, the children gathered at daylight to see the flag raised and a parade featured a Goddess of Liberty.[31] Lucy Fryer Vance described a Fourth of July in Mesa, Arizona. "We always had a long parade.... They had the militia perform. They chased the greased pig and had games, relay races and everything else in the park. They had concessions.... Believe me, that was a day! Then, of course, at night we saw fireworks."[32]

In Mexico, the Mormons observed Cinco de Mayo, a Mexican holiday that commemorated the victory over the French at Puebla during the time of Maximilian. Diez-y-seis de Septiembre, which Nelle Spilsbury Hatch saw as the equivalent of the United State's Fourth of July, celebrated Miquel Hidalgo and Grito de Dolores's success in gaining independence for Mexico in 1810, with parades, patriotic speeches, games and other activities. Rita Skousen Johnson recalled, "On the 16th of September we always had a program to commemorate these historic days in Mexico; so the children could grow up to know that independence was brought on by strife and by people giving their blood and dying for the liberty that we have now."[33]

Not all the Mormon settlers learned Spanish, and Mildred Call Hurst recalled that singing the Mexican anthem on Cinco de Mayo was often awkward. "Some of us could read it and say the words but most of us couldn't. There was a little Mexican town about two miles away and sometimes we would go up and listen to their programs." But usually they had little to do with the Mexicans.[34]

In Canada, the Mormons celebrated Dominion Day, July 1, with parades, speeches and games. The next day, the anniversary of Cardston's founding was also a holiday. Lawrence Lee dates the first celebration of Dominion Day, and then called it "a yearly observance to which Gentile ranch neighbors were invited. Arbor Day was also commemorated in the Canadian manner, for the local government authorities deliberately set about inculcating in the Mormons a patriotism for Canada and encouraging them to observe national holidays."[35] In fact, in order to show their patriotism, the Mormons almost went overboard in celebrating Canadian holidays. As R.C. Macleod explained in his history of the North-West Mounted Police, "Perhaps because of public hostility the Mormons made a considerable display of celebrating Dominion Day every July first. The police regarded this phenomenon with curiosity since instead of making the Latter Day Saints [sic] less conspicuous it only made them more so. Canadians generally tended to be undemonstrative on the occasion."[36]

There were unique Mormon holidays though. The Twenty-fourth of July, a Utah state holiday, commemorating the arrival of the Mormon pioneers into the Salt Lake Valley, was celebrated in much the same way, with parades, devotions, sports and dances. Cardston, with two days of celebration early in July, did not usually celebrate the Twenty-fourth of July, but the smaller Mormon communities in Alberta usually did. In describing the Twenty-fourth of July celebrations in Mexico, Winnie Haynie Mortensen said:

> We always looked forward to the Twenty-fourth of July for a celebration. Now that seems strange down in Old Mexico because we had to be careful to be sure and celebrate the Cinco de Mayo and the Diez-y-seis de Septiembre. We used the Mexican flag and we were not supposed to put out the American flag at any time. During the Twenty-fourth of July we had our flags so we would get them out.[37]

The Twenty-fourth was also an important holiday for Latter-day Saints in the United States outside of Utah. Lucy Fryer Vance remembered, "The Twenty-fourth was just as big as the Fourth in Mesa because the vast majority were members of the Church."[38]

Holidays were, of course, not the only way the Mormons showed their loyalty to the country. Politics were also a visible sign. Although the Mormon Church had been founded in the United States, it was not always assumed that the Latter-day Saints were good citizens. In fact, the Mormons in Utah had a separate political party, the People's Party, which was organized in response to a party organized by ex- or non-Mormons, the Liberal Party. To show they supported the US government, the church disbanded the People's Party in 1891. Members of the church were encouraged in stake conferences to join one of the national parties, and when it appeared too many Mormons were being Democrats, some were encouraged to be Republicans.[39] Church leaders encouraged members to vote, but did not tell them how to vote. Wilford Woodruff stated in a General Conference in 1897, "I do not care whether a man is a Republican or a Democrat, but it is your duty in electing good men to govern.... Unite together within your party lines and appoint good men."[40]

Following all the problems surrounding polygamy and the political situation, when Utah finally became a state, the citizens were anxious to show they were loyal Americans. The Spanish-American War of 1898 provided one opportunity. The church supported and members responded to the government's request for volunteers. Within a short time, five hundred men had agreed to fight, which demonstrated the willingness of the Latter-day Saints in Utah to support their country in military action.[41]

Although Mormon settlers in Mexico had less involvement with the government than in the United States, they invited Mexican government officials to celebrations. For example, an article entitled "Our American Colony in Mexico Does Itself Credit" in the *Deseret News* described a harvest fair that was held in Colonia Diaz. The hall was decorated with a Mexican flag and mottos in Spanish; and a visiting Mexican official was quoted as saying, "The motto I see at the head of the hall, 'Long live our adopted country' gives me much pleasure and I can say in behalf of my people assembled here, we gladly welcome you to our midst and I hope we shall all grow together into one nation."[42] In 1899, residents formed a political club to gain greater status in Mexico. At the same time, they "presented a memorial to President Diaz praying him to accept renomination to the presidency of the republic as the desire of every Mormon colonist in Mexico." After some discussion, it was signed by every family head in Colonia Juarez. According to the *Deseret News* article that described the memorial, "To the wise and firm administration of President Diaz may be ascribed the wonderful prosperity and advancement of Mexico during recent years and his continuance in office for another term insures continued business stability and national prosperity for a time to come."[43]

Because of the cultural and language differences, many Mormons did not become Mexican citizens. Emma Romney Haymore Greetham said, "My father never took out papers for Mexico. He was always an American citizen."[44] Even if a father took out Mexican citizenship, usually the mother did not. The children born in Mexico had dual citizenship because of one of their parents' citizenship and their place of birth. Ara O. Call, who grew up in Mexico, explained, "Predominately the culture and the members of the Church at that time were Americans."[45]

The confusion of the Mexican Revolution created problems for the Mormon colonists. Although they tried to remain neutral, bandits from both sides raided them for needed supplies. Finally, when the rebels demanded that they take sides and surrender their guns, Stake President Julius Romney decided that it was time to leave. In July 1912, the women and children took the train to El Paso, Texas, and most of the men followed overland. Because of the unstable government situation, most chose not to return to Mexico. For those who did return, many made several other exoduses. Those who remained became Mexican citizens so they could own land, but many still considered the United States home.

In Canada, the Mormons were more comfortable with the culture and committed to the Canadian federal government (which was also more stable). Many became Canadian citizens. No doubt such loyalty was encouraged earlier by statements by the minister of Agriculture and Customs encouraging the Mormons to settle in Canada, though they did not include permission to bring in plural wives. When the apostolic delegation returned from Ottawa in 1888, Francis Lyman told the Saints, "We must comply with every law of the land and the Priesthood would not accept breaking the law and fellowship would be withdrawn from those who violated the laws." When John W. Taylor visited the colonies, on 30 June 1889, he "said we would have opposition, as in other lands. Exhorted the saints to observe the laws of the land scrupulously. Advised those who came here to take a definite stand whether they would be citizens of this land or of the U.S."[46] In 1890, Charles Card encouraged the settlers to become citizens of Canada "in order that they might have all of the privileges of citizenship and show their loyalty to the government which had granted them a new home."[47] At the dedication of the Cardston Temple, Edward James Wood, the stake president, led his co-believers in a cheer that included loyalty to Canada: "God bless our temple, God bless our builders, God bless our Church, God bless all people, God bless Canada, God bless the British Empire and Save our King."[48] Although some of the new citizens found it hard to determine the differences between the Liberal and Conservative parties, they voted in the elections and office seekers actively sought their vote.[49] Mormons from Alberta have played prominent roles in both provincial and federal governments.

In appraising the experience of polygamous Mormons in Canada, Mexico and the United States, the impact of law and culture must be seen as more decisive than the peculiar institution of polygamy. In Mexico, the differences in culture and language and the unstable government kept the Mormons separate from the Mexicans, and eventually forced many to return to the United States. In contrast, similar cultural backgrounds to the United States and a more stable government enabled Mormon settlers in Canada to become a more integral part of the community. Although both Colonia Juarez and Cardston look like transplanted Utah communities, Cardston blends in more with the Canadian surroundings, whereas Colonia Juarez and Colonia Dublan look completely out of place. Cultural differences, rather than polygamy, are the major reasons. Motivated by the same desires for safety, based on the same potent belief in the righteousness of polygamy and equally important parts of the Mormon tradition, the Mormon settlements in the United States, Canada and Mexico are a study of environmental influences.

NOTES

1. Cardston Ward Minutes, 3 November 1889, LDS Church Archives, LDS Historical Department, Church of Jesus Christ of Latter-day Saints, Salt Lake City, Utah. (Hereinafter LDS Church Archives.)

2. Quoted in Gustive O. Larson, "Government, Politics, and Conflict," in Richard Poll, et al., eds., *Utah's History* (Provo: Brigham Young University, 1978), p. 244.

3. Quoted in Richard Van Wagoner, *Mormon Polygamy: A History* (Salt Lake City: Signature Books, 1986), p. 111.

4. Larsen, pp. 244-92.

5. Torrey L. Austin, oral history, interviewed by Jessie Embry, 1976, LDS Polygamy Oral History Project, Charles Redd Center for Western Studies, Manuscript Division, Harold B. Lee Library, Brigham Young University, Provo, Utah, 4. (Hereinafter LDS Polygamy.)

6. Truman Call, oral history, interviewed by Laurel Schmidt, 1981, pp. 1-2, LDS Polygamy.

7. Christopher Layton, autobiography, n.d., LDS Church Archives, pp. 51-52.

8. David Boone and Chad J. Flake, "The prison diary of William Jordan Flake," *Journal of Arizona History*, 24 (Summer 1983), pp. 145-70.

9. Quoted in Carmon Hardy, "Cultural 'Encystment' as a Cause of the Mormon Exodus from Mexico in 1912" (doctoral dissertation, Wayne State University, 1963), p. 72.

10. Hardy, pp. 78-79; Nelle Spilsbury Hatch, *Colonia Juarez: An Intimate Account of a Mormon Village* (Salt Lake City: Deseret Books, 1954), p. 11; Hardy, "Mormon Polygamy in Mexico and Canada: A Legal and Historiographical Review," in this volume.

11. Hardy and Victor Jorgenson, "The Taylor-Cowley affair and the watershed of Mormon history," *Utah Historical Quarterly*, 48 (Winter 1980), pp. 17-18.

12. Jane è Woolf Bates and Zina Woolf Hickman, *Founding of Cardston and Vicinity* (n.p., William L. Woolf, 1960), p.1; Leo Stutz, dictation, 1981, LDS Church Archives, p. 1.

13. *Statutes of Canada*, 1890, 53 Vic., c. 37.

14. Canada, House of Commons, *Debates*, 10 April 1890.

15. Genealogical Department, Church of Jesus Christ of Latter-day Saints, Salt Lake City, Utah.

16. Van Wagoner, pp. 159-60; D. Michael Quinn, "LDS church authority and new plural marriages, 1890-1904," *Dialogue: A Journal of Mormon Thought*, 18 (1985), pp. 10-105.

17. Van Wagoner, p. 169.

18. Georgina Bolette Critchlow Bickmore, oral history, interviewed by Stevan Hales, 1982, 1, LDS Polygamy, p. 20.

19. Jessie L. Embry, "Is One Wife Enough? The Effects of LDS Polygamy on an Idaho Family," unpublished manuscript.

20. Marcus Hart, oral history, interviewed by Jessie L. Embry, LDS Polygamy, 1976, p. 7.

21. Thomas G. Alexander, *Mormonism in Transition: A History of the Latter-day Saints, 1890-1930* (Champaign: University of Illinois Press, 1986), p. 68.

22. Karl Skousen, oral history, interviewed by Leonard Grover, 1980, LDS Polygamy, p. 4.
23. Author unknown, "Polygamy in Mexico," n.d., Anthony W. Ivins Collection, Box 16, Folder 17, Utah State Historical Society, Salt Lake City, Utah.
24. Winnifred Newton Thomas, oral history, interviewed by Jessie L. Embry, 1982, LDS Polygamy, p. 27.
25. William L. Woolf, oral history, interviewed by Maureen Ursenbach and Gary L. Shumway, 1972, LDS Church Archives, p. 18.
26. Bates and Hickman, *Founding of Cardston and Vicinity*, p. 74.
27. Lawrence B. Lee, "The Mormons come to Canada, 1887-1902," *Pacific Northwest Quarterly*, 59 (January 1968), p. 11.
28. Cardston Ward Minutes, 31 August 1890, LDS Archives.
29. Ellice Marie Bentley LaBaron, oral history, interview by Charles Ursenbach, 1973, LDS Archives, pp. 6-7.
30. Interview with Grant Ivins, 21 June 1971, Grant Ivins Collection, Utah State Historical Society, p. 10.
31. Zina Patterson Dunford, oral history, interviewed by Jessie L. Embry, LDS Polygamy, p. 4.
32. Lucy Fryer Vance, oral history, interviewed by Jessie L. Embry, 1982, LDS Polygamy, p. 8.
33. Rita Skousen Johnson, oral history, interviewed by Chris Nelson, 1981, LDS Polygamy, p. 11.
34. Mildred Call Hurst, oral history, interviewed by Jessie L. Embry, 1976, LDS Polygamy, p. 9.
35. Lee, p. 16.
36. R.C. Macleod, *The NWMP and Law Enforcement, 1873-1905* (Toronto: University of Toronto Press, 1976), p. 156.
37. Winnie Haynie Mortensen, oral history, interviewed by Leonard Grover, 1979, LDS Polygamy, p. 15.
38. Vance, p. 8.
39. James B. Allen and Glen M. Leonard, *The Story of the Latter-day Saints* (Salt Lake City: Deseret Books, 1976), pp. 343 and 417.
40. Ibid., p. 438.
41. Ibid., p. 437.
42. Journal History, 20 September 1894, LDS Church Archives, p. 8.
43. Ibid., 29 November 1899, p. 8.
44. Emma Romney Haymore Greetham, oral history, interviewed by Jessie L. Embry, 1976, LDS Polygamy, p. 21.
45. Call, p. 10.
46. Cardston Minutes, 25 November 1888, LDS Church Archives.
47. Hudson, p. 128.
48. Edward James Wood Journal, 13 September 1920[?], LDS Archives.
49. Journal History, 27 April 1900, p. 11; 12 November 1900, p. 19.

10 Mormon Polygamy in Mexico and Canada

A Legal and Historiographical Review

B. CARMON HARDY

THE CRUSADE AGAINST Mormon polygamy in the United States a century ago largely followed passage of the 1882 Edmunds Act. In writing the law, Congress amended existing legislation so as to forbid what it called simply, "unlawful cohabitation." Anglo-American legislators, in favoring monogamous marriage, had been traditionally content to erect criminal barriers only to the attempt at formalizing bigamous or other irregular liaisons. Mormons succeeded in escaping the penalties of such enactments by resorting to entirely private devices, such as religious performances when contracting plural unions. The 1882 revision made it possible to prosecute, fine, and send to prison Mormons who had been joined in polygamous relationships as the result of such informal ceremonies.[1]

One of the consequences of this legislation was that, beginning in 1885, lands were found south of the US border where polygamous families could locate away from the reach of the new law. By 1890, when Mormon President Wilford Woodruff issued the Manifesto advising against further polygamous contractions in violation of the law, three communities had been founded in Mexico, with another six destined to appear in the next 15 years. From these early years, until the exodus of the colonists at the time of the Mexican Revolution, it was clear to every Mormon involved that the church's wish to foster and protect the institution of plural marriage was the primary reason for the existence of such colonies in Mexico.[2]

This notwithstanding, and despite the fact that this was one of the largest colonization efforts undertaken by the Great Basin church, Mormon

186

writers and representatives did everything they could to mute the significance of the project, both at the time and for some years after. Every attempt was made to say as little as possible to journalists and outsiders about it. The church's official newspaper and individual spokesmen denied that anything like a large-scale movement of Saints to Mexico was occurring or planned. Members, it was said, who had moved in that direction were only responding to crowding in the United States. Mormon farmers were simply trying to improve their circumstances and were doing so as individuals. Most importantly, all connection between their migration southward and the practice of polygamy was not only ignored but also explicitly denied.[3]

Similar efforts were made within the colonies to minimize visibility and reduce attention to the real reason for their presence there. The colonists were encouraged to conduct themselves carefully. Apostle George Teasdale, the authority responsible for directing affairs in Mexico during the first years of the colonies' existence, upon hearing that a stranger was visiting one of the settlers, immediately summoned the owner of the home to explain who the visitor was and why he was there. The outcome of the episode was that an official "entertainer of strangers" was appointed and colonists were instructed neither to associate nor communicate with outsiders any more than was necessary.[4] Men intending to reside in Mexico were asked to sign restrictive covenants agreeing not to sell property to non-Mormons. Women were told to give no information to strangers and to avoid mingling with Mexican neighbors.[5] For years, plural wives were instructed to identify themselves to non-Mormons as single women, as sisters, or as relatives visiting temporarily.[6] The colonists were told to be discreet about what was said in letters to friends in the United States, and sometimes were forbidden to take jobs outside the colonies.[7] W. Derby Johnson, Jr., Bishop in Colonia Díaz, summarized in his diary the substance of talks that he gave to church members there as follows, "Those who come to join us must have recommends. Parties in School House Mexicans must not be invited [n]or we go to their dances." And, "Keep our mouths shut."[8]

The reasons for such reticence are easily adduced. The national campaign to abolish Mormon polygamy in the United States had reached such proportions during the 1880s that church leaders were doing everything possible to survive as a church while, at the same time, preserving the principle of plural marriage.[9] Statements were made by church authorities to the effect that the actual number of Mormons practising polygamy was greatly diminished, and by the mid- and late 1880s amounted to no more than 2% or 3% of the church's membership. Beyond this, on more than one occasion during

these years, the public was told that Mormon leaders were no longer permitting the performance of polygamous contractions at all.[10] The church
was doing everything it could to give the impression that it was bending to
demands that plural marriage be discontinued. Clearly, it was important
that the public know as little as possible about those communities in Mexico
where such marriages were still occurring and would continue to be performed with church approval for more than a decade after the 1890
Woodruff declaration.[11]

There is another reason why Mormon spokesmen were anxious to
obscure the nature of marital patterns in the Mexican colonies; one that will
occupy a significant portion of this paper. This has to do with what was
and was not permitted by Mexican law. Numbers of Mormon writers have
stated that polygamy was permitted legally in Mexico.[12] This has been a
comfortable assumption for church members because it seemed to satisfy
the requirements of the Woodruff Manifesto. The truth is that not only were
formal bigamous contractions forbidden in Mexico but also privately solemnized polygamous marriages, as performed by the Mormons, fell athwart
Mexican legal *intent* as well. This is most easily explained by a review of
Mexico's legislation on the subject.

Relevant Mexican statutes were based on Spanish codes. Although the
sources of Spanish law were of a mixed and sometimes conflicting nature,
the influences of Roman and canon law combined to produce a vigorous
condemnation of polygamy. It was considered a heinous crime, "*sumamente
perniciosa.*" Spanish laws authorized condign punishment for polygamy,
including branding, imprisonment, loss of property, and being forced to
serve in the galleys of the Spanish navy.[13] The reason for such hostility was
undoubtedly rooted in ancient Spanish concern for unsullied lines of
patriarchal descent. Additionally, those commenting on Spanish law justified
the aversion to polygamy by saying that it was unfair to women, reducing
them to slaves; that some men would have several wives whereas others
would have none; and, most importantly, that it was contrary to the tradition of the Christian monogamous home.[14]

Mexican national law was slow to take form due to repeated paroxysms
of political disturbance. But even with the changes of the late 1850s—
secularizing the marriage ceremony—there was no departure from the traditional Spanish commitment to matrimony as an ideal, "uniting one sole man
to one sole woman."[15] Spanish compilations, with their opposition to
polygamous marriage, served as the basis for legal procedure everywhere
in the republic.[16] Mexican federal codes not only reiterated Spanish

concern with and opposition to polygamy but also declared their allegiance to monogamous marriage as an obligation of high importance by forbidding divorce except under narrowly defined circumstances.[17] Frequently, the federal codes doubled as the basis for law in the states. Chihuahua, for example, adopted the federal criminal code for its own use in 1883, two years before the Mormons began arriving in large numbers. Sonora, where additional Mormon colonies came to be located, contrived a document more closely adapted to its particular needs in 1884.[18] Both states issued new penal codes of their own in 1897 and 1909 respectively. And both included absolute prohibitions against *bigamia* or *matrimonio doble*, that is against formally contracted plural marriages.[19]

But, it may be said, Mormon polygamous unions were not formally contracted by public magistrates. Therefore, as the products of private religious ceremonies, Mormon polygamous arrangements were not, strictly speaking, in violation of Mexican law. This, unquestionably, is the reason that some have alleged that those Latter-day Saints who went to Mexico to practise plural marriage did so legally. The difficulty with this argument is that it confounds the very purpose for which the Mexican statutes were drawn. This is illustrated by what the laws did with adultery. Determined as they were to preserve the traditional monogamous household against such things as polygamy and divorce, Spanish and Mexican legal authors made special allowances for sexual irregularities. They recognized that men were likely sometimes to lapse in sexual fidelity to their wives. Consequently, if they were discreet, men were permitted to consort with mistresses without calling into question the structural durability of their monogamous unions. Adultery, in the case of men, did not categorically constitute grounds for dishonor or divorce.[20] And formal provision was made for heritable rights by children born outside of marriage as the result of such alliances.[21] For men, as one authority put it, the act of adultery was not always the crime of adultery. But, we repeat, the reason for incorporating such blinds into the law was that, by so doing, the monogamous home would remain formally intact, in spite of whatever personal crises arose to assail it.[22]

Something of a parallel existed in the United States. After anti-polygamy legislation was passed by the Congress, many Mormons were outraged at what they considered to be the hypocrisy, the double standard, of those who made and enforced such laws against them. To the Mormon, vast numbers of homeless children, widespread prostitution, adultery and sexual deceit constituted a standing rebuke of those who condemned the Mormon marriage system which, the Saints alleged, had largely eliminated such evils.[23]

What Mormons seemed unable to grasp fully, although it was explained on several occasions, was that it was not the sexual derelictions of individuals with which the law was concerned so much as with preserving the *form* of the monogamous home. The purpose of the laws, as explained by legislators and judges alike, was to expunge the "semblance" of a competing and threatening order of American home life. This is why, in the face of Mormon consternation, convictions for plural marriage were allowed even when no sexual relations between spouses existed. The intent was to obviate, in the words of the Utah Commission, "the assault made by the Mormon Church upon the most cherished institution of our civilization—the monogamic system."[24] In other words, as in Mexico, legislators were relatively indifferent to sexual misbehavior, or the lack of it, so long as the monogamous home remained unchallenged as a social ideal.

It is also important to remember that advocates of Mormon polygamy in the last century believed that monogamy was an inferior contrivance, that it resulted in moral decline, and that it was largely responsible for many of the sexual ills of the day, including prostitution and abortion. Plural marriage, on the other hand, was the order of heaven and, when properly lived and understood, would redeem mankind both physically and socially. In other words, the Saints believed fully that polygamy, rather than monogamy, must be cultivated as the preferred marital arrangement in the home.[25] Inasmuch as it was the Mormon support for and participation in this domestic pattern that chiefly accounted for their presence in Mexico, and given the commitment to monogamy inherent in Mexican law, Mormon polygamy clearly violated the intent of the statutes involved. It was not simply a matter of the Mormons taking advantage of Mexican moral laxity as permitted by loopholes in their laws.[26] By ignoring the historical purposes that lay behind the loopholes, the Mormons were attempting to supplant those purposes with an order of marriage that the loopholes were designed to prevent.

Evidence that Mormon polygamy was considered morally and legally unacceptable in Mexico is to be found in responses by the Mexican press to Mormon colonization. Even before the colonies were established, fear was expressed that, if Mormon immigration to Mexico should prove true, Mexican society would suffer because Mormon customs were so out of step with Mexican "principles of both public and private morality."[27] After the first migrants arrived, the public was warned by Mexican writers that the sect, because of its practice of polygamy, was guilty of violating the laws and was a scandal to traditional Christian morality.[28] Such comments were made for years, characterizing the Saints as fanatical, anti-social, anti-family and disobedient to the laws.[29] As the editor of a prominent Mexican journal put it in the late 1880s, "If the Mormons on coming here practice polygamy they certainly are not submissive to the law of the land nor to the precepts of Christianity."[30]

Further evidence that Mormon polygamy in Mexico was looked upon as unapproved legally arises from admissions to this effect by Mormons themselves. In 1891, for example, Apostle Brigham Young, Jr., admitted to reporters that polygamy was against the law in Mexico and that Mormons living there were abiding by those laws "in every particular."[31] W. Derby Johnson, Jr., a Mormon bishop in Colonia Díaz, and the husband of three living wives, told a journalist from the United States the same thing, that polygamy was not being practised by the colonists because it was against Mexican law.[32] In yet another interview, Bishop Johnson reassured Mexican reporters that "there is neither intention nor possibility of introducing the practice of polygamy in Mexico. That is as impossible under Mexican laws as under those of the United States."[33] Anthony W. Ivins, chief ecclesiastical authority over all Mexico Mormons, warned settlers in 1901 to take care for they were living in a land where plural marriage was in violation of the law.[34] And, in 1906, a Mormon from Colonia Dublán, another of the colonies, "roundly denied" to a Mexican newspaper that any of the colonists were living in polygamy because, as he expressed it, although Mormons believed plural marriage to be a divine institution, it was no longer practised because it was against the laws of both Mexico and the United States.[35]

At this point of our investigation, we must ask how it was that Mormon polygamy succeeded in being tolerated if, in fact, it contradicted Mexican legal intentions? To answer this, we must explore an episode that took place shortly after the first Mormon camps were established in the Casas Grandes Valley in the spring of 1885. At that time, local Mexican officials issued an order expelling the settlers from the country.[36] While there were several reasons that accounted for this development, at least one of them is likely to have been hostility towards polygamy as incompatible with Mexican law.[37] Hoping to have the expulsion order rescinded, two Mormon Apostles, Erastus Snow and Moses Thatcher, travelled to Mexico City for talks with national officials. Once there, and with the assistance of Mission President Helaman Pratt as translator, they gained an audience with cabinet level officers and with Mexican President Porfirio Díaz.

We have Pratt's diary, and in it the most complete summary of what the

Mormon leaders were told over the several days they were in the capital. In the first place, Secretary of Public Works Carlos Pacheco directed that the expulsion order be cancelled.[38] A major part of Díaz's plans for developing the nation's economy involved the establishment of foreign colonists on Mexican soil, especially on arid lands of the northern provinces. The Mormon reputation for being good farmers filled the prescription Mexican leaders and planners had built into the laws governing the stimulation of Mexican agriculture through colonization.[39] Whatever local authorities in Chihuahua might have felt about the Mormons, Díaz's ministers were determined to implement their leader's economic policies. The Saints were assured that they could remain.

According to Pratt's account, it was not until the third day, again in a meeting with Secretary Pacheco, that the subject of polygamy was discussed. The minister told the Mormon leaders that they could bring their plural wives and families to Mexico, but they were to do it quietly. He indicated that he wished personally that Mexico's laws could be changed so as to permit plural marriage to be practised openly. That not being possible, he made it clear that if charges were brought against the Saints because of their marriage practices, they would likely be taken to court and have to defend themselves there. He assured them, however, that those Mormons who were monogamous need have no fear of persecution in Mexico. Pratt's final entry concerning this conversation was to paraphrase Secretary Pacheco as repeating again that the Mormons and their plural families were welcome, they could come and colonize in peace, but they were to do it quietly.[40]

This interview is significant for a number of reasons. In the first place, the meeting with Pacheco in which polygamy was discussed did not include President Díaz. It was more than a week after this occasion before the Mormons were introduced to the nation's president. And when this occurred, Pratt's notes give no indication that anything at all was said on the subject of plural marriage.[41] This does not mean that the president would have opposed the Mormons as colonists on account of their polygamy. It is only that, contrary to later Mormon comments, there is no firsthand evidence that President Díaz ever personally gave them permission to ignore Mexican law. This is reinforced by comments made to Anthony W. Ivins by George Q. Cannon when Ivins was instructed in the manner by which couples would be sent to him to be married in plural relationships. According to Ivins's son, Cannon said, "Now Brother Ivins, if you have occasion to meet Porfirio Diaz...we want you to tell him that we are NOT practicing polygamy in Mexico."[42]

Secondly, it is clear from Secretary Pacheco's advice to the Mormons that he knew that what they were doing in their family affairs contravened Mexican legal intentions. This is why he repeatedly counseled them to be private and quiet about it. This would agree with a statement credited to Joseph F. Smith shortly after the Manifesto was drafted, in which he is supposed to have remarked, "There is a tacit understanding between the church and the Mexican government, that we may practice plural marriage but must outwardly appear to have but one wife."[43] We can also understand better why, immediately after its issuance, a copy of the 1890 Manifesto was sent to representatives of the Mexican government.[44] This gave support to the image cultivated by the Mormons of being law-abiding settlers.[45]

We must also take notice that Pratt's account of this conversation refers only to the safety that colonists might feel in bringing their already existing plural families to Mexico. Nothing of an equally explicit nature was said in connection with new plural marriages. Some might have believed that they had been given the right to marry new wives because of the welcoming spirit of government officials. If this was the case, however, it was entirely inferential. Some years later, Burton Hendrick, a non-Mormon journalist, claimed to have information that supports this view. Mexican officials, he said, gave the Mormon representatives to understand that they could bring already existing polygamous wives to Mexico, but there were to be no new polygamous unions contracted on Mexican soil.[46]

Finally, these interviews with Mexican leaders were important because they provided a pattern for Mormon encounters with government officials in Canada. In that regard, it is significant that Apostles John W. Taylor, Francis M. Lyman and Brigham Young, Jr., were sent to the border region shortly after the time of these meetings and were apprised of the conversations that Snow, Thatcher and Pratt had held with Mexican authorities.[47] Apostles Lyman and Taylor were the Mormon leaders who later conferred with Canadian political officials in connection with the settlement of Mormons in Canada.

What we know of negotiations between Mormon authorities and government leaders in Mexico gives support to what we said earlier about the subdued nature of Mormon statements concerning their settlements in Chihuahua and Sonora. Efforts made to disguise the movement as inconsiderable and denials concerning the practice of polygamy not only comported with Mormon strategies of defense in the United States but also were in harmony with what they had been advised to do by Mexican officials as well. We can conclude also, at this point, that a good deal of myth grew up

John W. Taylor, 1858-1916, son of President John Taylor, church apostle and land developer in Canadian Mormon settlements. LDS Archives.

in connection with the toleration of plural marriage in the Mexican colonies. There is no evidence, for example, as one account has it, that the Mormons approached Porfirio Díaz to ask about the legality of plurality of wives. The story goes that Díaz said no legal limitations existed, quipping, "It does not matter to Mexico whether you drive your horses tandem or four abreast."[48] Rather, we can be sure that what the Mormons were doing, through the encouragement of polygamous family life, was quite out of harmony with at least the purpose, if not the letter, of laws south of the border, and that, despite a long tradition in Mormon history asserting otherwise, both Mexican officials and Mormon leaders at the time knew it.

Latter-day Saint settlement in Alberta commenced in 1887, only two years after the first Mormon camps were established in northern Mexico. As with those in Chihuahua and Sonora, Canadian Mormons located sites close to the international border. And, as in Mexico, the Mormons in Canada both prospered and multiplied. In little more than a decade, seven settlements were founded, with others to follow in succeeding years. Most importantly, as with those who went to Mexico, the search for refuge from the crusade against polygamy in the United States constituted a major reason for the move there by those Mormons who located in the region.[49]

Once again, church leaders denied that Mormon interest in Canada had anything to do with polygamy. Every effort was made to represent the migration north as inconsequential, as but the result of farmers looking about to improve their lot. The Mormons were quite content with life in Utah, it was said. It was only that, being cultivators of the soil, some were naturally attracted to the fertile lands of the Canadian West.[50] And similar to Mormon polygamy in Mexico, there has also been misunderstanding as to what the Saints encountered in Canada in connection with its laws. Some, for example, have said that prior to the Mormon entry, anti-polygamy legislation did not exist in Canada.[51] Because of this, as with Mexico, it will be helpful to examine the Canadian legal experience relating to polygamy.

To begin with, as in the case of Spain, there existed from the time of early modern England a strong statutory tradition opposing plural marriage. The practice was criminalized in the first years of the Stuart reign.[52] Educated sentiment was often expressed against it. As an eighteenth-century polemicist put it, it was nothing less than "self-evident" that England, with its monogamy, was superior to India with its polygamy.[53] Blackstone, writing at about the same time, noted that bigamous relationships were properly punished as felonies because they constituted "so great a violation of the public economy and decency of an well ordered state."[54] And midway through the nineteenth century, the case of *Hyde* v. *Hyde and Woodmansee* (1866), involving a former Mormon polygamist living in England, held that such contractions were neither Christian nor licit.[55]

English law and custom exercised an important influence on Canadian legal practice. As with Mexico in its borrowings from Spain, conformity to the British model was a conscious legislative policy by Canadians.[56] By the time of the Mormon arrival, not only had the "British North America Act" lodged the regulation of marriage throughout the dominion with the central government but also the "Consolidation Act" of 1869 reaffirmed the most recent English statute prohibiting polygamy.[57] Beyond this, in 1886, one year before the Mormon migration began, Parliament declared, "Every one who being married, marries any other person during the life of the former husband or wife, whether the second marriage takes place in Canada, or elsewhere, is guilty of felony, and liable to seven years' imprisonment."[58]

At the same time, the area embracing what is now Alberta was subject to a federal agency, the Council of the North-West Territories. A lieutenant-governor, in concurrence with this council, was authorized to issue such ordinances as were necessary for the government of the region.[59] Pursuant to this authority, and nearly a decade before the first Mormon pluralists arrived, a decree was issued declaring that "precontract," or previous marriage to a living spouse, constituted an impediment to another legal marriage.[60] These enactments, in company with the English statutory and judicial traditions, clearly condemned formally contracted plural marriages. The question was whether privately arranged bigamous unions, as by the Mormons, would be any more acceptable to Canadian authorities than officially solemnized multiple marriages disallowed by their laws. In other words, Canada was faced with the same circumstance confronting Mexico at the time of the Mormon arrival there in 1885, and by the United States prior to 1882.

Similar to what happened when the Saints began colonizing in Mexico, dominion journalists raised questions about the suitability of Mormons as settlers on Canadian soil. Referring to the repeated problems Mormons had had with the law in the United States, the *Edmonton Bulletin* called them "treasonous" and as "nasty as Chinamen and more dangerous than...Nihilists." However industrious they may be as farmers, it was essential, said the *Bulletin*, that they be given to understand that they must behave as Canadian citizens if they were to live in Canadian society. Similar fears were expressed on the floor of Parliament, urging that Canada's legal condemnation of men taking multiple spouses be strictly enforced upon the new settlers.[61] While it was not the single issue involved, plural marriage, more than anything else, was what concerned Canadians when the first Mormon colonists began crossing the Canadian-American border.[62]

Although the intent of Canada's anti-bigamy laws undoubtedly was to prevent the kind of marriages practised by the Saints, as in the United States before passage of the Edmunds Act, Mormon use of private ceremonies left them technically exempt from the letter of Canadian statutes. Because of the alarm raised in the press, however, and because of their experience in the United States, where after 1882 the laws were changed to comprehend private contractions, Mormon leaders took steps to obviate such a development in Canada. Reminiscent of their experience with the Mexican government at the time of the expulsion order in 1885, church authorities decided to approach Canadian officials directly and ask for permission to bring their plural families into the dominion. Mormon leaders unquestionably hoped that they would be given the same kind of blind from the Canadian government that they had obtained in Mexico. Canada, like Mexico, was anxious to encourage immigration to and development of its vast lands in the central and western parts of the nation. Perhaps, as in Mexico, the prospect of establishing a hardy population of Mormon farmers in those regions could be used to persuade government leaders to leave the laws as they were and to ignore their intent in exchange for the otherwise good citizenship the Mormons were sure to bring. Their request, however, was refused.

Not only did the Mormons fail with their petitioning in Ottawa but also a later report by the mounted police indicating that they had certain knowledge that Mormon colonists were practising polygamy in Canada led to demands that, in the words of the *Winnipeg Free Press*, "The law in this country is that a man shall have but one wife at a time, and that law must be made to apply to Mormons as well as the Gentiles."[63] The result was, just as had been done in the United States, Canada's 1886 anti-bigamy statute was amended to criminalize such unions when contracted "in any...manner or form whatsoever, and whether in a manner recognized by law as a binding form of marriage or not." This amendment, if anything, was more particular and careful in its language than the Edmunds law in the United States from which it was borrowed. But to make sure there was no confusion, the enactment specifically indicated that it was "persons commonly called Mormons" and their practice of "spiritual or plural marriage" with which it was concerned.[64] Finally, illustrating Canadian congruence with views in Mexico and the United States that it was the *appearance* of plural family life that must be repressed, provision was made for convictions with or without evidence of sexual relations between spouses.[65]

Despite efforts to imitate and profit from their experience, the Saints in Canada failed to obtain the license granted them in Mexico. With the amendment of Canadian law in 1890, identifying the private ceremonies employed in Mormon multiple marriages as prohibited, the intent of the earlier Canadian statutes was made explicit. Unlike in Mexico, where legal intent also existed but was never reified, the Canadians moved to meet Mormon plural marriage in the same way as it had been done in the United States with the Edmunds Act of 1882. The result was that, although plural family life existed in Canada after 1890, as it did in the United States, it was both less frequent and less openly acknowledged than in Mexico.[66]

It was undoubtedly due, in part at least, to their efforts to conceal such things that the Canadian colonists were criticized for displaying isolationist tendencies. While it was admitted that he made a good farmer, as one commentator put it in 1902, the Mormon simply was not to be trusted. "There is," he said, "a mystery in his life which baffles the observer."[67]

Ironically, the large influx of Indian and other Oriental peoples into commonwealth nations since World War II has resulted in a liberalization of attitudes, especially regarding the heritable rights of polygamous wives and children.[68] Hence, although the Mormon community in Canada acquired increasing respect as years passed, lineaments of the old prejudice remained. For more than a half-century, Canada's Criminal Code continued to preserve not only the ban on polygamous marriages but also the 1890 law's specific reference to Mormons as a group with which the law was especially concerned.[69]

Having discussed similarities in Mormon efforts to perpetuate polygamy in Mexico and Canada, we can conclude with some observations regarding Mormonism's own historical treatment of these attempts. We have already shown that, at the time these colonizing efforts began, the church did everything it could to obscure polygamy as a reason accounting for members moving out of the United States. As we suggested, this was done, in Mexico at least, because government leaders suggested that they be "quiet" about such things. It was also consonant with the image cultivated by Mormon leaders who, through the end of the century, denied that new plural marriages were yet authorized or performed anywhere in the church.[70]

At the time of the Smoot investigation in 1904, and consistent with the policy followed during the 1890s, President of the Church Joseph F. Smith repeatedly denied that he or either of his predecessors (Wilford Woodruff and Lorenzo Snow) had authorized new polygamous unions since the Manifesto. No such marriages had occurred, he declared, with the approval of the church anywhere in the world.[71] Later, after Senator Smoot was accepted into the Senate, a special address by the First Presidency in 1907 again alleged that, except for some few cases on the part of recalcitrants, the church had been "true to its pledge respecting the abandonment of the practice of plural marriage."[72]

As a rule, Mormon commentators have tended to perpetuate the silence of those difficult, transitional years around the turn of the century. The modern church displays a distinct sensitivity to the entire question of its polygamous past. Although the number of exceptions has increased in recent years, the works of respected scholars treat plural marriage as an aberration whose significance for nineteenth-century Mormonism is minimized.[73] So far as continuation of the practice after 1890 is concerned, when acknowledged, it is usually said to have occurred in Canada and Mexico because laws prohibiting polygamy did not exist there.[74] In most instances, however, like churchmen of a century ago, when discussing Mormon settlement in these countries, plural marriage is given little attention, or simply avoided. Mormon migration is explained primarily as a response to the need for economic improvement or the wish to carry Mormon teachings to foreign lands.[75] This same defensiveness no doubt lay behind the successful attempt by Latter-day Saint political leaders during the 1950s to remove from Canada's laws the old references linking the Saints to polygamous ways.[76]

The memory of polygamy, as Thomas Cheney put it, has been an "incessant thorn-prick" in the side of the twentieth-century church.[77] Yet, to the degree that Mormonism's nineteenth-century commitment to plural marriage is screened by students of the Mormon past, to that same degree we defraud our knowledge not only of Mormonism in its earlier years but also of Mormonism today. Institutions, like men, can only be comprehended when the integrity of their full experience over time is understood. By restating, as accurately as we are able, the devotions that compelled men and women to leave their homes for new, difficult beginnings in Mexico and Canada, and by recalling both the subterfuge and the courage employed to deal with the circumstances they encountered, we do them, as well as ourselves, greater honor than by silence and denial.

NOTES

1. The original law is found at U.S., *Statutes at Large*, Vol. 12, chapter 126, pp. 501-02 (1862). The amendment, or Edmunds law, with its use of the term "cohabitation," is at U.S., *Statutes at Large*, Vol. 22, chapter 47, pp. 30-32 (1882).

2. The Woodruff Manifesto was first published under the title of "Official Declaration," in *Deseret News*, 25 September 1890 (hereafter, DN). So far as the purpose of the colonies was concerned, in the words of Anthony W. Ivins: "the condition of marriage existing among the Latter-day Saints was the main factor in bringing the Saints to Mexico." "Juarez Stake High Council Historical Record, 1895-1903," 21 February 1896, Latter-day Saint Historical Archives, Salt Lake City, Utah (hereafter, LDSA).

   Standard historical treatments of the Mexican colonies are Thomas Cottam Romnev. *The Mormon Colonies in Mexico* (Salt Lake City: Deseret Book Co., 1938); Nelle Spilsbury Hatch, *Colonia Juarez: An Intimate Account of a Mormon Village* (Salt Lake City: Deseret Book Co., 1954); the excellent study by Moisés González Navarro, *La coloniación in México 1877-1910* (México, 1960), pp. 63-70; and the recent but discursive work by Agricol Lozano Herrera, *Historia del Mormonismo en México* (México, D.F.: Editorial Zarahemla, 1983), pp. 6-51.

3. Henry Lunt, as quoted in Warner P. Sutton [United States Consul-General at Matamoros, Mexico], "Mormons," Consular Reports, No. 97, U.S. Congress, *House Miscellaneous Documents*, 50th Cong., 1st Sess.,

1887-1888, 23, p. 576; "The Mormons are not Gone Yet," DN, 4 February 1885; "Expressions From the People", ibid., 8 April 1885; "Expressions From the People," ibid., 14 April 1885; letter to United States Secretary of the Interior Lucius Q.C. Lamar from George Ticknor Curtis, ibid., 1 December 1886; the comments of John W. Young cited in *Evening Sun* [New York], 10 November 1888; clippings in "Journal History of the Church," 14 September 1885, p. 11, and 7 October 1888, p. 7, LDSA; "President Woodruff His Views on the Present Situation," *Woman's Exponent* 18 (February 1890), p. 141.

4. Nelle Spilsbury Hatch, "George Teasdale," in Nelle Spilsbury Hatch and B. Carmon Hardy, compilers, *Stalwarts South of the Border* (Anaheim, Calif.: Shumway Family History Publishing Co., 1985), p. 683.

5. Joel H. Martineau, "The Mormon Colonies in Mexico 1876-1929," typewritten manuscript, part 4, pp. 6, 8, 19-20, and 35, LDSA.

6. See, for example, Emily Black, "Mary Eliza Tracy Allred," typewritten manuscript, pp. 6-7, in "Collection of Mormon Biographies," 19/11/5, LDSA.

7. "Juarez Stake High Council Minutes, 1895-1917," 29 September 1900 and 25 May 1901, LDSA.

8. Diary of W. Derby Johnson, Jr., part 8, p. 17, 25 December 1887; part 8, p. 32, 15 July 1888, in possession of Mrs. Beth Simper, Holbrook, Arizona. This theme was pursued at greater length in B. Carmon Hardy, "Cultural 'Encystment' as a cause of the Mormon exodus from Mexico in 1912," *Pacific Historical Review*, 39 (November 1965), pp. 439-54.

9. Among the best studies of the crusade against Mormon polygamy are Nels Anderson, *Desert Saints: The Mormon Frontier in Utah* (Chicago and London: University of Chicago Press, 1942), pp. 166-333; Leonard Arrington, *Great Basin Kingdom: An Economic History of the Latter-day Saints 1830-1900* (Cambridge, Mass.: Harvard University Press, 1958), pp. 353-79; all of Gustive O. Larsen, *The "Americanization" of Utah for Statehood* (San Marino, Calif.: The Huntington Library, 1971); James B. Allen and Glen M. Leonard, *The Story of the Latter-day Saints* (Salt Lake City: Deseret Book Company, 1976), pp. 377-434; Leonard J. Arrington and Davis J. Bitton, *The Mormon Experience: A History of the Latter-day Saints* (New York: Alfred A. Knopf, 1979), pp. 161-84; and all of Edward Leo Lyman, *Political Deliverance: The Mormon Quest for Utah Statehood* (Urbana and Chicago: University of Illinois Press, 1986).

10. "Epistle of the First Presidency," 4 April 1885, in James R. Clark, compilers, *Messages of the First Presidency of The Church of Jesus Christ of Latter-day Saints 1833-1964*, 6 vols. (Salt Lake City: Bookcraft, 1965-1975), 3, p. 11; and the comment of John T. Caine, Utah's territorial delegate to Congress, that polygamy was a "dead issue" in Utah, that it would not be revived, and that less than 1% of the people living in Utah had ever been polygamists. U.S., Congress, House, *Congressional Record*, 50th Cong., 1st Sess., 1888, 19, pt. 8, pp. 7949-7953. For two independent studies indicating that, as late as 1880, polygamy was both more common and that it played a greater role in Utah's social life than heretofore believed, see Larry Logue, "A time of marriage: Monogamy and polygamy in a Utah town," *Journal of Mormon*

History 11 (1984), pp. 3-26; and Lowell "Ben" Bennion, "The incidence of Mormon polygamy in 1880: 'Dixie' versus Davis Stake," ibid., 11 (1984), pp. 27-42.

11. For discussions of the use to which the Mexican colonies were put in perpetuating polygamous marriage after the Manifesto of 1890, see Victor W. Jorgensen and B. Carmon Hardy, "The Taylor-Cowley affair and the watershed of Mormon history," *Utah Historical Quarterly*, 48 (Winter 1980), pp. 16-19; D. Michael Quinn, "LDS Church authority and new plural marriages, 1890-1904," *Dialogue: A Journal of Mormon Thought*, 18 (Spring 1985), pp. 15-19 and 57-98 (hereafter *Dialogue*);and Richard S. Van Wagoner, *Mormon Polygamy: A History* (Salt Lake City: Signature Books, 1986), pp. 152-53 and 161-94.

12. As but a sample of the many who have since accepted this view, see the inference of such belief in Romney, *The Mormon Colonies*, pp. 51-52 and 267; and Kimball Young, *Isn't One Wife Enough?* (New York: Henry Holt and Company, 1954), p. 419. Direct affirmations of the legality of polygamy in Mexico can be found in Jerold A. Hilton, "Polygamy in Utah and Surrounding Area Since the Manifesto of 1890" (master's thesis, Brigham Young University, 1965), pp. 6, 13 and 18; James B. Allen and Richard O. Cowan, *Mormonism in the Twentieth Century*, rev. edn. (Provo, Utah: Brigham Young University Press, 1969), p. 19; Kenneth W. Godfrey, "The coming of the Manifesto," *Dialogue*, 5 (Autumn 1970), p. 15; Annie R. Johnson, *Heartbeats of Colonia Diaz* (Mesa, Arizona: published by the authoress, 1972), p. 14; and Davis Bitton, "Mormon polygamy: A review article," *Journal of Mormon History*, 4 (1977), p. 111.

13. The canons of the church had a direct influence on the compilations of many European and New World nations, transforming monogamy into what one scholar has called the "Grundsatz" of Western Christian society. Erich Vogel, *Das Ehehindernis des Ehebruchs. Eine rechtsvergleichende Arbeit* (Heidelberg: inaugural dissertation, 1928), p.92. The Catholic emphasis on monogamous marriage was especially great in Spain. Joaquin Francisco Pacheco, *El Código penal concordado y comentado*, rev. edn., 4 vols. (Madrid: Imprenta de Manuel Tello, 1870), 3, p. 226; Rafael Altamira y Crevea, *Cuestiones de historia del derecho y de legislación comparada*, 4 vols. (Barcelona: Herederos de Juan Gile, Editores, 1913), 2, pp. 98-100, sec. 463; Luis Fernández Clérigo, *El Derecho de familia en la legislación comparada* (México: Union tipografica editorial Hispano-Americana, 1947), p. 37. For statutory examples of repeated sanctions against polygamy in Spanish law, see "De los adúlteros, y bígamos," with references to earlier codes, in *Novisima recopilación de las leyes de España...* (Madrid, 1805-1807), lib.12, tít. 28, leyes 6-9.

14. See, for example, the note attached to Carlos III's castigation of bigamy in 1770, at *Nov. recop.*, lib. 12, tit.28, ley 10; also discussion of the subject in J. Francisco Pacheco's commentaries on the Spanish legal reform of 1870, in his *El Código*, 3, p. 21; the same in Pedro Gomez de la Serna, *Elementos del derecho civil y penal de España...*, rev. edn. by Juan Manuel Montalban (Madrid: Libería de Sanchez, 1877), 3, pp. 348-49 and 364; and Joaquin Escriche,

Diccionario razonado de legislación y jurisprudecia, rev. edn. (Paris and México: Libería de Ch. Bouret, 1888), pp. 378 and 1356.

15. Jorge Vera Estañol, "Juridical Evolution," in Justo Sierra, ed., *Mexico, Its Social Evolution...*, trans. G. Sintiñón, 2 vols. in 3 (Mexico: J. Ballescá and Co., 1900-1904), 2, p. 742.

16. D. Manuel Mateos Alarcon, *La Evolución del derecho civil Mexicana desda la independencia hasta nuestros dias* (México: Tip. Vda. de F. Díaz de Leon, Sucs., 1911), pp. 5-7; Toribio Esquivel Obregón, *Influencia de España y los Estados Unidos sobre México* (Madrid: Casa Editorial Calleja, 1918), p. 22; Miguel S. Macedo, *Apuntes para la historia del derecho penal Mexicano* (México: Ed. "Cultura", 1931), pp. 199-210 and 272; Jose Ma. Ots y Capdequi, *Historia del derecho Español en America y del derecho indiano* (Madrid: Aguila, 1969), pp. 30-36, 43 and 45-48.

17. *Redacción del código civil de México que se contiene en las leyes Españolas...por...Vincente González Castro*, Vol. 1 (Gudalajara: Mario Melendez y Muñoz, 1839), lib. 1, tít. 4, cap. 2, sec. 1, arts. 60, 63, 99, and 102; *Código civil del imperio Mexicano* (México: Imprenta de M. Villanueva, 1866), lib. 1, tít. 4, cap. 6, arts. 185 and 191; *Código civil del Distrito Federal y Territorio de Baja California* (México: Imprenta José Batiza, 1870), lib. 1, tít. 5, cap. 1, arts. 159 and 163, secs. 4-5 and 9; *Código penal para el Distrito Federal y Territorio de Baja California sobre delitos del fuero común, y para toda la república sobre delitos contra la federación* (México: Imprenta del gobierno, en palacio, 1871), lib. 3, tít. 6, cap. 7, arts. 831, 832 and 838; *Código civil del Distrito Federal y Territorio de la Baja California reformado en virtud de la autorización concedida al ejecutivo por decreto de 14 de Diciembre de 1883* (México: Imprenta de Francisco Díaz de Leon, 1884), lib. 1, tít. 1, cap. 1, arts. 155 and 159, sec. 9; cap. 6, art. 268.

    In Mexico, as in Spain, divorce was not legally possible until the twentieth century. See, for example, the *Código civil* [Mexico, 1884], lib. 1, tít. 5, cap. 5, art. 226. To have allowed divorce, as to permit polygamy, it was believed, would corrupt the family and, perforce, society. Alberto Gaxiola G., "Notas sobre la evolución juridico-social de la familia en México," (thesis, U.A. de México, 1936), p. 28.

18. *Código penal para el Distrito Federal y territorio de la Baja California...* (Chihuahua: Libería de Donato Miramontes, 1883); *Código penal del estado de Sonora* (Hermosillo: Imprento del gobierno, 1884).

19. *Código penal del estado libre y soberano de Chihuahua*, primera edn., oficial (Chihuahua: Imprente del gobierno en palacio, 1897), lib. 3, tít. 6, cap. 7, arts. 781-88; *Código penal del estado de Sonora* (Hermosillo: Imprenta del gobierno, 1909), lib. 3, tít. 6, cap. 7, arts. 724-27.

20. Spain: *Nov. recop.*, lib. 12, tít. 26, art. 1; and the commentaries of Pacheco, *El Código*, 4, pp. 292-94; Gomez de la Serna, *Elementos*, 3, pp. 343-44; and, Rafael Altamira y Crevea, *Historia de España y de la civilización Española*, rev. edn., 4 vols. (Barcelona: Herederos de Juan Gili, Editores, 1913), 1, pp. 462-63, sec. 307.

    Mexico: *Código penal* (1871), lib. 3, tít. 6, cap. 6, art. 821; *Código civil*

(1884), lib. 1, tít. 5, cap. 5, art. 228. See also Manuel Andrade, *Código civil del Distrito Federal y territorios reformado...* (México: Botas é hijo sucs., 1925), p. 41; Gaxiola G., "Notas," 27; and Francisco Gonzalez de la Vega, *Derecho penal Mexicanos los delitos*, 3 vols. (México: Editorial Porrua, 1944-1945), 3, pp. 232-33.

21. As regards mistresses and their children in Spain, "las barraganas" and "los hijos naturales," see Gomez de la Serna, *Elementos*, 1, pp. 95 and 308n; 2, pp. 75-82; In Mexico, see the provisions at *Código civil* (1884), lib. 4, tít. 1, art. 3236; lib. 4, tít. 4, cap. 3, art. 3592; and the discussion provided by Don Luis Mendez et al., *Código civil del Distrito Federal anotado y concordado con...otras códigos Mexicanos y extranjeros...* (México: Imprenta de Escalante, 1871), p. 31; Mateos Alarcon, *La Evolución*, pp. 22-41.

22. D. Yndalecio Sanchez et al., *Código penal para el Distrito Federal y territorio de la Baja California...anotado y concordado* (México: Imprenta de Ignacio Escalante y Cia., 1872), p. 11. See also Pacheco, *El Código*, 3, pp. 108-09; Gomez de la Serna, *Elementos*, 1, p. 308n; Escriche, *Diccionario*, p. 98; "Adulterio," in Antonio de Jesús Lozano, *Diccionario razonado de legislación y jurisprudencia Mexicanas...* (México: J. Ballescá y Cia., 1905), pp. 95-96; and Gonzalez de la Vega, *Derecho*, 3, pp. 228.

23. For a sample of the Mormon volley on Victorian hypocrisy, see *Journal of Discourses by Brigham Young, President of the Church of Jesus Christ of Latter-day Saints, His Two Counsellors, The Twelve Apostles, and Others*, 26 vols. (Liverpool: published by F.D. Richards, 1855-1886), 20, pp. 308-09; 23, pp. 56-57; "The Way of the World," DN, 2 September 1879; "Discourse," DN, 13 June 1885; "New England Bigamy and Utah Polygamy," DN, 22 June 1882; "Discourse by Apostle Erastus Snow," DN, 13 June 1885; "Utter Depravity," DN, 3 December 1885.

24. "Report of the Utah Commission," *Report of the Secretary of the Interior; Being Part of the Message and Documents Communicated to the Two Houses of Congress at the Beginning of the Forty-ninth Congress*, 5 vols. (Washington, DC: GPO, 1885), 2, pp. 887-88. For rulings by the courts emphasizing this same point, see *United States* v. *Musser*, 4 Utah 153, 7 Pac. 389 (1885); *Cannon* v. *United States*, 116 U.S. 55 (1886); *United States* v. *Smith*, 5 Utah 232, 14 Pac. 291 (1887); and Mr. Justice Field's opinion in *Davis* v. *Beason*, 133 U.S. 341-342 (1890). As Mark S. Lee has pointed out, it was the high priority attached to the ideal of the monogamous home by Victorian society that best explains the reasoning in the famous Reynolds case of 1879. "Legislating morality: Reynolds v. United States," *Sunstone*, 10 (April 1985), pp. 8-12.

25. It was the problems of widespread immorality and attendant ills that Apostle Moses Thatcher spoke to in recommending Mormon polygamy to the consideration of Mexican readers when he opened the Mormon mission in Mexico City in 1879. *La Poligamia Mormona y la monogamia Cristiana comparadas...por el Elder Moisés Thatcher* (México: Imprenta de E.D. Orozco y Cia., 1881), pp. 19-33. The question of polygamy's presumed social and hygienic superiority, and the expectation of its eventual displacement of

monogamy, was the subject of the author's "Mormonism's Nineteenth Century Socio-Biological Critique of Monogamy" (paper delivered before the Mormon History Association, Salt Lake City, 2 May 1986).

26. Franklin Spencer Gonzalez, "The Restored Church in Mexico," typewritten manuscript, pp. 23-24, LDSA.

27. "Mormones," *El Monitor Republicano*, 5 February 1880. The first exploring party of Mormons to enter Mexico in 1876, if we believe the account of their leader and chronicler, were castigated upon their appearance in Paso del Norte as heralds of a plague of immorality. Daniel W. Jones, *Forty Years Among the Indians: A True Yet Thrilling Narrative of the Author's Experiences Among the Natives* (1890; reprint edn., Los Angeles: Westernlore Press, 1960), pp. 242-43.

28. "Teorías mormonicas," *La Patria Diario de México,*" 30 Julio 1886; "Mormonism in Mexico," *Mexican Financier*, 31 January 1885; editorial, ibid., 2 May 1885; editorial, ibid., 14 March 1885; and the summary of editorial opinion provided in Warner P. Sutton, "Mormons," p. 576.

29. "Chihuahua antes y hoy," *El Correo de Chihuahua*, 27 February 1905; "La Poligamia en México," ibid., 30 Enero 1906; "Doce mil mormones para México," *El Tiempo Diario Católico*, 14 September 1906; the letter from the Mexican minister of public works in William Alexander Linn, *The Story of the Mormons from the Date of Their Origin to the Year 1901* (New York: Macmillan, 1902), pp. 614-15; and the citations and comments of Moisés González Navarro, *La Vida Social: Historia moderna de México. El Porfirato*, ed., Cosío Villegas et al., 8 vols. (México: Editorial Hermes, 1948-1965), 4, pp. 179-180.

30. As reported in Sutton, "Mormons," p. 576.

31. "The Mormons in Mexico," *Deseret Weekly*, 17 January 1891; the interview between Luis Hüller and the *Chicago Tribune*, reported in "The Colonies and Railroads in Mexico," DN, 2 February 1891; and that with John W. Young, in "Chihuahua, Sonora and Sinaloa," *Mexican Financier*, 7 March 1891.

32. Reported in "Information about Mexico," *Deseret Weekly*, 24 January 1891.

33. "The Mormon Colonies," *Mexican Financier*, 7 February 1891.

34. "Historical Record, Juarez Stake, 1901-1906," 23 February 1901, LDSA. See also the comments of Apostle John Henry Smith, in "Juarez Stake Historical Record, 1907-1932," 7 March 1908, LDSA.

35. "La Poligamia en México," *El Correo de Chihuahua*, 30 Enero 1906.

36. A translated copy of the expulsion order is found in Andrew Jenson, compiler, "Juarez Stake Manuscript History and Historical Reports, 1895," 17 March 1885, LDSA.

37. "Mormones," *La época*, 5 Mayo 1885; "The Mexican plan for settling the Mormon question," *Mexican Financier*, 2 May 1885; and "Against the Mormons," *Salt Lake Herald*, 27 September 1885.

38. Helaman Pratt Diaries, 3, 12 and 13 May 1885, Helaman Pratt Collection, LDSA.

39. "Ley sobre colonización y deslinde de terrenos baldíos," in *Legislación Mexicana; ó, colleción completa de las disposiciones legislativas expedidas desde*

la independencia de la república...1867-1910. Edn. oficial...[Vols. 1-34 (1876-1904) by Manuel Dublán and José María Lozano; Vols. 31-42, edited as "Colección Legislativa" by Agustín Verdugo, A. Dublán and A. Esteva], 42 vols. in 50 (México: Imp. gob., 1876-1912), 16, pp. 663-67, núm. 8887, 15 Diciembre 1883.

40. Helaman Pratt Diaries, 3, 14 May 1885.

41. Ibid., 3, 22 May 1885.

42. H. Grant Ivins, "Polygamy in Mexico as Practiced by the Mormon Church, 1895-1905," typewritten manuscript, p. 5, Special Collections Department, Marriott Library, University of Utah.

43. Joseph Henry Dean Diary, p. 107, 24 September 1890, LDSA.

44. Although I have not found anything comparable in the case of Canada, it seems likely that copies of the Manifesto were sent to members of the Canadian diplomatic corps in the United States, just as they were to Mexican authorities. The official publication of the Mexican government acknowledged formally that their ambassador in Washington, DC, had received a copy. See *Diario oficial*, núm. 102, 27 Octobre 1890.

45. At least one American observer, writing at the time of the Mexican Revolution, believed that had Díaz's successor, Francisco I. Madero, survived as president, he would have required that the Mormons discontinue polygamy and obey the law. John Lewin McLeish, *Highlights of the Mexican Revolution Some Previously Unwritten History of the Beginning and Growth of Constitutional Government in the Southern Republic* (n.p.: Menace Publishing Co., 1918), p. 133.

46. Burton J. Hendrick, "The Mormon revival of polygamy," *McClure's Magazine*, 36 (January 1911), pp. 459-60.

47. Jenson, "Juarez Stake Manuscript History," 5 June 1885. Later that summer, Apostles Lyman, Young, Taylor and Snow all made additional trips to Mexico City, where they discussed land matters with cabinet members and were confirmed in their sense of welcome as colonists. I find no record dealing with these meetings that would indicate additional conversation about polygamy. Ibid, 3 July 1885, 15 July 1885, 13 August 1885; and Albert R. Lyman, *Biography of Francis Marion Lyman 1840-1916 Apostle 1880-1916* (Delta, Utah: published by Melvin A. Lyman, 1958), p. 108.

48. Annie R. Johnson, *Heartbeats of Colonia Diaz*, p. 14. The same story, as told by the daughter of one of the colonists, is found in Elva R. Shumway, oral history, interviewed by Leonard R. Grover, 24 April 1980, Mesa, Arizona, p. 8, BYU. A similar tradition also persists among Mormon Fundamentalists. See Verlan M. LeBaron, *The LeBaron Story* (Lubbock, Texas: Keels and Co., 1981), p. 45.

49. Those accounts, on which I have relied, concerning early Mormon colonization in Canada are chiefly "Brief Account of the Early History of the Canadian Mission, 1887-1895," Alberta Temple Historical Record, typewritten manuscript, LDSA; and the excellent, but often ignored, study of Lowry Nelson in C.A. Dawson, *Group Settlement: Ethnic Communities in Western Canada*, Vol. 7, *Canadian Frontiers of Settlement* (Toronto: Macmillan, 1936), pp.

175-272. I have also consulted Andrew Jenson, "Alberta Stake," *Encyclopedic History of the Church of Jesus Christ of Latter-Day Saints* (Salt Lake City: Deseret News Publishing Co., 1941), pp. 8-10; Archie G. Wilcox, "Founding of the Mormon Community in Alberta" (master's thesis, University of Alberta, 1950); Lowry Nelson, *The Mormon Village: A Pattern and Technique of Land Settlement* (Salt Lake City: University of Utah Press, 1952), pp. 219-71; Melvin S. Tagg et al., *A History of the Mormon Church in Canada* (Lethbridge Herald Co., 1968); Lawrence B. Lee, "The Mormons come to Canada, 1887-1902," *Pacific Northwest Quarterly*, 59 (January 1968), pp. 11-22; and L.A. Rosenvall, "The transfer of Mormon culture to Alberta," *American Review of Canadian Studies*, 12 (Summer 1982), pp. 51-63.

50. "Not an exodus," *Deseret Weekly*, 22 June 1889. For yet other examples of the Mormon attempt to mask the connection between the flight of those moving to Canada and the anti-polygamy crusade, see "The 'Mormons' in Canada," DN, 26 August 1889; "Mormons in Canada," *Deseret Weekly*, 7 September 1889; "Mormons in Canada," ibid., 14 December 1889; "Mormons in Canada," DN, 25 November 1889; "The 'Mormons' in Canada," ibid., 20 December 1890.

51. Brigham H. Roberts, *A Comprehensive History of the Church of Jesus Christ of Latter-day Saints Century I*, 6 vols. (Salt Lake City: published by the Church, Deseret News Press, 1930), 6, pp. 259 and 276; Austin and Alta Fife, *Saints of Sage and Saddle* (Bloomington: Indiana University Press, 1956), p. 171; Hilton, "Polygamy in Utah," pp. 6, 13 and 18; Lee, "The Mormons come to Canada," p. 16; Godfrey, "The Coming of the Manifesto," p. 15; J. Max Anderson, *The Polygamy Story: Fiction and Fact* (Salt Lake City: Publisher's Press, 1979), p. 122; Brian Champion, "The Press, Parliament and polygamy: The Mormons come to Canada," *Thetian* (1981), p. 24.

52. "An Acte to restrayne all psons from Marriage until their former Wyves and former Husbands be deade," 1 Jac. 1, ch. 11 (1603-04); 26 Geo. II, ch. 33 (1740); and, 9 Geo. IV, ch. 31, sec. 1 (1833). See also the overview provided under "Bigamy," *Encyclopedia of the Laws of England*, ed., E.A. Jelf (London: Sweet and Maxwell, 1938-1941), 2, pp. 73-38.

53. James Cookson, *Thoughts on Polygamy, Suggested by the Dictates of Scriptures, Nature, Reason, and Common-sense;...* (Winchester: Printed by John Wilkes for the Author, 1782), p. 61.

54. William Blackstone, *Commentaries on the Laws of England* (Oxford: printed at the Clarendon Press, 1769), 4.13.2.

55. Kenneth L. Cannon II, "A Strange Encounter: The English courts and Mormon polygamy," *Brigham Young University Studies*, 22 (Winter 1982), pp. 73-83. Another study, in 1966, found the Hyde ruling, with its refusal to entertain such a marriage for purposes of dissolution, general and binding in the British Commonwealth. D. Mendes Da Costa, "Polygamous marriages in the conflict of laws," *The Canadian Bar Review*, 44 (May 1966), p. 293.

56. See, for example, the "Colonial Laws Validity Act," 28 & 29 Victoria, ch. 63. For his assistance in connection with the Canadian legal background on polygamy, I wish to thank Mr. Vincent M. Del Buono, Senior Counsel, Human Rights and Criminal Law, Department of Justice, Ottawa.

57. "British North America Act," 30 Victoria, ch. 3, sec. 91. The "Consolidation Act," with its condemnation of bigamy, is at 32-33 Victoria, ch. 20, sec. 58. And the slightly older English prohibition is to be read at 24-25 Victoria, ch. 100, sec. 57, Imp.

58. "An Act Respecting Offenses Relating to the Law of Marriage," 49 Victoria, ch. 161, sec. 4.

59. "An Act to make further provision for the government of the Northwest Territories," 34 Victoria, ch. 16.

60. "An Ordinance Respecting Marriages," no. 9, 1878, in David Laird [lieutenant-governor], *Ordinances of the Northwest Territories, Passed in the Years 1878 and 1879* (Regina: printed by Nicholas Flood Davin, 1884), p. 45.

61. Untitled, *Edmonton Bulletin*, 3 September 1887; untitled, ibid., 31 March 1888; and the comments of M. Doyon in Canada, House of Commons, 28 *Debates*: 980, 3 April 1889.

62. The Mormons were not without journalistic support. See "Mormons All Right," *Manitoba Daily Free Press*, 3 January 1888; and the account of the visit to Mormon settlements by Minister of Customs Mackenzie Bowell, in "That Mormon Visit," *Macleod Gazette*, 31 October 1889. Some Mormons were reported to have told all who inquired that they had "eschewed polygamy." "Lee's Creek Mormons," *Calgary Tribune*, 14 November 1888.

63. Editorial, *Winnipeg Free Press*, 18 October 1889. Also, "That Mormon Visit," *Macleod Gazette*, 31 October 1889; untitled, ibid., 6 February 1890; "Mormons in Canada," *Edmonton Bulletin*, 21 December 1889; editorial, *Regina Leader*, 17 February 1890; editorial, *Saskatchewan Herald*, 19 March 1890. A brief account of the surveillance conducted by the North-West Mounted Police and their continuing suspicions of the Mormons is found in R.C. Macleod, *The NWMP and Law Enforcement 1873-1905* (Toronto and Buffalo: University of Toronto Press, 1976), pp. 155-56.

64. 53 Victoria, ch. 37, sec. 11, subsections a-d. This enactment was incorporated into Canada's first Criminal Code (55-56 Victoria, ch. 29) in the *Revised Statutes of Canada*, part 5, sec. 278, pp. 104-05 (1892) (hereafter RSC). Despite the Canadian statute's greater particularity, there is no doubt that it was inspired by the purpose, if not the language, of the Edmunds law. See the comments of Sir John Thompson, minister of justice and author of the law, in House of Commons, 31 *Debates*, 3173, 10 April 1890; and James Crankshaw, *The Criminal Code of Canada and the Canada Evidence Act...*, rev. edn. (Toronto: Carswell, 1910), p. 349.

To assure further that plural marriages as performed by the Mormons, could not legally occur, an 1892 law was added prohibiting the "solemnization" of any marriage except by those officers properly authorized by the state. 55-56 Victoria, ch. 29, sec. 279; RSC, part 22, sec. 279, p. 288 (1892). That this was aimed directly at polygamous Mormons from Utah, see W.J. Tremeear, *The Criminal Code and the Law of Criminal Evidence in Canada...* (Toronto: Canada Law Book Company, 1908), p. 255. The United States Congress had placed a similar provision in the Edmunds-Tucker Act: U.S., *Statutes at Large*, Vol. 24, ch. 397, sec. 9 (1887).

65. 55-56 Victoria, ch. 29, sec. 279; RSC, part 6, sec. 311, p. 255 (1892).

66. Jessie L. Embry, "Exiles for the principle: LDS polygamy in Canada," *Dialogue*, 18 (Fall 1985), pp. 108-16; idem, "Two Legal Wives: Mormon Polygamy in Canada, the United States and Mexico" in this volume.

67. John Davidson, "The foreign population of the Canadian West," *The Economic Journal*, 12 (March 1902), p. 102; all of Edgar E. Folk, *The Mormon Monster, or, The Story of Mormonism...* (Chicago and Toronto: Fleming H. Revell Co., 1900); Herbert Wesley Toombs, *Mormonism* (Toronto: The Board of Home Missions and Social Service, Presbyterian Church in Canada, 1916), pp. 26-27; the brief sensation created when marriages performed by Mormon elders in Toronto in 1924 were temporarily invalidated, "Journal History of the Church," 18 June and 1 July 1924, LDSA; and the chronicle of anti-Mormon publications for this period provided by Howard Palmer in his "Polygamy and Progress: The Reaction to Mormons in Canada" in this volume.

68. See J.H.C. Morris, "The recognition of polygamous marriages in English law," *Harvard Law Review* 66 (April 1953), pp. 961-1012; and T.C. Hartley, "Bigamy in the conflict of laws," *International and Comparative Law Quarterly*, 16 (July 1967), pp. 680-703.

69. For example, RSC, part 6, ch. 146, sec. 310, pp. 253-54 (1906); and, in the 1927 general revision of the Criminal Code, it was preserved in "Offenses Against Conjugal Rights," RSC, part 6, sec. 310, pp. 404-05.

70. See testimony given before the master in chancery, as published in "The church cases," *Deseret Weekly*, 24 October 1891. For more denials, later in the decade, see "The Brigham Young of 1896," DN, 10 October 1896; "Polygamy not the Issue," ibid., 22 October 1898; "The Manifesto," ibid., 15 July 1899; "Polygamy and Unlawful Cohabitation," ibid., 8 January 1900.

71. U.S., Congress, Senate, *Proceedings Before the Committee on Privileges and Elections of the United States Senate in the Matter of the Protests Against the Right of Hon. Reed Smoot, a Senator from the State of Utah, to Hold His Seat*, 59th Cong., 1st Sess., Doc. no. 486, 4 vols. (Washington, DC, GPO, 1906), 1, pp. 102, 143, 177, 178, 184, 211, 317-18, and 485.

72. Clark, *Messages*, 4, p. 151.

73. For example, James B. Allen and Glen M. Leonard, *The Story of the Latter-day Saints* (Salt Lake City: Deseret Book Company, 1976), p. 278; Leonard J. Arrington and Davis Bitton, *The Mormon Experience A History of the Latter-day Saints* (New York: Alfred A. Knopf, 1979), p. 185 (in the case of the latter volume, see Bitton's comment that he and Arrington were "advised" to excise a chapter on polygamy from their book); "Ten years in Camelot: A personal memoir," *Dialogue*, 16 (Autumn 1983), p. 13.

74. See above at note 51. See also First Presidency of the Church of Jesus Christ of Latter-day Saints, "Official Statement," in Clark, *Messages*, 5, pp. 324 and 330; John A. Widtsoe, *Evidences and Reconciliations: Aids to Faith in a Modern Day* (Salt Lake City: The Bookcraft Co., 1943), p. 310; the

comments and quotations provided in William E. Berrett and Alma P. Burton, eds., *Readings in LDS Church History from Original Manuscripts...*, 3 vols. (Salt Lake City: Deseret Book Co., 1953-1958), 3, pp. 109, 117 and 124; Hyrum M. Smith and Janne M. Sjodahl, eds., *The Doctrine and Covenants Containing Revelations Given to Joseph Smith, Jr., The Prophet with an Introduction and Historical and Exegetical Notes*, rev. edn. (Salt Lake City: Deseret Book Co., 1957), p. 837; Paul E. Reimann, *Plural Marriage Limited* (Salt Lake City: Utah Printing Co., 1974), pp. 28-29, 93, 109 and 178-79; and the astonishing statement by a daughter of President Joseph F. Smith, who claimed to have researched the subject, in Edith Smith Patrick, oral history, interviewed by Leonard Grover, 19 July 1980, Orem, Utah, p. 20, LDS Polygamy Oral History Project, BYU.

75. Roberts, *A Comprehensive History*, 6, pp. 259 and 276; Ralph B. Keeler, "Un estudio social, económico, y educativo de las colonias mormonas en el Estado de Chihuahua" (Col. Juárez, Chih., México, n.d.); Albert Kenyon Wagner, "Chihuahua, Our Home" (field project, master's degree, Brigham Young University, 1957), p. 49; Russell R. Rich, *Ensign to the Nations: A History of the LDS Church from 1846 to 1972* (Provo, Utah: Brigham Young University Publications, 1972), p. 406; Clifford J. Stratton and Marsha Romney Stratton, "Catherine's Faith," *Ensign*, 11 (September 1981), pp. 53-54; LaVon B. Whetten and Don L. Searle, "Once a haven, still a home," ibid., 15 (August 1985), p. 43; Glenna M. Hansen, "Mexico: a Timeless past merges with a teeming present," *This People*, 4 (February / March 1983), pp. 31-34.

    Canada: Wilcox, "Founding of the Mormon Community in Alberta," pp. 9-10, 15, 120 and 133; Tagg et al., *A History of the Mormon Church in Canada*, pp. 24 and 49-53; William E. Berrett, *The Latter-day Saints A Contemporary History of the Church of Jesus Christ* (Salt Lake City: Deseret Book Co., 1985), pp. 272-73 and 306-07; Richard O. Cowan, *The Church in the Twentieth Century* (Salt Lake City: Bookcraft, 1985), p. 32; Dean Hughes, *The Mormon Church: A Basic History* (Salt Lake City: Deseret Book Co., 1986), p. 184; and Don L. Searle, "Cardston harvesting a pioneer heritage," *Ensign* 17 (April 1987), pp. 36-41.

76. This was due chiefly to work by John Horne Blackmore and Solon Low. See 2-3 Elizabeth II, ch. 51, sec. 243 (1953-54). I am indebted to Professor Brigham Young Card of the University of Alberta for bringing this revision to my attention. I also wish to acknowledge Mrs. Dawn Monroe of the Public Archives of Canada in Ottawa for further assistance on the subject.

77. Thomas E. Cheney, Austin E. Fife and Juanita Brooks, eds., *Lore of Faith and Folly* (Salt Lake City: University of Utah Press, 1971), p. 133.

Cardston, c.1893, showing transition from log "first" homes to frame houses. Lee Creek divides the community from the farmland. The Card home, termed "the canton flannel palace" because of cloth which Zina Card hung on the inside walls, is in the centre of this photo, on the town's Main Street. NA 237-42 Glenbow Archives.

11 Mormon Women in Southern Alberta
The Pioneer Years

MAUREEN URSENBACH BEECHER

"SISTER HAMMER PUT her head through the tent opening the first morning after her arrival at Lee's Creek, surveyed five inches of newly fallen June snow, and called out, 'Brother Card, is this the kind of place you have brought us to?' 'Yes,' he shouted back, 'did you ever see anything like it?' 'No, I certainly never did,' was her scathing reply."[1] That Sister Hammer and Brother Card were seeing the same scene through different eyes is obvious; that one of those differences is based on their gender suggests an approach to the Mormon experience in Canada that is relatively new to the study, that of women's history. The history of Mormon settlement in Canada has for the most part been written by and about men and their concerns; even the splendid account that underlies so many of the studies of the Cardston settlement, that of the Woolf sisters, Jane and Zina, deals more with kings and counselors than with the homely aspects of people's experience, women included.[2] This essay is an attempt towards a more inclusive view.

Men and women experienced the settlement process differently; Sister Hammer was not just complaining at the cold and the snow. While her husband, Josiah, would engage in tasks of cattle herding, exploring, logging and building, normal outdoor activities little affected by the new snow, she and her sisters would be expected to prepare and serve food, wash clothes, provide sleeping quarters, and organize household goods, all of them indoor tasks done only with great difficulty out of doors or in a tent in inclement weather. Even though there was some crossover of sex roles in western pioneering, primary responsibility was still gender oriented, women doing women's work, men doing men's work, as nineteenth-century American culture defined them.[3]

211

Women's and men's initial responses to the western prairie were shaped by their expectations of their future lives there. All that space delighted Richard Harvey as "paradise indeed," room to expand as he could not in Utah's tiny Heber Valley. And all that prairie grass, belly-high to his horse, he saw as "the abundance of feed and grass everywhere and nothing to feed but my cattle." To his wife, Millie, arriving in a snowstorm, with babe in arms and three more clinging to her skirts, the vastness meant distance from food supplies, medical help, schools and companionship. And the tall grass threatened her children—the girls grew up wearing bright red sunbonnets, so as not to be lost in the fields. For Richard, Canada was a brave new world; for Millie it was exile, and she longed all her life to return "home to Utah."[4]

The immigrants' reasons for coming were varied over the various periods of settlement,[5] but the one that instigated the initial influx, the prosecution of polygamists in Utah, was experienced as intensely, if differently, by women as by men.[6]

The first Mormon settlers of southern Alberta were polygamists and members of their families fleeing from prosecution in the United States under the stipulations of the Edmunds Act. Deputy marshals in Utah and surrounding states tracked down offenders with increasing vigor—and success—and forced men into the "underground," such that by 1885 it was obvious to several of the polygamous patriarchs that they must flee or face the fines and imprisonment. The jeopardy that led the men into hiding is considered fully in the literature; only recently have studies dealt with the experiences of their wives sought as witnesses against their husbands, and likewise forced out of sight.[7]

A few letters of Charles Ora Card and his third wife, Zina Young Williams Card, principals in the initial Mormon venture to Alberta, serve to demonstrate the tensions that led women to join their husbands willingly in the flight to Canada. Widowed ten years earlier, Zina had married Card in June 1884 at the height of the "raid" against polygamists. Residing under her Williams name in Provo, where she taught at Brigham Young Academy, and even in Logan, where Card was stake president and father of an already large family, Zina did not risk discovery as a plural wife until she became pregnant with their first child. Then she had to go underground, living with trusted friends. "Where are you darling today, I wonder for in your last [letter] you had to change," wrote her mother in April 1885, indicating that Zina had had to be secreted away. "How are the times?" she added, cryptically inquiring about the intensity of the federal officers' pursuit.[8] That same month, Card wrote from his hiding place, "Not knowing whether I will be at home tomorrow or not," his encouragement to Zina in her pregnancy, "I crave blessings upon you from the Lord and hope your body may continue to strengthen for its burthen...." Card expressed hope "that my wives will comfort one another."[9] His desire might have been less than fully realized. Zina wrote later:

> S[arah] and I have good times, and I have done as near right as I know how by all. She has the red cow & I shared the apples with them. Sister S[arah], what shall I say, only this, that I have done by her as I would like to be done by, and I leave the rest in the hands of God.

In contrast to the apparent cool civility she expressed toward Sarah Painter, Zina added in the same letter, "I love Vinie...," Card's recently acquired wife Lavinia Rigby.[10]

Following his oft-told escape from the deputy marshals, Card himself again hid out, writing on one occasion to Zina that "I never knew how to sympathize with you in your exile as I do today...."[11] Under various names, the two corresponded, conducting necessary business and arranging clandestine meetings as opportunity permitted. By the time a September 1886 letter arrived from Moses Thatcher in Colonia Juarez, advising Card how to travel there, he was planning the Canada exploration;[12] by mid-September he and his two companions were out of Utah, headed north.

Once Card was beyond the marshals' reach, Sarah, Zina, and Vinie were no longer in jeopardy of having to testify, though they could still be questioned about Card's whereabouts. They spent the winter in comparative peace. "Don't worry about me for God has given me power over my own self, and I am happy and contented," wrote Zina in November.[13] By the time of Card's return, prosecution had lessened—"the deps [deputy marshals] are out of town, so Br. Kimball says," Zina wrote—so meetings could be arranged. "If you feel to send for me I will leave our darling [baby Joseph] with mother." Nevertheless, "To be safe I shall stay from home for a few days."[14] By spring, as plans were materializing for the family's move to Canada, Card, having spent the early spring on the underground, wrote, "You say you miss me, I confess it's mutual, for these days are long and dreary... I shall be glad when I am on English soil again."[15]

Women, then, as well as men, saw the risk of emigration as less than the danger of remaining in Utah. Even so, there is an element of the "reluctant pioneer" stereotype in the attitudes of Mormon women pioneers to Canada, an element exacerbated, in many cases, by the men going on ahead and leaving their wives the responsibility of tidying up affairs at home, providing the clothing and foodstuffs necessary, packing the wagons, and bringing the children. "Father came in March," wrote Louisa Grant Alston, "and I with my seven girls and one boy got here June 11, 1900."[16] In most cases, there were men in the companies, often young boys along to herd the cattle; usually the women drove their own wagons as well as carrying out their domestic responsibilities. "Sarah [Daines] drove a very spirited team and it often caused the other members of the party to hold their breath in anxiety while she drove over some of the terrible perilous roads," reads one account. The Woolf-Card-Farrell company, among the first to Lee Creek, had likewise fewer men than wagons and "Mamie or I [Mary Lula or Jane Woolf] cared for young Joseph [Zina Card's two-year-old] while his mother drove team and Sterling [Zina's teenaged son] drove cattle."[17] Card met the company at Helena, Montana, about halfway to their destination; other husbands met their wives near the Canadian-US border or at the sometimes treacherous St. Mary River crossing.

Most, but not all the women who came, were met by husbands. One spunky young woman, Sarah Ann Hinman, came in 1889 to spend an anticipated few months with her sister's family. The older woman with whom she had traveled turned back at Helena, after which the seventeen-year-old drove the wagon while her brother-in-law's sons drove the cattle. At the nooning, besides preparing the midday meal—"I had to learn to cook over a campfire"—Sarah would bake the bread which had risen from the morning's mixing. "Can't say I enjoyed my trip," she commented later. Absence of female company was part of the discomfort, it seems, "After the lady who was with me had to go back I was very lonesome. I had no idea it was such a long ways when I left home, or I guess I never would have left."[18]

Even for those who came with their husbands, the journey was not easy or pleasant. Hannah Anderson was forced to leave her three-year-old Annie behind in Cache Valley with "the aunt," presumably one of her husband's other two wives, because of the difficulty of caring for her other five children, including Mary, a toddler who learned to walk along the wagon tongue.[19] Adeline Greene, setting out with her husband and children, underestimated the severity of the Idaho-Montana mountain climate, "It blowed and rained like sixty. Could not get much fire—could not bake bread—had a serious time," she wrote. As helpful as her husband was with the family—he often cooked, or purchased food or medicine, or found a small cookstove to make the work easier—she commented in her diary, "I had thought to have had some pleasure out of this trip but I have not seen any yet." Her spirits were

Cardston's first women, c.1900. Back row, l-r: Elizabeth Hammer, Zina Y. Card, Lydia J. Brown; middle row: Catherine Pilling, Rhoda Hinman, Mary L. Woolf, Jane Hinman, Sarah Daines; front row: Mary L. Ibey, Jane Eliza Bates. NA 147-4, Glenbow Archives.

further dampened by their frequent meetings with returning emigrants who had found Canada not up to expectations. "We met four teams coming back from Cardston all sick of the country. I feel sick of it too," she wrote.[20] Her husband's parallel account of the journey makes no mention of discouraging reports.

Although most of the immigrants came in small groups in horse-drawn wagons, various railroad connections were possible, even from the first year of settlement.[21] Prices were exorbitant to settlers coming from an agricultural economy, however, and, there was the matter of cattle and household goods as well. By 1893, when the Woolf family was returning from a visit to Utah for the dedication of the Salt Lake Temple, the "Turkey Trail" narrow-gauge line was in full operation, however slow.[22] Millie Harvey, emigrating by train in 1900, was forced to ride with her infant and three children in the caboose, since there was a passenger car only twice a week. The train stopped frequently to let cattle feed, and finally disgorged its passengers, two- and four-legged kind, on the bald prairie at Stirling, where there was only a station house for shelter until a way could be found to a hospitable neighbor.[23]

The usual settlement pattern adopted by Mormons, the "nucleated" village described by Lynn Rosenvall as having its roots in New England models, was well suited to the needs of women.[24] Those "rituals" of family and community life that women used to cement the society are enhanced by the proximity of their homes. One need but contrast the recorded activities of Mormon women with those of Alberta ranch wives, as described in the writings of Sheilagh Jameson, to recognize the advantages to women of hamlet over homestead settlement.[25] While describing the lengths to which ranch women went to maintain social connections, Jameson observed that "particularly during the early years of settlement, there were women who felt the weight of loneliness. Often it was the lack of feminine companionship they found most wearing."[26]

The assumption that Mormons in Alberta followed the pattern established in Utah, where unclaimed lands could be freely distributed among settlers, is flawed, however. When the first Mormons in Cardston settled on a half section registered in the name of Charles Ora Card, it was made clear that title to surrounding lands could not be purchased by the group co-operatively, and that the Saints, like other immigrants, would be required to abide by homesteading regulations or purchase land at going rates.[27] The settlement pattern of "carelessly scattering out over a wide extent of country," decried by an 1882 First Presidency letter, would seem unavoidable by the stipulations of the 1872 Dominion Lands Act.[28]

What actually occurred in Mormon settlement was a combination of homesteading and hamlet dwelling, of land obtained by pre-emption and homestead claim, as when the Leavitts settled Buffalo Flats west of Cardston; and of purchase, as when the Pillings bought Section 25 of Township 2, Range 24, southeast of Cardston.[29] Those two families formed the nuclei of the towns of Leavitt and Aetna respectively; however, others, such as Johnny and Lucinda Woolf, established a ranch eight miles south of Cardston, but so the nearest neighbors were "no more than a couple of miles away."[30] Cardston was the still point in this moving world, but the experiences of those whose residence was there and those who only visited were quite different.

It is difficult to surmise what proportion of the total Mormon population lived in what circumstance at any given time. According to the 1891 Canadian Census, 341 people gave their religion as "Mormon." The census taker gave no indication of the location of the families listed, and a comparison of the lists with available ecclesiastical lists suggests that a number of settlers were not accounted for. The Young Ladies' Mutual Improvement

Association minutes of that year, for example, show 31 young women enrolled, only 19 of whom appear on the Census. By rough guess, then, one-third of the population might have been living out of reach of the Census, probably on remote homesteads.[31] That estimate is confirmed by Card himself, writing in 1894, "About a third of our people live out upon their ranches and are scattered for several miles around."[32]

What is indicated by the population registered in that Census is that the Mormon settlers, as might be expected, did indeed immigrate as families. Impressions from the Census groupings themselves are borne out by the attached population distribution graph, in which the group as a whole, with its almost equal balance of men and women, fits the model of a community characterized by families in single units. The group, of course, is extremely small, and the graph is representative of nothing beyond that one group. There are only two skews on the graph. One indicates that adult males are older than adult females in the 35-and-older bracket, a phenomenon explained for this group by the preponderance of polygamists who brought with them a second or third, and therefore younger, wife, leaving the older wife or wives in Utah.[33] The other shows a marked absence of females in the 15-to-19-years group. There seems to be no immediate explanation for the latter gap.[34] The evenness of the graph in its first three segments suggests that emigration caused no disruption in family growth; by actual count, 45 children had been born to Mormon families in Alberta by the spring of 1891.[35]

Just as it is easier to count people living in villages, so it is easier to assemble evidence of their lifestyles, and so existing studies of Alberta Mormons have taken that bias. But there are now sufficient records of Mormon women who spent their lives in the homestead-like circumstances to contrast their experiences with those of women in the towns. In that pattern of contrasting and comparing, let us look at some aspects of the lives of Mormon women in the first few years of Canadian settlement.

Those "rituals" of community interaction mentioned earlier give shape to a woman's life, no matter where she is. In a landmark study of nineteenth-century American women, Carroll Smith-Rosenberg demonstrated a "female world" in which women bonded to other women created the basis upon which the kinship networks were built after industrialization drew men into a remote workplace. The home place became women's center, and the rituals of the life cycle the events through which they interacted.

Weddings, for example, bring women into close contact over a period of weeks, even months. Mother and daughter, sisters, neighbors and friends

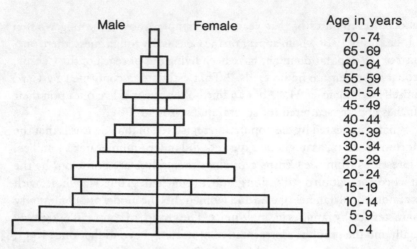

Figure 11.1: Population Distribution: Mormons of Cardston area, Canada Census 1891.

Source: Based on manuscript census, microfilm, Glenbow-Alberta Institute, Calgary, Alberta. Total Mormon population, 341.

gather over preparations. Jane Bates interrupts her discourse of crops and commerce for two pages of detailed description of Amy Leonard's and Heber Allen's 1889 wedding—the first celebrated in Cardston. The account could have come from a Salt Lake newspaper and the dress from the pages of *Godey's*, so elaborate was the affair:

> The long table was centered by a seven layer wedding cake, beautifully decorated...the lovely blue cashmere, lace trimmed wedding dress, the goods of which were the first bought from the Card store, were made and decorated by Aunt Margaret Leonard. The fashionable wedding dress consumed ten yards in the making. The upper part was a basque with five seams and four darts, all of them boned. The skirt was heavily draped. Ruchings and shirrings of the same material adorned both basque and skirt, with a dainty chiffon ruching around the neckband. Cascades of the material were draped over the back to fit over the bustle. There were puffs, folds, pleats and ball buttons set closely together to complete the trimming.[36]

All this, just two years into settlement, suggests several things: that the rituals of giving and taking in marriage had been imported whole cloth from Utah, where such elaboration would have been much easier to arrange; that the women felt themselves every bit as genteel as their southern and eastern sisters; and that the community would continue to bind itself by intermarriage.

Another marriage, also in Cardston, suggests that not only the Mormon community but also the gentile one paid attention to such matters: Margaret May Frank, of United Empire Loyalist stock, and educated in a country school near Strathroy, Ontario, qualified as a schoolteacher in Toronto. Through a teachers' agency, she applied for, and received, a teaching post in Cardston. She arrived in August 1899, surprised to discover a Mormon community, but relieved to be welcomed into the manse as part of the Presbyterian minister's household. Members of his family would tease Margaret, telling her how "all the non-Mormon bachelors would be coming around to get a look at the new teacher," as indeed they did. She finally chose to marry Verne Shaw, the son of a nearby rancher. "The church was jammed to the doors," she reported of the wedding, the first among Presbyterians in Cardston. "I wore a white organdy floor length gown and a net veil." "Among the guests were 'Aunt Zina' Card and Sterling Williams and his wife. I got a kick from writing home and telling my people that Brigham Young's daughter had been one of my wedding guests. Mrs. Card gave us a beautiful big lamp with china base and shade."[37] The comparison with the Mormon wedding is obvious. What their weddings do to bind Mormon communities in the larger Canadian society, they also do to cement the minority Protestants in the Mormon community. One would like to believe that the wedding served the larger purpose of building bridges between parts of the community, Mormon and gentile; however, that only three of the guests seem to have been Mormon suggests the exclusiveness of the two groups.

There are few examples of homestead marriages in the sources. One suggests the lack of amenities, however, not only of ceremony but also of daily life. Mary Aldridge grew up second in a family of 13 children on the outskirts of Cardston community life. Coming into town with her bridegroom-elect to be married by Bishop Woolf, she was surprised with a wedding supper, "with all the trimmings," prepared by the Woolf women, and a gift of "home-made, lace-trimmed under things. I've never had anything as nice as these," she responded.[38] Where there was no female network, it would seem, the rituals were normally slighted and only the bare forms observed.

Birthing, in a time before the practice of hospitalization, was another opportunity for ritual observance among women. Indicative of the women's interdependence is the oft-repeated account of the first Mormon birth in Canada, when Mrs. Roberts, Sarah Daines and Zina Card, schooled in midwifery only by her mother's hastily written notes, delivered Mary Woolf of her daughter Zina Alberta. As the crisis neared, runs the account, Zina's "interest was anxiously divided between the notes on the table and her patient in the bed." Finally, the patient, already a mother nine times over, called, "Zina for pity's sake leave your notes alone and come here. I'll tell you what to do." Later that day, the same three women presided over a second birth, a son to Mrs. Samuel Matkin. In a village where homes are close, such sisterhood is natural and easy.

Birthing on a homestead is another matter, however. There are the accounts of last-minute attempts to reach the town, where the midwife could be found, and of expecting mothers spending two or three weeks in town in order to be close when their time arrived.[39] A more standard approach was to hire a midwife from whatever distance—Catherine Pilling at Aetna is credited with 526 births and Ann Eliza Baker at Leavitt with 600, numbers always followed by the standard claim of "never losing a mother or child."[40] Mildred Harvey's birthing of her fifth child is illustrative of the usual procedure for homestead wives:

> Sister Hannah Russell came out from Stirling to care for the mother and baby. Sister Russell was a wonderful midwife, and probably ushered into the world more babies than did any doctor or other nurse in those early days. She stayed as long as was deemed necessary, and then [a neighbor] Sister Kesler walked, or rode if a horse was available, the mile and a half, daily to help Mother with the work for a week or two. So, when the Kesler babies were born...Mother walked or rode to their house to give similar help.[41]

Remote as they were, the women still found ways of being supportive to one another in times of need.

One practice among Mormon women seldom found mention in even the most personal sources. It was an ordinance deemed sacred by both practitioners and recipients: the ceremonial washing and anointing of a woman before her confinement. Two sisters, often members of the Relief Society, or under its direction, would visit the home of the expecting woman and, with appropriate prayers, bless her for her safe delivery. The practice continued as late as the 1930s when it was discontinued in favor of blessings pronounced by male priesthood holders.[42]

In the observances surrounding death, too, there was sisterhood. Often the ritual became an office considered part of the Relief Society work. Mary Layton recalled that part of her task as president of that organization was to sit up with the sick, and, after preparing the body for burial, with the dead. The task could be shared among several women in a village setting; among remote or sparse settlements it became problematic. Mary E. Smith died in Orton, forty miles from Cardston. Rhoda Hinman, 73-year-old matriarch among the Cardston women, and Elizabeth Hammer drove their horses through a blizzard, laid out the woman in appropriate Mormon ceremonial clothing, and returned home, still through the blowing snow.[43] The same service that the two women did for their distant coreligionist, one had done for the other. Hinman had earlier recorded in her diary that "Aunt Lizzie Hammer lost her baby this morning. It died very suddenly they sent for me but it was dead when I got there I dressed it. Poor folks I feel so sorry for them.... We made the clothes for the baby today as they intend to bury it tomorrow."[44] It would be hard to overestimate the effect of such service on the bonding of woman to woman.

Those vital events, marriage, birth and death, were always times of community interaction. But the daily affairs of living in hamlet and homestead also served to bind the women in a compassionate sisterhood. The simple tradition of visiting, "that endless trooping of women to each other's homes,"[45] fostered bonding among contiguously dwelling women. Among the homestead women, Sunday meetings, when the family would drive several miles to services, provided contact. Rhoda Hinman's diary, sketching her daily activities, demonstrates the frequency of such visits: between 21 May and 16 August 1897 she records making 28 visits to other people's homes, and entertaining others in her home 33 times, which averages out to sixty visits in ninety days. While her own visits were mostly in Cardston—her husband Morgan had died in 1891, and so her travel was somewhat restricted—her visitors were often people from the surrounding farms and ranches, and their stay generally involved at least a meal, if not overnight hospitality. Such visits were needed breaks in the isolation for the visitors, and provided to the widow a testimonial to the continuing importance of her service.[46]

Even so, for the ranch or homestead-dwelling Mormon woman, as for her non-Mormon correspondents, there would be long times of loneliness, lessened for some by the presence of a sister, grown daughters, a mother or, in the case of Nora Ross, a mother-in-law. Arriving at the Alberta homestead, the Ross women had found not even the beginning of a home, nothing except a pile of lumber slabs and a tent that the men had been using. Mother Ross and I sat and hugged each other and cried out our hearts, after which she said: "Well, Nora, that's enough of that, if this is our home, let's make the most of it."

Even when the house was finished, Nora recalled,

It really wasn't much of a home and I was very homesick.... I had left my own parents and everything that was dear to me in Utah and longed to return. I never could have stayed except for my wonderful mother-in-law, who was an Angel stright [sic] out of Heaven.[47]

Educational opportunities at home were at best difficult for homestead and ranch families. Mothers usually began their children's instruction in the rudiments, or arranged to transport them daily to country schools. Mary Nilsson Hansen, raising her children near Aetna, recorded the difficulty of seeing her daughters taken by wagon across the St. Mary River to the nearest schoolhouse. "One afternoon the river had risen so high that the wagon box nearly swam off. The men were standing at the edge ready to swim for [the children]."[48]

In many instances, family life would necessarily be disrupted, as one or more members would move into town for school. In the case of Willie Woolf, for instance, homestead life meant living and working as a team with his parents, until additional purchases expanded the ranch beyond "what one man, his wife, and a six-year-old boy could work." But when that boy turned seven, his mother moved with him into Cardston, where they lived in two rooms built onto her parents' home. And though Willie worked summers at the ranch after that, his mother "never returned to live at the ranch."[49]

Cultural opportunities on the land were homemade. Often there was a musical instrument—organ, violin or, failing that, comb and tissue paper—that could fill the long evenings. Lucile Ursenbach remembers that:

Evenings at home were quiet, games or reading or sewing, or Mother playing the organ for Father or for the family to sing, then early to bed, for the day started early. There were hired men, and sometimes one would become more or less part of the family for a month or two. He might even have a talent and be able to play a mandolin or to give readings—"Curfew shall not ring tonight!" or "The highwayman came riding, riding"—while four children lay on the floor [of the sleeping loft above], leaning over the open stairway, listening, entranced.[50]

Meanwhile, in the village, even before the meetinghouse was completed, there were dramatic productions which advanced in sophistication as the population grew and facilities and materials became available. Zina Card, who in her teens had acted in the Salt Lake Theatre, is perceived as the leading light in Cardston dramatics; certainly, the performing arts tradition had been encouraged among Mormons since the early 1840s.

For the Mormons, as for other frontier people, there were the grand celebrations. From the first there was the Dominion Day observance, a Fourth of July imported and translated, as much as political statement as a heartfelt commemoration. The Lee Creek Mormons hosted visitors from neighboring ranches and the Indian reservation for sports and horse racing, with dinner in a bowery followed by speeches, songs, recitations and toasts.[51] Later, remembered Rega Card:

We would have a big parade in the forenoon, with a Marshal of the Day leading,...followed by the brass band, beautiful floats and other entries. Some summers the Indians joined the parade on their horses. Then we had horse-racing, roping contests, wrestling, baseball, etc.[52]

As the community grew, team sports of baseball and basketball became important American imports, contrasting with the tennis and polo more popular with the English-born ranchers to the north. With some exceptions, Mormon women participated in the outdoor events as spectators and food providers; some girls played team sports, although for basketball games— played outdoors—wearing skirts was less than comfortable for most. And there were family trips to the nearby mountains at Kootenay, now Waterton. Again, women played the typical role. "We had a large wooden chest that Mamma would fill with provisions," remembered Rega Card, "and we would take two days to make the 35 mile trip, camping by the Belly River the first day out."[53] Generally more appropriate to women's tastes were the indoor events: balls, banquets, literary societies, dramatic productions and recitals; these, too, were part of the community life, attended where possible by the ranch dwellers.

Among Mormon women, however, their ecclesiastical practices provided the strongest binding force. Organizationally, the apparatus was in place before most of the Cardston women were born: the Female Relief Society had been organized in Nauvoo, Illinois, in 1842, and re-established in Utah in 1867 as the official body of Mormon women; in 1869 and 1878 respectively, the Young Ladies' Mutual Improvement Association and the Primary Association (then under the umbrella direction of Relief Society leadership) had also been founded. The Cardston Relief Society was formally organized in November of the town's first year, and later in two satellite communities, Fish Creek (Mountain View) and St. Mary River (Aetna), each with about ten women. In each case, the Relief Society organization preceded ward organization, a precedent not unfamiliar in women's history where evidence is extensive to show that most women's co-operative activities begin as grass roots movements. More patterned organization of relief societies followed the establishment of the Alberta Stake (diocese) and the appointment of Mary Woolf as Stake Relief Society president. Rhoda Hinman records in 1896 that "Sis Mary Woolf Uncle Henry Hinman Aunt Jane [Bates] and myself went up to the Leavitt Ward Organized a Relief Society had a good meeting a nice ride and returned home late at night."[54] It is significant in Mormon organizational structure that the women effected their own organization; Henry Hinman, a patriarch but not a line officer, was probably along to drive the wagon.

The 1842 beginning of Relief Society, where church founder and prophet Joseph Smith had presided at its organization "after the order of the priesthood," and the near simultaneous introduction of temple ordinances in which women shared equally with men, had left with Mormon women a legacy of personal worth, self-determination and organizational autonomy. "I now turn the key to you," Smith had told the women, having set up a presidency and instructed them in procedure. And in the same address, speaking to nineteenth-century women whose legal status made them almost entirely dependent on their husbands, he proclaimed, "After this instruction, you will be responsible for your own sins. It is an honor to save yourselves—all are responsible to save themselves."[55] In that and other contexts, Smith had encouraged the women in their spiritual exercises, in expression of the gifts of healing, tongues, prophecy, and in blessing one another's lives, both temporally and spiritually. Their charitable instincts, as he considered them, he put to use, assigning the women to see to the needs of the poor, and Relief Society, on both general and local levels, in conjunction with the presiding and ward bishops, became the church's welfare agency.

Relief Society came into the Alberta colonies as part of a network of Mormon women reaching from Canada to Mexico, from California to Colorado.

Even before the railroad reduced the three-to-seven-week journey to three days, there had been a surprising amount of noncommercial travel over the Alberta-Utah route. Karel Denis Bicha's observation that "Mormons remained tied to Salt Lake City instead of Alberta and Canada"[56] is certainly born out in the connection maintained by the Alberta women with their Utah sisters. Frequent visits of the Utah-based "leading sisters" to the outlying settlements were augmented by the semimonthly distribution of the *Woman's Exponent*, the quasi-official organ of the Relief Society. Used, along with the *Young Woman's Journal*, as discussion material in church classes, it carried accounts of activities in all its branches, instructions from presiding officers, editorials on feminist issues, news about and writings by its subscribers, and biographies of exemplary Mormon women. "A soldier— mounted police—just rode up and brought papers for us. A Deseret News from you and two Exponents....We are pleased to get the news," wrote Mary Woolf to her mother Elizabeth Hyde in Utah.[57]

Nevertheless, it was the visits themselves that provided the strongest bond. Zina Card, though not the Cardston president of Relief Society, was its chief link to the governing network in Utah; her mother, Zina Young, being the Relief Society general president for the first 14 years of the Alberta settlement. "Aunt Zina's" visits to Alberta were as frequent as her daughter's to Utah. In 1897, Zina Card received her husband's blessing to return to Utah to act as her mother's aid and secretary.[58] Occasions that took other Cardston women to Utah likewise strengthened the ties: Elizabeth Hammer's trip south to study midwifery; the Woolf family's excursion to the dedication of the temple; the trips of several young couples to be "sealed" in the Logan temple; the Leavitt wives' changing places, and Harriet's final move back to Canada; and Mildred Harvey's journey south to tend her ailing mother.

And there were the letters. If the Card family's trove of correspondence, preserved over five generations, is indicative, the women—for most of the letters are by and to women—must have spent some time almost every week corresponding with family and friends "back home" in Utah.[59] The establishment of a post office in and mail route to Lee Creek was a matter of importance from the beginning. The contacts with Utah kin strengthened not only the familial ties but also the ecclesiastical ones.

The Mormon women brought with them not only the organizations as formally established in Utah but also the charismatic practices of the women in the early church. In Relief Society, as in the Young Women's meetings, there were occasional outpourings of spirit manifested by speaking in tongues and prophesying, expressions seldom found among Mormons in the present church. Healing was exercised singly or in groups, as in some occasions recorded in the Relief Society minute book. On one such, some 27 women, having fasted prior to the meeting, assembled in the home of Elizabeth Hammer to bless chronically ill Mary "Mamie" Steed. Zina Card, conducting, had the women kneel facing Utah and the temple, "as our President Woodruff" had suggested.[60] Sister Steed began with prayer on her own behalf, followed by 19 others. The women sang a hymn, and then two of the older sisters, Sarah Daines and Rhoda Hinman, performed the washing and anointing ordinance, a symbolic reminder of covenants taken and blessings promised. All the women gathered around Sister Steed and laid hands on her head in blessing. About this time, Sister Hammer, who had been "attending the sick" in her role as Relief Society president, returned home. The rhetoric of the minute-taker suggests the intensity of the occasion. "Sister Hammer arose her face beaming with the Spirit of God and blessed Sister Mamie Steed in tongues the spirit was so powerful it ran like electricity to the hearts of all present. [T]he gift of interpretation rested upon Sister Nellie Taylor. She arose filled with power that caused her voice to sound like a clarion...." More blessings followed, and then benediction. "[T]he Sisters remained enjoing [sic] the gifts of prophesies prayers, tongues, and interpretation. A spiritual feast never to be forgotten," concluded the minute-taker.[61]

While such charismatic manifestations had occurred in the early years of Mormonism, they had since been replaced at the church's center by more patterned forms; however, here, on the outskirts of Mormondom, there seemed to be a need for a more potent expression of God's approval, and the women created the circumstances that would foster it.[62] Such shared experience—added to the bank of shared homes, shared food, shared hardship, shared success and shared hope for the future—bonded the Mormon pioneer women of southern Alberta to each other, to their faith, and eventually to the new land.

As their sisters to the south had done a generation earlier, Mormon women in southern Alberta molded a new identity based on their experiences with the western prairies and the people who were there. They came as Mormons among gentiles; the debates carried on about them between the initially pro-Mormon editor of the Macleod Gazette and the generally anti-Mormon editor of the Lethbridge News could not but have created in the women a sense of isolation from the mainstream of Alberta society. To find themselves, daughters of New England gentry in some cases, compared with Mennonites and Hutterites added to the sense of difference. Nevertheless, they were Mormon first, and genteel second.

But genteel they were, their model in that, as in ecclesiastical practice, being Zina Young Card. With a persistence grown of a generation of struggle before them, they pulled themselves as quickly as the new land permitted out of the fields, the barn, and even the chicken coop, into the kitchen, and finally into the front parlor for an evening soiree featuring a guest pianist from Lethbridge. The "cult of true womanhood," encompassing the virtues of purity, piety, submissiveness and domesticity enjoined upon nineteenth-century American women, became their self-definition, the values they would pass on to their daughters "unto the third and fourth generation."[63]

The point at which they also included "Canadian" in their self-definition was, however, an individual matter of sorting out loyalties: Mildred Harvey might long have cried to return to Utah; but her Utah-born daughter proclaimed in the face of a citizenship struggle, "In my heart I've always been Canadian."[64]

NOTES
1. Jane E. Woolf Bates and Zina Woolf Hickman, *Founding of Cardston and Vicinity: Pioneer Problems* (n.p.: William Woolf, 1960), p. 22.
2. Besides the Bates and Hickman, *Cardston and Vicinity*, which, despite its limitations, has proven the most useful source for this study, there are the following: *A History of the Mormon Church in Canada* (Lethbridge, Alberta: Lethbridge Stake, 1968); Howard Palmer, "Mormons," in *Land of the Second Chance: A History of Ethnic Groups in Southern Alberta* (Lethbridge, Alberta: *Lethbridge Herald*, 1972), pp. 137-65; John R. Hicken, "Events Leading to the Settlement of the Communities of Cardston, Magrath, Stirling and Raymond, Alberta" (master's thesis, Utah State University, 1968).
3. Maureen Ursenbach Beecher, "Woman's work on the Mormon frontier," *Utah Historical Quarterly*, 49 (Summer 1981), pp. 276-90.
4. Lucile H. Ursenbach, "The Life of Richard Coope Harvey," p. 16, and "The Life of Mildred Cluff Harvey," in *Four Leaves from History* (Calgary, Alberta: privately published, 1973). See also Maureen Ursenbach Beecher and Richard L. Jensen, "The Oft-Crossed Border: Canadians in Utah," in *The Peoples of Utah*, edited by Helen Zeese Papanikolas (Salt Lake City, Utah: Utah State Historical Society, 1976), pp. 294-98.
5. *The Mormon Church in Canada*, chapters 3 and 6.
6. The more exact term here would be *polygyny*, since Mormon belief allowed a man to have more than one wife, but not the opposite. Years of usage, however, have settled the more general term *polygamy* as describing the practice of the Latter-day Saints.

7. Recent studies of the plight of women during the raid include Kimberly Jensen James, "Between two fires: Women on the 'Underground' of Mormon polygamy," *Journal of Mormon History*, 8 (1981), pp. 49-62; Lorie Winder [Stromberg], "Prisoners for Their Patriarchs: Plural Wives in the Penitentiary, 1882-1890," typescript in the author's possession; Martha Sonntag Bradley, " 'Hide and Seek': Children on the Underground," unpublished MS, copy in the author's possession; and Julie Roy Jeffrey, "If Polygamy Is the Lord's Order, We Must Carry It Out," in *Frontier Women: Trans-Mississippi West, 1840-1880* (New York: Hill and Wang, 1979), pp. 147-78.

8. Zina D.H. Young to Zina Young Williams, 3 April 1885, Zina Young Card Papers, Brigham Young University Library, Provo, Utah (hereafter cited as BYU).

9. "Somebody" [Charles Ora Card] to Zina Young Williams, 20 April 1885, Zina Young Card Papers, BYU.

10. "G. Ross" [Zina Young Card] to "My Dear Charlie" [Charles Ora Card], 5 November 1886.

11. [Charles Ora Card] to [Zina Young Card], 13 June 1886, Zina Young Card Papers, BYU.

12. Moses Thatcher to Charles Ora Card, 9 September 1886. Zina Young Card Papers, BYU.

13. G. Ross [Zina Young Card] to [Charles Ora Card], 5 November 1886.

14. Zina Young Card to "Dear Heart" [Charles Ora Card], 9 January 1887, Zina Young Card Papers, BYU.

15. Charlie Peterson [Charles Ora Card] to Zina [Young Card], 3 March 1887, Zina Young Card Papers, BYU.

16. Louisa Grant Alston, Autobiographical Sketch, typescript, Glenbow-Alberta Institute, Calgary, Alberta (hereafter cited as Glenbow).

17. Bates and Hickman, *Cardston and Vicinity*, p. 9.

18. Sarah Ann Hinman Card, recorded interview, Glenbow.

19. Mary Layton, recorded interview by M.M. Merrill, 4 May 1961, Glenbow.

20. Adeline Greene, Diary, 29 April-19 June 1898, as published in Gordon Kay Greene, *Daniel Kent Greene: His Life and Times* (n.p.: privately published, n.d.), 3 and 14 June 1898, pp. 98 and 101.

21. Zina Young Card to Zina D.H. Young, 6 October 1887, photocopy of holograph courtesy Mary Brown Firmage; R.F.P. Bowman, *Railways in Southern Alberta*, Occasional Paper No. 4 (Lethbridge, Alberta: Whoop-Up Chapter, Historical Society of Alberta, 1973), p. 10.

22. Bates and Hickman, *Cardston and Vicinity*, p. 119.

23. Ursenbach, "Mildred Cluff Harvey," *Four Leaves from History*, p. 8.

24. L.A. Rosenvall, "The transfer of Mormon culture to Alberta," *American Review of Canadian Studies*, 12 (1982), p. 56.

25. Sheilagh S. Jameson, "Women in the Southern Alberta Ranch Community," in *The Canadian West*, edited by Henry C. Klassen (Calgary, Alberta: University of Calgary, 1977), pp. 63-78. See also Eliane Leslau Silverman, *The Last Best West: Women on the Alberta Frontier, 1880-1930* (Montreal: Eden Press, 1984); also Mary W.M. Hargreaves, "Women in the agricultural settlement of the northern plains," *Agricultural History*, 50 (1 January 1976), pp. 179-89.

26. Jameson, "Women in Southern Alberta," p. 71.

27. *Lethbridge News*, 29 March 1888; Bates and Hickman, *Cardston and Vicinity*, pp. 73-74.

28. As quoted in Rosenvall, "Mormon culture to Alberta," p. 58. The best study of the Canadian homestead system is Chester Martin, *"Dominion Lands" Policy* (Toronto: Macmillan, 1938).

29. *The Life of Thomas Rowell Leavitt and His Descendants* (Lethbridge: privately published by the Leavitt Family Organization, 1975), p. 41; Maxine Pilling Rodgers, *Richard Pilling: A Family Heritage* (Red Deer, Alberta: privately published, 1980), p. 51.

30. *The Autobiography of William L. Woolf* (Salt Lake City, Utah: privately published, 1979), p. 4.

31. Manuscript Census of Canada, 1891, microfilm, Glenbow.

32. Charles Ora Card to Hon. A.M. Burgess, 22 February 1894, as quoted in Bates and Hickman, *Cardston and Vicinity*, pp. 123-24.

33. See Jessie L. Embry, "Exiles for the principle: LDS polygamy in Canada," *Dialogue*, 18 (Fall 1985), pp. 108-16. Of the 49 polygamists in her study who lived in Canada, 43% lived with second wives there, 20% with first wife, and 18% with third wife.

34. Sarah Ann Hinman Card, "Sketch."

35. To calculate actual fertility patterns would require more data than the census provides. Four years later, in 1895, Card would talley 548 Mormons in Canada, 337 adults and 211 children. Bates and Hickman, *Cardston and Vicinity*, p. 141.

36. Bates and Hickman, *Cardston and Vicinity*, pp. 80-81.

37. "Autobiography of Margaret May Frank Shaw," typescript, Glenbow, pp. 3-10.

38. Bates and Hickman, *Cardston and Vicinity*, pp. 151-52. For gentile marriage traditions on the Alberta frontier, see Eliane Leslau Silverman, "Women's Perceptions of Marriage on the Alberta Frontier," in *Building Beyond the Homestead: Rural History on the Prairies*, edited by David C. Jones and Ian MacPherson (Calgary: University of Calgary Press, 1985), pp. 49-64.

39. Margaret Shaw Autobiography, p. 14.

40. Rodgers, *Richard Pilling*, p. 55; *Thomas Rowell Leavitt*, p. 50.

41. Ursenbach, "Mildred Cluff Harvey," *Four Leaves from History*, pp. 11-12.

42. Linda King Newell, "A gift given, a gift taken: Washing, anointing, and blessing the sick among Mormon women," *Sunstone*, 6 (September-October 1981), pp. 16-25. A more complete consideration of her subject is found in *Sisters in Spirit: Mormon Women in Historical and Cultural Perspective*, edited by Maureen Ursenbach Beecher and Lavina Fielding Anderson (Urbana: University of Illinois Press, 1987), pp. 111-50.

43. Bates and Hickman, *Cardston and Vicinity*, pp. 176-77.

44. Rhoda Hinman, Diary, 21 March 1897, Archives, the Church of Jesus Christ of Latter-day Saints, Salt Lake City, Utah (hereafter cited as LDS Church Archives). All materials from the LDS Church Archives are used with permission.

45. Carroll Smith-Rosenberg, "The female world of love and ritual: Relations

between women in nineteenth century America," *Signs* 1 (Autumn 1975), p. 9.

46. Rhoda Chase Stoddard Hinman, Diary, 21 May-16 August 1896, LDS Church Archives.

47. Eileen Ross Lott to Maureen Beecher, 19 June 1986. Lott is quoting from *Stirling, Alberta: Its Story and People* (Stirling: Stirling Sunset Society, 1981).

48. Mary Nilsson Hansen, "My Story," typescript, LDS Church Archives.

49. *William L. Woolf Autobiography*, pp. 6-8; William L. Woolf, *Johnny 'n Cindy, Biographies of the Honorable John William Woolf and Lucinda Marie Layne* (n.p.: privately published, n.d.), p. 80.

50. Ursenbach, "Mildred Harvey," *Four Leaves from History*, p. 15.

51. *Lethbridge News*, 5 July 1888.

52. Orson Rega Card, "Memories," p. 10, photocopy of typescript in the author's possession, courtesy Rega Card.

53. Rega Card, "Memories," p. 9.

54. Rhoda Chase Stoddard Hinman, Diary, 27 December 1896.

55. Minutes of the Female Relief Society of Nauvoo, 1842-44, 28 April 1842, LDS Church Archives.

56. Karel Denis Bicha, *The American Farmer and the Canadian West, 1896-1914* (San Diego, California: Coronado, 1968), p. 101.

57. Mary L. Woolf to Elizabeth Hyde, 2 August 1887, as quoted in Bates and Hickman, *Cardston and Vicinity*, p. 31. The policeman would have been a member of the North-West Mounted Police.

58. Charles O. Card to Zina Y. Card, 16 June 1897, Zina Huntington Young Papers, LDS Church Archives.

59. Mary Brown Firmage, into whose hand most of such materials came, is most generously donating the letters to various archives. At this writing there are Card family collections in the LDS Church Archives and Brigham Young University Library.

60. James E. Talmage, *The House of the Lord: A Study of Holy Sanctuaries, Ancient and Modern* (Salt Lake City, Utah: Bookcraft, 1962), p. 170.

61. Cardston Ward, Relief Society Historical Record Book A, 1890-1898, 14 November 1895, LDS Church Archives.

62. See Hannah Adeline Hatch Savage, Journal, 7 May 1896, holograph, LDS Church Archives.

63. These are impressionistic observations from the sources at hand; a continuation study might parallel, among Mormon women, Eliane Leslau Silverman's excellent study, "Women and the Victorian Work Ethic on the Alberta Frontier: Prescription and Description," in *The New Provinces: Alberta and Saskatchewan, 1905-1980*, edited by Howard Palmer and Donald Smith (Calgary, Alberta: University of Calgary, 1980), pp. 91-99. How those values have changed and how they have been retained since the 1890s is analysed in Gisela Demharter's "Die Sozialisation von Mädchen bei kanadischen Mormonen," doctoral dissertation, Ludwig-Maximilians Universität, München, 1987.

64. Unrecorded interview of Lucile Harvey Ursenbach by Maureen Beecher, reaffirmed 4 May 1987. See also the discussion in Beecher and Jensen, "Canadians in Utah," p. 297.

IV | MORMONS IN THE ECONOMY AND IN GOVERNMENT

IN THE ALBERTA setting, Mormons were sufficiently concentrated and culturally distinct to have a significant impact on the local economy. Their participation was particularly important in agriculture, since they were crucial to the development of irrigation. This was a major undertaking with important economic and social consequences for Alberta. The CPR and Galt coal interests owned large tracts of land in southern Alberta and saw irrigation as a means of colonizing this land. During the 1880s and 1890s, the federal government, coal-mining interests, the Mormon Church, the CPR and local boosters, all worked together to bring large-scale irrigation to southern Alberta.

In the 1880s, C.A. Magrath of the Galt interests in Lethbridge favored large-scale irrigation and colonization. Magrath formed a close partnership with Mormon leader C.O. Card, who also saw the potential for a major colonization scheme that could meet the needs of land-hungry Mormon farmers in the American Great Basin. In 1898, the Galt interests signed a contract with the Mormon Church to build an irrigation system. This led to the influx of a new wave of Mormon settlers.

Irrigation made possible the development of a wide variety of crops. Sugar beets were an ideal crop for making intensive agricultural use of irrigation. Begun by Mormons, and dominated until the 1940s by Mormon growers, the sugar beet industry has remained an important part of southern Alberta's economy to the present day.[1]

During the 1930s, Mormon farmers helped establish a vegetable canning industry in southern Alberta. Thereafter, Lethbridge developed as a major canning, freezing and food distribution center for the entire province. In addition, the by-products of the sugar beet and vegetable-processing

231

industry—beet pulp, molasses, pea vines—made possible the development of a prosperous cattle-feeding industry on irrigated farms. The paper by Byron and Craig Palmer is based on biographies of Mormons in agriculture, and discusses their contribution not only in these areas of irrigation, sugar beets and cattle-feeding but also in grain milling, ranching, agricultural research and education.[2]

Mormons have also played a significant role in the oil industry in Alberta from its beginnings. The first oilwell in Alberta, drilled in 1899 at Oil City, was developed by Mormon William Aldridge.[3] Other Mormons have been involved as entrepreneurs and public servants, or as technicians and researchers. The most prominent include Glenn Nielson, who left a sheep ranch in southern Alberta to build a major integrated American-Canadian oil company—Husky Oil.[4] Cardston school principal and Mormon bishop N.E. Tanner served as Alberta's minister of Lands and Mines in the Social Credit government during a crucial stage in the industry's development, from the late 1930s to the early 1950s. He was then asked, in 1954, by Alberta Premier Ernest Manning and Canada's economic "czar" C.D. Howe, a Liberal cabinet minister, to head TransCanada PipeLines, a massive government-industry venture. In what to non-Mormons was a strange transformation, but to Mormons a logical progression, Tanner left the oil industry in 1960 to become a Mormon apostle.[5] Jack Armstrong's position as president of Imperial Oil of Canada during the 1970s and early 1980s is a reminder of the Mormon role in the industry,[6] though the history of Mormons in oil and gas has still to be written.

The appointment of N.E. Tanner to the First Presidency of the Mormon Church in 1963 aroused interest in Mormon political behavior in Canada. Although Alberta Mormons have not been innovators of economic or political ideas, they have regularly adapted ideas that appear to offer solutions to the problems facing a hinterland economy. Mormons in Alberta have in the past been able to reconcile their religious beliefs with political ideas ranging from the moderate left to the extreme right. They have supported and run as candidates for a variety of political parties—Liberal, United Farmers of Alberta, Co-operative Commonwealth Federation, Social Credit, Progressive Conservative and Western Canada Concept parties. Two Mormon Members of Parliament, John Blackmore and Solon Low, served as leaders of the national Social Credit Party; four occupied posts in provincial Social Credit cabinets; and one was a prominent leader in the separatist Western Canada Concept Party during the early 1980s.

In his wide-ranging paper, David Elton discusses Mormon political behavior at the municipal, provincial and national levels. He places the subject within the larger context of the relationship between religion and politics in American and Canadian societies.

The paper by Elton points to interesting questions about the relationship between Mormons and Canada's political culture in general and Alberta's predominantly right-wing political culture in particular. Although Elton shows that overall voting trends in the Mormon communities differ little from the rest of Alberta, the level of Mormon involvement in the WCC leadership (including at one point almost half the directors, as well as the leader Gordon Kesler) suggests a stronger right-wing orientation than the larger Alberta political culture.

Elton's paper offers scope for speculation about future political behavior of Mormons. Will geographic dispersion coupled with the strong time demands on the lay leadership of the Mormon Church further erode their level of political activism? Has the growing pluralism and secularization of Canadian society made it less likely that Mormons could be elected to public office outside their own geographical concentrations? Since Mormons hold strong views on many moral issues now facing Canadian society, will the depth of their convictions on these issues eventually draw them into new political activity and coalitions?

NOTES

1. Though there is no overview study of the sugar beet industry to date, two studies that discuss the role of Mormons are John Thompson and Allen Seager, "Workers, growers and monopolists: The Labour Problem in the Alberta Beet Sugar Industry During the 1930s," *Labour*, (1978) and Melvin S. Tagg and Asael E. Palmer, *A History of the Mormon Church in Canada* (Lethbridge: Lethbridge Stake Historical Committee, 1968), pp. 105-06.

2. See Charles Ursenbach, "R.C. Harvey and his Romnellet sheep," *Alberta History* (Autumn, 1982), pp. 31-37; Peter Hawker, "Sheep and sheep men in Alberta," *Alberta History* (Spring, 1988), pp. 20-29.

3. George de Mille, *Oil in Canada West* (Calgary: Northwest Printing and Lithographing, 1970), Chapter 4.

4. Earle Gray, *The Great Canadian Oil Patch* (Toronto: Maclean-Hunter, 1970), pp. 251-55.

5. G. Homer Durham, *N. Eldon Tanner; His Life and Service* (Salt Lake City: Deseret Book, 1982); William Kilbourn, *Pipeline* (Toronto: Clarke, Irwin, 1970), Chapter 5, which discusses Tanner's career, is entitled "A Strange Story."

6. Peter Foster, *The Blue-Eyed Sheiks* (Don Mills: Collins, 1979), pp. 72-77.

12 Mormons in Western Canadian Agriculture

From Irrigation to Agribusiness[1]

BYRON C. PALMER
CRAIG J. PALMER

SINCE 1887, THE Mormon presence in Canada has been characterized by strong leadership and productivity in agriculture. A hundred years later, the majority of Mormons in western Canada, particularly in Alberta, still derive their income, either directly or indirectly, from this field of endeavor.

Since both authors are professional agriculturalists and have many contacts with Mormons in agriculture, we selected from a roster of over fifty names a sampling of 11 whom we consider to be especially interesting, and for various reasons, outstanding in their contributions to Canadian agriculture. We have also drawn attention to seven Canadian-born Mormon expatriates, who have risen to prominence in American and international agriculture.

We adopted a biographical approach, so that interplay of the many factors entering into Mormon contributions to agriculture could be recognized. Three values run as common threads throughout the lives of these men: adherence to the Mormon ethic of hard work and industry; an attitude of service, rather than the accumulation of personal wealth; and vision—the willingness to see their work and lives in a broad context and a long-term perspective.

We have defined a Mormon as one with Mormon heritage, roots or experience, whether or not they were active participants in the Mormon faith throughout their lives. We have selected persons from three time periods: an initial pioneering period beginning in 1887 and extending to the 1920s; an intermediate period, when the children of the pioneer period or converts of their generation began taking their places in Canadian agriculture; and the current period, beginning in the 1950s, when Canadian Mormon contributions began to take on international significance. The contributions of some of the persons selected span two and, in the case of Asael Palmer, all three periods.

Another challenge to selection concerned what aspects of agriculture should be emphasized: production, food processing, research, education, organizational development or political activity. We have chosen those who represent all these varied endeavors within agriculture, though because of their visibility, especially in recent years, our selection favors those connected with research and education.

One issue that we were unable to deal with adequately is the role of women in agriculture. Their important supporting role can be inferred from mention of the wives and mothers in some of the biographies presented. Their actual contribution in various branches of agriculture deserves more careful study and better documentation, however, than this limited introduction can provide.

It is our hope that the combined biographies will give a broader picture that will transcend sample size, methodology and other limitations. There is still a rich harvest of history that has not been told and deserves more scholarly attention.

THE PIONEER PERIOD—1887 TO THE 1920s

Agriculture was the dominant economic concern and activity of Mormon settlers in Canada, influencing the selection of sites for colonization, the selection of settlers from Utah, and the directions for community and economic expansion once initial settlements were successfully launched. Although some of those prominent in the intermediate or, what we have chosen to call the Emerging Technology Period, had begun to make significant contributions by the mid-1920s, we focus here on four of the early pioneers who had an acute interest in the role of agriculture and left a lasting imprint on the industry. These were Charles O. Card, Jesse Knight, Edward J. Wood and George W. Green.

Charles Ora Card[2]

The key person in the earliest Mormon agriculture in western Canada was clearly C.O. Card. He was born in New York state in 1839. He migrated westward to Utah in 1856 and pioneered in agriculture, local industry and construction in Cache Valley from 1860 to 1887. Though he owned title to several small Cache Valley farms, he was not a farmer by occupation.

He was, however, deeply involved in irrigation projects upon which Cache Valley agriculture depended. Before coming to Canada, he helped create and operate three irrigation systems, with a total length of over 32 miles, that supplied water to over 11,000 acres. Most of the Latter-day Saints who migrated with him to Canada were experienced irrigation farmers. It is not surprising to find them involved in, or supportive of, irrigation projects.

In the early 1890s, Charles A. Magrath, as land manager of the North Western Coal and Navigation Co. of Lethbridge, proposed several different irrigation and immigration schemes to C.O. Card, who recognized their potential value to the Mormon colony and to solving recent problems of unemployment in Utah. Subsequently, he submitted a plan to the First Presidency of the church and contributed significantly to the final agreement reached on 14 April 1898. The church agreed to supply the labor to build an irrigation canal from the St. Mary River to the Lethbridge district, with payment to be half in cash and half in land. This made it possible for anyone who had a team of horses and a scraper to take a subcontract, acquire a farm, and, at the same time, earn a grubstake to live on while establishing the farm.

Card toured communities in Utah to recruit settlers and canal workers to meet this obligation. The church took the contract as a welfare project, "as there was still the effect of the 'Cleveland panic' or depression in Utah," named after the incumbent president of the United States. When work lagged, he called special meetings in all Canadian wards to encourage local members to help. By September 1900, all contracts were completed. It is interesting to note that one of the reasons for selecting the Mormons for this project in the first place was the perceived commitment of farseeing leaders such as C.O. Card.

Jesse Knight[3]

Jesse Knight was born in Nauvoo, Illinois, in 1845 and died in Provo, Utah, in 1921. With his parents, Newell Knight and Lydia Goldthwate, he immigrated to Utah; however, his father became ill and died en route. The rest of the family reached Utah in the fall of 1850. His early life was spent in Salt Lake City, and in Provo, where the family moved in 1857.

Jesse Knight began his ranching business in a small way soon after he was married in 1869. He invested his earnings in land and livestock, until he

Jesse Knight, center with hat, in the office of Reed Smoot, right, Mormon apostle, in Salt Lake City. P2483 LDS Archives.

finally acquired a good-sized ranch about two miles west of Payson, Utah, which he stocked with dairy cattle and horses. Several years later some mining men stopped at his ranch and interested him in a mining venture. He eventually struck several rich deposits of gold, silver and lead.

He became interested in the development of southern Alberta agriculture as a result of a visit by John W. Taylor, an LDS apostle, and Charles McCarthy of Cardston. They told him about the fertile lands of the area and urged him to buy some land. In January 1901, he sent his two sons to Canada to survey the situation. They bought 30,000 acres of land near Spring Coulee and set to work to stock it, initially with 4,000 head of cattle shipped in from Winnipeg. They called the ranch the Bar K2. Later in the year Knight joined his sons in Stirling, Alberta, and decided within a few days that he would build a sugar factory. On 10 July 1901, Jesse entered into a contract with the Canadian North-West Irrigation Company and the Alberta Railway and Irrigation Company to purchase an additional 260,000 acres of land in the area and to build a sugar beet factory that would be ready for operation to handle the beet crops of 1903. He further agreed to keep it open for at least 12 years. This agreement was guaranteed with a pledge of $50,000.

Following the signing of the contract a townsite was located and named

Raymond, after his eldest son. The town grew rapidly and boasted a population of over 1,500 people two years after settlement began.

Knight had promised to have 3,000 acres of land ready for planting to sugar beets when the factory was ready, so he immediately began hiring men with teams and plows to do the work, paying them $2.50 per acre for plowing. As dry weather came on, plowing got more difficult and Knight raised the price to $3.00. Finally, he was obliged to send his son, Ray, to Utah for larger teams and plows to do the work. Ray soon returned with a trainload of heavy horses and equipment and the plowing was completed on time. The plant began accepting beets in the fall of 1903. It operated for the promised 12 years. Why the plant was built and why it closed after 12 years are interesting stories. Magrath, who, with the Galts (all non-Mormons) was heavily involved in the development of southern Alberta at this time, is quoted in Jesse Knight's biography by his son J. William Knight as follows:

> My opinion is that Southern Alberta should never forget what it owes to Jesse Knight, because I happen to know from actual efforts, how impossible it was to get capital interested in such an enterprise in a new and sparsely settled country like our northwest until Mr. Knight came along.... Mr. Knight was the most unusual man I ever met, a man of the finest integrity. I would describe him as the poor man's friend.

> The Raymond sugar factory was not built as a commercial enterprise so much as for the benefit of the settlers in the surrounding country.

The basis for this philanthropic attitude was largely, according to Knight, the result of a "Greetings to the World," sent out at the beginning of this century by the president of the church, Lorenzo Snow. It said in part:

> Men and women of wealth, use your riches to give employment to the labourer! Take the idle from the crowded centres of population and place them on the untilled areas that await the hand of industry. Unlock your vaults, unloose your purses, and embark in enterprises that will give work to the unemployed, and relieve the wretchedness that leads to the vice and crime which curse your great cities, and that poison the moral atmosphere around you. Make others happy and you will be happy yourselves.

Farm of Edward J. Wood at Glenwood, Alberta, C.1932. ND 27-70 Glenbow Archives.

He was profoundly moved by this counsel and felt that it was a message from the Lord for him.

As to the reason for closing the factory, it seems that there was just not enough energy in the backs of the beet growers to produce enough beets to keep the factory running. With energy in short supply and raising beets a labor-intensive activity, farmers who had initially welcomed the factory with enthusiasm gradually moved into small grains and livestock, which, at the time of closing of the factory in 1914, were more profitable. Eventually, in the mid-1920s, the Utah-Idaho Sugar Company came back and set up another factory at Raymond, but concurrently with it, arrangements were made to bring in immigrant farm labor to help produce the beets.

Edward J. Wood[4]

Edward James Wood was born in Salt Lake City, 27 October 1866, to William Wood and Elizabeth Gentry. His biographer, Melvin Tagg, reports that his youth was filled with schooling, church activity and athletics. He excelled in swimming while attending the University of Deseret. He was also proficient in fencing, boxing and bicycle riding.

At the age of 35 he was called by President Joseph F. Smith to fill a mission to Canada. He and his family arrived in Cardston 7 November 1901.

In Canada, Wood was immediately recognized as a leader. He was asked first to be manager of the Cardston Mercantile Company, a general store owned by several of the leading church men of the stake. Before the first month had passed, he was appointed to the Stake High Council. On 31 August 1903, he was chosen to lead the Alberta Stake as its president. This he did for 39 years and was released on 17 August 1942. He served as president of the Alberta Temple from the time of its dedication in 1923 until his release from that calling in 1948 at the age of 82.

As a church leader in an area where the Mormon faith predominated, he had tremendous influence on not only religious but also on economic developments. Shortly after he became stake president, he undertook a major task on behalf of the people. This project was one of the most important steps in the colonization of southern Alberta by the Latter-day Saints. "President Wood realized that the Mormons would soon be hemmed in if they did not buy more land and expand their boundaries."

The West was being divided up into small farms and ranches and the big rangeland ranches were dying out. One of the largest of these was the Cochrane Ranch, a large 66,500-acre unfenced ranch adjacent to the LDS settlements. Many Saints were immigrating to Canada from the center of Mormondom and desired farms close to other Mormons. Wood recommended to the First Presidency that this great ranch, which could serve many families, be purchased by the church for colonization purposes. This they did. The ranch included all the land between the Belly and Waterton rivers, six to eight miles wide and 28 miles long. Wood was given power of attorney by the First Presidency to act as agent for the church in administering the affairs of the ranch and in dividing it up and selling it to Latter-day Saint settlers.

A series of dry years created much hardship on the newly arrived farmers. With the planning assistance of John A. Widtsoe, a noted irrigation expert from Utah and apostle of the church, irrigation canals were laid out and built.[5] The work started in 1921 and was finished in two years.

He helped to organize a creamery co-operative to promote local dairy products. He raised sugar beets and invested in a butcher business and a packing plant. Other businesses that attracted his investment were banking, real estate and the Cardston Oil and Gas Society, of which he became president. He was also president of two coal-mining companies. In 1903, he helped to organize the Cardston Agricultural Society and became its first president.

He never aspired to political office, but because he was held in such great respect by the people in the Cardston area he wielded a great influence on the local political scene. Perhaps his greatest contribution to agriculture was his strengthening of the faith of farmers in themselves with God's help to meet the many challenges of pioneer life.

George W. Green[6]

George W. Green was born at Enterprise, Utah, 27 February 1868. His schooling included one year at the University of Deseret (now the University of Utah).

In 1902, Ephraim Ellison, a prominent Utah miller, encouraged by Joseph F. Smith, President of the Mormon Church, set up the Raymond Milling and Elevator Company in the rapidly growing new town of Raymond. By the fall of 1902, there was enough wheat being produced in the area to keep the mill running. Green, Ellison's representative in Salt Lake City, was sent from Utah in 1902 to manage the new mill at Raymond.

Under his management, the milling industry grew rapidly. It expanded to Magrath, where a mill was built in 1906. In that year, the Raymond Milling and Elevator Company's name was changed to the Ellison Milling and Elevator Company. A mill was also built in Lethbridge in 1907, on the invitation of C.A. Magrath who had become a director of the company in 1904. In 1914, the company purchased the H.S. Allen Mill at Cardston. The products of Ellison Mills were not only marketed intensively in Alberta and British Columbia but also went to England, Scotland, Norway, Hong Kong and mainland China.

In 1935, Green resigned his position as manager of Ellison Mills to devote more time to an alfalfa meal plant and freight forwarding enterprise. Several years later, he launched another business, the Green Star Mill Ltd., which specialized in cereals, graham, whole wheat and rye flour, and later produced potato chips, puffed wheat and rice, flaked wheat cereal, mixed grain cereal, and other cereal products.

Green was extremely civic minded and served as mayor of Raymond for two terms. While in that position, he brought electric power to the Knight Sugar Factory and later to the entire town. He served on the Raymond School Board for several terms. With his wife, Mary E. Nalder, he moved to Lethbridge in 1911, and was called to serve in the first Bishopric of the Lethbridge Ward in 1912. He was called to be bishop in 1914, then in 1921 when the Lethbridge Stake was organized, he served as first counselor in the Stake Presidency.

As these biographical sketches show, this pioneer period was characterized by strong leadership in land settlement, diversified production, irrigation,

Ellison Mill and Elevator A
at Raymond, Alberta,
c.1930. First built 1902,
burned and rebuilt twice,
1924-25 and 1937.
Courtesy Reed C. Ellison,
Lethbridge and J.O.
Hicken et al., *Roundup:
Raymond 1901-67*, p. 275.

Ellison Mill and Elevator B
at Magrath, Alberta, 1906,
burned down in 1916.
Courtesy Reed C. Ellison,
Lethbridge.

Ellison's Mill at
Lethbridge, Alberta, 1906
and continuing. Courtesy
Reed C. Ellison,
Lethbridge.

capitalization of farms, new industry, the introduction of sugar beet and the development of a milling and elevator complex. These developments represented a great deal of co-operation among individual Mormon farmers and workers, the LDS church and its leadership (locally and in Utah), and non-Mormon entrepreneurs, financiers and government officials.

THE EMERGING TECHNOLOGY PERIOD

Although there were many innovations in the technology of agricultural production and processing during the pioneer period, the innovation, evaluation and dissemination of new technology did not get into full gear until the mid-1920s. The major actors during this period were primarily the sons, born in Utah or in western Canada, to parents from the pioneering era. They began their careers when the supporting institutions of universities and experimental stations for the agricultural industry were well in place in the United States and were being developed in Canada. It was also a period of market expansion and upheaval, and of political and organizational developments related to agriculture as a national and international concern. Five biographies characterize this middle period, when science became wedded to husbandry, and the polity.

Frank Wyatt[7]

One discipline of agricultural science in which the Mormon presence in Canada has been widely recognized is soil science. It is not surprising therefore that in 1919, when Dean Howes of the University of Alberta decided to establish the first separate soils department in Canada, he selected Dr. Frank Wyatt. Wyatt was born in 1886 and raised on an irrigated farm near Wellsville, Utah. He graduated from the College of Agriculture at Logan, Utah, in 1910 and received his doctorate from the University of Illinois in 1915. He remained on staff as an assistant professor until 1919.

Dr. Howes wanted Wyatt to do research on dryland farming and irrigated farming, with some consideration of the question of drainage. Wyatt remained as head of the Soils Department until his death in 1947.

In response to concern about the soil problems from drought and wind erosion, Wyatt initiated a soil survey of the Fort Macleod district in 1921. Wyatt is credited with organizing the soil survey program for Alberta, which he directed for the remainder of his life. In the late 1920s, new settlers were

Asael E. Palmer, left, examining sugar beets with W. H. Fairfield, center, and Herbert Chester, right, Lethbridge Experimental Station, 1956. NA 4704-5 Glenbow Archives.

beginning to establish homesteads in forested areas where soils were not as fertile or as easy to manage as the rich prairie soil. In 1930, he was instrumental in having long-term fertility plots established on a grey, wooded soil near Breton. It is likely that he was the first soil scientist to do research on the effects of atmospheric deposition on soils.

Asael E. Palmer[8]

Historian James H. Gray portrays Asael E. Palmer as one of six men whose contributions were indispensable in saving the agricultural industry in the

Palliser Triangle during the 1930s, and states that he knew more about soil drifting than any other Canadian. But his influence on agriculture was much broader.

He was born in Salt Lake City, Utah, on 26 November 1888. His early years were spent on an irrigated mountain valley farm near Aurora in Sevier County. He came to Alberta with his parents in 1903, where they bought a 480-acre dryland and irrigated farm, eight miles northwest of Raymond. His father, William Moroni, was not well after they moved to Canada, so his sons had to run the farm. By the time Asael was 17, two of his brothers had died from typhoid fever and the residual effects of rheumatic fever. This left him to run the farm.

In 1909, he and his half brother, Wilford, filed for a homestead fifty miles northeast of Lethbridge, near the present town of Turin. These pioneer farming experiences were hard but exciting times, and they set the stage for his later career in agriculture. Because of his farming obligations, he did not enter high school until 1910, when he was 22 years old. After graduating from the church-owned Knight Academy in 1914, he continued his education at the Utah Agricultural College and was granted a bachelor of science degree in agriculture in June 1917. The previous October, he had married his former high school teacher, Maydell Cazier. Among his college days' activities were public speaking and debating, and this aptitude for public speaking was one of the reasons that he was so successful in the role he played in persuading farmers to change some of their farming techniques.

Upon graduation, he took a position with the Canadian Pacific Railway as a soil chemist and irrigation investigator, and took up summer residence at Tilley, a village in the Eastern Irrigation District. His assignment was to advise the CPR on the suitability of lands in that area for irrigation. Government officials considered most of the lands east of Brooks as unsuitable for irrigation because of a relatively high concentration of salts in the subsoil. He was able to show that most of these salts were calcium sulphate (gypsum), and this was not only nontoxic to plants (as was feared) but also had an ameliorating effect on the harmful properties of other salts present. He seems to have been the first scientist to have discovered this phenomenon. He received "a great deal of help and encouragement from Drs. John A. Widtsoe and Franklin S. Harris," two of his UAC instructors. This research was undoubtedly the major deciding factor in persuading the CPR to proceed with the development of the Eastern Irrigation District. This land has been a successful irrigation enterprise for over fifty years.

In the fall of 1918, Asael and Maydell both accepted teaching positions at the Raymond Knight Academy, a church-operated school, where they remained for two years. For the final year, Asael Palmer was its principal. In 1921, he applied for and was offered a position at the Dominion Experimental Farm at Lethbridge. His first assignment was to direct the irrigation investigations. Later, he was made responsible for dryland work as well.

He set up a series of controlled field-plot experiments to determine appropriate irrigation practices for prairie irrigated agriculture, crop water use, optimal frequency of irrigation, and soil moisture-holding capacities. He was the author of the first comprehensive report in Canada on on-farm irrigation practices. It was accepted by the University of Alberta as a master's thesis in 1927, and later it was expanded into a bulletin that was published by the Canada Department of Agriculture.

Palmer maintained close contacts with other government officials and irrigated farmers and was a strong supporter of the irrigation industry. He was instrumental in re-establishing the sugar beet industry in Alberta in the mid-1920s. He was one of the original directors of the Alberta Sugar Beet Growers Association and later an honorary president.

He is probably best remembered for his efforts in the fight against wind-induced soil erosion. This was and remains a serious problem in southern Alberta and southwestern Saskatchewan. He became acquainted with all the areas in southern Alberta that were experiencing soil drifting. His responsibility was to find out which farming practices were effectively controlling erosion. The struggle to develop dryland farming technology is chronicled in his book, *When the Winds Came*.[9] Many techniques were tried, but the most successful was found to be leaving a stubble mulch on the soil surface to bind the soil particles together. He called it "trash cover farming." This method completely changed traditional farming practices that had been imported from the east, where a clean, well-plowed field was considered a mark of successful farming. A number of other techniques, such as strip farming, basin listing, and weed control using blade cultivators, were tried successfully. Palmer and his staff kept in close contact with all efforts to control erosion and encouraged, through frequent field days at the experimental station, at several substations and personal visits to farms, adoption of promising new techniques. Each has found an appropriate place in farm technology.

Many people participated in this work, both at the farming level and in the mobilization of financial and human resources, but the contribution of Asael Palmer stands out in all facets of this effort.[10]

After he retired from the Experimental Station in 1953, he was sent by the federal government to Pakistan to take over the direction of an agricultural research station in a northwest frontier province near the city of Peshawar. He was also successful in introducing a sugar beet industry to Pakistan that is still flourishing.

After his return, he continued to be actively involved in community, church and agricultural activities. He ran unsuccessfully in the Lethbridge riding as the Liberal candidate in the 1957 federal election. For six years, he served on the board of trustees of the Alberta Agriculture Research Trust Fund. He represented the Alberta Chamber of Commerce at a Prairie Provinces Water Seminar. This was established by the governments of the three prairie provinces to study the waters and the future uses of the Saskatchewan and Mackenzie watersheds.

He was given a number of consulting assignments during his later years and served as an expert witness at several court cases. His last professional consulting assignment came in his 91st year. This was as a special adviser to a consulting firm that had been commissioned by the Alberta government to evaluate the potential expansion possibilities of irrigation.

During all of these activities, Palmer was active in administrative activities in the LDS church. From 1921 to 1926, he was a counselor to the president of the Lethbridge Stake of Zion. In 1926, he was called to be the stake president, which he carried out for the next twenty years. This was during his most active years in agricultural research.

After returning from Pakistan, he served on the Lethbridge Stake High Council, was agricultural adviser on the Stake Welfare Committee, was chairman of the Agricultural Advisors of the Canadian Welfare Region, managed a 443-acre irrigated welfare farm, was a stake missionary for two years, and directed the establishment of the Lethbridge Stake Genealogy Library. He chaired a committee in 1966-67 which compiled the histories of the Canadian LDS church units and published them as a Canadian centennial project.[11]

Charles Owen Asplund[12]

Charles Asplund was born 27 December 1899 in Fairview, Utah, the son of Olof Peter Asplund, who was born in Sweden, and Jeannette Christina Anderson, who was born in Fairview. His family moved to Alberta in 1902, settling in Raymond. His father soon secured a homestead in the Barnwell area, however, so Charles went to school in Barnwell, during the time of farming operations, and in Raymond during the winter.

After completing high school, he attended the Agricultural College in Raymond. He was on a livestock judging team from the college that won a provincial championship. This was an important learning experience for his subsequent career.

The University of Alberta agreed to accept graduates of the five agricultural colleges in the province and Charles decided to enrol there in 1923. He received his degree, a bachelor of science in agriculture, in three years. He graduated at the head of his class and received the Governor General's gold medal for the highest marks in the school. In the fall of that year, he secured a teaching position at the Raymond Agricultural College. He taught animal husbandry and was farm manager of the College's irrigated farm.

The Great Depression came, and with it the closing of the school. The government rented the college farm to the Asplunds, and they ran it until 1935. During the winter, Asplund worked for the government in the Brooks-Vauxhall area, distributing relief seed and feed to the people. Other activities during this time were livestock feeding and raising sheep. In 1935, he was appointed district agriculturalist for the Cardston area. He was still responsible for giving out seed and feed but took on the job of determining the sex of chickens.

He and his brother, Chester, who lived at Glenwood, began operating a small feedlot, with cattle and a little flock of sheep. The family moved to Lethbridge in 1940, and over the next 15 years he played a major role in consolidating eight small feeder associations into one large one called the Chinook Feeders. These associations, which received their initial impetus from the provincial government, were a joint effort between ranchers and farmers. The ranchers furnished the livestock, and the farmers the feed and care. Under Asplund's management, the association grew into a multimillion-dollar business. It shipped cattle to all the biggest markets on the continent, and it was known from coast to coast. A drop in the market in the mid-1950s, however, created a serious financial strain on the association. He found himself without a job. Not long after, the new association manager made some unfortunate decisions and the business folded. He continued privately in the livestock business by buying cattle and then putting them out with various farmers to fatten.

Asplund is well remembered as an organizer of youth in the field of agriculture. He organized and supervised many youth clubs, such as the Swine, Calf and Sheep clubs. He was often called to be judge at school fairs and other livestock exhibits. He was active in the Alberta Beet Growers

Association, was on the Raymond and Cardston school boards, and the Lethbridge Municipal Hospital Board. He was always active in his church and served in many callings, including being bishop of the Lethbridge Ward.

Lalovee Rogers Jensen[13]

Lalovee Jensen was born at Magrath, Alberta, on 9 June 1907, to Christian and Allie Rogers Jensen, who had immigrated to Canada from Utah in 1902 and bought a farm southwest of Magrath. He received his elementary and secondary schooling in Magrath. Following a church mission in Texas from 1926 to 1929, he studied animal science at Brigham Young University.

He was active in Canadian agriculture and many civic organizations for over thirty years. He was a trustee of the Magrath School District for one term, was a member of the founding board of directors of Unifarm, which succeeded the Alberta Federation of Agriculture, and represented the Alberta Sugar Beet Growers on Unifarm from 1970 to 1974. He was a director of the Alberta Sugar Beet Growers from 1944 to 1975 and served as its president from 1954 to 1975. He was vice-president of the Canadian Sugar Beet Producers from 1954 to 1961, and president from 1961 to 1975.

For thirty years, he also provided leadership to sheep and wool producers. He was director and executive director for the Canadian Co-operative Wool Growers from 1949 to 1968, and president from 1968 to 1979. He was the first president and founding director of the Canadian Sheep Marketing Council, from May 1972 to June 1976. During that same period, he was the first president and founding director of the Alberta Sheep and Wool Commission. From 1973 to 1977, he was the founding director and first president of the Lamb Processors Co-operative Ltd. He also served as a member of the Federal Government Sheep Survey Committee, which tendered an official report to the Federal Cabinet in 1958, dealing with the needs of the Canadian sheep industry. He was a member of the Senate of the University of Lethbridge from 1973 to 1976, was an original member of the Alberta Agricultural Research Trust, and an original member of the Advisory Committee to the Agricultural Economics Division of the University of Alberta.

In spite of his heavy commitment to the operations of these producer organizations, he developed a highly successful farming operation—Happy Valley Farms Ltd. In 1949, he and his family received the highly valued "Master Farm Family" award. In October 1974, he was inducted into the Alberta Agricultural Hall of Fame. (His father Christian Jensen had earlier been named to the Canadian Agricultural Hall of Fame.)

He won international recognition for his achievements in a 37-year breed improvement program, which has resulted in a unique strain of polled Rambouillet sheep. He did this through selection within the breed, rather than by crossbreeding, and thereby has removed the horns, opened the face, removed the wrinkles, and improved the meat qualities of the breed. In March 1980, Jensen was made Honorary Knight of the Golden Fleece by the Canadian Co-operative Wool Growers.

Reed C. Ellison[14]

Reed C. Ellison, born in Layton, Utah, 28 December 1909, did not arrive in Alberta until 1933. He had a strong connection with the pioneer period, however, through his parents, Morris Heber Ellison and Margaret Jane Cowley, and his grandfather, Ephraim Ellison. His great-grandfather brought with him to Utah his eastern American farming skills. He and his son Ephraim, Reed's grandfather, started several businesses, which included a major role in building the Weber County Canal in Utah. In addition, they were heavily involved in cattle and sheep production. Although Reed never became seriously involved in these aspects of the family's enterprises, he did become involved in enterprises in which church influence was critically important. The Church focused his father's and grandfather's attention on opportunities for the Saints to colonize and develop the southwestern part of Alberta.

After graduation from high school, he attended the University of Utah for five years, the first three years in the School of Business, and then in the School of Law for two years. The family owned and operated a farming business.

After two years of law, he expected to finish law the next year. But this was in the worst of the Great Depression years. Without a source of income, he accepted an offer from his father to go to Canada and work in the milling business. To prepare himself for this move, he learned cereal chemistry by going to a flour mill in Salt Lake City where he learned the whole milling process. He moved to Canada in 1933.

He has always had a strong desire to promote agriculture. His company was responsible for the introduction in the 1920s of Soft White Wheat, which has grown to a sizable industry in southern Alberta. It makes the best kind of flour for producing pastry and cake products. Seed was brought in from Idaho, but the available varieties were not well suited to local conditions and rust was a major problem. Plant breeding, however, has overcome most of these problems.

There was little Durham wheat grown in Alberta prior to the 1940s. The company brought in seed from Manitoba and distributed it to farmers. During the first years of its trial in the area, if the farmer's crop did not do well, the company did not invoice them for the seed. There is now a good acreage of Durham and Soft White in southern Alberta. The latest figures show about 400,000 acres of Soft White (practically all on irrigated land). Reed was also involved in the promotion of mustard as a viable crop.

After George W. Green's retirement as manager of Ellison Mills, Reed's father, Morris, took over the management, until 1942 when Reed became manager.

During the war years, all mills in Canada were operating at full capacity to supply flour to Great Britain. This resulted partly because of damage to mills in Great Britain by bombing. Following the war, the company, under Reed Ellison's direction, experimented to produce a loaf of bread that met changing government standards for vitamin-enriched flour. They found that leaving much of the wheat germ in white flour was difficult. This improved the vitamin content but had some effect on the baking quality.

He and his company were heavily involved in promoting the production of mustard seed. L.B. Knowlton, an LDS associate of Green's was also a major actor in the promotion of mustard. In 1949, Ellison Mills bought out the George W. Green Co. that Knowlton managed. Lethbridge became the center of mustard seed production for Canada. Ellisons did not start its production, but they did much to promote it.

Ellisons also became involved in the handling of wheat for export. The Canadian Wheat Board allowed Ellisons to buy pedigreed seed wheat direct from the producer. Practically all of it went to Saudi Arabia. In this way, producers were able to deliver over quota direct to the company rather than through Wheat Board channels. Most of it was winter wheat, cleaned and bagged locally and shipped out of Vancouver. This business was phased out in 1977.

In addition to making a major contribution in the development of grain processing and marketing in southern Alberta and to Canadian overseas markets, Reed C. Ellison has had a long and effective involvement in the business and educational sectors of Lethbridge and in his church. He has been actively involved in Chamber of Commerce work, was one of the first senators for the University of Lethbridge, and was also a member on the University's Board of Governors. He and his wife, Eva, have served in practically all the ward and stake administrative callings in the LDS church.

This period, from the 1920s to the 1960s, and continuing beyond in the lives of Lalovee Jensen, Asael Palmer and Reed Ellison, reflects Mormon contributions in the scientific side of agriculture, as well as processing, market development, and the forming of strategically important associations for the agricultural industry, especially in Alberta. While some devoted themselves completely to an agricultural profession, as in the case of Dr. Wyatt, others combined professional and church roles. Mormon agriculture and agriculturalists emerged from a relatively isolated pioneer past and were gradually integrated into the larger Canadian agricultural scene.

THE RECENT PERIOD

The third generation of Mormons in agriculture is made up of persons whose parents, and more often grandparents, helped establish Mormons in Canadian agriculture, plus others who became Mormons. This has been a dynamic period for agriculture, as it retreated from being a dominant occupation to becoming one of lesser importance numerically in the face of technological advance, corporatism, urbanization and swelling government employment. For this period, we have selected two who have made their careers primarily in Alberta, and seven, treated briefly, who have moved from Canada; a group we refer to as "the expatriates."

D. Tracy Anderson[15]

Tracy Anderson, the third of eight children, was born in Magrath, Alberta, on 27 June 1916, to John Forbes Anderson, Jr. and Sarah Elizabeth Tracy, who were both born in Utah. His grandparents came to Canada in 1903. Later, they moved to Raymond, where Tracy took his first seven years of schooling. The family moved to Lethbridge in 1928, where he graduated from high school in 1934. He attended the Calgary Normal School for a time, then in 1939 he enrolled at the University of Saskatchewan, where he graduated in agricultural engineering and agriculture.

Anderson served in the Canadian armed forces during World War II, after which he returned to the research station and became heavily involved in the evaluation of basic techniques of dryland farming. Although earlier studies had pointed farmers away from some eastern cultivating techniques, there was still much to be done in matching farming technologies with the specific needs of each piece of land. He became well acquainted with equipment that was being developed to help control soil drifting and perform other on-farm work. This was near the end of the period of transition between horse power and tractor power.

Work at the Lethbridge Research Station on land reclamation, especially as it applied to wind erosion control, did not go unnoticed in other parts of the world. Anderson spent many years spreading the gospel of "trash cover." During the 1950s and 1960s his major research and development interests led to participation in international conferences on trash cover farming.

Kenneth P. Anderson[16]

Kenneth Anderson was born in Barnwell, 22 November 1925. His parents were Hillman Monroe Anderson and Merle Johnson. His father's family came from Utah in 1902. His mother came with her parents from Arizona in the same year.

He received his early education in Barnwell, graduating from high school in 1944. He received a military call in 1945 and spent a year in the army. Following the army, Radio College in Toronto, a mission to Denmark and work as an announcer with CJOC Radio Station in Lethbridge, he was invited by the chairman of the board of the Taber Irrigation District (TID) to accept an administrative position under the supervision of Ted Sundall, the district manager. He accepted the offer, and began work in June 1951 as the district's assistant manager. The timing was appropriate, since a new area north of Taber called the "Big Bend" was just coming into the district, and the assessment roll of the district moved from 21,500 acres to about 32,000 acres. He soon became acquainted with all the irrigation system components, including the farms and farm families in the district.

Upon Sundall's retirement, Anderson was appointed manager. He attributes his interest in irrigation to his Mormon antecedents, since he grew up on an irrigated farm among experienced irrigators who had brought their irrigation technology with them from Utah and Idaho. He believes this background helped to get him invited to work with the district.

Shortly after he joined the TID staff, a new technology began to appear, sprinkler irrigation. This had an impact on the district; by the early 1960s from 40% to 50% of the land was then being irrigated by sprinkler. This required a reclassification of the new lands. Farmers were now able to irrigate land that they previously could not cover with gravity irrigation. By about 1964, the assessment roll had reached 40,000 acres. This meant that he had to renegotiate farmer/district agreements with all the farmers. This was a pioneering exercise. Although more acres were added, the farmers found that because of the increased efficiency of the sprinklers, their water use dropped from about 2.3 to 1.4 acre feet per acre.

During his tenure as manager of the TID, he participated actively in helping to put the case for cost sharing of the irrigation system rehabilitation to the government. It had been known for a long time that the benefits of irrigation do not stop at the farm gate. For example, the Taber industrial park does about 80% of its business with the irrigation industry. An Alberta government-sponsored study in the mid-1960s demonstrated that only about 14% of the benefits from the irrigated areas in Alberta accrue to the farmer, with 86% being distributed throughout the country.

As a result, the province established its Irrigation Capital Works program, which provided for 86% of the cost of rehabilitation of the irrigation systems in the districts, with the water users contributing the remainder. This has resulted in a multiyear reconstruction program, beginning in 1969 and continuing through to the present. This has put a great additional burden on the irrigation district managers, since it has been up to them to plan how to schedule the program (now operating at a level of about $30 million annually), get board and provincial approval, raise the farmers' share of the costs, get the engineering and construction work done, while at the same time meeting the districts' commitments to supply water to users.

A further challenge for Anderson and his district has been to ensure proper co-ordination with three other irrigation districts that take water from the Waterton, Belly and St. Mary storage and distribution systems. Anderson and his board members have made major contributions toward the solution of the many issues related to water sharing during reconstruction of their main canal, and in developing long-term agreements that meet the needs of the districts and the Alberta Departments of Agriculture and the Environment.

THE EXPATRIATES

As mentioned in the introduction, there are a number of Canadians who have spent most or all their careers outside Canada. They add to the total picture of Canadian Mormons in agriculture.

William H. Bennett[17]

William H. Bennett was born in Taber, 5 November 1910, to William A. Bennett and Mary Walker. He attended Taber schools, the Raymond School of Agriculture, and Utah State University.

He was a professor on the faculty at USU, where he served as associate professor of agronomy, dean of the College of Agriculture, and director of extension services. He was called by the church in 1970 to serve as an assistant to the Quorum of the Twelve Apostles and then in the First Quorum of Seventy. He died in 1980.

Kenneth W. Hill[18]

Dr. Hill spent his childhood in Taber. He received his bachelor of science in agriculture from USU, his master of science from the University of Alberta in 1947, and his doctorate from the University of Nebraska in 1951. He had made a name for himself in Canada with the Rogers Sugar Company at Vancouver, and with Canada Agriculture in sugar beet research at the Lethbridge Research Station, where his major focus was on sugar beet nutrition. He did pioneering work on establishing relationships between nitrogen fertilizer application and beet sugar content. He also spent 12 years at the Central Experimental Farm at Ottawa before accepting a faculty position at USU in 1963 as director of the Agricultural Research Station. Later, he served as department head of their Department of Plant Science. His last major assignment at the university before retiring in 1980 was to write the history of the USU Agricultural Research Station for the period 1928 to 1978.

James Austin Bennett[19]

Dr. Bennett, a brother of William Bennett, was born in Taber in 1915. Practically all his career has been at USU, where he served for many years as head of the Department of Animal Science.

James Wood[20]

James, born in 1915, son of Harold Wood, is another product of Taber whose professional life was principally tied to USU. Like many other faculty members in agriculture, he served several overseas tours in Africa and the Middle East.

Bruce H. Anderson[21]

Dr. Anderson was born in Raymond in 1917, a brother of Tracy Anderson whose biographical sketch appears earlier. He received his bachelor of science and master of science from USU in the late 1940s and a doctorate from the University of California, Davis, in the 1950s. His career has been devoted almost entirely to overseas irrigation, project administration and consulting engineering. In addition to many short-term overseas assignments, he has been resident in Iran, Venezuela and the Dominican Republic. He served as the executive director of a consortium of western American universities (Consortium for International Development), for about ten years, while on the faculty of USU.

Glen Stringham[22]

Dr. Stringham was born and raised in Welling, Alberta, on an irrigated farm. He did his undergraduate work at USU and postgraduate work at Colorado State University. He has spent most of his career in teaching and administration in USU's Department of Agricultural and Irrigation Engineering. He has completed a number of overseas assignments in Latin America and Africa, particularly in connection with assisting developing countries to prepare and implement irrigation engineering training programs in their universities.

J. Paul Riley[23]

Dr. Riley was born in British Columbia and took most of his undergraduate and postgraduate work at USU. Most of his career has been as a water research scientist at the Utah Water Research Laboratory. He is internationally recognized for his many research papers on agricultural water quality.

CONCLUSION

In the recent period, one begins to see the intense changes affecting Mormons in agriculture in southern Alberta, and at the same time the spread of highly trained agricultural specialists to the United States and other countries. The third generation has built on the humble beginnings of farming, ranching and irrigation in the tiny Alberta Mormon settlements, and moved their influence firmly onto the national and international stages.

In considering a century of Canadian Mormons in agriculture, some patterns begin to emerge. One, with a few notable exceptions, is the involvement of Mormon agricultural leaders in civic and church affairs. Another is the prominent role of the Utah Agricultural College, later Utah State University, in the preparation of Mormon agricultural leaders,[24] especially in irrigation engineering, a specialization whose development in Alberta universities has lagged. One consequence of USU's prominence has been a migration, especially in the recent period, of southern Albertans to fruitful agricultural careers in Utah and elsewhere. All of the "expatriates" received at least one university degree from USU. This, plus the international reputation of the university, especially in irrigation-related programs, and the Mormon culture in Logan, Utah, were undoubtedly the principal reasons for their continued involvement with USU.

A third pattern, evident from the start and continuing to the present, is the vision that has characterized Mormon agricultural endeavors and personnel, a vision that has taken the western Canadian Mormon experience and motivations, translated into the various aspects of agriculture, to much of the modern world. Agriculture is one field where the Mormon presence in Canada has had an important impact. It will continue no doubt in the future to have its own unique story to tell.

NOTES

1. We express appreciation to Dr. Brigham Card for encouraging us to undertake this paper, and to Dr. Card and Dr. Howard Palmer for editorial suggestions. Dr. Palmer arranged for financial help that facilitated several of the interviews through the University of Calgary's oral history project, "Peoples in Southern Alberta." Debra Hadley assisted in interviewing and extracting pertinent information from the personal histories of several people whose biographies are in this paper.
2. See B.Y. Card, "Charles Ora Card and the Founding of the Mormon Settlements in South-Western Alberta, Northwest Territories," in this volume for further background on C.O. Card. The best biographical source, apart from C.O. Card's own journals, is A. James Hudson, *Charles Ora Card: Pioneer and Colonizer* (master's thesis, Brigham Young University, 1961, and published privately, 1963). See pp. 20-21 for Card's Cache Valley background in irrigation.
3. For further background on Jesse Knight, a basic work is Jesse William Knight,

The Jesse Knight Family (Salt Lake City: Deseret News Press, 1941).

4. The best reference for Edward J. Wood is Melvin S. Tagg, *The Life of Edward James Wood: Church Patriot* (master's thesis, Brigham Young University, and published privately, 1959). All the material on him used in this paper is from this source.

5. John A. Widtsoe, mentioned in the Wood biography and in the biography of Asael E. Palmer that follows, as an agricultural scientist from Utah, exerted a strong influence on Mormon and Canadian agriculture from 1900 to the 1950s.

6. The sources used for George William Green were from news clippings and biographical notes possessed by his son, Thomas N. Green, and from a taped interview with Reed C. Ellison.

7. Frank Wyatt is the first Mormon background agriculturalist in Canada to be listed in *American Men of Science*, 7th edition, 1944.

8. Information relating to Asael E. Palmer came from James H. Gray, *Men Against the Desert,* (Saskatoon: Modern Press, 1969), and from *Palmer, Asael E. Oral History,* interviews by Charles Ursenbach, Lethbridge, Alberta, 1973. Typescript. Oral History Program, Archives, Historical Department of the Church of Jesus Christ of Latter-day Saints, Salt Lake City, Utah.

9. A.E. Palmer, *When the Winds Came* (published privately, no date).

10. The honors include Fellow of the Agricultural Institute of Canada; Distinguished Service Award from Utah State University; honorary degree, Doctor of Laws (LL.D) from the University of Lethbridge; Alberta Agricultural Hall of Fame; Award of Merit from the Canadian Horticultural Council; the Water-Wheel Award of Merit from the Alberta Irrigation Projects Association, and on the occasion of his 95th birthday, honorary membership in the Association.

11. Melvin S. Tagg and Asael E. Palmer, *A History of the Mormon Church in Canada: A Canada Centennial Project* (Lethbridge: Lethbridge Stake Historical Committee, 1968). Chapters 5, on early settlement, and 6, on irrigation and Mormon expansion in Alberta, deal with early Alberta Mormon agricultural developments.

12. *Asplund, Charles Owen, Oral History*, Interviews by Eva R. Ellison with Julia Ellen Russell Asplund, his wife, April 1985. Typescript. Oral History Program, Archives, Historical Department of the Church of Jesus Christ of Latter-day Saints, Salt Lake City, Utah.

13. Information on Lalovee Rogers Jensen was provided in typescript by his daughter, Sylvia Bullock, 2720 South Parkside Dr., Lethbridge, Alberta.

14. Information on Reed C. Ellison was provided in a personal taped interview with this essay's authors in April 1987.

15. Information on D. Tracy Anderson was provided in a personal taped interview with Debra Hadley in April, 1987.

16. Information on Kenneth P. Anderson was provided in a personal taped interview with Debra Hadley in April 1987.

17. See William Hunter Bennett entry in *American Men of Science*, 11th edition, 1967.

18. Kenneth Wilford Hill entry in *American Men of Science*, 11th edition, 1967. Other sources, personally known to authors.
19. James Austin Bennett, entry in *American Men of Science*, 11th edition, 1967.
20. James Wood, personally known to senior author.
21. Bruce H. Anderson entry in *American Men of Science*, 11th edition, 1967. Other sources, personally known to senior author.
22. Glen Stringham, personally known to authors.
23. J. Paul Riley, in *American Men and Women of Science*, 16th edition, 1986.
24. The high productivity of Utah State Agricultural College, USU for doctorates, 1920-1961, has been noted by Kenneth R. Hardy, "Social origins of American scientists and scholars," *Science*, Vol. 185 (1974), pp. 497-506, especially Table 4.

13 Political Behavior of Mormons in Canada

DAVID K. ELTON

THE POLITICAL BEHAVIOR of Mormons in Canada has attracted
but little interest among writers on Canadian government and politics
during the past three decades. Four possible reasons for this state of
affairs come to mind. First, with but minor idiosyncrasies, the political
values, attitudes and behavior of Mormons have not set them apart from
other Canadians. Second, from a national or regional political perspective, Mormons as a group make up an insignificant segment of the Canadian population (.4%), and politically a relatively unimportant proportion
of the population of Alberta (1.9%). There is, therefore, little likelihood
that Mormons, as a group, would play a significant role in setting or
influencing either the Canadian or Alberta political agenda. Third, those
Mormons who have obtained leadership positions within the Canadian
political system have not drawn attention to their religion by articulating
beliefs inconsistent with the larger political constituencies they represented,
or undertaken actions that would focus attention upon their religious
affiliation. Fourth, political behavior at the provincial constituency or
municipal level, where Mormon populations in southern Alberta are
politically significant, are seldom analyzed by anyone but writers for small
town weeklies, or the patrons of local restaurants, pool halls or conve-
nience stores in the small Mormon communities of Cardston, Raymond
and Magrath in southern Alberta.

A search of the literature on Mormons and politics in Canada located
but one published article, written by Howard Palmer in 1969.[1] This article
outlines the history of the Mormon settlement in southern Alberta from
the early 1900s to the late 1960s, identifies Mormons who were elected

to Canada's Parliament (MPs), or as members of the Legislative Assembly of Alberta (MLAs), and examines the politically relevant issues related to national and provincial policies, particularly during the 1930-1960s period.

Four aspects of Mormon political behavior in Canada will be addressed in this essay. First, to place Mormon political behavior in perspective, a brief summary of the research findings on religion and politics in the United States, with emphasis on Mormon political behavior, will be presented. The second section will provide an overview of Mormons' participation in Canadian national politics. The third section examines Mormon activity within Alberta provincial politics, focusing primarily upon the Cardston constituency, the only provincial riding in Canada in which Mormons constitute a religious majority. The fourth section focuses upon municipal politics in the only three towns in Canada in which Mormons make up a religious majority: Cardston, Magrath and Raymond. Conclusions drawn from this survey of Mormon political behavior constitute the fifth and final section.

MORMON POLITICAL BEHAVIOR IN THE UNITED STATES

A considerable amount of research on religion and politics in general, and Mormon political behavior in particular, has been conducted in the United States.[2] Yet, there is little consensus on the significance of religion upon political behavior.[3] While there is clear evidence that party identification (i.e., an individual's sense of identity with either the Republican or Democratic parties) is the most important predictor of vote, the only consistent generalization about the relationship of religion to political behavior seems to be that it is inversely related to the individual's overall political involvement.[4] As one author pointed out, "The more politically involved the voter, the less religious pull he would feel, the less politically involved, the higher the effect of religion."[5] Thus, notwithstanding considerable discussion about religion and politics in the US since 1980, given the role of the moral majority and Christian fundamentalism, particularly in presidential politics, there is still no consensus on the significance of religion on voting behavior.[6]

One of the more recent comprehensive studies on Mormon political behavior was undertaken by A.O. Miles at New York University.[7] The study analyzed church pronouncements on politics. It was also based upon a mail survey in 1968 (2000 questionnaires mailed with 743 completed), followed by another mail survey in 1977 (1500 mailed with 508 completed). These questionnaires were mailed to a cross-section of Mormons in the United States. The purpose of the study was basically threefold: to determine the level of political participation among Mormons and the extent to which the Mormon Church encouraged this activity; to examine whether Mormon voting behavior and political attitudes are predictable more on the basis of socioeconomic and demographic factors than on the basis of religious affiliation and level of church commitment; and to differentiate between the individual's attribution of church influence, and actual positions taken by the church on political candidates and issues. The Miles study came to the following conclusions:

1. The Mormon Church regularly (i.e., annually) encourages political participation, particularly with regard to voting in national, state and local elections.

2. Mormons react to changing times and conditions in much the same way as other American voters.

3. Voting turnout in Utah is always higher than the US national average:

Year	National average	Utah average
1970	43.5	64.0
1972	55.5	68.5
1974	36.1	55.7
1976	53.1	66.5

4. Mormons indicate higher levels of political participation than the national average by from 8% to 13%, depending upon the activity (i.e., campaign contributions, attendance at political meetings, volunteer work for a candidate, membership in political club, etc.).

5. Few Mormons identify church leaders or membership as a significant source of guidance in political matters. For example, when asked, "Whose opinion on political issues and candidates do you rely on most?," only one in ten (10% in 1968 and 13% in 1977) identified church leaders or "church and others." This compares to two in three respondents who identified "self" as the primary source of influence. In the 1977 survey, significantly more respondents (20%) identified the mass media as the primary source of influence.

6. Mormon Church leaders have not endorsed candidates (e.g., Presidential candidates) since 1960 when President David O. McKay personally

endorsed Richard Nixon against John Kennedy. The church has, however, made policy statements to their members on such issues as the Equal Rights Amendment, abortion, liquor sales, etc.

7. The Mormon Church seeks to distance itself from political movements or partisanship.

8. Approximately one in five (19% in 1968 and 17% in 1977) church members feel adherence to church doctrine influences party identification considerably, while another five of ten (44% in 1968 and 59% in 1977) feel it has some influence on one's choice of party.

9. Mormons tend to identify more frequently with the Republican Party (55% in 1968 and 49% in 1977) than the Democratic Party (22% in 1968 and 20% in 1977). Approximately one in four Mormons (22% in 1968 and 29% in 1977) did not identify with either party.

10. The stronger a church member's commitment to LDS doctrine and principles, the more likely is the member to vote Republican (approximately 80% of those with a strong commitment to the church voted Republican, compared to approximately 45% of those inactive).

11. Mormons often impute church advocacy or endorsement of political issues when in fact it has not taken a stand (e.g., support for the granting of amnesty to Vietnam War draft resisters).

The general conclusion to be drawn from the current literature on religion and politics in the United States is that under "normal circumstances" (i.e., voting in a general election or on most plebiscites) religion seldom plays a significant role in influencing the political behavior of voters in general, or Mormons in particular. The tendency for Mormons to identify more with the Republican Party than Democratic Party might well be more a function of a more general conservative commitment that influences both religious affiliation and activity and partisan identification.

CANADA'S NATIONAL POLITICAL STAGE

Religion is a powerful predictor of party preference in Canada. Time and again, analysis of survey research data indicate that Catholics tend to support and vote Liberal, while Protestants tend to vote Conservative.[8] Unfortunately, analysis on religion and politics in Canada has not dealt with the many denominations that are lumped under the general heading "Protestant." Further, while the correlation between being Catholic and voting Liberal is clearly significant, there is no clear explanation of this cleavage.

As one author noted, "The persistence of an apparent religious cleavage was due less to religion than to something else, whose nature was open to conjecture, which coincided with religion."[9]

Because research regarding the individual political behavior of Mormons in Canada has yet to be conducted, discussion of Mormons and national, provincial and local politics is limited in this essay to aggregate voting behavior and the career patterns of individuals affiliated with the Mormon Church.

The impact of Mormons upon Canada's national political stage has been limited. There are a number of possible reasons for this state of affairs. First, in a parliamentary political system that emphasizes parliamentary majorities, it would be most unusual to find the specific religious concerns of less than 1% of the population influencing the political agenda. Indeed, if all Mormons in Canada lived in one geographic area, numerically they would make up the equivalent of but one riding in the national Parliament. A second factor limiting religious related behavior in Canada is, with the exception of special privileges given religious schools in some provinces (particularly Newfoundland), that religious affiliations in general are seldom considered politically relevant. Third, only rarely do Mormon church leaders take a specific stand on Canadian political issues (eg., prohibition in the early 1900s, and family allowances in the 1940s). This does not mean to suggest that the church's stand on abortion, Sunday opening laws, pornography, capital punishment, etc., are not relevant political issues for Canadian Mormons, but rather to point out that the church's decision to take a stand on these issues is oriented primarily to the American political agenda and all but oblivious to political events in Canada. Church leaders in Ontario did take a stance on the entrenchment of women's equality in the Canadian Constitution in 1981 by making a presentation to the parliamentary committee examining the issue, but there was little notice made of this intervention either in the Canadian media or among members of the church.[10]

The fourth possible reason that Mormons have had relatively little impact upon national politics is that few Mormons have either sought or been elected to Canada's Parliament. Two plausible explanations for the lack of Mormons in Canada's Parliament come to mind. First, because of their small numbers, the pool of people from which to draw possible MPs is small. Second, and, perhaps most importantly, because of the lay nature of the Mormon Church, individual members of the church with leadership abilities are almost always assigned church leadership positions. These positions take up a great deal of time and effectively preclude these individuals from

TABLE 13.1 Lethbridge Constituency Voter Participation Compared to Provincial and National Voter Participation in National Elections

	Mormon Communities			Lethbridge	Alberta	National
DATE	*CARDSTON*	*RAYMOND*	*MAGRATH*	*Constituency*	*Constituency*	*Average*
1957	81%	75%	75%	74%	73%	74%
1958	78%	80%	73%	80%	74%	79%
1962	74%	82%	75%	79%	74%	79%
1963	77%	80%	72%	81%	79%	79%
1965	67%	76%	73%	76%	74%	75%
1968	65%	72%	74%	74%	73%	76%
1972	72%	82%	72%	73%	76%	77%
1974	61%	69%	71%	67%	67%	71%
1979	69%	66%	66%	68%	68%	76%
1980	63%	64%	64%	61%	61%	69%
1984	63%	75%	65%	67%	69%	75%
Average	70%	74.6%	70.9%	72.7%	71.6%	75.5%

SOURCES: Report of the Chief Electoral Officer, Minister of Supply and Services, Ottawa, 1957-84.

committing the amount of time necessary to take an active role in other community activities that might lead to nomination and election to public office.

Little can be said about the contemporary electoral behavior of Mormons in national politics based upon aggregate data because they are dispersed throughout the country. The one exception is the Lethbridge, Alberta, constituency, where Mormons make up between 20% and 25% of the eligible voters. The aggregate national election voting data of the three predominantly Mormon communities in the Lethbridge constituency (Cardston, Magrath and Raymond) in Table 13.1 suggest that unlike Utah Mormons, who tend to vote more frequently than non-Mormons, Canadian Mormons do not tend to vote any more frequently than do other Albertans. Indeed, in two of the three communities, the average voter turnout was somewhat lower than the national average (i.e., Cardston 70% and Magrath 70.9%, Canadian average 75.5%). The data in Table 13.1 do contain one interesting anomaly. In the 1957 election, the turnout in all three Mormon communities barely exceeded that of both the provincial and national averages for that year. This unusual turnout is understandable, given that the candidates for both the leading parties, the Social Credit Party and the Liberal Party, were Mormons. This is the only time in Canadian history that the candidates of the two major parties within a particular riding were Mormon.

In addition to sharing similar voting turnout characteristics with those of the Alberta population, Mormon communities also tend to share the same national party preferences as do other southern Albertans. In the early 1900s, when southern Albertans were electing Liberals, so were the residents of the Lethbridge riding. When southern Alberta swung their support behind the UFA, following World War I, so did the residents of Lethbridge constituency. When southern Alberta abandoned the UFA in the midst of the Great Depression and embraced Social Credit, so did the residents of the Lethbridge riding, even though Mormons were advised by a church leader, Apostle Melvin J. Ballard, not to support parties with "unsound" economic policies.[11] Finally, the most recent switch in partisan loyalties, to the Progressive Conservatives (1958), took place in the Lethbridge constituency the same time as it did in the rest of southern Alberta. In sum, the evidence available from the Lethbridge constituency suggests that as far as national politics are concerned Mormon political behavior is indistinguishable from that of other southern Albertans. This voting record suggests that the political behavior of Mormons is probably primarily a function of regional environmental factors.

Attainment of high profile positions within the national political system, be they elected or appointed, by individuals affiliated with the Mormon Church on the national political stage has been limited. During this century, only two Mormons have been elected to Parliament, Solon Low (1945-58) and John Blackmore (1935-58). Both were not only members of the Social Credit Party but also the party leader. While these men did receive some publicity because of their status as leader of a small protest party, neither ever moved far from the obscurity of the opposition backbenches in Ottawa.

No member of the Mormon faith has ever been elected to the governing party at the national level, or for that matter the official opposition party. In a parliamentary system where cabinet members are always chosen from the governing party, this means that no Mormon has ever served in the central decision-making body of the Canadian government—the cabinet. No Mormon has ever been appointed to the Canadian Senate, or been appointed head of a federal crown corporation or regulatory agency. N. Eldon Tanner's position as the head of TransCanada PipeLines in the mid-1950s is the

John H. Blackmore, Social Credit M.P. for
Lethbridge, 1935-58. P 1975 2909347
The Archives, Sir Alexander Galt
Museum, Lethbridge, Alberta.

only instance in which a Mormon has held the senior position in a high profile national quasi-government organization.

While there have been individuals affiliated with the Mormon Church
who have attained responsible positions in the national public service (e.g.,
Alex Morrison was an assistant deputy minister in the Department of Health
and Welfare; Tanner Elton was an assistant deputy minister in the Department of the Solicitor General, and is currently deputy attorney general of
Manitoba; and Doug Bowie was assistant deputy minister in the Department of the Secretary of State), no Mormon has ever attained a high profile
public office in Canada's national government structure.

ALBERTA PROVINCIAL POLITICS

Although slightly more than one in every two Mormons live outside the province of Alberta (46,890 of 89,870), with but one exception no record has
been found of a member of the Mormon Church who has been elected to
public office, been appointed to head a provincial crown corporation, or
having attained the position of deputy minister of a provincial department
of government. (The exception is the appointment of Jim Matkin as a deputy
minister of Intergovernmental Affairs in British Columbia.) The record is
somewhat different in Alberta.[12]

John W. Woolf, nonpartisan MLA for Cardston, Assembly of the Northwest Territories, 1909-05 and Liberal MLA, Alberta, 1905-12. NA 114-13 Glenbow Archives.

Martin Woolf, Liberal MLA for Cardston, 1912-21. A 2748 Provincial Archives of Alberta.

George L. Stringham, United Farmers of Alberta MLA for Cardston, 1921-35. A 3629 Provincial Archives of Alberta.

TABLE 13.2   Voting Turnout — Cardston Provincial Constituency

Date	Cardston Constituency	Provincial Average	Winning Candidate	Political Affiliation	Religious Affiliation
1905			John Woolf	Liberal	Mormon
1909			John Woolf	Liberal	Mormon
1913			Martin Woolf	Liberal	Mormon
1917			Martin Woolf	Liberal	Mormon
1921	79.3%		George Stringham	UFA	Mormon
1926	77.4%	67.0%	George Stringham	UFA	Mormon
1930	65.4%	66.7%	George Stringham	UFA	Mormon
1935	95.4%	81.8%	N.E. Tanner	S.C.	Mormon
1940	81.9%	74.8%	N.E. Tanner	S.C.	Mormon
1944	72.2%	69.2%	N.E. Tanner	S.C.	Mormon
1948	60.0%	63.4%	N.E. Tanner	S.C.	Mormon
1952	56.0%	59.4%	Edgar Hinman	S.C.	Mormon
1955	61.8%	68.0%	Edgar Hinman	S.C.	Mormon
1959	66.2%	63.9%	Edgar Hinman	S.C.	Mormon
1963	56.1%	56.1%	Edgar Hinman	S.C.	Mormon
1967	62.1%	64.3%	Alvin Bullock	S.C.	Mormon
1971	58.9%	72.0%	Edgar Hinman	S.C.	Mormon
1975	56.8%	59.6%	John Thompson	P.C.	Non-Mormon
1979	58.6%	58.7%	John Thompson	P.C.	Non-Mormon
1982	64.8%	66.0%	John Thompson	P.C.	Non-Mormon
1986	46.3%	47.3%	Jack Ady	P.C.	Mormon

SOURCES: Report of the Chief Electoral Officer, Government of Alberta, Edmonton, 1905-86.

Since Alberta became a province in 1905, 17 members of the Mormon faith have been elected to the provincial legislature. Many of these individuals were re-elected several times. To put the above data in perspective, during the course of the 21 general provincial elections, a Mormon has been elected 34 times out of a possible 1,215, or 2.8% of the time. This figure is slightly higher than the proportion of Albertans who are affiliated with the Mormon Church (1.9%). Of the 34 constituency elections won by Mormons, 18 of them were won in the Cardston constituency, where a majority of the population (approximately 65% at the present time) are members of the Mormon Church. Not surprisingly, in only 12 (1975-86) of the 82 years has a non-Mormon served as MLA for Cardston. In this individual's case, John

Thompson, members of his immediate family were active members of the church.

The data in Table 13.2 tell basically the same story as the national voting data discussed earlier. Voting turnout in the Cardston constituency is similar to that of the province as a whole. In addition, changes in party support took place the same time as did party fortunes throughout southern Alberta: from Liberal to UFA, from UFA to Social Credit, and from Social Credit to Progressive Conservative. There is, therefore, no evidence in these provincial voting data that Mormons behave any differently from other Albertans living in the same region of the province.

A closer look at political activity within the Cardston constituency suggests that on occasion there are unusually high levels of participation. The 1986 Progressive Conservative candidate nomination meeting is an excellent example. As in many Alberta constituencies over the past decade, winning the PC nomination is for all practical purposes a guarantee of one's subsequent election to the provincial legislature. Thus, the real competition takes place at the PC nomination meeting several months prior to the election, and not on election day. Four candidates contested the PC nomination, which was held on 12 February 1986 in Magrath. Three of the candidates were Mormons: Jack Ady and Broyce Jacobs from the Cardston area, and Dick Williams from Raymond. The fourth candidate, Bob Grbavac, was Catholic and from the Raymond area. The results of the three ballots used to declare a winner, under the 50% plus one rule used in nomination meetings, are provided in Table 13.3. A superficial examination of these data would suggest that Bob Grbavac lost the nomination because of an unwillingness by Mormons to support a Catholic candidate. This conclusion oversimplifies reality. In fact, a large proportion (estimated to be in excess of 50%) of Bob Grbavac's initial 700 supporters were Mormon. Furthermore, while Grbavac was well known in the Raymond area, he was a relatively unknown figure forty miles away in the Cardston area. The same was true for each of the other candidates. While well known in their own communities, they were not well known throughout the constituency. Thus, when Broyce Jacobs was eliminated on the first ballot, it was not particularly surprising that many of his supporters moved to support Ady, a well-known local county official. Dick Williams, while not as well known as Jack Ady, had been born and raised in the Cardston area, and thus it was no surprise that he too picked up support from former Jacobs supporters. It was thus only on the third ballot, where former Williams supporters moved in a ratio of three to one to support Ady over Grbavac, that religious considerations might have

TABLE 13.3　　Cardston P.C. Constituency Nomination — February 1986

Candidate Name	Residence	First Ballot	Second Ballot	Third Ballot
Dick Williams	Raymond	461	541	
Jack Ady	Cardston	505	693	1049
Broyce Jacobs	Cardston	399		
Bob Grbavac	Raymond	700	720	836
Totals		2065	1954	1885

SOURCE: Data obtained from two candidate's campaign workers.

played a prominent role in influencing some former Williams supporters to choose Ady over Grbavac. The ability to isolate religious considerations in this final balloting is further complicated by the considerable style and personality differences between Ady and Grbavac.

Perhaps the most important element of this nomination meeting is to be found in the number of people who participated in this political event, rather than the balloting itself. In 1986, there were 9,611 eligible electors in the constituency. Of this number, 1,556 were residents of the Blood Indian Reserve, who historically have not participated much at all at either the nomination or election stages in provincial elections. This means that 2,065 of the 8,085 non-natives in the constituency, or one in four eligible voters (25.5%) participated in the PC Party nomination. While there are no known statistics on participation levels at nomination meetings in Canadian provincial or national politics, it is unlikely that there are many (if any) nomination meetings in the past three decades that a similar or larger proportion of the total electorate participated in.

Of the 17 Mormons elected to the Alberta Legislature since 1905, four have been appointed to the provincial cabinet: Solon Low was appointed provincial treasurer, and later became minister of Education. N.E. Tanner was appointed speaker of the Alberta Legislature in 1935, and two years later was appointed minister of Lands and Forests, a position he retained until he left provincial politics in the early 1950s. E.W. Hinman held the position of provincial treasurer during the late 1950s and early 1960s. Bill Payne, the only Mormon to serve in the Alberta cabinet during the past two decades, held the position of minister without portfolio from 1982 to 1986.

N. Eldon Tanner, Social
Credit MLA, Minister of
Lands and Mines,
1937-52.

Solon E. Low, Provincial
Treasurer, 1937-44,
Minister of Education,
1943-44. MP for Peace
River, and national party
leader, 1945-58. PA600
Provincial Archives of
Alberta.

Edgar "Ted" W. Hinman,
Social Credit MLA,
Minister of Municipal
Affairs, 1954. Provincial
Treasurer, 1955-64. A10,
654 Provincial Archives of
Alberta.

William "Bill" E. Payne,
Progressive Conservative
MLA, Minister without
portfolio responsible for
Public Affairs Bureau,
1982-86. Alberta Govern-
ment Audiovisual Services.

Because Alberta did not utilize a cabinet committee system until the 1970s, it is impossible to identify Low, Tanner and Hinman formally as members of the Alberta inner cabinet. There is no doubt, however, given the central position of the portfolios they were given, provincial treasurer, minister of Mines and Forests, and minister of Education, that they held one of the top four or five most important positions within the provincial government.

Relatively few Mormons have attained senior positions in the Alberta senior civil service. Over the past two decades, for example, only seven Mormons have attained one of the two top positions in any department—assistant deputy minister or deputy minister. These individuals are: H. Jensen and V. Wood, Lands and Forests; G. Purnell, Agriculture; B. Gehmlich, Public Works; D. Salmon, Auditor General; D. Wood, Public Affairs; and W. Payne,

Public Affairs. This number of senior public servants is approximately what one would expect, given the size of the Mormon population in the province.

A preliminary search of appointments to senior positions on government boards and agencies identified two Mormons: Bob Lundrigan, who served a term as chairman of the Human Rights Commission, and Cec Purves, chairman of the Surface Rights Board.

A discussion of Alberta politics and Mormons in the 1980s would be incomplete without mention of the central role that a Mormon played in the western separatist movement that flared up overnight in the fall of 1980 and spread quickly through the rural areas of central and southern Alberta. The catalyst for this political movement was the announcement and implementation of the federal government's National Energy Program and constitutional initiatives. In the eyes of many western Canadians, both of these policy initiatives were thinly disguised attempts to confiscate resource revenues and increase the federal government's effective control over western Canada.

This frustration with national policy culminated in the surprise election of Gordon Kesler, of the separatist-leaning Western Canada Concept Party (WCC), in a by-election in the central Alberta constituency of Olds-Didsbury in February 1982. Inasmuch as Kesler was the first western separatist ever elected, he became an overnight folk hero among the radical conservative element of Alberta politics and obtained considerable regional and national media attention. In 1982, Kesler was clearly the best known Mormon in Canada.

Nine months following Kesler's victory in the Olds-Didsbury by-election, a provincial general election was held, and Kesler, as leader of the newly formed WCC, was successful in recruiting candidates in all but one Alberta riding. On 9 November 1982, the WCC obtained 11.8% of the popular vote but failed to elect anyone to the Alberta Legislature. Given the conservative sentiments in the Cardston constituency, the highest proportion of votes (36.7%) obtained by any WCC candidate was by a Mormon candidate in this predominantly Mormon riding.

The most significant aspect of this brief, overt flirtation with separatism by a segment of the Alberta electorate was that there was little if any reference made to Kesler's religious affiliation. Time and again Kesler was identified by his occupation (oil company scout), and place of residence (High River), but his religious affiliation was seldom considered relevant.

The above record of Mormon participation in provincial politics and government in Alberta is not extraordinary, but rather is well within the

L. Gordon Kesler, Western Canada Concept Party MLA for Olds-Didsbury, 1982. *Alberta Report* photograph.

norms one would expect from a group of people that make up approximately 2% of the province's population. While people such as N.E. Tanner, Solon Low and E.W. Hinman clearly played a pivotal role in Alberta politics during the 1940s and 1950s, no Mormon has reached equivalent stature in Alberta politics during the past twenty years. There have been numerous issues particularly relevant to Mormons, such as Sunday opening laws, the sale of liquor, abortion, pornography, etc., where opinion within the Mormon community was predominantly on one side of the issue. Yet, Mormons in Alberta have always found themselves as one group among many religious and nonreligious groups supporting or opposing these issues, and have seldom, if ever, been singled out as a dominant political force. As Bill Payne, a former cabinet minister and current Calgary MLA, pointed out, the stereotype of Mormons among Alberta government leaders is that of self-reliant, patriotic, fundamentalist Christians with "right-wing" political values.[13]

David H. Elton, Mayor of
Lethbridge, 1935-43.
Courtesy David K. Elton,
Lethbridge.

Don H. MacKay, Mayor of
Calgary, 1950-59. NA
277501 Glenbow Archives.

Cecil J. Purves, Mayor of
Edmonton, 1977-83. A
86-30 City of Edmonton
Archives, Alberta.

MUNICIPAL POLITICS

While Mormons have played a modest role in national and provincial politics, in each of Alberta's three largest municipalities a Mormon politician has, for two or more terms, occupied the mayor's chair. In Lethbridge, D.H. Elton was a prominent member of the Lethbridge city council and mayor during the 1930s and early 1940s. In Calgary, Don MacKay was an alderman and mayor during the late 1940s and 1950s. In Edmonton, Cec Purves was an alderman and mayor during the 1970s and 1980s. While there is no evidence that religion played any role in the election of any of these men, that all three were mayor for several terms in predominantly non-Mormon communities has been a source of civic pride for members of the Mormon community throughout Alberta. The election of these three men also indicates the extent to which Mormons were considered an acceptable subset of these larger Alberta communities.

Municipal politics within the three "Mormon towns" of southern Alberta suggests a different pattern of political behavior than that found at the national or provincial level of political activity.[14] In all three towns, Mormons have been disproportionately overrepresented on town councils. In Cardston, there is no record of a non-Mormon ever being elected mayor, even though non-Mormons currently make up almost 30% of the town's population. In Raymond, on only one occasion has a non-Mormon been

TABLE 13.4   Aldermanic Elections in Mormon Towns 1971-1976

Religious Affiliation of Constituents	Cardston		Magrath		Raymond	
	NO.	%	NO.	%	NO.	%
Mormon Candidates	73	90	40	65	56	90
Mormons Elected	36	100	26	72	33	92
Non-Mormon Candidates	5	7	22	38	6	10
Non-Mormons Elected	0	0	10	28	3	8

SOURCES: Personal interviews with town secretaries in Cardston, Magrath and Raymond.

elected mayor, even though currently over one in every four residents are non-Mormon (27%). Mormon overrepresentation on the Magrath town council has not been as prevalent. For example, the current mayor of Magrath is non-Mormon, even though the ratio of non-Mormons to Mormons is about the same as that of Cardston and Raymond (approximately 30%).

An examination of the religious affiliations of individuals nominated and elected for the town councils of Cardston, Magrath and Raymond over the past six municipal elections (1971 through 1986) indicates the extent to which Mormons have been disproportionately overrepresented. As shown in Table 13.4, 93% (73 of 78) of the candidates for alderman in Cardston during the 1971-86 period have been Mormon, and all those elected have been Mormon. In Magrath, 65% (40 of 62) of the candidates for alderman have been Mormon, and 72% of those elected have been Mormon. Comparable figures for Raymond are 90% of the candidates Mormon, and 92% of the aldermen Mormon. These data suggest that the overrepresentation of Mormons on two of the three town councils might be more a function of the number of non-Mormons running for office than the voting behavior of the town residents.

There are a number of factors that might discourage non-Mormons from contesting town council elections. First, given the dominant visual (church buildings), social and economic (ownership of local businesses by Mormons) aspects, non-Mormons might feel that their chances of being elected are slim and therefore do not even bother contesting the elections. Second, because the Mormons tend to associate primarily with one another, due to the extensive social activities sponsored by the church (e.g., sports leagues, boy scouts, dances, picnics, overnight campouts, etc.), non-Mormons might not have occasion to socialize adequately with their neighbors, and thus fail to establish a network of friends and associates adequate enough to encourage political participation. Third, Mormons are often perceived by non-Mormons to treat fellow Mormons preferentially; thus, a folklore, based in part on experience, has developed about Mormons being unwilling to support non-Mormons in local elections in Mormon communities.

CONCLUSION

Research on religion and politics indicates that in our contemporary society religion is seldom a fundamental determinant of political behavior. Recent research on Mormon political behavior in the United States indicates that while Mormons tend to participate in politics to a greater extent than their fellow countrymen, and tend to support the Republican Party disproportionately, there is little evidence to indicate that their religious beliefs influence their political behavior to a greater extent than other socio-demographic characteristics or attitudinal frameworks, such as political conservatism.

The data available regarding the political behavior of Mormons in Canada indicate their political behavior is indistinguishable from that of other Canadians. Mormons in Alberta tend to participate in politics in similar proportions to other Albertans, and hold similar views to those expressed by non-Mormons within their local communities. Their choice of political parties is similar to that of other members in their community. From a political behavior perspective, Alberta Mormons are as typically Albertan as are the adherents of any religious group in the province.

NOTES
1. Howard Palmer, "Mormon political behavior in Alberta," *Tangents* 1, Brigham Young University, 1969, pp. 85-112.
2. For a review of the literature, see David B. Magleby, "Religion and voting behavior in a religiously homogeneous state," 1987, Working Paper, Department of Political Science, Brigham Young University.
3. Robert Axelrod, "Where the votes come from: An analysis of electoral Coalitions, 1952-1968," *American Political Science Review*, Vol. 66 (1972), pp. 11-20.
4. See Philip E. Converse, "Religion and Politics: the 1960 Election," in Angus

Campbell, Philip E. Converse, Warren E. Miller and Donald E. Stokes, eds., *Elections and the Political Order* (New York: John Wiley and Sons 1967).

5. Magleby, op. cit., p. 9.
6. Jeffrey Brudney and Gary Copeland, "Evangelicals as a political force: Reagan and the 1980 religious vote," *Social Science Quarterly*, Vol. 65 (1984), pp. 1072-79.
7. A.O. Miles, "Mormon Voting Behavior and Political Attitudes" (unpublished doctoral thesis, New York University, 1980). See also Magleby, op. cit., p. 17.
8. Richard Johnston, "The reproduction of the religious cleavage in Canadian elections," *Canadian Journal of Political Science*, XVIII:I (March 1985), pp. 99-113.
9. W.P. Irvine, "Comment on 'The reproduction of the religious cleavage in Canadian elections'," *Canadian Journal of Political Science*, XVIII:I (March 1985), p. 117.
10. Although a good cross-section of Mormon leaders and scholars were interviewed in preparing this paper, only one person indicated an awareness of this event.
11. Palmer, op. cit., p. 101.
12. Information for this section of the paper was obtained by checking government records and interviewing church leaders, academics and Mormons active in political affairs.
13. These comments are based upon an interview between the author and Bill Payne, April 1987.
14. The data used in this section were obtained from the town offices in Cardston, Magrath and Raymond, from church leaders in the area, and from the participants in the events discussed.

V | SOCIAL AND DEMOGRAPHIC PERSPECTIVES

THIS SECTION IS a first response to the scholarly challenge of delineating and assessing the contemporary Mormon presence in Canada. Its two chapters are comparative, inclined to statistical description, sensitive to the interaction of values and behavior, and note further research needs.

George Jarvis is one of the first social scientists known to have examined the demographic characteristics of the present-day Canadian Mormon family by making use of the 1981 Census of Canada. This is the first Census to classify members of the Church of Jesus Christ of Latter-day Saints (Mormons) separately from the Reorganized Church of Jesus Christ of Latter-day Saints in Canada. With such improved Census classification of Mormons, other studies of Mormons in Canada can now follow, using the full range of Census variables, as Jarvis has begun to do.

As a sociologist, Jarvis uses the terms and skills of demography, scarcely disguising that he is dealing with important human considerations: Marriage at what age? With whom? When to begin sexual relationships? How long does marriage last? What are the rates of marriage dissolution? What are the prospects for remarriage after divorce or widowhood? How is family life affected by gender roles? How long does one live? In Jarvis's work, statistics and life are not far apart.

The close-up view of the Canadian Mormon family that Jarvis provides, sharpened through comparisons with other populations in Canada and in the United States and Utah, contributes to an understanding of contemporary families generally. His work also provides a contemporary view against which the historical Mormon family in Canada can be compared. His attention to similarities and differences among Mormons

279

internally in Canada, as well as in relation to other groups, adds insight into the degree of distinctiveness Mormons have as a people in present-day Canada, where most families are caught up in, and influenced by, the currents of late twentieth-century change.

Dean Louder's innovative inquiry into the Canadian Mormon identity also begins demographically, using data adjusted to reflect accurately Mormon population in Canada from 1921. He compares graphically the numbers and distribution of Mormon and non-Mormon populations in Canada and the United States. This comparison makes vivid the disproportions of Mormons in both countries, which are inevitably reflected in multiple Mormon identities underlying a popularly perceived, taken-for-granted common identity.

Of greater interest to Louder, however, is the combination of demographic, social, historical, institutional and language factors that tend to differentiate Mormons and their identities. He raises pertinent issues and candidly explores new lines of thought about Canada's Mormons. Is there a similarity between Mormons and nineteenth-century Metis in their patterns of international border crossings? Are Mormon attempts to be a durable people similar to Quebec values and activities associated with "survivance"? Is it possible for center-periphery relationships among Mormons, continentally and in Canada, to be exacerbated by the neglect of languages and cultures of Canadian Mormons, especially of francophones? In comparison with federal Canada and its countervailing provinces, how does Mormon authority in Canada function without structures for countervalence? Louder anticipates these and other challenges to the study of Canada's Mormons.

Louder introduces an unmistakable scholarly style prevalent in Canada, that of creative criticism within a bilingual, bicultural and multicultural frame of reference. Where this style and the challenges it presents to Mormons generally and to Mormon studies in particular can lead in scholarship and social development might well portend a next step into the future.

Jarvis and Louder have begun an important research path that others will follow as they probe the nature of the contemporary Mormon presence.

14 Demographic Characteristics of the Mormon[1] Family in Canada

GEORGE K. JARVIS

LATTER-DAY SAINTS HAVE come to be known as family people. It is difficult to say exactly when this perception originated, although it perhaps began in the late nineteenth century, when Mormons became famous for large families made up of a man, multiple wives, and many children. At one time a cartoon appeared in eastern newspapers that depicted Brigham Young in a gigantic bed, with many wives on each side. Under the bed were numerous trundle beds full of their offspring. Many persons, even today, do not know that only a small minority of nineteenth-century Mormon families were polygynous, and that this practice ended officially in 1890. Alternatively, perhaps Mormons became linked with family in the public eye, as it became known that Mormons favor a form of marriage that may last beyond death, even forever. The Mormon practice of family home evening requires family members to remain home one night per week and engage in family-centered activities. Mormons have also produced a series of television advertisements that promote good parenting and happy family life.

Visitors are restricted from entering Mormon temples while they are in active operation, although a temple may be visited before its dedication. This is due to the sacred nature of ordinances that occur there. The private nature of the Mormon temple has furnished endless stories, which might be disquieting to persons not familiar with the Mormon faith. Thirty years ago, in West Germany, the author received a tract that had been given to the local members of the *Evangelische Kirche*. The tract alleged that 1,000 young women had been lured away from Switzerland by Mormon missionaries to remote Utah. Too late, they realized their mistake and were forced to go through the temple. One of the unfortunates was depicted standing on top of the Salt Lake City Temple about to take the long plunge into Great Salt Lake. This would have been a remarkable athletic achievement, as the distance is approximately seven miles from the temple to the lake.

Despite the mistaken content of such stories, the interest of Latter-day Saints in marriage, temples, children and families has become well-known. This interest is expressed continually in statements from church leaders. LDS ideology about the family and the image of the church conveyed in the media calls to mind the picture of a middle-class family consisting of husband, wife and at least two happy children. A more balanced view can be obtained from social science surveys and censuses, which gather data from all people not just those with whom one has contact or who conform to the ideal of the LDS family. In this essay, I shall consider LDS beliefs about family life, as well as evidence from social science research from the United States and Canada as to whether the Mormon family today conforms to its popular image. Although data from the United States and Canada will be used, special emphasis will be given to the Canadian version of the LDS family. This essay will emphasize demographic data on family characteristics, highlighting such areas as sexuality, marriage, fertility, family patterns and mortality.

SELECTED DEMOGRAPHIC CHARACTERISTICS

The nature of the family life of LDS Canadians is influenced by a number of demographic factors, including the relative size and growth rate of the LDS population, together with its regional distribution, urban-rural residence, ethnic origin, age composition and sex ratio. It should be pointed out that these data on Canadian LDS are from the Census of Canada which, unlike the United States Census, asks for religious preference. Therefore, the data represent those who express a preference for the Mormon faith, a population not necessarily identical to those who are in the continuous registry that the LDS Church keeps on those who have in the past been baptized into the church.

SIZE OF GROUP   Although Canada was the first country outside the United States to receive LDS missionaries, and Canadians have always been represented among the leaders of the central Church, in 1981 LDS Church membership included only 82,000 members, 0.3% of the Canadian population. These data are from the Census of Canada. A 1986 estimate of 90,945 Mormons has been generated from LDS Church records by B.Y. Card. This is a small minority and demonstrates the relatively slow growth of the church in Canada compared to that in the United States and some other countries. Because there are relatively few LDS persons, chances for marriage within the group are affected, as are chances for social relationships with those of similar belief. A mentality of "we" and "they" tends to emerge. Many LDS children outside of southern Alberta find themselves, with their siblings, the only Mormon children in a school. Occasionally there is open prejudice displayed by classmates or teachers, usually a result of inadequate knowledge about the religion. Families find solidarity in their religious uniqueness, but this solidarity is sometimes strained, even broken, as children reach the age of marriage, perhaps choosing spouses outside the religion or opting for a style of life incompatible with the faith. The church sponsors special youth and educational programs to combat this tendency.

GROWTH   Although Mormons are a small religious group in Canada, today the LDS religion is one of the fastest-growing churches. Between 1971 and 1981, the total Canadian population grew at an annualized rate of 1.1%. Mormons grew almost three times as fast (3.0%). Only a few religious categories, such as "no religion" (6.6%), the residual category of "other religions" (4.5%) and Pentecostals (4.3%), increased at a more rapid rate. Rapid growth among Latter-day Saints reflects relatively high birth rates and the efforts made by many families to introduce their friends to the church. Families also spend time getting to know and associate with new families in their congregations, which helps converts to remain affiliated with the church.

REGIONAL DISTRIBUTION   Latter-day Saints are not spread uniformly throughout the country. Of all major denominations, LDS are the most regionally concentrated, as measured by the index of dissimilarity. Only the small, communal groups of Hutterites are more concentrated, with 98.8% living in the Prairie provinces. The regional pattern in Canada shows that 56.6% of LDS membership in Canada live in the Prairie provinces, most of these in Alberta. Approximately three-quarters of LDS live in western Canada.

Comparing the three-quarters of LDS members who live in western Canada with those living in eastern Canada, one can see that the eastern population is much more urban, and the ratio of men to women is more disproportionate in the East and more balanced in the West. Interfaith marriages occur much more often in the East, although some of this is probably due to individuals being converted without their spouse. In eastern Canada, 38.9% of female members are married to a nonmember; only 25.3% of male members are in such mixed marriages. In western Canada, rates of interfaith marriage among LDS are much lower. The proportion divorced or separated is also much higher in eastern Canada, as is the percentage who are single-parent families. Whereas in the West more families fit the Mormon stereotype of husband-wife and children, in the East this pattern is found less often. Fertility is also lower in the East, being only a little above average. Both high and low extremes of education are much more common in the East than in the West, and average income is lower in the East.

In recent years, the LDS population is becoming more scattered. In 1981, almost one in five LDS (19.8%) lived in British Columbia and more than one in six (17.6%) lived in Ontario. Much smaller numbers lived in Quebec and the Atlantic provinces. This growing dispersion has occurred as youthful families moved from southern Alberta in search of educational and occupational opportunity. As the families are usually emotionally close to those they leave behind, the result is a great deal of long-distance phoning, visiting and other communication over wide distances among members of the dispersed extended family. There is also growing exposure of dispersed Mormons to the potentially secularizing influence of life remote from established congregations of LDS.

RURAL-URBAN RESIDENCE   Religions vary as to whether their membership is predominantly rural in residence or whether they tend to live in cities. In 1981, the Jewish population was the most likely to live in cities of more than 500,000 population (92.4%), and Hutterites were most likely to live in rural areas (98.9%). The total population of Canada was divided into 40.1% living in large cities, 35.0% living in other urban places, and 24.9% living in rural areas. Mormons were similar but not identical to the national distribution. Over 31.3% of LDS lived in cities of 500,000 and over, slightly less than average. Mormons were somewhat overrepresented in smaller urban places, with 42.6% of members living there. This reflects the original Mormon settlement pattern, which tended to be in small towns, not on isolated farmsteads. In rural places in 1981, they were about average with 26.0%. In the United States, LDS have in the past had a rural or small-town base in the mountain states, and elsewhere have lived in the larger cities. Canadian LDS have also had a southern Alberta heartland, but in other places in Canada tended to populate the largest cities. Over the past few decades, in both the western United States and Alberta, there has been considerable urbanization of the LDS population.

ETHNICITY   Many religions in Canada are identified with a particular ethnic group. For instance, 86.6% of those in the Reformed churches are Dutch in ethnic background; 83.5% of Ukrainian Catholics are Ukrainian; and 78.5% of Anglicans are British. No single ethnic group is as dominant among Mormons, the largest representation being of British ethnic origin, 59.2%. No other single ethnic origin or combination, such as Scandinavian, totaled more than 5% of the Latter-day Saint population.

AGE DISTRIBUTION   The age distribution of a group largely reflects past fertility; a group with relatively low average age has had high birth rates in the past. It will also have a low proportion of older persons. The age distribution of the LDS population seems to have been affected by past high fertility. The age distribution might also have been affected by large numbers of persons immigrating to or emigrating from Canada, or converting to the religion from other faiths, given that both immigrants and converts tend to be younger adults and younger families. Currently, Mormons have large numbers of children less than 15 years of age (33.6%) compared to the total population (22.8%). Young adults are found in about the same proportion as in the rest of Canada. Persons aged 35 to 64 are less common among Mormons (23.8% compared to 31.6%), as are old persons aged 65 or more (5.8% compared to 9.0%).

SEX RATIO   The ratio of males to females in a population is 1.000 if there are exactly as many males as females. Canada's population has a ratio of 0.986 males to each female, indicating fewer males than females. Some groups, such as those of no religion (1.376), other religions (1.105), Eastern Orthodox (1.063), Reformed bodies (1.043) and Ukrainian Catholic (1.026), have more males than females. But Mormons have a ratio of 0.919, indicating substantially more females than males. In this, they are similar to Jehovah's Witnesses (0.832), Pentecostals (0.883), Baptists (0.912) and Anglicans (0.919). It should be remembered that this is the ratio of males to females for all ages. As age increases, the sex ratio decreases due to the longer life expectancy of females in comparison to males, so that, at older ages, there are even fewer Mormon men relative to Mormon women. Given the relative shortage of Mormon men, and given that Mormon men have a high rate of marriage as well, an unmarried female convert's chances to marry are reduced, as are the chances of a divorced or widowed LDS female member.

SEXUALITY

BELIEFS   Sexual activity is portrayed in a positive light by LDS leaders, indeed as something sacred and beautiful, but it is only permitted with one's lawfully wedded spouse. Sexual relations are viewed as valuable both for the sake of procreation and for the cultivation of love between spouses. Before marriage, church members are urged to adhere to a single standard of chastity. Boys and girls are given identical instruction on this subject. If sexual transgressions occur, repentance is urged, which includes sorrow for the act, prayer, confession to one's bishop, and not doing the act again.

SEXUAL BEHAVIOR   Several studies of nonmarital sexual activity among Mormons provide consistent evidence that not all Mormons conform to the church's teachings about sexual relations outside of marriage; nonetheless, fewer LDS than average engage in either premarital or extramarital sexual intercourse.

Christensen[2] found that Mormons at a university in the western United States had lower approval of intercourse and lower rates of participation in nonmarital intercourse than did students at several other universities. The only persons who had lower rates of nonmarital sexual behavior were students at a midwestern Mennonite college. Heaton[3] reported similar findings from a subset of adolescent Mormons in the 1971 National Survey of Young Women. In this sample, 15% of Mormon teenage women had engaged in premarital sexual relations compared to 26% for the entire sample. Miller and co-workers[4] surveyed students in high schools in three states in the western United States. Seventeen percent of Mormon students reported premarital sexual intercourse, compared with 48% of Catholics, 51% of those with no religion, and 67% of Protestants. In this study, multiple regression confirmed the powerful effect of religious attendance and affiliation as determinants of sexual experience.

Religious activity should also be taken into account in these results. For instance, Smith found that fewer Mormon college students experienced intercourse than their Catholic and Protestant counterparts. But the most powerful finding in his study is that the LDS who attended church often were much less likely to have sex outside of marriage than those who never attended church.[5] Moreover, the difference between actively participating Mormons and those who did not participate was greater for Mormons than for the other religions. Exposure to the community, its teachings, and general social control produced much greater conformity. Among Mormons who frequently attended church, 15% of men and 9% of women reported nonmarital intercourse. Although Mormons who did not participate in church activities have been influenced by increasing sexual permissiveness since 1950, and have increased their rates of sexual experience between 1950 and 1972, Mormons who actively participated were insulated from these trends and did not increase rates of nonmarital intercourse. In other words, it does not seem to be true that participating Mormons are only lagging behind and will some day catch up to the national trend to greater sexual permissiveness. Nor does the consistency of these comparative results indicate that Mormons are more reticent to report sexual behavior than are members of other faiths, although this possibility should be studied.

Canadian rates of sexual behavior among LDS have not been studied systematically to date, but there is no evidence that patterns are dissimilar to LDS in the United States. In future research, Mormons in Canada should be studied. They should also be compared to members of other small, active denominations, such as Pentecostals, Jehovah's Witnesses, Mennonites, and other groups with strong social control and conformity. It seems quite clear, however, that most Mormons, especially those who actively participate in church activities, follow the moral code of the church. This sets the tone for other church teachings about the family.

MARRIAGE

BELIEFS ABOUT MARRIAGE   All Latter-day Saints are encouraged to marry, preferably in a temple; a temple marriage is believed to have the potential to last not only during this life but also forever. In order to qualify for temple marriage, a couple must be interviewed by church leaders. In the interview, probing questions are asked about beliefs and actions, questions that tend to weed out those who are not serious in their commitment to the church and to each other. It has been argued that the belief that marriage is eternal demands and fosters strong commitment from those who are thus sealed together.[6] If making such a commitment translates into willingness to sacrifice for the marriage, to overcome difficult problems, to live by a strong

Generation One: Seated: David Allen Pitcher, b. 1882, migrated to Cardston to farm from Utah, 1903, and Elsie Mae Peterson, b.1887, migrated to Cardston with parents, 1889, married in Logan Temple, Utah, 1907. Nine children. Standing, l-r: David DeCon, Berniece, La Reine, Mary Elizabeth, Venna May and Willis Allen. Not shown, Marjorie and Lorin, died in infancy, Walter Martin at age 26. Photo courtesy Willis A. Pitcher, Cardston.

code of ethics, including sexual fidelity and participation in the same religious group, it is easy to see why temple marriage is strongly correlated with low divorce rates.

Other elements of church life also contribute to the solidarity of marriage. Sexual fidelity is promoted, and if adultery occurs, the offender's repentance is sought. If it does not occur, he or she might be punished by removal of church privileges. Obligations of mothers and fathers are frequently reinforced from the pulpit and in church classes. Families are also visited each month by church members. Activities are strongly couple oriented, and if a man and woman have difficulty, they can go to their bishop or to LDS Social Services for counseling.

The Latter-day Saint believes that after death the place of greatest reward in the afterlife is a condition called exaltation. A man or woman cannot reach this state alone. Only those who have been sealed in eternal marriage and who have remained faithful to all the promises they have made to each other and to the church can qualify for this status. Such a belief further increases marital commitment and underlines the importance of marriage. It also makes life difficult for single and divorced persons in the church. Much social life is oriented to couples and families. Recognizing this problem, the church has organized special groups and activities for single persons. There are congregations made up solely of the unmarried, both among student and nonstudent populations. Church-sponsored universities, colleges, institutes (at other universities) and seminaries (near high schools and junior high schools) help young people to marry endogamously. But some whose plans do not include marriage or family might find themselves increasingly separated from mainstream activity in the church.

NUPTIALITY   Studies in the United States have found that a higher proportion of Mormons get married at some time in their lives than either Catholics or Protestants.[7] Data from the Census of Canada also provide support for this pattern. Of those who have ever married, Mormons in Canada are the second most married group, with 95.1% of males having married by age 30 (91.1% for the total population), and 96.0% of females having married (92.5% for the total population). Only Reformed churches have greater proportions married.

AGE AT FIRST MARRIAGE   Age at first marriage is an important predictor of marital success. Research indicates that those who marry too young or too old have less chance of a successful marriage. Those who review these matters, however, believe that it might not be the age *per se* but factors related to age, such as premarital pregnancy, education, and rebellion against parents, that reduce chances for successful marriage among those who marry extremely young. The reduced odds for success for those marrying later in life are less well understood.

Mormons in Canada have a rather youthful marital pattern. Males are more likely than average to marry at less than 20 years of age (12.0% compared to 7.0% in Canada as a whole). Females are also more likely than average to marry while young (40.2% compared to 29.0% in Canada). This pattern operates in spite of many young LDS men going on missions for the church. The modal age for entry to this service is 19, which keeps many from marrying at that time. Fewer females serve such missions. Mormons are a basically pronuptial population, where the "push" is to get on with marriage and rearing a family. It is likely that this tendency to early marriage is not so great in urban Mormon populations, where educational levels are higher.

INTERMARRIAGE   An important measure of assimilation for a group is the extent to which its members marry outside the group. The Census of Canada shows what proportion of persons in each religion are married to a person of their own faith. In this case, the total number of mixed religious marriages is composed of at least two categories: those who originally married someone of a different faith; and those who were originally of the same faith, but one spouse or both chose to change to a different denomination. This complicates further the picture of interfaith marriage. From these data such differences cannot be unraveled; therefore, one must take the proportions in interfaith marriage at face value, realizing that their meaning is somewhat obscure.

The average proportion of interfaith marriage for all groups is 21.9% for men and 21.3% for women. There are major differences among religious groups, however. Jewish persons (10.2% for men and 7.6% for women) and those in Reformed churches (8.6% for men and 8.3% for women) have the fewest interfaith marriages. Eastern non-Christians (13.9% for men and 8.1% for women), Jehovah's Witnesses (9.2% for men and 27.7% for women) and Roman Catholics (10.9% for men and 12.8% for women) also have overall low rates of interfaith marriage, although the rate of such marriage is higher than average for female Jehovah's Witnesses. Mainline Protestant denominations have rather high rates of interfaith marriage, usually averaging between 30% and 40% interfaith marriage. Those in "other religions" and persons who prefer no religion are the most heterogamous of all, averaging over 40% "interfaith" marriage. Although Mormons have strong norms towards endogamy, the statistics show that they have slightly higher than average rates of interfaith marriage, especially LDS women (22.1% for men and 30.2% for women). Mormons in western Canada (21.2% males and 27.5% females) have fewer interfaith marriages than in eastern Canada (25.3% males and 38.9% females). It is quite likely that many of the Mormon interfaith marriages reflect conversion patterns among adults, rather than Mormons choosing to marry outside the fold. Nevertheless, it is also reasonable to assume that in areas where there are fewer LDS available for marriage, such as in eastern Canada, the pressure to marry someone of another faith might be substantial.

DIVORCE AND REMARRIAGE   Divorce is not forbidden, but it is discouraged among LDS, as among members of most churches. Couples are encouraged to make every attempt to overcome their problems and build their families for eternity.

Divorce rates are low among Latter-day Saints, but especially among those married in the temple. Studies in the United States show that Mormons are less prone to divorce than are Catholics and Protestants, and are far less likely to divorce than those who have no church. Recently, however, attention has been centered on what appears to be a high divorce rate in Utah, a state made up predominantly of Mormons. Goodman and Heaton[8] comment that the above average divorce rate is essentially attributable to Utah's liberal divorce laws; to the concentration of married persons in Utah in the younger ages, when divorce risks are the greatest; and to a high rate of remarriage in Utah with inflated risks of multiple divorces occurring to the same persons. When these facts are controlled, the percentage in Utah who will ever get divorced is well below the average of the United States.

Full religious participation is related to lower than average divorce rates among Mormons. Heaton and Goodman[9] report results from a survey of 7,446 Latter-day Saints aged 18 and over in the United States and Canada. They indicate that of Mormons who attend church regularly, 10.2% of men and 15.2% of women have experienced divorce, compared to 21.6% of men and 26.3% of women who attend less frequently. It is not clear whether church attendance reduces the likelihood that divorce will occur or whether divorce reduces the likelihood of church attendance. The relationship is clearer when one considers temple marriage. Of respondents 30 years of age and over who had ever been married, 53% indicate they had been married in the temple.[10]

Among Mormon men who have ever been married, only 5.4% of those married in the temple have been divorced, compared to 27.8% of those not married in the temple. Of women married in the temple, 6.5% have been divorced, compared to 32.7% of those not married in the temple. In short, non-temple marriages run a more than five times greater risk of divorce than do temple marriages.

Less is known about individuals who have become estranged from the LDS Church. The number and identities of those whose names are formally removed from the rolls of the church are kept confidential. A larger number remain on the rolls of the church but do not actively participate. These less active persons have not been as much studied as participating Mormons, and some of them in time change status to greater activity or, alternatively, have their names removed from the records.

In the Census of Canada, data on divorce are expressed as the percentage of those in the population who are currently divorced or separated. In this report, the data are refined further to the proportion of those who have ever been married and who are currently divorced or separated. It should be noted that those who have at one time been divorced and who are currently remarried are eliminated from this statistic, even if they have had multiple divorces. If one could assume, which one cannot, that all groups remarry at the same rate, this statistic would still not be a good measure of the amount of divorce in a population. As some religious groups have substantial numbers of proselytes, the marital status of these persons must also be taken into account. If, for example, large numbers of divorced persons were to join a church, this would inflate the proportion divorced or separated in that group. Furthermore, not all separations are recorded in the Census, only those that have become relatively permanent. Despite these handicaps, Canadian Census data on divorce and separation are reported because they provide a unique view of the entire population and permit a description of smaller religious groups such as Mormons.

What appears is a different picture for males and females among the LDS population. Only 5.8% of LDS males are currently divorced or separated, less than the 6.6% divorced or separated in the Canadian population; however, 11.9% of LDS females are currently divorced or separated, compared to only 8.9% of the total population. Contrary to expectation, LDS females have a higher than average proportion currently divorced or separated. Different explanations might account for this in a population thought to have less divorce than average. One explanation is that there actually is a higher divorce rate, which might reflect, in part, the stress on marriages when one partner joins the church and the other does not. The high proportion of interfaith marriages among Mormon women might put them at particular risk of divorce. Another explanation is that substantial numbers of females, already divorced, join the church. Perhaps some of these are specifically attracted to the image of a church that stresses strong families. Adding to this would be the difficulty in remarriage that would be experienced by females in a population already experiencing a female imbalance and with a high proportion of already married males. The newly converted, divorced females would initially seek to marry within the group. A few would succeed, but others would remain single or eventually remarry with someone who is not a Mormon. These patterns would contribute to the higher proportion of female divorced persons among LDS. In general, remarriage occurs more rapidly among Latter-day Saints than among adherents of other religions, following a divorce or the death of a spouse, which shows the high value placed on marriage. The chances for remarriage are much better, however, for men than for women.

In order to explore these relationships further, the percentage divorced was examined by region in Canada. Either explanation of the large proportion divorced—stress on marriage caused by conversion, or the large number of already divorced persons joining the church—would lead to a greater proportion divorced in regions with a larger proportion of converts to the church, and would be lower in the prairies, where there are proportionally more members born to LDS parents. This seems to be the case. The lowest proportion of LDS divorced persons, both male and female, is found in the Prairie region, even though overall divorced proportions are not the lowest in this region for the total population. In areas such as Quebec, with more recent converts, the percentage divorced among LDS is almost twice as high. In eastern Canada, the ratio of LDS males to females is only .84, reflecting both the large numbers of female converts and their reduced chances to marry within the LDS population. In western Canada, the ratio is much more equal, (.94).

FERTILITY

BELIEFS   Once married, an important obligation of couples is to have relatively large families. In a recent address, Mormon prophet Ezra T. Benson[11] said, "Husbands and wives, as co-creators, should eagerly and prayerfully invite children into their homes. Then, as each child joins their family circle, they can gratefully exclaim, as did Hannah, 'For this child I prayed; and the Lord hath given me my petition which I asked of him'." Careful inspection of this quote illustrates that, while contraception is not prohibited, positive reasons are cited to encourage Mormon families to have children. To multiply and replenish the earth is a biblical injunction that Mormons take seriously. LDS leaders today encourage large families. This stems in part from the belief in a pre-existence, in which all inhabitants of the world lived as spirits with God, and a belief that all the righteous spirits are to come to this world through birth. Latter-day Saint families, by having more children, speed this process and ensure that a larger proportion of spirits will be born to Mormon families. Bahr and co-workers[12] interviewed LDS women in the United States who had at least seven children and found some of the major reasons for high fertility were the beliefs that each family has a predestined number of children; having large families conforms to the counsel of church leaders; interference in the reproductive process is wrong; and spirits in heaven should have the opportunity of coming to good Mormon families. In short, fertility has religious meaning for Latter-day Saints.

Generation Two: Family of Willis Allen Pitcher and Ethel Caldwell, each of Cardston, married in the Alberta Temple, 1933. Six children. Standing, l-r: Allen Kent, Karen, Ethel (mother), Willis (father), Willis LeRon, Rhea Margaret: seated, l-r: Dee LeVern, Gladys Charlene. Photo courtesy Willis A. Pitcher, Cardston.

FERTILITY DATA   Even in the nineteenth century, when fertility was high throughout the United States, Mormons had more children than average.[13] Thornton[14] shows that Utah fertility, often accepted as a proxy for LDS fertility, remained above average throughout this century. Despite these differences, trends in LDS fertility and that for the United States have often paralleled each other. Nevertheless, during the 1970s, Utah fertility increased while the national rate decreased. Since 1980, Utah fertility has dropped substantially, but Utah still has the highest fertility of any state in the United States. In 1984, Utah's crude birth rate was 23.7 per thousand, 50% higher than the United States as a whole.[15] At about the same time, a national sample of Mormons also indicated roughly 50% higher numbers of children ever born than members of other major religious groups, excluding nonwhites.[16] As to the future, a study of fertility expectations among Mormon high school students in Utah predicts that high fertility will continue.[17]

According to a study in the United States, high Mormon fertility is not due to lack of knowledge or unwillingness to use contraception,[18] although it does in part reflect a strong resistance to abortion as birth control. Mormons are just as likely as others ever to have used contraception, although they often delay its use until child rearing has begun. Further, Mormons tend to use contraception less frequently than others.

Mormon fertility is related to determinants such as income and education, but in a different way than among other Americans. Typically, studies in the United States find that those with more income and education have lower fertility. Mormons show a contrasting pattern, as both high family income and high wife's education are related to higher fertility.[19] Perhaps this is due to the strong efforts made by the LDS Church to provide religious education, supportive of family and fertility norms, for those who attend secondary schools and universities.

Religious activity has a stronger effect on fertility among Mormons than among other groups.[20] As with sexual activity, greater involvement with the church is associated with greater conformity to its teachings. In this case, more activity leads to higher fertility.

In Canada, Mormons demonstrate higher fertility, as measured by children ever born, than do most other groups. For years, Catholics have been looked to as the religion with high fertility. In 1981, Roman Catholics still had more children born per 1,000 women (2,702) than the national average (2,493). But several religious groups, including Hutterites (5,281), Reformed bodies (3,368), Mennonites (3,308) and Mormons (3,044), had even higher fertility than Catholics. The lowest fertility was recorded by those with no religion (1,845) and Jewish (1,970), followed by mainline Protestant groups (Presbyterian, 2,195; Lutheran, 2,268; United Church, 2,313; Anglican, 2,330; and other Protestant, 2,457). Mormon fertility is much greater in western Canada, at 3,170 children born per 1,000 ever-married women, compared to 2,670 in eastern Canada, hardly above average. Some converts might have already largely completed their fertility by the time they join the church in eastern Canada, so that LDS doctrine has less effect on their fertility. Moreover, the church is more scattered, and social norms for smaller families might be more influential on Mormons in places where the church is small, such as eastern Canada. This should be studied more intensively.

Generation Three: Allen Kent Pitcher and Donna Delphine Diebert, each of Cardston, married in the Alberta Temple, 1963. Six children. L-r: Shawn Edward, Gregg Allen, Kent Allen (father), holding Tiffany Delphine, Angela Dawn, Donna Delphine (mother), Timothy Kent, Daniel Todd. Photo courtesy Willis A. Pitcher, Cardston.

FAMILY PATTERNS

FAMILY TYPE   If the traditional family is defined as consisting of husband, wife and children, one would expect Mormons to have more of such families than most other religions. In part, this is true, in that 62.8% of Mormon families are of this traditional type, compared to 56.9% in the total Canadian population. Fewer families than average consist of husband and wife only (23.5% compared to 31.8% in Canada as a whole), which reflects high fertility that lasts over a longer part of the life cycle for Latter-day Saints. What might surprise some is that Mormons have one of the highest proportions of lone female parents, constituting 11.9% of all families, above average for Canada (9.3%). Families consisting of lone male parents are not more frequent than average (1.8%, compared to the average of 2.0%). This tendency to lone-parent families is probably linked to the large proportion of female divorced persons in the Mormon Church in Canada. It should be noted that this pattern is even more pronounced in eastern

Canada, where 19.3% of families are made up of single parents. This is a major departure from the media image of the traditional Mormon family and is probably due to some of the factors mentioned in the section on divorce.

GENDER ROLES   Little is known of Mormon gender roles and division of labor in Canada, which are often thought to be traditional with respect to their basic attitudes towards women. The fact that the priesthood (to which most males over age 12 belong) is solely male in the LDS Church has encouraged such thinking. Mormon males are advised to take their responsibility as breadwinner seriously and to support the family. They answer this challenge by heavy involvement in work. More LDS men than average are employed (79.6% compared to 73.1% in Canada); fewer are unemployed (3.2% compared to 5.0%). The remainder are students, retired, and otherwise not in the labor force.

Gender roles with regard to employment affect family patterns in important ways. Certainly, one of the most sweeping changes of the past forty years has been the movement of females into the labor force. Whether a woman works outside the home or not is important, because, for women, it provides alternative means of supporting herself and increases freedom and status. Among Mormons, it is not forbidden for women to work outside the home, but they receive periodic encouragement not to work unless they need to. In Canada, LDS women are employed at approximately the national average (46.5% compared to the Canadian average of 47.3%); however, of the number working, more than an average number (39.5% compared to 30.8% in total population) work part time. More careful and complete study of Mormon division of labor, employment patterns and family power structure is needed in Canada.

MORTALITY

HEALTH RULES   Latter-day Saints from 1833 have had a set of health rules called the Word of Wisdom. They are counseled not to drink alcoholic beverages, not to use tobacco in any form, not to drink hot drinks (interpreted to mean coffee or tea), and are urged to eat whole grains, fruits in season, and meat in moderation. Mormons are less likely than average to engage in nonmarital sexual relations. They fast from food and drink once a month, encourage regular exercise, have well-organized support groups to assist in time of crisis, and encourage the involvement of members in the provision of many types of services for each other.

LIFE EXPECTANCY   Studies of length of life among Mormons have been undertaken since the 1970s.[21] Jarvis and Northcott[22] have recently written a review of this literature. Studies show consistently that Latter-day Saints live several years longer on average than other members of the population. This has been found to be true in Utah and California in the United States, in Alberta, Canada, and in New Zealand. Actively participating Latter-day Saints receive much greater advantage than those who do not participate. Men are benefited to a greater extent than are women. In middle age, Mormon male mortality is approximately half that of similar non-Mormons. Actively participating LDS men in Utah and California live on average six years longer than other United States white males and about three years longer than United States white males who have never smoked tobacco. The reasons for this longer life expectancy are not fully known, but it is probably due to a combination of life style, support groups, and a greater chance to participate in families and to give meaningful service throughout life.[23]

The outcomes for the family are several. First, in Canada and in Alberta, non-Mormon women outlive non-Mormon men by between seven to eight years. Add to this that women are usually two to five years younger than men when they marry, and this means that the average woman has to expect many years of widowhood. Among Mormons, by contrast, this sex mortality differential is greatly reduced, as are the years of widowhood. Second, a terrible burden for many families is the suffering due to disease and the "premature" death of middle-aged men. Loss of earning power, as well as medical costs and uncertainty, add to the suffering. There is evidence that LDS families are at less risk of morbidity and mortality at all ages.[24] Third, in families with lower male mortality in middle-age, as among typical Mormon families, the children have a better chance to get to know their grandparents, and even their great-grandparents. Indeed, as more persons live to become great-grandparents, there is the potential for conflict, as renewed dependency in extreme old age might sandwich the grandparental generation between the needs of the extremely old and those of younger generations that still require assistance. The opportunity for gains is also present, however, as the generations have the opportunity to link together in new ways. Such family patterns have the potential to foster personal bonding and support between the generations. Moreover, the link with one's own ancestral roots is more apparent, as the younger generations are more likely to know the older and hear their recollections of the family's past firsthand. The old are able to renew themselves through contact with youth, as the young are able to grow through service to those who have preceded and previously served them.

CONCLUSIONS

National data on Mormons in Canada obscure what seems to be two quite different populations: the LDS population that has been established for several generations in Alberta, and the scattered population living in the major cities of the country. In the West, most members have been born into LDS families; in the East, a much larger proportion have been converted to Mormonism during their own lifetimes.

Among scattered Mormons in the East, a further division exists between, on the one hand, lifetime or longtime LDS, often displaced from Alberta or Utah in a sort of Diaspora, far from their roots in the West, and on the other, new converts who are in the process of adjusting their adult lives and family patterns to the Mormon model, an adjustment that might take many years, and if begun late enough, perhaps more than one generation.

Apart from such geographical differences, however, certain issues face all Mormon families in Canada. Canadian trends towards secularization, more frequent nonmarital sexual behavior, lower nuptiality, lower fertility, more divorce, more nontraditional family types, and altered gender roles are firmly entrenched, and in many cases influence LDS families. Exposure to these trends is increasing as the LDS population of Canada disperses to large cities throughout the country.

After an examination of the characteristics of Mormon families in Canada, one might say that in some respects, such as rural-urban residence, and ethnicity, Mormons are similar to the general population. Other writers have commented on similarity in socioeconomic characteristics as well.[25] In other respects, such as small, overall size of group; high rates of growth; youthful age structure; female population imbalance; regional concentration; conservative sexual behavior; high fertility; low mortality; and pronuptial marriage patterns, they seem to be acutely different. In most ways, their actual behavior seems to approximate their image and indicates consistency with their beliefs, but in the large number of divorced females, female lone-parent families, high proportions of working females, and interfaith marriages, there are surprises that should, after study, be addressed by the Mormon community.

Even in marriage, fertility, sexuality, family patterns, and mortality risks, where Mormons are notably different from others, they are influenced by national trends. Their patterns, although different from others in degree, parallel the trend line of the general population. It is most likely that, in the future, continued pressure will be experienced by LDS in Canada to conform to emerging norms of sexual permissiveness, single living, intermarriage, altered gender roles, low fertility, frequent divorce, and nontraditional family patterns. The ability to resist these tendencies will depend on the church's ability to keep the loyalty of its members and adapt its techniques of securing conformity to the changes of the future.

NOTES
1. The term Mormon, throughout the essay, refers to members of the Church of Jesus Christ of Latter-day Saints and is used interchangeably with the terms Latter-day Saints and LDS.
2. Christensen, Harold T., "Mormon sexuality in cross-cultural perspective," *Dialogue*, 10 (2), pp. 62-75, 1976.
3. Heaton, Tim B., "The Four C's of the Mormon Family," Address given at Brigham Young University, Provo, Utah, 11 October 1985.
4. Miller, Brent C., J. Kelly McCoy, Terrance D. Olsen and C.M. Wallace, "Background and Contextual Factors in Relation to Adolescent Sexual Attitudes and Behavior," unpublished manuscript, 1985.
5. Smith, Wilford E., *Social Disorganization and Deviant Behavior* (Provo, Utah: Brigham Young University Press, 1974).
6. Broderick, Carlfred, *Marriage and the Family* (Scarborough, Ontario: Prentice-Hall, 1988).
7. Heaton, "The Four C's of the Mormon Family."
8. Goodman, Kristen L., and Tim B. Heaton, "Divorce," in Bahr, S., T. Heaton and T. Martin, eds., *Utah in Demographic Perspective* (Salt Lake City, Utah: Signature Books, 1986).
9. Heaton, Tim B., and Kristen L. Goodman, "Religion and family formation," *Review of Religious Research,* 26 (4), pp. 343-59, 1985.
10. Heaton, T.B., and K. Goodman, "Religion and family formation," *Review of Religious Research*, Vol. 26, no.4, pp. 343-59, June 1985.
11. Benson, Ezra T., "To the Mothers in Zion," Address given at a fireside for parents, the Church of Jesus Christ of Latter-day Saints, Salt Lake City, Utah, 22 February 1987.
12. Bahr, Howard M., Spencer J. Condie and Kristen L. Goodman, *Life in Large Families* (Washington, DC: University Press of America, 1982).
13. Mineau, G.P., L.L. Bean and M. Skolnick, "Mormon demographic history

II: The family life cycle and natural fertility," *Population Studies*, 33 (3), pp. 429-46, 1979.

14. Thornton, Arland, "Religion and fertility: The case of Mormonism," *Journal of Marriage and the Family* (February), pp. 131-42, 1979.
15. It should be noted that, as Mormons are a youthful population, these differences in crude fertility rates might be somewhat exaggerated.
16. Heaton and Goodman, "Religion and family formation," pp. 343-59.
17. Toney, Michael B., Ban Golesorkhi and William F. Stinner, "Residence exposure and fertility expectations of young Mormon and non-Mormon women in Utah," *Journal of Marriage and the Family*, 47 (2), pp. 449-56, 1985.
18. Heaton, Tim B., and Sandra Calkins, "Family size and contraceptive use among Mormons: 1965-75," *Review of Religious Research*, 25 (2), pp. 103-14, 1983.
19. Thomas, Darwin L., "Correlates of Religious Commitment in Mormon Families: Some Preliminary Findings and a Challenge," Presented at the Fourteenth Annual Virginia F. Cutler Lecture, Brigham Young University, Provo, Utah, 1979. Heaton, Tim B., "Sociodemographic characteristics of religious groups in Canada," *Sociological Analysis*, Vol. 47, no. 1, Spring, pp. 54-65, 1986.
20. Heaton and Goodman, "Religion and family formation," pp. 343-59.
21. Jarvis, George K., "Mormon mortality rates in Canada," *Social Biology*, Winter, 24 (4), pp. 294-302, 1977.
22. Jarvis, George K., and Herbert C. Northcott, "Religion and differences in mortality and morbidity," *Social Science and Medicine*, Vol. 25, pp. 813-24, 1987.
23. Ibid.
24. Ibid.
25. Heaton, Tim B., "How does religion influence fertility: The case of Mormons," *Journal for the Scientific Study of Religion*, 25 (2), pp. 248-58, 1986.

ACKNOWLEDGEMENT

Special thanks are due to Professor Tim B. Heaton of the Department of Sociology, Brigham Young University, who has generously provided substantial, invaluable information on demographic and family patterns of Latter-day Saints from the United States and Canada.

15 Canadian Mormon Identity and the French Fact[1]

DEAN R. LOUDER

"I LOVE CANADA, but I get goose bumps all over when I hear the *Star Spangled Banner* and see 'Old Glory' floating...."[2] These words, pronounced by a prominent Alberta-born Latter-day Saint educator, reflect the cultural dilemma of a large number of Latter-day Saints in Canada whose roots and primary symbolic resource field lie south of the border. Outnumbered thirty to one by their American coreligionists, Canadian Mormons, perhaps more than Saints of any other "foreign land," pledge a degree of allegiance to the United States. Traditionally, they have observed with great pride their elites called southward (witness, for example, the long and distinguished church careers of Nathan Eldon Tanner and Hugh B. Brown). Until the recent nomination of Alex Morrison to the First Council of Seventy, Latter-day Saint folk heroes in central Canada have typically been American mission presidents such as Thomas Monson and Russell Ballard, who have since taken their places in the high tribunes of the church. For decades, Alberta Saints have watched their children seek educational and marriage opportunities at church institutions in the United States only to remain afterward as Americans. Canadian Mormons who wish to affirm a separate national identity face a special set of circumstances and a challenge even greater than that of their fellow Canadians.

The physical geography of North America, in light of its human geography, has not facilitated the blossoming of a clear-cut cultural identity on the northern half of the continent. The powerful north-south-oriented economic and cultural forces have consistently threatened to put asunder the flimsy east-west loyalties that characterize the narrow, sporadically inhabited band of effectively settled land that has for six score years been Canada.[3] The issue of Canadian survival in the shadow of the American giant is not new. It has perplexed politicians, professors and other public figures for generations. The recently signed and ratified Free Trade Agreement constitutes the most recent evidence. In this essay, I will first summarize rapidly the recent attempts by the federal government to bring Canada together and to create a new Canadian identity in which the French language plays a fundamental role, and then illustrate the presence of Canadian Mormons in their North American context. Third, I will examine Canadian Mormon identity within a regional context and, fourth, assess the institutional reaction of the Church of Jesus Christ of Latter-day Saints to the "New Canada"—a different kind of place from the one left behind by Eldon Tanner and Hugh B. Brown.[4] In conclusion, I will comment upon the relevance and importance of the study of Mormon life in Canada.

TOWARD NATIONAL UNITY AND A SEPARATE IDENTITY

To those who frequently asked him how Canada was different from the United States, the late Honorable Lester Pearson had a pat answer which he used and encouraged Canadians to use "When they ask you how Canada is different from the United States, answer them in French!"[5] Owing to his penchant for emphasizing the linguistic aspects of Canadian identity and for his role in bringing Pierre Elliott Trudeau, his eventual successor, into government as justice minister, to Pearson is usually attributed credit for the recent transformation of the Canadian symbolic order.[6] While Pearson might have been the author and Trudeau certainly the enforcer of sweeping cultural reforms, closer examination reveals much deeper roots, going back at least to the hanging of the French Métis leader Louis Riel, two years prior to the 1887 arrival of Mormons in Alberta, and to a succession of events that confirmed the systematic opposition in English Canada to the extension of French-language rights.[7] A Canada that would integrally respect the rights of two founding peoples and bear a bilingual label had been called for at the beginning of the current century by Québec nationalists, who suggested that if English were to become Canada's only official language the country was destined to become nothing more than a small part of the American whole.[8]

Apparently more preoccupied by the French Canadian than the American threat to national identity, these appeals went unheard in English Canada.

Nevertheless, between 1921 and World War II cautious modifications were brought to a few "Canadian" symbols theretofore resolutely British: a bilingual postage stamp in 1923, all stamps and money orders in 1926, bilingual paper money in 1936. The severing of the umbilicus with Great Britain in 1931, with the passing of the Statute of Westminster which granted effective political autonomy to Canada, should logically have given impetus to further Canadianization of the symbolic order, but the Great Depression and the advent of war provided excellent excuses for doing little.

At mid-century, as Canada entered a period of unprecedented prosperity and growth, the issue of national identity loomed large. The Royal Commission on National Development in Arts, Letters and Sciences, the first of three major royal commissions formed to examine the issue, was created. It identified clearly what would come to be the primary source of concern for later commissions—NATIONAL UNITY. It reiterated the fragility of English Canada and the risk of cultural, if not political, assimilation by the powerful neighbor.[9] The report concluded that Canada was seriously menaced by a process of Americanization and that the federal government should intervene to promote a distinctive, bicultural Canadian identity. A decade and a half later, rich with the findings of the Royal Commission on Bilingualism and Biculturalism established by Pearson in 1963, and threatened by a political crisis in Québec, the central government proceeded at an accelerated pace with the transformation of cultural symbols to accommodate better the French segment of the population. The Official Languages Act granting equal status to English and French; the new red and white maple leaf flag (down with the Union Jack); "O Canada" as national anthem in lieu of "God Save the Queen"; and Trans-Canada Airlines resurrected as the bilingual Air Canada are but a few of the more visible elements of this recent cultural metamorphosis.[10]

Thus, today's Canada was born out of a dual strategy: to establish and promote a distinct Canadian identity on the northern half of the continent; and to quell rising Québec nationalism (separatism) by affirming unequivocally and concretely the right of the French to be at home everywhere in Canada.

What has all this to do with the Mormon Church? At the very moment that Ottawa was working feverishly to create a new bilingual Canada and Québec nationalism was reaching its apogée with the eventual election of a sovereignist government, which succeeded in establishing for the first time the unequivocal primacy of the French language, *at all levels*, within *la belle province*, LDS membership was enjoying unprecedented growth throughout

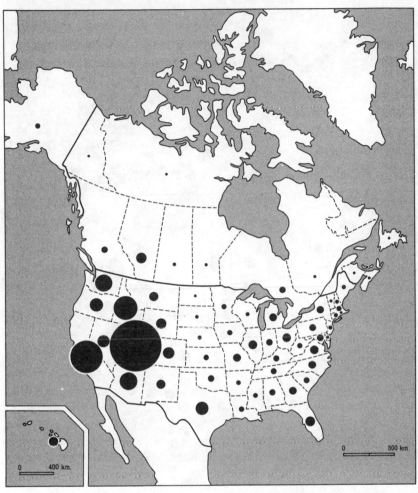

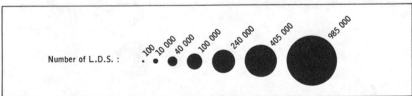

Number of L.D.S. : 100 10 000 40 000 100 000 240 000 405 000 985 000

Figure 15.1: Latter-Day Saints in Canada (1981) and the United
States (1980) by province and state.

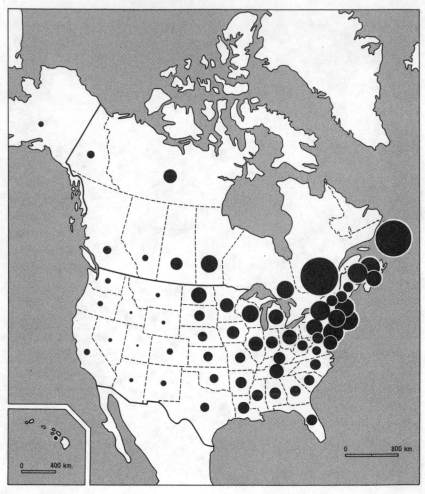

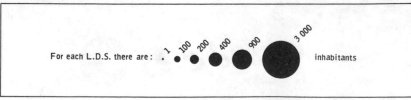

For each L.D.S. there are: .1 100 200 400 900 3 000 inhabitants

Figure 15.2: Ratio of total population to Latter-day Saint population, Canada (1981) and United States (1980) by province and state.

the country and more particularly in Québec. It is useful at this point to examine this growth and to situate Canadian Mormons in their North American context.

CANADIAN MORMONS IN THEIR NORTH AMERICAN CONTEXT

A century after their humble beginnings in Alberta in 1887, Mormons in Canada are nearing the 100,000 mark (Figure 15.1). Outnumbered by their counterparts in the United States by 30 to 1, they represent approximately one-fiftieth of the world's Mormons. The western preponderance of the faith is clearly apparent. Utah still led the way in 1980 with 985,070 Latter-day Saints, followed by California (405,411), Idaho (240,843) and Arizona (139,178). Alberta was home to approximately as many Saints as Wyoming (40,368) and more than neighboring Montana (26,035) and New Mexico (28,804).

Despite its remarkable growth rate, Mormonism remained, at the beginning of the current decade, a minority religion in every state and province except Utah (Figure 15.2). Only in this state and Idaho is the ratio of total population to Latter-day Saints under five. In the densely settled northeast and in Canada's easternmost provinces, this ratio is particularly high.

If Mormons were distributed as the population in general, the index of geographic concentration would be zero for every state and province, but since they are not, it is instructive to examine where their numbers are larger (positive index) and smaller (negative index) than expected given the population size of each province or state (Figure 15.3). In all western states, including Alaska and Hawaii, Latter-day Saints are overrepresented in the population of the United States. In only one Canadian province, Alberta, is this the case. The surplus here compares with that of the next door neighbor, Montana, and Colorado. For the eastern reaches of the continent, the higher the total populaton of each state and province, the greater the underrepresentation of the Latter-day Saints.

The LDS population of Canada has grown from approximately 12,000 in 1921 to 90,945 in 1986. During the critical periods alluded to earlier (the 1960s and 1970s), LDS membership increased by 20,000 and 25,000 respectively (Table 15.1).[11] Of particular note is the nearly tenfold increase in Québec, a relatively "Mormon-less" region in 1961, and the decrease in the Canadian cultural hearth of Alberta between 1981 and 1986, the only province to exhibit such a decline (Table 15.2).[12]

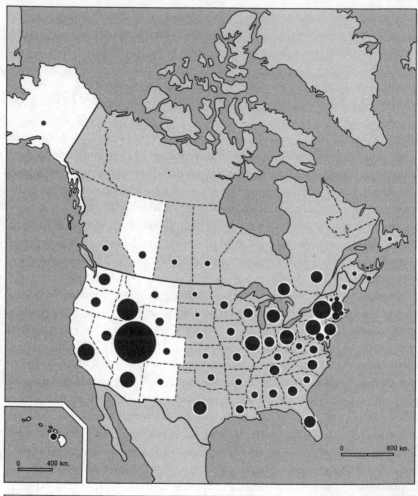

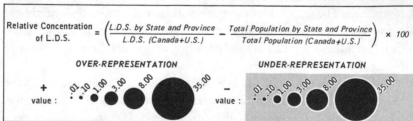

Figure 15.3: Relative geographic concentration of Latter-day Saints in Canada (1981) and the United States (1980).

TABLE 15.1   Latter-Day Saint Membership in Canada, 1921-1981

Year	Membership
1921	12,257
1941	16,468
1961	38,748
1970	57,633
1981	82,090
1986	90,945

SOURCES: (1986) B. Card, Mormons in Resource Hinterlands: Sociological Perspectives
(1981) Statistics Canada, 1981, Cat. 92-912
(1961) Dominion Bureau of Statistics, 1961, Cat. 92-546
(1921) Census of Canada, 1921, Vol. 1, Table 31.

See also note 12.

TABLE 15.2   Latter-Day Saint Membership by Province,
1961, 1981 and 1986

Province	1961*	1981	1986
Newfoundland	76	195	349
Prince Edward Island	8	140	300
Nova Scotia	393	1,570	2,466
New Brunswick	161	810	1,228
Québec	557	2,121	4,536
Ontario	6,466	14,505	18,357
Manitoba	714	1,780	2,389
Saskatchewan	886	2,580	3,114
Alberta	24,529	42,185	41,838
British Columbia	5,124	15,925	16,147
Yukon	25	165	127
Northwest Territories	20	185	94

* 1961 census figures for Latter-day Saints less RLDS membership for the
same year.

SOURCES: (1986) B. Card, Mormons in Resource Hinterlands: Sociological Perspectives.
(1981) Statistics Canada, 1981, Cat. 92-912.
(1961) Dominion Bureau of Statistics, 1961, Cat. 92-546.

TABLE 15.3   Distribution of Latter-Day Saints According to Size of Place, Canada 1961, 1981

Size of Place	Percentage 1961	Percentage 1981
1,000	33.1	26.6
1,000 - 1,999	7.7	3.2
2,000 - 4,999	8.2	9.0
5,000 - 9,999	2.2	4.1
10,000 - 29,999	5.9	5.9
30,000 - 99,999	11.9	13.1
100,000	31.2	38.1

The Latter-day Saint population of Canada, as the population of the country as a whole, is overwhelmingly urban.[13] In 1961, two-thirds of Canada's Mormons lived in urban places (Table 15.3). By 1981, the urban percentage had risen to 73%. Nevertheless, the figures are considerably lower than those for Canada as a whole. The strong rural tradition of Mormondom in southern Alberta with spillover into Saskatchewan and British Columbia has clearly had an impact.

Of note also is the Mormon presence in Canada's urban centers. In 1981 (Table 15.4), 27 cities of 50,000 inhabitants or more had LDS "congregations" of at least 250 Latter-day Saints. These places accounted for 53% of the total Mormon population in Canada. The western cities of Calgary (9,670), Vancouver (5,030) and Edmonton (4,810) surpassed all others. The leading eastern center, Toronto (4,295), is in fourth position.

Latter-day Saints are present, to varying degrees, throughout Canada. To what extent do they share a common identity?, a Mormon identity?, a Canadian identity?

MORMON IDENTITY IN THE CANADIAN MOSAIC [14]

Clearly, Alberta, and the Cardston region in particular, has had great meaning for the LDS Church. As an outlier of the Mormon cultural region in the United States,[15] it has played a vital role in the expansion of the faith in English Canada.[16] Despite the urgings of early leaders to become naturalized citizens of Canada, to meet the homestead requirements and to be unswerving

TABLE 15.4   Census Metropolitan Areas and Census Agglomerations of 50,000 Population and over with at Least 250 Latter-Day Saints, 1981

Calgary	9,670
Vancouver	5,030
Edmonton	4,810
Toronto	4,295
Montreal	1,500
London	1,480
Winnipeg	1,325
Victoria	1,280
Hamilton	1,195
Ottawa-Hull	980
Regina	835
Kitchener	815
St-Catharines-Niagara	655
Saskatoon	635
Windsor	590
Halifax	575
Kelowna	525
Oshawa	505
Sarnia	440
Prince George	440
Nanaimo	435
Kamloops	435
Thunder Bay	300
Sault Ste. Marie	290
Saint John	280
Brantford	265
Kingston	250

SOURCE: Statistics Canada, 19B1, Cats. 93-922 to 93-934.

in their loyalty to Canada and British institutions,[17] those early Saints exhibited rather ambiguous relations with and divided loyalties towards the mother country.

In their outstanding study of Canadians in Utah, Ursenbach and Jensen cited William Woolf, born in Cardston in 1890, who remembered that, "We never spoke of 'Utah'; it was always 'down home.' "[18] Hugh B. Brown's mother was deeply hurt at leaving Utah and Mildred Cluff Harvey vowed to be "a Utahn to her death."[19] The midsummer celebrations in southern Alberta were a curious mix of American patriotism and Canadian festivities, the latter designed as much to win the approval and gain the confidence of the non-Mormon settlers as to instill loyalty for Canada in the Mormon:

> From July 1 to July 4 became one long celebration, including a program of speeches praising, on the First, Canada's fair government and good land; on the Third, Cardston's founding; and on the Fourth, the American heritage of freedom and liberty dating back to the Revolution.... And later the same month on July 24, the entrance of Brigham Young into the Salt Lake Valley would be celebrated with equal enthusiasm.[20]

That all these loyalties could be maintained in the consciousness of a single community, conclude Ursenbach and Jensen, attests to the basic similarity of the mores and customs of Canadians, Americans and Mormons.

Despite this similarity, Alberta Mormons do *apparently* differ in subtle yet noticeable ways from fellow Albertans and Canadians. For instance, how does one explain the preference for basketball in southern Alberta at the expense of the national sport, hockey, except by the presence in every Mormon chapel of a "cultural hall" and access to the US college network where the Karens and the Tollestrups have starred over the years?[21] A "Mormon drawl," according to Ursenbach and Jensen, sets Alberta Mormons apart from their Canadian compatriots, but facilitates their passage undetected in Utah.[22]

The ultimate study of Alberta Mormon identity has yet to be undertaken, although, bit by bit, the pieces seem to be falling in place. Projected research by Elton in the area of Mormon political behavior in Alberta is particularly promising.[23] What seems abundantly clear, however, is that Alberta Mormons, and probably those in the neighboring provinces, which they have in large part spawned, continue to enjoy a symbiotic relationship with the mother country. Unlike the descendents of American Loyalists who fled the United States 120 years before the Mormon exodus to Alberta and turned their back on the fledgling American nation, the Saints of Alberta resemble more the nineteenth-century Métis of the prairies, for whom the international boundary was essentially nonexistent and hence "oft-crossed."

To highlight further the permeability of this boundary, the address of the Cardston temple, the only universally acknowledged parcel of Mormon

Toronto, Ontario Temple in Brampton, dedicated 1990, architect's rendition. Copyright 1988, The Church of Jesus Christ of Latter-day Saints, used with permission.

sacred space in Canada should be noted. In official church publications, it is listed as Babb, Montana, USA?[24] Perhaps inspired by the frequent Canadian postal strikes, but just as likely to facilitate dissemination of temple information to the vast American clientele, church officials have chosen to maintain a Cardston temple postal box outside the country. Such decisions reflect cultural insensitivity and reveal a corporate behavior not unlike that of US firms that consider Canada merely another part of their domestic markets.[25]

In Ontario, despite being peppered by western Canadian Mormons having direct ties to Utah, the Latter-day Saint population is nevertheless dominated by a "non-western" ideology. Ontario Mormons do not suffer from the well-known syndrome of western alienation as do their counterparts in Saskatchewan, Alberta and British Columbia. Cultural loyalties are not split across the international boundary to the same extent. Their political loyalties are focused upon a nearby capital, Ottawa, and reinforced by proximity to the financial center of Canada, Toronto. In dealings with nearby American Mormons, the Canadians frequently speak from a position of strength, being more numerous and better organized than their brothers and sisters residing in the backwaters of upstate New York, and they enjoy parity with those facing them across the Great Lakes or straits or locks or rivers. In October of 1987, ground was broken for a temple in Brampton, Ontario. Completion of this edifice in the Greater Toronto area should logically reinforce a Canadian Mormon identity. No longer will it be necessary to make the 600- to 1000-kilometer trek to Washington, DC, to seek the highest blessings.

Of all Canadian Mormons, as for all Canadians, it is easiest for Ontarians, especially those without western origins, who have joined or whose parents joined the LDS church since World War II, to express a Canadian identity.

The Maritime provinces of Nova Scotia, New Brunswick and Prince Edward Island, once integral parts of early Canada are today, along with Newfoundland, quite marginal relative to central Canada (Ontario and Québec) and the more prosperous western provinces. They are likewise peripheral within Canadian Mormondom. The 3% or 4% of Canadian Mormons who have always resided in the Maritime provinces, especially in Nova Scotia, have drawn little strength from the old-line Mormon settlements in the West. Their Mormon ties have been southward to the United States, homing in on Boston or, precisely, Cambridge, site of the mission home of the New England States Mission, which for a half century furnished Maritime Saints with missionaries and spiritual sustenance. The brief period that the Canada-Halifax Mission has been in existence has contributed to a reorientation and perhaps a Canadianization of LDS identity in Atlantic Canada. Here, as will be shown in the case of Québec, the mission is faced with the delicate problem of dealing with an official-language minority, the Acadian population of northeastern New Brunswick, which falls under its ecclesiastical jurisdiction, but would be more logically placed in a unilingual French Mission headquartered in Quebec City.[26] Alas, the linguistic question returns. It is impossible to avoid it in the Canadian context. It is also impossible to avoid it in the Canadian Mormon context. Nowhere is this more obvious than in Québec where the LDS Church is young and where the confrontation between the "two solitudes" has been played and replayed throughout its history.[27]

The total sum of information on the church in Québec does not fill one page in the 300-page volume *A History of the Mormon Church in Canada*, published in 1968 as the Latter-day Saint contribution to the centennial of Confederation. A rather unusual declaration, even amusing, if not faith promoting, concerns the Montréal chapel:

The chapel is on Rue St. Joseph. It is one of the very few LDS Chapels that has a cross on it. It is a cement cross and is embedded in the brick work. The chapel was purchased years ago and the expense of removing the cross was prohibitive.[28]

The chapel had been purchased from the Syrian Orthodox faith in 1942 and served well, until a firebombing of the foyer in the late 1970s by a man and his son, disgruntled over their wife's and mother's new religious affiliation, led church authorities to abandon it. Into the 1970s, it served primarily an English-speaking congregation. Of the 900 Québec Mormons cited in the centennial volume, probably no more than 100 were French speaking, despite the overwhelming French majority in Québec and Montréal.[29] Only one French branch existed, consisting of approximately 80 members. Two other English units are mentioned, Greenfield Branch on the southshore and Pointe Claire Branch in West Island.[30]

The brief treatment given Québec in this quasi-official history is consistent with the degree of proselytizing carried on among French-speaking Quebeckers up until that time. Owing to the rigid control over public and private life exercised by the Catholic Church, no concerted missionary effort was pursued among the French in Montréal or the rest of the province until the early 1960s when major societal reforms, termed the Quiet Revolution, heralded the advent of sudden secularization and swift modernization of Québec society, accompanied by a rapid rise in nationalism.[31]

The Saints of the early 1960s in Québec were served by the unilingual Toronto-based Canadian Mission, which, in light of the "enlightenment" taking place in Québec, designated a few missionaries, with essentially no prior experience in the French language, to proselytize. Their modest success created a base to which a sprinkling of Mormon immigrants from France and Belgium was added to fill out the ranks of the embryonic branch in Montréal. By 1965, missionaries had finally drifted 150 miles downriver to the provincial capital and second-largest city, Quebec City, where a minuscule branch was created in 1969.

It is noteworthy that in French Québec, unlike other much more exotic regions of the world that are documented in the work of Garth Jones, culturally steeped Mormons from the western Zions have played a relatively small role in the establishment of their faith.[32] Canadians, primarily from Alberta, have always constituted a disproportionate share of the rosters of the various French missions of the church. Benefiting from earlier and more constant exposure to French as a second language, the young men and women from Raymond, Magrath, Hill Spring and Calgary, to name but a few places on the Mormon map of Canada, frequently exhibited greater linguistic skills than their more numerous American companions. On this basis, it might be expected that, once returned home, these former French missionaries would profit from the official bilingualization of their country to drift eastward to take advantage of their linguistic skills and, as a result, take up activity in the fledgling branches of the Québec church that were emerging. Such was not the case, however. There appears to be little evidence that the former French missionaries have served as emissaries for the church in Québec.[33] They have tended to remain in their regions or have gone to the United States. In the instances of those few who have migrated to Ottawa or Montréal, they have gravitated to English wards or branches. Their role as blacksmiths in forging a new Canadian identity has been minimal.

INSTITUTIONAL REACTION TO THE NEW CANADA

In the midst of the linguistic turmoil surrounding the passage of the Official Languages Act of 1969, the transformation of the Canadian symbolic order, and the rise to unprecedented heights of Québécois nationalism, attempts by the French-speaking Saints in Québec to obtain services in their own language from the unilingual Canadian Mission in faraway Toronto met with little success. Locally, priesthood leadership lay in the hands of the anglophones whose Latter-day Saint antecedents in Québec reached back at least a generation further.[34] Montreal district conferences, which included Saints from both linguistic groups, were held at three-month intervals in the St. Joseph street chapel, located on "le plateau Mont-Royal" in the heart of French east-end Montréal. Prayers, speeches and songs were offered with little regard to the French members whose responsibility it was to "rig up" their own translation system and furnish the translator if they were to enjoy a semblance of fellowship. Not until the first district conference of 1972 were a speech and choral presentation in the French language permitted.

Quite naturally, rumors circulating in the fall of 1971 to the effect that a French mission in Québec was in the offing were met with jubilation. A genuine commitment on the part of the church to Québec and the New Canada with a strengthened French presence seemed forthcoming. As a result, the presidency of the tiny LDS branch in Québec City, established two years earlier, audaciously proposed to church headquarters, without passing through the conventional district and mission channels dominated

Mormon 'local' or meeting place in Quebec City, 1973-83, on third floor above Roy Accessories. Photo by Dean Louder.

by English speakers, that the site of the new mission headquarters in the *belle province* be *la vieille capitale* and not *la metropole*. A lengthy excerpt from this letter, addressed to Elder Delbert Stapley of the Quorum of Twelve Apostles, is instructive and echoes the philosophy of *survivance*:[35]

> Undoubtedly many considerations suggest that the mission should be headquartered in Montréal, but, we believe that such a selection might place a significant psychological burden on missionary activity throughout the province. The reasons for this are primarily historical and cultural. For three centuries French Canada has succeeded in preserving its language and cultural heritage in the face of sometimes formidable obstacles.... French Canada constantly feels overwhelmed and frequently threatened by their Anglo-Saxon neighbors. As one after another of its cherished institutions becomes anglicized through English Canadian and American influences, the Quebecker, possessing a keen sense of self-preservation and patriotism, comes to be very suspicious and distrustful

toward foreign organisations. We believe that the Church can do much to minimize the impact of this attitude on missionary work by a few simple acts which overtly demonstrate the desire and intention of the Church to become an integral part of the local scene. To Americans and other foreigners, Montreal may well represent French Canada, but the French Canadian, especially the Quebecker, has quite a different perception. To him, Montreal is a great cosmopolitan city, the home office for myriad world-wide corporations, a city where the French language and Québec traditions are important to an increasingly small proportion of the population, both in numbers and influence. To him, Montreal represents the incursion of Anglo-Saxon influence into the French Canadian cultural realm. To our way of thinking, to place the provincial headquarters of the Church in Montreal affirms in the French Canadian mind that here is another American institution which has only token interest...in that which is French Canadian.[36]

Elder Stapley acknowledged receipt of the letter, confirmed the creation of a separate Québec Mission, and expressed appreciation for the ideas put forth, mentioning that they would be taken into consideration.[37] The search for a mission homesite proceeded, focusing, however, upon the upper-class English neighborhoods of Beaconsfield, Westmount and Town of Mount Royal, all in the Montreal area. This seeming contradiction with what had been stated in Stapley's initial response generated a second missive:

> We have learned indirectly that President Olsen (the mission president to be) and a representative of the church office responsible for the acquisition of new property have visited Montreal.... We find it difficult to understand how the factors which resulted in the choice of Montreal over a more representative French-Canadian city would also prompt this even closer identification with the English speaking community, an association we believe will be detrimental to the future success of the work....We understand that he (President Olsen) met with the Montreal District Council during his short visit.... It is important to recognize, however, that the French-Canadian community is not represented on the District Council. Perhaps President Olsen is not aware that a prerequisite for a French-Canadian to serve in that position is a bilingual competence. The same requirement is NOT in effect for English speakers.[38]

Nevertheless, Town of Mount Royal was chosen. As though to prove the Quebec City branch presidency wrong, the French membership of the church continued to increase in the province, to the extent that a decision was reached in 1974 to create a separate French district consisting of the entire French-speaking membership. A second decision, the effects of which were much more far-reaching, was made almost simultaneously. The new mission boundaries, which had corresponded to the political boundaries of the province of Québec, were redefined to include eastern Ontario, with its large—relative to Québec—Latter-day Saint populations concentrated in Ottawa and Kingston and northern New York state. Figures are not available to indicate whether or not French members had by 1974 attained majority status within the original mission, but it is clear that they were relegated, in dramatic fashion, to minority status within the new Canada-Montreal Mission. Indeed, 13 years later (in 1987), 2,753 (41%) people were members of French-language wards or branches (all in Québec), as compared to 3,835 (56%) in English units. Within Québec, 1,236 (29%) belonged to English wards; the 2,753 French constituted 65% of the total Québec membership.[39] Just as Québécois are a majority in Québec, but a minority in Canada,[40] French-speaking Latter-day Saints are a majority within Québec, but a minority within the Canada-Montreal Mission.[41]

The impact of this decision was significant not only for members who observed their status as minority or majority change in the twinkling of an eye but also for the missionary effort as well. Missionaries serving could expect to spend at least five or six months in English areas. Combined with the short-lived shortening of missionary service for men to 18 months, few missionaries acquired the linguistic skills necessary to carry on anything more than a rudimentary conversation in Québécois.

In 1987, 3,771 (88.5%) of Québec's total Mormon population of 4,259 was located in the Montréal area, whereas only 57% of the total population was there. Two thousand, two hundred and sixty-five (82%) of its French Latter-day Saint population were there, but that same area includes only about one-third of Québec's total French-speaking population.[42] One can only speculate at this point as to how these numbers might be different today had the unsolicited grass roots advice offered by the Quebec City branch presidency been heeded and had the church maintained its apparent 1971 linguistic commitment.

The epilogue of the Quebec City branch history written in 1983 reiterated the need to re-establish an LDS Mission in North America where directives would be written in the language of Molière, where members could fill out tithing slips printed in their own tongue, where telephone communications

LDS 'Mormon' Chapel in Quebec City, 1983, serving la Branche de Québec and la Branche de Stadacone. Photo by Dean Louder.

to mission headquarters would be handled with ease at the other end.[43] Given the church's propensity to grant no particular importance to political boundaries, the epilogue goes a step further and suggests that the new mission include not only the province of Québec but also the Acadian portions of neighboring New Brunswick. This proposition had been rejected out-of-hand in 1981 by Charles Didier, the only francophone general authority of the church who manifested considerable dismay to learn that "they speak real French" in New Brunswick.[44]

Shortly thereafter, the area assignment of this the only francophone general authority was altered and French members locally could no longer speak to the ultimate authorities except via the language of Shakespeare.

A most disappointing event for French Latter-day Saints in Québec, besides the nomination in 1978 and 1981 of mission presidents scarcely able to communicate with them, occurred in September of 1979 when a regional conference of the church was held at Maple Leaf Gardens in Toronto. Spencer W. Kimball and other Latter-day Saint dignitaries, including Charles Didier, were present. The latter, after a brief word of greeting in his language, chose to (or was instructed to) speak in English, and nary a word of Canada's other official language was heard.

Insult was added to injury nine years later (19 September 1988) when another regional conference of the church was held, this time at Place des Arts, the cultural center for the Québec artistic community, in Montréal. Except for a strongly accented "bonjour" by the regional representative at the outset, no allowance at all was made for active French participation. French-speaking Saints were expected to participate passively by listening on an insufficient number of earphones to an all-English program. One hour and twenty minutes into the meeting, Russell Ballard, the presiding authority, sensed the malaise in the huge auditorium and asked, when it came his turn to speak, how many in the audience did not understand the proceedings. Overwhelmed by the sea of hands, he requested and obtained a translator to stand by his side. It is no wonder that following the final amen, a Saint in the upper balcony arose and screamed for all to hear, "Au Québec on parle français!"

The Murray-Corbin report on bilingual services concluded in 1981 that far too many institutions are all too frequently unable to provide services in the right place and the right time in the right language.[45] The church, in its dealings with its membership in the New Canada, can be numbered among these guilty institutions. A golden opportunity to rectify this situation is on the horizon. Ground was broken on 10 October 1987 for a temple in the Greater Toronto area. It will be the first universally accepted Mormon cultural symbol east of Cardston and the ultimate sanctuary for faithful Latter-day Saints.[46] The church has the opportunity of adopting the "federal model," which will require providing at all times bilingual services at all levels for all ordinances, or it can operate the temple as it does all other North American temples, furnishing non-English-language service upon request at specified hours. The unilingual English printed program provided for the groundbreaking ceremony might be indicative of the option selected.[47]

RELEVANCE AND IMPORTANCE OF MORMON STUDIES IN CANADA

Canadian Mormondom is, in many ways, a mirror image of Canadian society. It is fragmented, regionalized and driven by directives formulated by a central government, in this instance, located in Salt Lake City. Contrary to Canadian society, however, whose provincial governments serve as a counterweight to the federal heavyweight, there is no countervailing authority in Mormondom to temper decisions imposed from above. With respect to modern Canada, the central church seems burdened with its

Alberta legacy in the sense that Canada is often perceived as being synonymous with Cardston or southern Alberta generally. The cultural nuances of a bilingual and multicultural Canada, consisting of eight unilingual English provinces, one unilingual French province, one bilingual province, and two territories dominated numerically by native peoples, seem to escape it. In its policy decisions regarding Saints in Canada, the church appears guided primarily by practical and administrative considerations.

For 25 years now the Canadian nation-state has begun undergoing a mild cultural revolution, seeking to draw its peoples closer and to differentiate itself from its southern neighbor. More than any other, federal politicians have chosen to play the linguistic trump card. The French language has never been as strong in Canada as today. Once tightly entwined with religion at the heart of Québécois cultural identity, that identity today is expressed almost entirely in language. Once absent and scorned in English Canada, French occupies an ever larger place and constitutes the key component in the new Canadian identity.[48]

Canada, because of its similarities with the United States, its proximity, and reasonably common heritage, offers the church an excellent opportunity to divest itself of its American label. The authors of *America's Saints: The Rise of Mormon Power* argue that the Mormon church is pre-eminently an *American* church, that general authorities speak of a *domestic* church when referring to the US church, and *international* church when referring to any place outside their country's borders.[49] Gottleib and Wiley are wrong! The *domestic* church includes, in addition to the United States, Canada, and the *international* church refers to any place outside the United States *and* Canada. Thus, the official church and, by extension, its membership deny the cultural specificity of Canada and the existence of an international church within that country. By acknowledging and broadcasting the uniqueness of the LDS experience in all parts of Canada and "lengthening its stride" to get in step with recent events there, the church could symbolically separate itself from American policy, which views bilingualism or multilingualism as "divisive" and "dangerous,"[50] exercise leadership in facing culturally sensitive issues, and set a precedent for creative action in other diverse and pluralistic societies, many much more complex than Canada.

Canada is unique and relevant to the study of Mormon life in several ways. It was an early mission field whose converts, such as John Taylor, were rapidly absorbed into the immigration streams of the United States as they trekked southward and westward to join the Saints in Zion,[51] but it was also a haven a half century later for Mormon adventurers, entrepreneurs and harassed Utah pioneers.[52] Thus, it is a country—the only one in the world—with a relatively large indigenous Mormon population that traces its genealogical roots back to the United States. It sits beside, but is not literally a part of, the society that permitted the rise of Mormonism and then sixty years later obliged it to conform to societal norms. It is a land where old-line Mormons in and around Alberta's cultural hearth know much more about the activities of their faith in Latin America and Southeast Asia than east of the Canadian shield.

With the exception of Alberta, Mormon scholars and students of Mormonism have yet to discover Canada. The otherwise fine book *Mormonism: A Faith for all Cultures*, the proceedings volume of a 1975 Brigham Young University Centennial colloquium by the same name, has no place for Canada. The only non-English-language group in North America to merit attention is the Chicanos who have no geographic space to call their own. Charles Didier describes in four brief pages the church in French-speaking Europe, but there is nothing on French-speaking North America, despite its proximity and the presence of 6,000,000 people occupying a linguistic island of 636,400 square miles.

There exists no substantive overview, historical, sociological or ethnographic, of this so-called ethno-religious people in Canadian cultures.[53] Studies are punctual and sporadic, focusing above all on southern Alberta. Of the fifty papers presented at the 1987 national conference on the Mormon presence in Canada held in Edmonton, 22 studied Mormons located in the Alberta hearth. Two dealt with some aspect of Mormonism in British Columbia, one in Saskatchewan, one in Ontario, one in Québec, and one in the Atlantic provinces. The remaining papers were of a thematic nature, but still reflected, quite justifiably, a strong western Canadian bias.[54]

NOTES

1. This text is a revised version and fusion of two papers prepared for the National Conference on the Mormon Presence in Canada, Edmonton, Alberta, 6-10 May 1988.
2. Conversation with J.S. in Quebec City, April 1985.
3. In its annual report for 1984 (without date or place of publication), the Institute for Political Research mentions on page 2 that Canada represents "the triumph of politics over geography and economics, and sometimes, even over common sense."
4. Inasmuch as the evolution of federal policy has sought, above all, to placate

Québec, and given the relatively rapid growth of the LDS Church in this French province, the institutional reaction will be viewed principally from the Québec perspective.

5. See Marc Morin, "La langue au chat," *Le Devoir*, 5 April 1986.

6. R. Breton, "The production and allocation of symbolic resources: An analysis of the linguistic and ethnocultural fields in Canada," *Canadian Review of Sociology and Anthropology*, 21 (2, 1984), pp. 123-44.

7. For instance, the elimination of French from the Manitoba Legislature in 1890, and the abolition of educational rights for French minorities in the North-West Territories (1892), Ontario (1912) and Manitoba (1916). It is interesting to note in the present context the strong opposition in certain quarters of English Canada to Bill C-72, which would strengthen the current Official Languages Act.

8. The most prominent of these was Henri Bourassa, but there were others, for example, J.-M. Pénard, whose eloquent discourse is cited in G. Bouthillier and J. Meynaud, *Le Choc des langues au Québec, 1760-1970* (Montréal: Les Presses de l'université du Québec, 1972), pp. 382 and 384.

9. See B.K. Sandwell, "Present day influences on Canadian society," in *Royal Commission Studies* (Ottawa: Edmond Cloutier, 1951), pp. 2-6.

10. For an exhaustive treatment of these changes and their impact, see R. Breton, op. cit.

11. Reorganized Latter-day Saint membership has remained constant in Canada since 1961, with 11,268 members in 1961, 11,222 in 1971 and 11,472 in 1981, 65% of which are in Ontario.

12. With the notable exception of 1970, whose figures were furnished by Grant Allen Anderson, Manager of Library Services of the Historical Department of the Church of Jesus Christ of Latter-day Saints, statistics for periods prior to 1981, the year in which Statistics Canada first distinguished between Latter-day Saints and Reorganized Latter-day Saints, are derived by substracting RLDS membership as furnished by Barbara Bullard of the Independence(Missouri)-based church from census figures on "Latter-day Saints."

13. Statistics Canada defines as "urban" those residing in incorporated places of 1,000 or more.

14. In contrast to the American "melting pot," Canadian society is metaphorically referred to as a "mosaic." See, for example, J. Porter, *The Vertical Mosaic* (Toronto: University of Toronto Press, 1965); F.G. Vallée, "The Emergence of Northern Mosaic," in R. J. Ossenberg, ed., *Canadian Society* (Scarborough: Prentice-Hall, 1971); and L. Driedger, ed., *The Canadian Ethnic Mosaic: A Quest for Identity* (Toronto: John Wiley, 1975). In "Mosaic versus melting pot?: Immigration and ethnicity in Canada and the United States," published first in *International Journal* (Summer 1976), pp. 488-528, then in abridged form in E. Mandel and D. Taras, eds., *A Passion for Identity* (Toronto: Methuen, 1987), pp. 82-96, Howard Palmer argues that the mosaic/melting pot distinction has tended to be overstated.

15. See Donald Meinig, "The Mormon cultural region: Strategies and patterns in the geography of the American West, 1847-1964," *Annals of the Association*

of American Geographers*, 55 (1965), pp. 191-221.

16. Lynn Rosenvall, "The Transfer of the Mormon Village Pattern of Settlement to Southwestern Alberta," unpublished paper.

17. Melvin S. Tagg, and A. E. Palmer, *A History of the Mormon Church in Canada* (Lethbridge: *Lethbridge Herald*, 1968), p. 32; O. Kendall White, Jr., "Mormonism in America and Canada: Accommodation to the nation-state," *Canadian Journal of Sociology*, 3 (2, 1978), p. 172.

18. M. Ursenbach and R. Jensen, "The Oft-Crossed Border: Canadians in Utah," in *The Peoples of Utah*, ed., H. Papanikolas (Salt Lake City: Utah State Historical Society, 1976), p. 295.

19. Ibid., p. 297.

20. Ibid., p. 295.

21. Tom Karen of Magrath played for Brigham Young University in the 1950s, whereas the Tollestrup brothers, Phil and Tim, played in the 1970s at BYU and Utah State University respectively.

22. M. Ursenbach and R. Jensen, op. cit., p. 300.

23. D. Elton, "Political Behavior of Mormons in Canada" in this volume.

24. *New Era* (February 1987), p. 50.

25. This same conception is apparent as regards Canadian students at Brigham Young University and Ricks College, where they have not traditionally been considered a part of the international student contingent.

26. One-third of the population of New Brunswick is French speaking and concentrated in an arc stretching southeastward from Edmundston, near the Québec border, along Chaleur Bay and the Northumberland Straits to Moncton.

27. The English Canadian literary figure Hugh MacLennan popularized the usage of the term "two solitudes" in his classic novel of 1945 dealing with the French and English of Montréal, *The Two Solitudes* (New York: Duel, Sloan & Pearce, 1945).

28. *A History of the Mormon Church in Canada*, op. cit., p. 260.

29. In 1971, 79% of the population declared themselves to be of French ethnic origin and 11% of British. For Montreal, the percentages were 64% and 15% respectively. Statistics Canada, 1981, cat. 93-929.

30. *A History of the Mormon Church in Canada*, op. cit., p. 260.

31. In *America's Saints: The Rise of Mormon Power* (New York: G.P. Putnam's Sons, 1984), Gottlieb and Wiley assert that the church's two most clear-cut nemeses abroad are nationalism and Catholicism (p. 131). It is important to note that without nationalism in Québec and its replacement of Catholicism as the "national religion," Mormonism would likely never have penetrated *la belle province*.

32. Garth Jones, "Expanding LDS Church abroad: Old realities compounded," *Dialogue: A Journal of Mormon Thought*, 13 (Spring 1980), pp. 8-22.

33. John K.M. Olsen, first president of the Canada-Montréal Mission, founded in 1972, adopted as personal policy to instill in his missionaries of western Canadian origin the desire to build bridges between a little known and poorly understood Québec and their homelands in the West.

34. A tacit policy existed at the time that required a bilingual competence of French speakers in order to accede to priesthood leadership roles. The same requirement was not applicable to English speakers.

35. *Survivance* is the persistent ideology that has reigned in Québec and throughout the French diaspora in America since the fateful day in 1759 that culminated in the British Conquest. Characterized by some as a state of siege mentality, it consists of the predominant role accorded the preservation of language, culture and institutions. See D. Louder and E. Waddell, *Du continent perdu à l'archipel retrouvé: le Québec et l'Amérique française* (Québec, Presses de l'université Laval, 1983).

36. Letter from the Quebec City Branch Presidency addressed to Elder Delbert L. Stapley, 24 October 1971. Available as appendix A to Quebec City branch history. See note 43.

37. Letter addressed to Quebec City Branch Presidency, 3 November 1971. Available as appendix B to Quebec City branch history. See note 43.

38. Letter addressed to Delbert L. Stapley from Quebec City Branch Presidency, 5 May 1972. Available as appendix C to Quebec City branch history. See note 43.

39. Data on 1987 membership of all wards and branches in the Canada-Montreal Mission were furnished by stake and district clerks. In the absence of detailed ethnolinguistic data by branch, these serve as next best. Note that the membership of the Zarahemla Spanish-speaking branch in Montréal numbered 270.

40. According to social critic and journalist, Dominique Clift, it is this condition of living simultaneously in two situations diametrically opposed to each other that makes analyses of Québec ingenious and audacious. See his recent work, *Le Pays insoupçonné* (Montréal: Libre Expression, 1987), p. 142.

41. Justification was never offered for the 1974 decision. Two Machiavellian explanations suggest that it was done to prevent isolation of the LDS official-language minority (the English) in a province where the church's future was most assuredly a French one, or to maintain the French in a minority situation while awaiting the maturation of its leadership. A more probable theory holds that church administrators merely sought a more equitable distribution of membership between the two-year-old mission and the old one in Toronto.

42. The Montréal area is home to 74% of the province's English-speaking population and 88% of its allophone (non-English and non-French mother tongue) population. Statistics Canada, 1981, cat. 93-929.

43. D. Louder, *Film de la branche de Quebec, 1969-82* (unpublished branch history, September 1983). Available at the Harold B. Lee Library, Brigham Young University and the Marriott Library, University of Utah.

44. Conversation with Elder Charles Didier in Quebec City, April 1981.

45. "Minutes of Proceedings and Evidence of the Special Joint Committee of the Senate and House of Commons on Official Languages. First Report to Parliament" (July 1981: Murray-Corbin Report), p. 272.

46. Although delighted at the prospect of having a temple on Canadian soil, many Québec members are nevertheless disappointed that it is to be situated on the Detroit side of Toronto. For Mormons in the Quebec City region and the

handful residing farther north and east, the Washington Temple will be nearly as close and perhaps more accessible.

47. After reading a preliminary version of this text, John K. Carmack of the First Council of Seventy and current area superviser for northeastern North America instructed the church's regional representative in eastern Canada to be constantly sensitive to the need to have all matters pertaining to the Toronto Temple translated into French and available in that language. See letter to the author dated 6 January 1988.

48. Indicative of this is an article in the April 1987 issue (p. 3) of *University Affairs/Affaires universitaires*, the official publication of the Association of Universities and Colleges of Canada, on the subject of the level of interest in French among English-speaking Canadian university faculty, which bears the title, "Parlez-vous français? Oui, je suis un professeur canadien." The popularity and growth of French immersion schools in English Canada constitutes further proof.

49. Gottleib and Wiley, op. cit., p. 130.

50. Numerous newspaper articles or literature from the USENGLISH movement could be cited. Suffice it to mention just three of the more accessible: an unsigned article appearing in the influential *Washington Post* (28 July 1986), p. D2; Peter Brimelow, "A cautionary case of bilingualism," *Commentary*, 84, 5, November 1987; and Peter Brimelow, *The Patriot Game: National Dreams and Political Realities* (Toronto: Key Porter Books, 1986).

51. R. Bennett, op. cit.

52. L.J. Arrington, "Historical Roots of the Mormon Settlement in Southern Alberta" in this volume.

53. Armand Mauss in this volume argues that except for strategic purposes, as in the case of the organization of the first national conference on the Mormon presence in Canada around the theme "A North American ethno-religious people in Canadian cultures," it might be incorrect to consider Mormons an ethnic group.

54. Curiously enough, the organizers of the *national* conference gave only minimum attention to the bilingual nature of Canada in the preparation, organization and presentation of the Edmonton gathering.

VI | MORMONS AS AN ETHNIC PEOPLE
Two Viewpoints

IN ATTEMPTING TO make sense of the Mormon experience in Canada, one needs to be able to relate Mormon history to broader patterns of group experience. But which analytical tools are most useful for explaining and understanding that experience? Can Mormons be understood best through concepts developed within the sociology of religion that analyze the conditions under which sects, cults, denominations and churches begin and evolve over time? Is the history of Mormons in Canada simply another chapter in the migration of members of American-based religious denominations to Canada? Should it therefore be understood in the comparative framework of the history and evolution of Jehovah's Witnesses, Seventh-Day Adventists, Christian Scientists and Disciples of Christ? Or is there something qualitatively different about Mormons, given their American Great Basin homeland, their Alberta geographical base, their range of social institutions, and the nature of Mormon-non-Mormon relations? Do these factors make Mormon history more analogous to that of other ethno-religious peoples, such as the Jews, Hutterites, Mennonites and Doukhobors?

Sociologist Armand Mauss and anthropologist Keith Parry come to different conclusions as to whether or not Mormons can be seen as an ethnic group. Whatever the historical arguments for considering Mormons a people, Mauss argues that those conditions no longer prevail and that because of the growing internationalization of the Mormon church, it is no longer possible to conceive of Mormons in ethnic terms. Parry is not so sure, and shows that the nature of Mormon-non-Mormon interaction in southern Alberta suggests that Mormons regard themselves as a people—and are considered a people by others—thus fulfilling the key elements in most social science definitions of ethnicity. Certainly, historically in Canada, Mormons were considered a people by outsiders, as Howard Palmer's account (in this volume) of attitudes toward Mormons in Canada makes clear. Mormons were seen as an alien group, at least until the 1920s, and the comparisons drawn by outsiders were to Jews, Mennonites, Icelanders, "Galicians" and other ethnic groups. The study of the history of prejudice towards Mormons in Canada clearly fits into an ethnic relations perspective rather than one that would understand Mormon-non-Mormon relations simply as another chapter in the interaction among different Christian denominations.

The case for understanding Mormons as an ethno-religious people rather than simply as another religious group rests not only on historical arguments but also on the applicability of concepts from the field of ethnic studies to the contemporary study of the Mormon experience. Parry argues that Mormons' distinctive vocabulary; shared history; distinctive theological beliefs leading to a preoccupation with genealogy; and definite in-group boundaries (including prohibitions on the use of alcohol, tobacco, tea and coffee, and an emphasis on in-group marriage) contribute to a strong sense of peoplehood (which includes the universal usage of the "brother" and "sister" terminology). Parry's article shows how the nineteenth-century fusion of ethnicity and religion has continued up to the present day.

The range of concepts from the field of ethnic studies that can be applied to the Mormons can be extended further. Studies of the impact of prejudice, leading to a minority group psychology that overconforms to middle-class norms in order to find acceptance, might be used to help explain the Mormons' pronounced social and political conservatism throughout most of the twentieth century. The concepts of social marginality, ethnic pride and ethnic self-hatred, which are key elements in understanding ethnic group psychology, could also be used to understand important features of the Mormon experience in Canada.

The process of Mormons' accommodation to the economic, social and political context of Canadian society is also part of the larger process of the assimilation of many different ethnic and ethnoreligious peoples in Canadian society. Historically, the Mormon experience in Alberta has been shaped by many of the same dynamics that affected all ethnic and ethno-religious groups who came to the prairies in the massive waves of immigration at the turn of the century. Mormons' bloc settlement, their economic adjustment, their gradual transition to identification with Canada, and their rural-urban transition all parallel the history of many other ethnic groups.

The Mormons' agricultural skills, English-language background, and knowledge of North American culture made their transition easier than that of many
other European immigrant groups, but the broad processes of adjustment and
accommodation were universal elements of the immigrant experience. The
Mormons, like the central and eastern Europeans, found that despite initial
strong hostility, they were gradually accepted into the larger society because
of their economic contribution, their growing political power, and their own
accommodation to the underlying values of the dominant society.

Comparing the Mormons more directly with ethno-religious groups, such
as Hutterites, Doukhobors and Mennonites, reveals many similarities between these dissenting groups who came to western Canada as farmers to
preserve their identity. All these peoples came in groups to escape religious
persecution, and settled in blocs. They shared a common sense of history
as a "people," and a common concern with the preservation of their group
identity. They devoted a good deal of energy and attention to boundary
maintenance and social control, and to these ends established a wide range
of institutions geared to encouraging social relations primarily within the
group. Because of their distinctive beliefs and practices, all aroused a good
deal of public opposition when they first arrived, and all have remained
somewhat controversial, though to varying degrees. One of the most intriguing questions for students of ethnic studies is why the social outcomes of
these processes within the various groups have been so different. Why did
the Mormons become so highly urbanized, and how were they able to maintain and expand their presence in urban communities, whereas the
Doukhobors have not been able to maintain their hold over those who have
become urbanized? How have the Mormons been able to maintain such a
high rate of endogamy in urban centers? How have they avoided the factionalism of the Doukhobors and Mennonites? What social factors have
enabled them to establish strong organizations in urban centers and maintain the support of most urban Mormons?

Even if an historical case can be made for Mormons as an ethnic or ethno-
religious group, will they continue so in future, with (as Mauss notes) their
growing dispersion, their increasingly multiethnic character, and the growing
impact of converts who have no connection with the pioneer Mormon past?
The history of Mormons in Canada raises many interesting theoretical and
comparative questions in the fields of ethnic and religious studies and
intergroup relations. A growing knowledge of this history will enrich our
comparative understanding of the broader dynamics of minority groups in
Canadian society.

16 Mormons as Ethnics

Variable Historical and International Implications of an Appealing Concept

ARMAND L. MAUSS

INTRODUCTION

ONE OF THE by-products of the American Civil Rights Movement of recent decades has been the fostering of pride in one's own ethnic heritage. This pride was first asserted by black Americans in the 1960s, apparently as a reaction against the failure of the idealized American "melting pot" to include them significantly in the emergent cultural alloy.[1] In its more conspicuous and significant forms, this rising "black pride" expressed itself politically in movements for "black nationalism" or "black separatism," religiously in the formation of the Black Muslims, and academically in the establishment of black studies departments, programs and curricula on many college campuses.[2] Slogans such as "Black is beautiful" gained some currency. Alex Haley's prodigious research on his family origins produced the best-seller *Roots*, demonstrating that even the descendants of black slaves could recover their genealogical heritage to a large extent, as a basis for cultivating ethnic identity and pride.

Other American ethnic groups soon followed the black example with comparable or analogous expressions.[3] Eventually, even non-Anglo European ethnics, led by exponents such as Michael Novak, began to promote their own forms of ethnic pride and power.[4] One outcome of this collection of movements has been a growing disenchantment with the classical American metaphor of the "melting pot,"[5] and a newly fashionable emphasis on ethnic identity—indeed, in some quarters almost a desperation to establish such an identity! The Canadian counterpart can be seen in the relatively recent rise of "cultural pluralism," both as slogan and as explicit government policy in response to incipient separatist movements in Quebec and elsewhere.

It was in this context that the Mormon Church and culture entered a new scholarly and literary age of its own, called "Camelot" by Davis Bitton.[6] While Bitton applied this term mainly to the decade that began with Leonard Arrington's call as church historian in 1972, the flowering of the new Mormon literature, more generally, actually began a decade or so earlier, perhaps with the founding of *BYU Studies*, but certainly by the time of the emergence of *Dialogue* in the mid-1960s. The prodigious output since then of historical and other studies of Mormon life and culture, virtually all of it by Mormon authors, can be understood in part as an expression of a renewed appreciation (if not, indeed, pride) in the unique cultural and religious heritage and identity of the Mormon people.

Of course, the Mormons had long since appropriated the biblical phrase "peculiar people" to refer to themselves, but that peculiarity had been mostly a liability in Mormon relationships with others. It took the non-Mormon anthropologist O'Dea to translate the venerable Mormon folk concept of peculiarity into academically more respectable terms, such as "incipient nationality" or even "ethnicity."[7] Thus, by the 1960s, even the Mormons, with their highly assimilated northwest European genetic homogeneity, and their conservative brand of Americanism, could join in the increasingly fashionable celebration of unique "ethnic" identity! By 1980, such an identity was legitimated by the inclusion of the Mormons in the *Harvard Encyclopedia of American Ethnic Groups*,[8] along with Hutterites, Copts and Muslims. This essay will explore some of the implications, many of them only potential, of conceiving of Mormons as an "ethnic group" and will offer something of a demurral to such a conception.

ETHNICITY AS A CONCEPT IN THE SOCIAL SCIENCES

One can scarcely object to considering Mormons as an "ethnic group" on the basis of conventions in the professional literature of the social sciences, for those conventions are not at all clear or unanimous.[9] They run the gamut from what might be called "soft" to "hard" definitions of ethnicity or ethnic group. In an essay for the above-mentioned *Harvard Encyclopedia of American Ethnic Groups*, Abrahamson comes close to saying that a distinctive religion is a sufficient basis for assigning "ethnicity."[10] One venerable dictionary of anthropology defines ethnicity simply (and vaguely) on the basis of "common cultural characteristics," language being especially important.[11] A more recent anthropological encyclopedia emphasizes *self* identity in defining an ethnic group as a group of people within a larger culture "who identify themselves as a distinct entity," though usually other traits are also present, such as a certain language or dialect, traditions, customs, dress, etc.[12] A newer glossary of anthropology also emphasizes the self-consciousness of a people in the definition of "ethnic" as referring to "any group distinguished by a self-conscious awareness of common cultural, linguistic, or racial characteristics" (which the glossary does not otherwise define).[13]

To complicate matters further, some sociologists have stressed, correctly I think, that "ethnicity," like many other cultural conditions, is best understood not as categorical, but as "emergent"—that is, as waxing (and perhaps also waning) under certain social-structural conditions such as occupational homogeneity, residential concentration and mutual institutional dependence.[14] Finally, in its "checklist" of criteria used for its own inclusion of various peoples, the *Harvard Encyclopedia* sets forth 14 different traits, any one or more of which could be used to define an ethnic group, adding the caveat that even such a generous list of criteria "does not exhaust all possibilities or viewpoints."[15]

If almost any claim to ethnicity seems legitimate by such expansive definitions, the professional literature also contains some "harder" or more demanding conceptualizations of "ethnicity." These usually emphasize birth-related and biological commonalities, such as descent, time and locus of birth, and a sense of belonging based on such factors.[16] Kinship and language seem to be the two most critical ethnic "markers" for one sociobiologist, though other traits are relevant too.[17] Clearly, the appropriateness of terms such as "ethnic" and "ethnicity" will depend on how exacting a definition one wishes to use, and particularly on how much priority that definition accords to a commonality of biological, genetic or genealogical traits.

APPLYING THE "ETHNICITY" CONCEPT: THE MORMON/JEWISH PARALLEL

"Ethnicity" (or alternatively, "ethnic group") is one of those concepts that seem clear enough in their most typical usage but grow problematic at the margins of their meaning. The term has come largely to replace "race" or "racial" in the social sciences in part because of the undue reliance on skin color, which the latter has always had, at least in the conventional wisdom, and in part because "race" has tended to connote a false categorical precision that simply cannot be established on the basis of such widely diffused traits as "colored" skin, or any other one overriding criterion. If the term "ethnic group" is intended deliberately as more modest in its claims to precision, however, it might now be in danger of losing its meaning altogether, given the breadth of some of its recent applications. If Mormons of all colors, languages, cultures and geographic origins can constitute an "ethnic group," one wonders, who, then, indeed, cannot?!

One of the more successful applications of the term "ethnic group" is probably to be found in the case of the Jews, and I suspect that many who are inclined to use the same term for the Mormons might have the Jewish example at least in the backs of their minds.[18] It is an attractive example, for there are certain compelling parallels between the Jews and the Mormons. Both claim literal, Israelite origin. Both claim a special status in the divine historical scheme. Both cherish a history of having endured and prevailed over persecution. Each identifies to some extent with a certain homeland. Both possess a worldwide sense of community based on common teachings, rituals and definitions of reality. Both continue to be viewed with a certain suspicion or hostility, sometimes organized (as with the anti-Semitic and anti-Mormon movements that still occur in North America), sometimes only subtle or muted. (Indeed, I have been so struck with the parallel stereotypes I have heard applied to Mormons and Jews that I have come to think of Mormons as "the Jews of the Rockies"!).

On the other hand, we must not resort to so facile a parallel that we overlook the considerable differences.[19] The Mormon claim to an ultimate common ethnic origin of an Israelitish or any other kind is an article of faith among believers, having no scientific, historical or other external validation. It may be that a certain identifiable "genetic structure" (a synthesis from the waves of nineteenth-century migrations from the countries of northwestern Europe) can be found among Mormons in Utah.[20] Indeed, one journalist of dubious talent has caricatured Utah Mormons as having a pervasive blond, hulking, Viking "look."[21] That is a far cry, however, from the ancient common Semitic origins ascribed to the world's Jews and Israelites (and Arabs, for that matter). Even Mormon persecution, as cruel as it was in the nineteenth century, was of relatively short historical duration, more akin to that suffered by the various other heretical Christian movements of history and far short of the Jewish experience in either duration, severity or recency. While the Mormon "homeland" has its parallels to that of the Jews in its arid climate, its two lakes (one salty) joined by a river, and its settlement after an exhausting trek under a modern "Moses," etc., it is a homeland that is becoming less "Mormon" all the time, even as Israel has been growing more Jewish. After another hundred years, the Mormon "homeland" might well be seen in retrospect as paralleling more the erstwhile "Puritan homeland" of New England than that of modern Israel.

Another important difference between Mormons and Jews is to be found in the sources of growth; for the Jews, growth comes almost totally from natural increase, enhancing the likelihood of a fairly homogeneous ethnic subculture from one generation to the next. In contrast, the Mormons are an aggressively proselytizing body, with converts accounting for a large proportion of each year's increase. These converts, furthermore, are coming increasingly from so-called Third World cultures that are quite exotic relative to the North American homeland. Without meaning to minimize the differences that also exist among Jews in various parts of the world, we would still expect the Mormon culture across time to be far more influenced than the Jewish one by recruitment from the outside. Indeed, Mormons already lack the kind of common historic language and literature that the Jews have, both in Hebrew and Yiddish. The unifying ritual, doctrinal and epistemological heritage of the Mormons certainly remains important, as it does for any distinct religious community, but in that respect Mormons parallel the Jews no more than they do, say, the Catholics, whom we would not ordinarily consider an "ethnic group."

What is it, then, that ultimately identifies Mormons with other Mormons, beyond a shared religion, however distinct that religion might be? To Martin Marty, Mormons are best understood as "a people," rather than as a church or a religion, and it is a common "story" that makes a people, he says. [22] Surely it begins to become ludicrous if we go far beyond the *religious* tradition and attempt to define Mormons from all the cultures and colors of the world as somehow constituting a new and separate "ethnic" category! Why not just a new world religion, as Jan Shipps[23] or Rodney Stark[24] would have it? Indeed, there is something incongruous and antithetical about trying to be a universal world church and a separate ethnic group at the same time!

While scholars like Thomas O'Dea and Dean May have made the case for a separate Mormon "peoplehood" or "ethnicity" about as convincingly as it can be made, it remains essentially an *historical* case. True as it might have been that nineteenth-century Mormons were an "emergent" ethnic group, with a subculture increasingly divergent from the American mainstream, such trends have been reversed during the twentieth-century assimilation of Mormons in North America. To be sure, there have been some strenuous and partly successful efforts by Mormons, at both the official and the folk levels, to resist this assimilation and growing convergence with American culture more generally.[25] Nevertheless, the assimilation has proceeded apace, as amply described and documented elsewhere, especially in the most recent studies.[26] Another way of assessing the degree of homogeneity (versus distinctiveness) between Mormons and others in North America at the present time is to study the results of systematic social surveys, to which I will now turn for a portion of this essay.

MORMONS VERSUS OTHER AMERICANS: INDICATIONS FROM SURVEY DATA

Beginning in 1972, the National Opinion Research Corporation (NORC), in collaboration with other companies and with grants from the National Science Foundation, has conducted annual Spring Social Surveys in the United States. Each survey has been based upon a carefully selected representative sample of about 1,500 cases, and the data have been collected in face-to-face interviews with extensive instruments. Many of the items in the instruments have been repeated every year, and some every other year, so that trends can be followed across time in many of the variables. There never have been enough religion variables included to satisfy researchers in religion, but at least every denomination reported in the interviews has been recorded and coded for each respondent, not only as of the time of the interview but also as of age 16, so that it is possible to identify respondents whose religious preference has changed since youth. Church attendance has also usually been included, and in more recent years a few belief items have begun to appear. Aside from religious matters, the instrument each year covers an enormous range of social and political attitudes and sociodemographic variables. The methodology, from sampling design to data filing, features the most advanced survey technology, so the data would seem to be of unimpeachable quality. (For more information, see a recent NORC codebook).[27]

Strictly on a random basis, one could not expect to pick up many Mormons in an annual survey sample of only about 1,500, especially outside of the Far West, and, of course, one does not. By aggregating all the Mormons included in the surveys each year from 1972 to 1985, however, we can obtain a Mormon subsample of 189, which is quite large enough for certain kinds of statistical breakdowns (though, to be sure, the sample will not be that large for every item, since some items have not appeared in the instrument every year). Of the total Mormon N of 189, 113 were also Mormons at age 16 and can therefore be considered lifelong members (or "lifers"), while 76 had different religions at age 16 and can therefore be considered Mormon converts.

In an effort to assess whether aggregating a sample over a period of 13 years would obscure some relevant trends or changes across time, I broke the sample down into three time periods (1972-1976, 1977-1982 and 1983-1985) based on a certain cogent strategy and made certain crucial comparisons, not only *among* the Mormons in those three periods but also *between* the Mormons and a random subsample of the national (non-Mormon) data (N = 1,247), similarly aggregated and similarly broken down. No significant differences by time period were apparent, either for Mormons or others in the distributions of such basic socio-demographic traits as age, sex, occupation, occupational prestige, education, father's education, or subjective class identification, or in certain attitudinal traits such as civil libertarianism and "anomia."[28]

For the *Mormon* sample, however, (but *not* the non-Mormon one), there were noteworthy temporal differences in three kinds of distributions: in the third time period, there was a large increase in the proportion of the Mormon sample taken from the Mountain states and a corresponding decline in the proportion from the Pacific states; in the same period, there was a large decrease in the proportion of the Mormon sample taken from cities of 100,000 or larger and a corresponding increase in the proportion from smaller towns; and there was a large decline over the 13 years in the proportion of the Mormon sample identifying themselves as Democratic and liberal in political preference and a corresponding increase in those identifying themselves as Republican and conservative. The evidence suggests that the first of these changes (in regional distribution) was an artifact of a deliberate change in sampling strategy in the more recent surveys, while the other two changes were in large part artifacts, in turn, of the first. In other words, whereas the earlier surveys had undersampled the Mormon population from smaller towns in the Mountain states, the more recent surveys seem to have oversampled them.

The changes in the political preferences of the Mormon subsample consequent to the recent oversampling from the Mountain states serve to underscore the important *regional* differences among Mormons even in the United States. Other regional differences were also apparent: Although clear majorities of Mormons in every region expressed what might be called fashionably liberal attitudes toward blacks and women (surprising as that might seem to some), the Pacific states Mormons were generally more favorable than other Mormons towards modern definitions of women's roles (e.g., working outside the home, participating in politics, etc.), but much lower in church attendance and religious intensity than their Mountain states brothers and sisters. Both the Pacific and Mountain states Mormons (especially the latter) were relatively strong in favoring civil liberties for nonbelievers. Mormons in various other parts of the United States (outside the West), however, were noticeably more conservative in attitudes toward blacks, toward women's roles, and toward civil liberties, while also having the highest scores in anomia.

While regional diversity among Mormons in the United States might undercut somewhat the common image of a homogeneous, monolithic "ethnic group," it should not be a surprise to any who have known Mormons in various parts of the country. Such diversity, indeed, has been apparent at least since I published some of the results of my own extensive surveys of Mormons in Salt Lake City and San Francisco taken nearly two decades ago.[29] From those surveys, considerable variety was apparent between the two regional samples of Mormons in religious orthodoxy, church activity levels, racial attitudes, sexual attitudes, political attitudes, and even some basic socio-demographic variables. It is obviously risky to attribute too much "ethnic" or even religious homogeneity to Mormons in the United States, to say nothing of Canada, Europe and more exotic locales.

If there is noteworthy diversity *among* Mormons, how much similarity is there between Mormons and *other* Americans? Do Mormons, despite their internal differences, still stand apart from the rest of the nation in certain important characteristics that might be called "ethnic" in some sense? And what about the impact of the large convert segment of the Mormon sub-culture? Does it seem to be closing or widening the gap between Mormons and other Americans? The four accompanying tables bear upon such questions. In these tables, we can see some three-way comparisons of lifelong Mormons, convert Mormons and non-Mormons, aggregated across the same time period (1972-1985). While the picture is mixed in some ways, certain generalizations do seem reasonable as we study the tables.

If we look at Table 16.1, we can see that the Mormons, whether converts or "lifers," resemble other (non-Mormon) Americans fairly closely in most sociodemographic respects. Mormons, on the average, have somewhat higher levels of formal education, occupational prestige, income, and social class self-perceptions, but these are generally not statistically

TABLE 16.1   Basic Demographic Distributions for Life-Long Mormons
("Lifers"), for Mormon Converts, and for Non-Mormons

Demographic Traits	Lifers (N = 113)	Converts (N = 76)	Non-Mormons (N = 1247)	Prob. *
Occupation				
prof., tech., mgr.	35%	36%	29%	.192
clerical	15%	17%	22%	
Occup. Prestige				
(above middle)	47%	54%	48%	.581
Father's Occup.				
Prestige (>mid)	64%	61%	57%	.305
Education more				
than high sch.	41%	26%	26%	.009
Income >$25K/an.	34%	23%	19%	.118
Class self-ident.				
working class	39%	59%	47%	.127
middle class	55%	38%	44%	
Region				
Mountain	63%	42%	6%	.000
Pacific	21%	29%	16%	
Mid & So. Atl.	8%	17%	32%	
East So. Central	3%	5%	7%	
Age <40	68%	52%	44%	.000
Family >4 kids	31%	24%	20%	.003
Conservative polit.				
self-ident.	55%	31%	27%	.000
Party preference				
Republican	66%	30%	30%	.000
Democratic	26%	55%	56%	

* Probability of chance distribution by chi-square test. Ns here are the maximums for each
column. They change somewhat from one item to another but rarely fall below 50 for
either Lifers or Converts.

Used with permission of *Dialogue: A Journal of Mormon Thought.*

significant differences. Mormons (especially the "lifers") tend to be a younger population than the nation as a whole, a fact no doubt related to the tendency also apparent in the table for Mormons to have larger families. In their regional distribution, Mormons (even the converts) are disproportionately found in the Mountain and Pacific states, as we would expect. The largest single concentration of American Mormons *outside* the West is now found in the South.[30] In political preference, it is important to note that while *lifelong* Mormons fit the public image of strong Republican and conservative attachments, the *converts* are almost identical to the national distribution in their preferences.[31]

In religious matters, as Table 16.2 indicates, Mormons rate relatively high in church attendance, with the lifers having nearly double the national rate for "weekly or more often," and the converts only a little less than that. In religious beliefs or feelings, the converts tend to stand statistically in the middle, while in smoking and drinking the converts more closely resemble the lifers, as we might expect. In *social* beliefs and attitudes, which would be more reflective of cultural or "ethnic" differences, there are a few important variations among the three columns, though the general non-Mormon sample is resembled sometimes more by the lifers and sometimes more by the converts (Table 16.3). Mormon converts and lifers are quite close to each other (but tend to differ somewhat from non-Mormons) in their levels of advocacy of civil liberties for atheists, in approval of school prayer, and in disapproval of abortion, pornography and homosexuality.[32]

On the other hand, converts look statistically more like the general non-Mormon sample in some of their attitudes towards blacks, especially in their disapproval of black assertiveness ("pushing") and in their approval of laws against racial intermarriage, as shown in Table 16.4. Surprising as it might be to some, however, the *lifelong* Mormons appear more "liberal" than *either* the converts or the non-Mormons in most of their attitudes towards blacks and towards women's roles. The more comprehensive study by Roof and McKinney, based on similar NORC data, showed that, contrary to their long-standing public image, Mormons are among the more *tolerant and liberal* of all American denominations towards blacks, towards new role definitions for women, and towards all kinds of civil liberties.[33]

So what might we conclude from all these comparisons based on the national NORC surveys? Of course, many other kinds of comparisons might have been included here, but I chose those most likely to reflect underlying cultural differences between Mormons and others, where such differences were, indeed, apparent. On the whole, there were not many of a strictly

TABLE 16.2   Distributions by Religious Beliefs and Observances for Life-Long Mormons ("Lifers"), Converts, and Non-Mormons

Beliefs	Lifers (N = 113)	Converts (N = 76)	Non-Mormons (N = 1247)	Prob.*
Life after death	96%	88%	76%	.000
"Strong" feelings for relig. affil.	63%	48%	42%	.001
Observances				
Church attendance				
weekly or more	56%	49%	31%	.000
< annually	21%	29%	38%	
Smoker at present	16%	18%	38%	.002
Ever drink at all now	31%	38%	78%	.000
Ever drink too much? (drinkers only)	38%	38%	38%	.941

* See note on Table 16.1.

Used with permission of *Dialogue: A Journal of Mormon Thought*.

Mormon-versus-non-Mormon kind, given the frequent convert/lifer differences. Such general Mormon differences from others as there were (outside of the strictly religious) appeared mainly in the realm of personal sexual morality and family values, as we have seen in many other studies. Some of those studies have also examined Mormon family life, family stresses and divorce rates, with results showing that not many of the Mormon family values (however unique they might or might not be) are reflected in unique Mormon *behavior*. To be sure, the relatively high Mormon fertility rates have persisted over many generations, but otherwise the Mormon cultural uniqueness in family life is not so apparent: the Mormon divorce rate is as high as the nation's (though not so for temple marriages); Mormon wives and mothers work outside the home at about the same rates as other wives and mothers; and Mormons seem to be having about the same difficulties with child rearing and child abuse.[34]

All in all, I would interpret the survey data as indicating that Mormons do not reflect a separate "ethnicity" in the United States so much as they

TABLE 16.3 Distributions by Indicators of Social Conservatism for Life-Long Mormons ("Lifers"), Converts, and Non-Mormons

Beliefs/ Attitudes	Lifers (N = 113)	Converts (N = 76)	Non-Mormons (N = 1247)	Prob.*
Civil Libertarianism: Agree that atheists should be allowed to . . .				
Speak in public	78%	82%	63%	.001
Teach in schools	61%	43%	43%	.008
Have anti-religious books in library	68%	74%	61%	.075
Church/State Separation: Prayer in the public schools				
Approve	51%	50%	37%	.059
Sex-Related Issues				
Approval of abortion ...				
For any reason	22%	16%	36%	.000
If single woman	22%	28%	43%	.000
If married, not wanting more	19%	24%	41%	.000
Favor sex education in public schools	62%	75%	79%	.104
Favor general laws vs. pornography	62%	61%	41%	.015
Has seen X-rated movie during past year	15%	5%	19%	.293
Believe homosexual relations are always wrong	86%	93%	69%	.034
Would allow book by homosexual in public library	44%	46%	43%	.979
Cynicism or "Anomia": Agreement that ...				
The lot of the average man is getting worse	53%	61%	61%	.364
It's not fair to bring a child into this kind of world	19%	34%	43%	.000
Government officials, etc., are not interested in the average man	53%	63%	68%	.017

* See note on Table 16.1
Used with permission of *Dialogue: A Journal of Mormon Thought.*

TABLE 16.4   Distributions by Attitudes on Race and Gender Issues for
Life-Long Mormons ("Lifers"), Converts, and
Non-Mormons

Beliefs/ Attitudes	Lifers (N = 113)	Converts (N = 76)	Non-Mormons (N = 1247)	Prob.*
Race Attitudes: Agree strongly that ...				
Whites and blacks should attend separate schools	7%	4%	11%	.447
Whites have a right to segreg. nbrhoods.	10%	13%	15%	.568
Blacks should not push so hard	23%	41%	38%	.205
Favor laws against intermarriage	18%	29%	29%	.072
Favor school bussing for integration	23%	10%	20%	.123
Would vote for a black for president	87%	84%	78%	.357
Gender Attitudes: Agree that ...				
All right for women to work outside home	75%	58%	71%	.439
Women should take care of the home not the country	28%	43%	30%	.233
Women are not suited for politics	32%	61%	42%	.024
Would vote for a woman for president	79%	73%	81%	.204

* See note on Table 16.1.

Used with permission of *Dialogue: A Journal of Mormon Thought*.

resemble ordinary Bible Belt Christians in their sexual and family values and in their general social and political conservatism. This seems especially true of the *converts*, raising an interesting question of causality, which I posed also in an earlier paper:[35] Are converts drawn to Mormonism *because of* its resemblances to Bible Belt Christianity, or is the conversion from among such conservative Christians actually changing the subculture of Mormonism? This question takes on added significance in the face of the relatively rapid Mormon growth in the American South.[36]

In general demographic terms, the constituency from which the Mormon Church seems to be drawing its American converts is similar to that of the lifelong membership: While perhaps seeing *themselves* more as "working class" and as Democrats than do the lifers, the converts are actually quite upwardly mobile, for objectively they are solidly middle class in occupational prestige, in income and in educational attainment. Also, like the lifers, they have more children than average, and they hold relatively conservative social views relating to alcohol, sex and family. In these respects, the converts, even more than the lifers, resemble Bible Belt Christians, which might indeed be the constituency from which Mormon converts are disproportionately being recruited in the United States (cf. note 36). Obviously this causal relation cannot really be established with data such as these, collected after the fact. Due allowance must be made also for the well-known tendency of converts themselves to "assimilate" into the "mainstream" of adherents more generally and thus to lose some of their own zeal and peculiarity over time.

CONCLUSION: THE USES OF THE CONCEPT OF ETHNICITY

Should we conclude, then, that Mormons are or are not an "ethnic group"? Personally, I do not find this concept to be useful as applied to Mormons, whether in North America or elsewhere. In the "harder" or more biological applications of the concept, it clearly does not fit the increasingly genetically diverse Mormon populations. In its "softer" or more subcultural applications, the already fuzzy boundaries of ethnic taxonomies can only be further confused by trying to set aside a special category for Mormons. It seems to me that less pretentious terms like "subculture" or "cognitive minority" would give the Mormon case as much distinction as it either needs or deserves, whether in the United States or elsewhere. Nor do I think that the issue is resolved by Marty's rather cryptic suggestion that "[e]thnicity can be real or imaginary."[37]

Obviously, however, there is no reason to expect that my preferences will or ought to obtain over those of scholars and observers who find "ethnicity" meaningful in the Mormon case. Given the lack of scientific consensus about the exact criteria for ethnicity, reviewed at the beginning of this essay, no one is really in a position to resolve the question on objective grounds. That leaves us with a somewhat different and perhaps more interesting question: What *interests* might be served by the application of the "ethnicity" concept to Mormons, and what are some of the implications thereof? The answers to such questions will likely vary according to the time and location of the particular Mormons under discussion.

In North America

In twentieth-century North America, the ethnicity concept has served the *heuristic* interests of scholars such as O'Dea and May. Much of the scholarly orientation of Jan Shipps would also seem implicitly to portray Mormons on a similar conceptual basis. Of course, there is nothing wrong with that. Scholars need heuristic concepts and frameworks if their work is to rise above simple description. Like any heuristic device, however, this one of "Mormons as ethnics" will carry the risk of emphasizing some kinds of Mormon traits at the expense of other kinds. Specifically, this concept serves the intellectual and theoretical needs of those scholars whose focus is North American in location, historical as opposed to contemporary, and pointed more at Mormon cultural differences than at similarities with the surrounding culture.

That is true because almost all the unique Mormon traits that caught O'Dea's attention even thirty years ago had already been eroding for at least a generation, and they are even less conspicuous now. Not surprisingly, there is a strong parallel here to the experience of American Catholics in general, and even to the experience of the various Catholic nationality groups separately, despite the reluctance of Novak and others to acknowledge the rapid Catholic assimilation.[38] It is significant too that the overwhelming majority of May's essay on the Mormons in the *Harvard Encyclopedia of American Ethnic Groups*[39] is devoted to *historical* facts and details. Even in his section on "Mormon Culture," where one might expect to find some distinctively "ethnic" traits laid out, May reviews instead the history of Mormon artistic and literary accomplishments, thus using "culture" in the more popular sense.

Not that there is anything wrong with historical studies or with a focus on North America. After all, nearly all Mormon experience is both historical and North American, almost by definition. We are all immensely grateful for the rapidly accumulating historical literature on Mormons. The point here is only that to the extent that our scholarly attention remains focused on the distinctive "ethnic" traits of the Mormon past, we might be both less interested and less perceptive about the *assimilation* of Mormons and their religion, both in North America and elsewhere. There is the danger, in other words, of continuing to focus on the rapidly diminishing *differences* between Mormons and their "host societies," while neglecting the growing *similarities*.

Aside from the heuristic interests of scholars, the concept of ethnicity might also serve certain *political* interests of Mormons, ecclesiastically or collectively, at least in North America. As I observed early on, the term "ethnic group" might be seen as a fashionable counterpart of the Biblical term, "peculiar people." The historian Moore has argued that, even in the nineteenth century, it served the interests of Mormon leaders "to stress not what Mormons had in common with other Americans, which was a great deal, but what they did not have in common."[40] In modern public relations, Mormon claims to uniqueness as an "ethnic group" are more likely to be treated sympathetically by the media and the rest of the establishment than are the traditional Mormon claims to being the "peculiar people" or the "one true church" of the New Testament.[41]

In Canada, meanwhile, the current official and public sponsorship of Canadian cultural pluralism offers perhaps an even more favorable political climate within which to stress the "ethnic" aspects of the Mormon heritage. By way of illustration, in early May, 1987, an important and unprecedented conference on Mormons was held on the campus of the University of Alberta in Edmonton. Much of the financial and other sponsorship of this conference came from Canadian government sources: federal, provincial and local. It seems unlikely that such sponsorship would have been forthcoming without the strategic "packaging" of this conference under the title, "The Mormon Presence in Canada: A North-American Ethno-Religious People in Canadian Cultures." I do not mean to imply any impropriety in such uses of the "ethnicity" concept for Mormons, nor do I hold any cynicism about it. I am genuinely glad to see such uses. I am suggesting only that we be careful not to reify as "science" those conceptual tools that we put to essentially strategic uses.

These strategic uses at the corporate or institutional level have their counterpart in certain symbolic uses also at the social-psychological level, at least in North America, and perhaps in other English-speaking countries too. As Mormons are increasingly assimilated, especially in those countries where the Mormon presence has more than a century of history, it becomes increasingly difficult for Mormons to specify to themselves and to others just what the bases are for their own unique identity.[42] I have discussed this issue at some length elsewhere.[43] Here I shall observe only that during the past century there has been an obvious convergence between Mormons and their host societies in North America, so that Mormons are required to reach ever more deeply into their bag of cultural peculiarities to find traits that will help them mark their subcultural boundaries, and thus their very identity as a special people.

Some of the contrivances that result from this effort are themselves an interesting study in cultural innovation and adaptation to respectability. The old theological heresies of Mormonism no longer provide salient enough boundaries in societies that have become atheological. The "Word of Wisdom" is no longer enough in societies that now have national campaigns of their own against tobacco, alcohol, drugs, caffeinated drinks, poor nutrition and sedentary living. Even wholesome family life, once promoted as though it were a special Mormon invention, is becoming national policy. Under such circumstances, the Mormon folk, as well as Mormon leaders, can find a continuing sense of separate identity, and the psychological security accompanying it, much more readily if they can understand themselves as a separate "ethnic group," rather than as an increasingly respectable religion. Even the minuscule Mormon minority in Canada can feel a lot better as a constellation in the universe of Canadian ethnopluralism than as just another oddball religion to be tolerated.

Outside North America

Scholars who know the Mormon scene in other settings are better qualified than I to comment on the implications of conceiving of Mormons as an "ethnic group" in those cultures. In most places, though, it seems to me that the small Mormon population is likely to have a relationship with the surrounding society that is different from that in contemporary North America. Indeed, that relationship is probably more like what American Mormons experienced in the early twentieth century—namely, a struggle for respectability, or at least acceptance. In such a situation, the Mormon population, almost all converts, of course, needs no resort to "ethnic" definitions of itself in order to maintain a sense of unique identity at either the corporate or the individual level.

One finds few places in the world where "cultural pluralism" of an ethnic or any other kind carries the favorable connotation that it officially has in Canada or the United States. In most places, it is a problem, not a situation to be celebrated. In Spain, now in a tense relationship with its Basque minority, or in Japan, which has always had difficulty with its Korean minority, one wonders how the growing Mormon memberships in those countries will be appreciated if they are represented not merely as a new religion but as a whole new "ethnic" group! Indeed, relationships of Mormons with others in many countries is already complicated by the western American Anglo-Saxon ethnic biases imposed from church head-quarters on the Mormon populations there.

In short, it is difficult to see any strategic or heuristic advantages to con-ceiving of Mormons as any kind of "ethnic group" outside of North America, if there. I expect the Mormon religion to survive and prosper around the world for a long time, but I expect its future as an "ethnic group" to be quite contingent on the uses to which that concept can be put in specific cultural and historical contexts.

NOTES

1. George Breitman, ed., *Malcolm X Speaks* (New York: Grove Press, 1965); Melvin Drimmer, ed., *Black History: A Reappraisal* (Garden City, N.Y.: Doubleday, 1971); J.R. Howard, ed., *Awakening Minorities* (Chicago: Aldine, 1970); Minako Kurokawa, ed., *Minority Responses: Comparative Views of Reactions to Subordination* (New York: Random House, 1970).

2. For example, Breitman, *Malcolm X Speaks*; Howard, *Awakening Minorities*; Kurokawa, *Minority Responses*; Wm. Petersen, "Concepts of Ethnicity," in *Harvard Encyclopedia of American Ethnic Groups*, ed., Stephen Thernstrom (Cambridge, Mass.: Harvard University Press, 1980), pp. 234-42; Pierre L. Van den Berghe, *The Ethnic Phenomenon* (New York: Elsevier, 1981), Chapter 1.

3. For example, Howard, *Awakening Minorities*; Kurokawa, *Minority Res-ponses*; S. Levine and N.O. Lurie, eds., *The American Indian Today* (Baltimore: Penguin Books, 1970); Petersen, "Concepts of Ethnicity"; M.P. Servin, ed., *The Mexican-Americans: An Awakening Minority* (Beverly Hills, California: Glen-coe Press, 1970); Stan Steiner, *The New Indians* (New York: Dell, 1968).

4. Michael Novak, *The Rise of the Unmeltable Ethnics* (New York: Macmillan, 1972); Nathan Glazer and Daniel Patrick Moynihan, *Beyond the Melting Pot*, second edition (Cambridge, Mass.: MIT Press, 1970); Lionel Lokos, *The New Racism: Reverse Discrimination in America* (New Rochelle, N.Y.: Arlington House, 1971); Petersen, "Concepts of Ethnicity."

5. Harold J. Abrahamson, *Ethnic Diversity in Catholic America* (New York: Wiley Company, 1973); Milton M. Gordon, *Assimilation in American Life* (New York: Oxford University Press, 1964).

6. David Bitton, "Ten years in Camelot: A personal memoir," *Dialogue*, Vol. 16, no. 3 (1983), pp. 9-32.

7. Thomas F. O'Dea, *The Mormons* (Chicago: University of Chicago Press, 1957); E.Z. Vogt and T.F. O'Dea, "A comparative study of the role of values in social action in two southwestern communities," *American Sociological Review*, Vol. 18, no. 6 (1955), pp. 645-54.

8. Dean L. May, "Mormons," in *Harvard Encyclopedia of American Ethnic Groups*, ed., Stephen Thernstrom (Cambridge, Mass.: Harvard University Press, 1980), pp. 720-31.

9. Petersen, "Concepts of Ethnicity."

10. Abrahamson, *Ethnic Diversity in Catholic America*, pp. 869-75, "Religion" in *Harvard Encyclopedia of American Ethnic Groups*, ed., Stephen Thernstrom.

11. Charles Winick, *Dictionary of Anthropology* (New York: Greenwood Press, 1969 [1956]), p. 193.

12. D.E. Hunter and O. Whitten, eds., *Encyclopedia of Anthropology* (New York: Harper and Row, 1976), p. 146.

13. Roger Pearson, *An Anthropological Glossary* (Malabar, Florida: R.E. Krieger Publ. Co., 1985), p. 77.

14. W.L. Yancey, E.P. Ericksen and R. Juliani, "Emergent ethnicity: A review and reformulation," *American Sociological Review*, 41 (June 1976), pp. 391-403.

15. Stephen Thernstrom, ed., *Harvard Encyclopedia of American Ethnic Groups*, pp. v-ix.

16. C.E. Keyes, "Towards a new formulation of the concept of ethnic group," *Ethnicity*, Vol. 3 (1976), pp. 202-13.

17. Van den Berghe, *The Ethnic Phenomenon*, p. 35.

18. Calvin Goldscheider and Alan S. Zuckerman, *The Transformation of the Jews* (Chicago: University of Chicago Press, 1986), Chapters 1, 10 and 11.

19. Ibid.

20. L.B. Jorde, "The genetic structure of Utah Mormons: A migration analysis," *Human Biology*, Vol. 54, no. 3 (1982).

21. Peter Bart, *Thy Kingdom Come* (New York: Linden Press (Simon & Schuster), 1981), pp. 255, 260 and 302ff.

22. Martin Marty, "It finally all depends on God," *Sunstone*, Vol. 11, no. 2 (March 1987), pp. 42-48.

23. Jan Shipps, *Mormonism: The Story of a New Religious Tradition* (Urbana, Ill: University of Illinois Press, 1985).

24. Rodney Stark, "The rise of a New World faith," *Review of Religious Research*, Vol. 26, no. 1 (1984), pp. 18-27.

25. Armand L. Mauss, "Assimilation and ambivalence: The Mormon reaction to assimilation," *Dialogue: A Journal of Mormon Thought*, Vol. 22, no. 1 (Spring 1989), pp. 30-67; Grant Underwood, "When Latter-day Saint History Meets Latter-day Social History: Toward a Reconsideration of the Turn-of-the-century Transformation of Mormonism," paper presented at the annual meetings of the Mormon History Association (Provo, Utah, 1984).

26. Thomas G. Alexander, *Mormonism in Transition: A History of the Latter-day Saints, 1890-1930* (Urbana and Chicago: University of Illinois Press, 1986);

Shipps, *Mormonism*; Gordon Shepherd and Gary Shepherd, *A Kingdom Transformed: Themes in the Development of Mormonism* (Salt Lake City, Utah: University of Utah Press, 1984).

27. James A. Davis, *General Social Surveys 1972-1985* (data file codebook, 1985).

28. A similar use of aggregated NORC data has been made in a recent book by Roof and McKinney, yielding 176 cases of Mormons up through 1984. See Wade Clark Roof and William McKinney, *American Mainline Religion: Its Changing Shape and Future* (New Brunswick, N.J.: Rutgers University Press, 1987). Incidentally, the four tables presented here (above) were already presented for a somewhat different purpose in an earlier article (Mauss, "Assimilation and ambivalence") and are reprinted here by permission of the editors of *Dialogue*.

29. Armand L. Mauss, "Moderation in all things: Political and social outlooks of modern urban Mormons," *Dialogue*, Vol. 7, no. 1 (1971), pp. 57-69; idem, "Saints, cities, and secularism: Attitudes and behavior of modern urban Mormons," *Dialogue*, Vol. 7, no. 2 (1971), pp. 8-27; idem, "Shall the youth of Zion falter? Mormon youth and sex: A two-city comparison," *Dialogue*, Vol. 10, no. 2 (1973), pp. 82-84.

30. Roof and McKinney, *American Mainline Religion*, pp. 131-36.

31. The tables here have all been presented in three columns to obviate the need for two sets of tables (one each for the Mormon/non-Mormon comparison and for the lifer/convert comparison). This form of presentation actually *under*estimates the similarities between Mormons and non-Mormons, since the converts are usually closer statistically to the non-Mormons. Thus, if the convert and lifer data were merged into one Mormon column (as in the Roof and McKinney book), then the Mormon/non-Mormon differences would be even smaller, further undermining the case for a distinctive Mormon "ethnicity." Also, the total (merged) sample size for Mormons would be much larger than in either of the two existing Mormon columns, thereby enhancing the statistical significance of the comparisons.

32. For further evidence of the conservatism of Mormons compared to other denominations in matters of sex and the "new morality," see ibid., pp. 211-14.

33. Ibid., pp. 192-209.

34. Howard M. Bahr, "Religious contrasts in family role definitions and performance: Utah Mormons, Catholics, Protestants, and others," *Journal for the Scientific Study of Religion*, Vol. 21, no. 3 (1982), pp. 200-17; B.L. Campbell and E.E. Campbell, "The Mormon Family," in C.H. Mindel and R.W. Habenstein, eds., *Ethnic Families* (New York: Elsevier, 1981); Harold T. Christensen, "Stress points in Mormon family culture," *Dialogue*, Vol. 7, no. 2 (1972), pp. 20-34; Tim B. Heaton, "How does religion influence fertility? The case of the Mormons," *Journal for the Scientific Study of Religion*, Vol. 25, no. 2 (1986), pp. 248-58; T.B. Heaton and S. Calkins, "Family size and contraceptive use among Mormons 1965-1975," *Review of Religious Research*, Vol. 25, no. 2 (1983), pp. 102-13; Phillip R. Kunz, ed., *The Mormon Family* (Provo, Utah: BYU Family Research Center, 1977); T.K. Martin, T.B. Heaton and S.J. Bahr, eds., *Utah in Demographic Perspective: Regional and National Contrasts* (Salt Lake City: Signature Books, 1986); J.C. Spicer and S.D. Gustavus, "Mormon

fertility through half a century: Another test of the Americanization hypothesis," *Social Biology*, Vol. 21, no. 1 (1974), pp. 70-77; Darwin L. Thomas, "Family in the Mormon Experience," in W.V. Antonio and J. Aldous, eds., *Families and Religion* (Beverly Hills, California: Sage Co., 1983).

35. Mauss, "Assimilation and ambivalence."

36. Roof and McKinney, *American Mainline Religion*, pp. 131-36. Note also in Table 16.1 that the proportion of Mormon *converts* in the South Central/South Atlantic region (22%) is double the proportion of the Mormon lifers in that region, a disproportion much larger than that in either the Pacific or Mountain region.

37. Marty, "It finally all depends on God," p. 46.

38. Richard D. Alba, "Social assimilation among American Catholic national-origin groups," *American Sociological Review*, Vol. 4, no. 6 (1976), pp. 1030-46.

39. May, "Mormons."

40. R. Laurence Moore, *Religious Outsiders and the Making of Americans* (New York: Oxford University Press, 1986). See especially the chapter entitled "How to become a people: the Mormon scenario."

41. Indeed, as I have learned in personal conversations with staff members of the LDS Church Public Communications Department, the Mormon-Jewish "ethnic" parallel has already suggested itself to them in the form of the possible usefulness of a Mormon counterpart to the Anti-Defamation League of B'nai B'rith to deal with the current anti-Mormon campaign in the United States!

42. O. Kendall White, Jr., "Mormonism in America and Canada: Accommodation to the nation-state," *Canadian Journal of Sociology* Vol. 3, no. 2 (1978), pp.161-81.

43. Mauss, "Assimilation and ambivalence."

17 Mormons as Ethnics
A Canadian Perspective

KEITH PARRY

MORMONS DO NOT think of themselves as ethnics; nor do their neighbors label them as such; and, in Canada's Census reports, "Mormon" does not appear as an ethnic option. So is talk of Mormon ethnicity a fad? Is it a device used by professors to fund their academic games? Is it a public relations ploy, subtly designed to serve the Mormon Church? I do not believe it is any of those things; but let me rebut my own questions with an account of an incident that occurred while I was doing my first spell of anthropological fieldwork on the Blood Indian Reserve. Quite literally, the reserve is across the road from Cardston—the town founded in 1887 by Canada's first Mormon settlers. Twenty years ago, a handful of Bloods, a Catholic priest and I were sitting in a schoolroom on the reserve, ostensibly talking about co-operatives though our discussion ranged over various Indian issues as they came to mind. When we spoke of integration, an Indian stepped to the blackboard and made two marks. Here, he explained, were a Blood man and a Blood woman. He made two more marks, for a Mormon man and woman, then a final pair of marks that stood for a Hutterite couple. This is the way integration should be, he said, completing his diagram (see Figure 1).

The man at the blackboard argued that integration should not include intermarriage. But I do not wish to reiterate his position. I want to note instead that, in his argument, this man treated the Mormons, the Hutterites and the Bloods as three peoples. In contrasting "Blood" with "Hutterite" and "Mormon," he presented the latter two as ethnic rather than religious identities. Of course, I knew at the time that, in other contexts, Bloods identified Mormons as members of a church—only a few weeks before, a dead

353

Blood Indians from the adjoining reserve on Cardston Main Street, c.1917. NA 4611-27
Glenbow Archives.

Chief Shot-on-Both-Sides flanked by other prominent Bloods, presenting cheque to the
Canadian War Services Fund, 1941, in presence of local civic, educational, religious and
Indian administrative personnel, on steps of Cahoon Hotel, Cardston, Alberta. ND 27-61
Glenbow Archives.

Blood Indian
Man and Woman
o o

o o   o o
Mormon   Hutterite
Man and Woman   Man and Woman

FIGURE 1: A Blood Indian View of Integration

man's relatives had argued among themselves as to whether the Mormons or the Catholics should bury him. So, for me, the blackboard presentation pointed to the complexity of the Mormon identity, and even to its ambiguity: Mormons were to be thought of both as a people and as a church. This insight—however commonplace—allowed me to make better sense of my data. I had been documenting the work of Mormon missionaries on the reserve, and had observed that their successes were infrequent and hard won. I had seen, too, that Indian converts and investigators were often pressed by non-Mormon relatives and neighbors to sever their connections with the church. Though the missionaries brought religion, Bloods were likely to perceive them as the emissaries of a locally dominant ethnic group that had set out to serve its own secular interests. From this standpoint, converts and investigators appeared to other Bloods to be abandoning their own people.[1]

Now, embedded in the preceding argument are three points that deserve to be examined critically: that Mormons are a people as well as a church; that, on this account, they are to be thought of as ethnic; and that it is analytically useful to think of them in this way. As to the first of these points, I have suggested that, while Bloods certainly recognized Mormons in their religious aspect, the Indian at the blackboard implicitly accepted that Mormons were also in some sense a people like his own. That he should have done so is perhaps not surprising, since Mormons do speak of themselves as a people—this people, a peculiar people, Zion's people, for example. Visiting a ward meetinghouse, some students of mine were startled by a wall of posters that announced, among other claims, that "Zion's people quicken the pace" and "Zion's people are best." But these students were no less startled by a row of portraits on the opposite wall: first Jesus, then Joseph Smith and an appropriate sequence of prophets up to the present day. On the two walls, the duality and the complementarity of the Mormon Church and the Mormon people were explicitly juxtaposed. The same duality is expressed in the Mormon calendar: April 6 is a religious celebration, a celebration of Christ's birth and of the restoration of His church; July 24 is a celebration of the Mormon people, focused as it is upon their pioneer antecedents. Certainly, those Mormon pioneers were dedicated to the church, but on that day it is they who are honored for their faith, courage and endurance. Through the calendar, and in other ways, Mormons have ritualized their history in order to represent it to themselves—and so, in April and July, they celebrate their duality as a church and a people.

In passing to my second point, I should begin by noting that it is hardly original of me to conceive of ethnicity as the feeling of being a people. A number of writers have adopted such a definition. Referring specifically to the United States, one among them says:

> When I use the term "ethnic group"…I shall mean by it any group which is defined or set off by race, religion, or national origin, or some combination of these categories. I do not mean to imply that these three concepts mean the same thing.… However, all of these categories have a common social-psychological referent, in that all of them serve to create, through historical circumstances, a sense of peoplehood.[2]

Regarding American Mormons in particular, Dean May speaks of their "group consciousness" as he documents O'Dea's judgment that they "represent the clearest example to be found in our national history of the evolution of a native and indigenously developed ethnic minority."[3] The idea of ethnicity is implicit in Vogt and Albert's comparison of Mormons with Texan homesteaders, Spanish-Americans, Zunis and Navahos;[4] and it is assumed in the inclusion of the Campbells' essay on the Mormon family in a volume on "ethnic families in America."[5] Closer to home, the concept is explicitly employed in C.A. Dawson's study of "ethnic communities in western Canada," which deals with Doukhobors, Mennonites, German Catholics and French Canadians, as well as Mormons—all of them taken to exemplify " 'peculiar peoples' who have sought in bloc settlements to preserve their religion and their ways of life."[6]

But the writers I have just cited do not say how the ethnic and the religious are to be distinguished, nor do they tell us how the two are related—which brings me to my third point, and a preliminary caveat. I claim that the concept of ethnicity can be used to shed light upon Mormon institutions, and upon the interaction of Mormons among themselves and with others. But I have to warn that it might be better to speak of the concept in the plural, for its meaning is often vague or idiosyncratic. According to one account, out of 65 empirical studies dealing with some aspect of ethnicity, only 13 included any explicit definition of the concept;[7] while, among 27 definitions included in more theoretical works, 12 more or less distinct attributes of ethnic groups could be singled out.[8] Still, I believe that this hazy profusion can be turned to advantage, since each phrasing of the concept offers a particular view of the Mormon reality. I propose, then, to examine Mormon ethnicity from several standpoints: as a cultural phenomenon, as it relates to descent, and, finally, as a matter of boundaries. That choice reflects my anthropological background, my own ongoing approach to Mormon research, and the scanty literature that pertains to the contemporary Canadian Mormon scene. While much of what I have to say is drawn from American studies, and most of my argument applies to American Mormonism, I shall make as much use as I can of Canadian data.[9]

If ethnicity is held to depend upon cultural differences, then the case for Mormon ethnicity is a strong one—though, historically, it has been even stronger. With regard to the nineteenth century, I need only point to Klaus Hansen's study of the shadowy Council of Fifty,[10] which stood at the heart of Mormon political structure; to the various dimensions of the Mormon economy, which Leonard Arrington has examined in *Great Basin Kingdom*[11] and elsewhere; to Young's account of the radical innovation of polygyny;[12] to the manner in which the mission served as an agency of Mormon expansion, spelled out so clearly by Charles Peterson;[13] and to Lowry Nelson's study of the Mormon village, which reaches into this century.[14] As to the present, Meinig speaks of the Mormon "culture region,"[15] Francaviglia of the "Mormon landscape,"[16] the Fifes of "Mormon folklore,"[17] and so on. Connecting the past to the present, Davis Bitton points to the "ritualization of Mormon history" in pageants, parades, monuments and other forms[18]—the calendar among them, as I have shown. In these forms, history itself is a Mormon cultural artifact.

Fortunately for Canadians, Lowry Nelson's selection of Mormon villages includes Cardston, Stirling and Orton; and, as historical background to Nelson's chapters, we have studies by Lawrence Lee[19] and John Lehr,[20] which together give an account of the role of the church in the settlement of southern Alberta—describing, for instance, the complex political and economic arrangements that provided the railway and irrigation companies with Mormon labor in exchange for allotments of land designed to accommodate the Mormon farm village. As well, Lehr has described the settlement morphology and cultural landscape of Alberta's Mormon country.[21] But the most fundamental features of Mormon culture are less palpable than these, whether in Canada or in the Mormon heartland. Outsiders need never realize that Mormon bumper stickers mean what they say when they declare that "Families are Forever." Nor are strangers to Mormonism likely to understand the significance of the priesthood for the Mormon family, which might well resemble the gentile family in its outward appearance. Certainly, such strangers are unlikely to notice that kinship itself has a different value for Mormons in that it should include service to the dead, though a concern for the dead is evident in genealogical research and in the related activities of family organizations. In Cardston, for example, a cluster of Mormon families combine from year to year to send a representative to Europe to do genealogical research. Their co-operation in this task ensures that these families know each other not simply as neighbors and as brothers and sisters in the church but also as relatives through ancestors long dead.

From the standpoint of its purpose, this Mormon work for the dead illuminates the problem of the inheritability of ethnic group membership. Ethnicity is usually taken to involve an identity that is acquired by descent—a definition that hardly seems applicable to the Mormons, who proselytize actively for a church that can excommunicate its members. But the definition of ethnic identity as an inheritance begins to blur as soon as it is recognized that ethnic groups commonly recruit and lose members, by marriage, adoption and in other ways;[22] and, with regard to Mormons in particular, the definition is clearly compromised once it is acknowledged that, through their service to the dead, they hope to bring their lines of descent into the Mormon community. In effect, they offer their Mormon identity to gentile ancestors—for Mormons seek their roots, whether Welsh or Norwegian, so as to gather them to Zion.

Yet, from a different standpoint, the definition of ethnicity as inherited fits well with Mormon teachings. In the words of a General Authority:

Because the blood of Israel has been scattered among the Gentile nations, nearly all who came into the Church are in greater or lesser degree of the house of Israel literally. But if someone whose blood was wholly of Gentile lineage were converted, he would be adopted into the lineage of Abraham and Jacob and become of the house of Israel.[23]

So, for the convert as well as for the Mormon born in the faith, a patriarchal blessing will "contemplate an inspired declaration of the lineage of the recipient"[24] in the house of Israel. As a second church authority says, "It really makes no difference if the blessings of the house of Israel come through lineage or through the spirit of adoption."[25]

In a narrower view, the strong Mormon preference for endogamy will soon ensure that the descendants of a convert have pioneer forebears in some other line of descent, as well as a network of Mormon kin that can never be mapped in its entirety. Recurrently, then, the convert's progeny will be able to engage with other Mormons in a search for common ancestors, an activity that gives historical depth to the Mormon identity. Still, consistent with the view that, at the least, an ethnic identity is *ideally* inherited, "born" Mormons do sometimes distinguish themselves from converts: I have heard a wife suggest that her convert spouse was inflexible in applying Mormon values to his everyday life because he had not learned to be Mormon by experience; on the other hand, a woman who thought that a deacon's hair was too long noted also that he came from a convert family. Apparently, converts can be too rigid and too lax. In any event, on the basis of the arguments I have now mustered, I conclude that the definition of ethnicity as an inheritance need not deter me from thinking of Mormons as ethnics.[26]

I have already suggested that, when Mormon ethnicity is approached from a cultural standpoint, it draws attention to much that is recurrent, significant and distinctive in Mormon life; and I have used the specifics of Mormon culture to counter the view that Mormon ethnicity is spurious in that it is not rooted in descent. Now I shall approach Mormon ethnicity from the standpoint of the ethnic boundary and its processes. Anthropologists who employ the boundary approach hold that ethnicity does not depend on objective cultural differences but upon an understanding of *selected* differences— upon the meaning that is given to those differences.[27] To focus my discussion of this approach, I shall present a brief analysis that was written for me by a student in an introductory class, towards the end of the semester, when he had become acquainted with some basic anthropological concepts. Apart from some editing, which leaves his analysis intact, I use his words:[28]

As you walk along the sixth floor hallway of the University of Lethbridge, you will notice a set of carpeted steps in each of the hallway's five lettered sections. One set of steps may seem very similar to any other, but there are important differences in the groups of people who choose to congregate at each. The differences associated with the third set are more noticeable than the others. That set is known to many as "Mormon corner."

Mormon corner is found in section C of the sixth floor hallway, right in front of the glass-walled Media Centre. You might ask what makes Mormon corner different from any of the other sets of carpeted steps. This is the area in which the majority of students who are members of the Mormon faith choose to gather between classes and during the periods when they do not have classes.

The group of Mormon students at the University of Lethbridge represents a cultural minority in relation to the student body as a whole. This group differs from the remainder of the student population in many ways. Before they arrive at the university, the Mormon students have accepted or internalized a set of beliefs that could be called the norms of Mormon society. The most relevant norms in the case of Mormon corner are probably those concerning abstinence from tobacco and coffee. These substances can be thought of as two of the taboos of Mormon society.

We could also think of this cultural phenomenon in terms of structure and antistructure. If we look at the Mormon students who congregate at Mormon corner as a structure, we will notice a set of related statuses. First is the status of "member" or simply "Mormon." Outside of the structure is the status of "non-member" or "non-Mormon." There is another status also, termed "inactive" or "Jack Mormon." An individual who has this status is probably best described as between structure and antistructure. He is a Mormon but does not adhere to the norms of Mormon society. His counterpart in the structure would be termed an "active" or a "good Mormon."

Although it is common to see Mormon corner completely empty of smokers or coffee drinkers, there are no visible reasons for smokers or coffee drinkers to avoid this set of steps. The sanctions involved are internal sanctions such as "feeling out of place" or not being on the "in." There are several factors involved in the sanction of "feeling out of place." One is that of being the only person smoking, which is a symbol of structure elsewhere but a symbol of antistructure on Mormon corner. Another factor is language. There are words in the vocabulary used at Mormon corner that either do not exist or do not mean the same thing in the vocabulary of the non-Mormons. Such terms as institute (a place where Mormon students go for classes concerning their religion), stake or ward (divisions in the organization of the Mormon Church) may mean little to a person who is not a part of the Mormon student population. This lack of communication contributes to the separation of the Mormon and non-Mormon factions of the university.

There are certain rituals associated with Mormon corner, though they are not formal. One of these is gathering up all the ashtrays and placing them elsewhere. This ritual can be seen each time the cleaning lady distributes them—usually with a puzzled look, wondering no doubt where the last ones went. Any remaining ashtrays are usually torn, bent or mutilated in some other way that renders them almost useless. Another ritual is that each time a Mormon student walks past Mormon corner he or she is expected to stop and exchange a few words or jokes with those who are already seated there.

A feeling of territoriality prevails at Mormon corner. It is for that reason that those who frequent this area and are part of the Mormon corner culture feel free to destroy or remove the ashtrays. They refer to it often as Mormon corner as it is a common place to meet. Any new Mormon student coming to the University of Lethbridge is soon introduced to Mormon corner. Through a process of socialization, he or she begins to frequent Mormon corner with the other Mormon students. The new student soon realizes that his most common acquaintances spend much time there, and he follows suit because he feels "in place" as he conforms to the norms of the Mormon corner structure.

The phenomenon of Mormon corner is an example of a culture within another culture. Its existence shows the way in which the Mormon students, who could be classified as fictive kin as they consider each other as brothers and sisters, have formed a social network within the university.

The student who wrote that paper showed that he could interpret a familiar situation in such a way that it could usefully be compared with one that was apparently extremely different—a situation involving Mormons and Bloods, for example. So, when I place my own account of the Indian at the blackboard next to my student's analysis of Mormon corner, the latter suggests some answers to the question: Why did the Indian think of Mormons as a people? A tentative response might begin with territoriality: like the Bloods, and for that matter the Hutterites, Mormons seem to occupy a clearly defined space. As well, like the Bloods (and the Hutterites too), they are bound together by a pervasive sense of kinship—not only the fictive kinship of brothers and sisters in the church but also "real" kinship based on birth and marriage. For, like the Blood at the blackboard, Mormons favor endogamy, and their culture makes them aware of ancestral ties to each other. Then again, like the Bloods—though more successfully, both as a people and in their local communities—Mormons press for "institutional completeness."[29] In these ways and others, Mormons tend to be self-segregating;[30] and here they are served by certain symbols—among them, the avoidance of cigarettes and coffee. Such symbols might also serve their neighbors. When I began my research on the Blood Reserve, the first Blackfoot phrases I found it useful to learn were "No, I don't smoke" and "No, I am not a Mormon." At a coffee urn, I heard one Blood taunt another with "I guess you can't drink this stuff." The second man was known to be "seeing the missionaries"; so the Indian who taunted him was maintaining the boundary between two peoples.

Of course, brief as it is, the "Mormon corner" analysis can only point to the issue of boundary processes. A developed study of ethnic relations would detail the ways in which Mormons and others were systematically related: through avoidance, reciprocity, superordination-subordination, competition, conflict and so on. Much of my own research has taken this direction.[31] In a paper on the Mormon approach to the Indians during the Joseph Smith years,[32] I found it productive to envisage Mormons and Indians as members of an ethnic system in which gentiles were the third party, the better to understand the shifting patterns of alliance among the three.[33] The same basic model of ethnic relations permits a coherent approach to various aspects of Mormon-Indian relations in southern Alberta, for instance, the ambivalence that Bloods have shown towards the Cardston school system;[34] the way in which Indians used the media to recruit gentile sympathy for their blockade and boycotts at Cardston in 1980;[35] and the contest between Cardston and the Blood tribe for federal funding, a contest that brought school facilities to Cardston and "seed" money for Kainai Industries to the Blood Reserve.[36]

So, do I conclude that Mormons are really ethnic? Faced with such an inquiry, I should say that the question is not to the point. Mormons are really Mormon, and that is the reality. Still, I hope to have shown that ethnicity is a useful concept in that it highlights and clarifies the significance of aspects of Mormon life that might otherwise evade our attention.

NOTES
1. See Keith Parry, "To Raise These People Up": An Examination of a Mormon Mission to an Indian Community as an Agent of Social Change (doctoral dissertation, Department of Anthropology, University of Rochester, Rochester, N.Y., 1972).

2. Milton M. Gordon, Assimilation in American Life: The Role of Race, Religion, and National Origins (New York: Oxford University Press, 1964), p. 27.

3. Dean L. May, "Mormons," in Harvard Encyclopedia of American Ethnic Groups, ed., S. Thernstrom (Cambridge: Harvard University Press, 1980), p. 720.

4. Evon Z. Vogt and Ethel M. Albert, People of Rimrock: A Study of Values in Five Cultures (Cambridge: Harvard University Press, 1966).

5. Bruce L. Campbell and Eugene E. Campbell, "The Mormon Family," in Ethnic Families in America: Patterns and Variations, ed., C.H. Mindel and R.W. Habenstein (New York: Elsevier, 1976).

6. Carl A. Dawson, Group Settlement: Ethnic Communities in Western Canada (Toronto: Macmillan, 1936), p. ix.

7. Wsevolod W. Isajiw, "Definitions of ethnicity," Ethnicity, Vol. 1 (1974), p. 111.

8. Ibid., p. 117.

9. Using American data, Dean May approaches Mormon ethnicity in greater detail, though with an emphasis upon culture in its historical aspect, and upon the "prestige" culture of the "cultured" person in particular. See May, "Mormons." An anthropologist might pay more attention to contemporary everyday "folk" culture, or else treat Mormon ethnicity as a sociopolitical phenomenon.

10. Klaus J. Hansen, Quest for Empire: The Political Kingdom of God and the Council of Fifty in Mormon History (East Lansing: Michigan State University Press, 1970).

11. Leonard J. Arrington, Great Basin Kingdom: An Economic History of the Latter-day Saints, 1830-1900 (Cambridge: Harvard University Press, 1958).

12. Kimball Young, Isn't One Wife Enough? (New York: Henry Holt, 1954).

13. Charles S. Peterson, Take Up Your Mission: Mormon Colonizing Along the Little Colorado River, 1870-1900 (Tucson: University of Arizona Press, 1973).

14. Lowry Nelson, The Mormon Village: A Pattern and Technique of Land Settlement (Salt Lake City: University of Utah Press, 1952).

15. D.W. Meinig, "The Mormon culture region: Strategies and patterns in the geography of the American West, 1847-1964," Annals, Association of American Geographers, Vol. 55 (1965), pp. 191-219.

16. Richard V. Francaviglia, The Mormon Landscape: Existence, Creation, and Perception of a Unique Image in the American West (New York: AMS Press, 1978).

17. Austin Fife and Alta Fife, Saints of Sage and Saddle: Folklore Among the Mormons (Salt Lake City: University of Utah Press, 1980).

18. Davis Bitton, "The ritualization of Mormon history," Utah Historical Quarterly, Vol. 43 (Winter 1975), pp. 67-85.

19. Lawrence B. Lee, "The Mormons come to Canada, 1887-1902," *Pacific Northwest Quarterly*, Vol. 59 (January 1968), pp. 11-22.

20. John C. Lehr, "The sequence of Mormon settlement in southern Alberta," *Albertan Geographer*, Vol. 10 (1974), pp. 20-29.

21. John C. Lehr, "Mormon settlement morphology in southern Alberta," *Albertan Geographer*, Vol. 8 (1972), pp. 6-13; John C. Lehr, "The Mormon cultural landscape in Alberta," *B.C. Geographical Series, Occasional Papers in Geography*, Vol. 17 (1973), pp. 25-33.

22. Fredrik Barth, "Introduction," in *Ethnic Groups and Boundaries: The Social Organization of Culture Difference*, ed., F. Barth (Boston: Little, Brown, 1969), p. 21.

23. Bruce R. McConkie, *Mormon Doctrine* (Salt Lake City: Bookcraft, 1958), p. 357. Taking a more extreme position, McConkie then asserts, "That this adoption involves a literal change in the convert's blood was plainly taught by the Prophet." Ibid.

24. Ibid., p. 504.

25. James E. Faust, "Patriarchal blessings," *New Era*, Vol. 12 (November 1982), p. 7.

26. I am tempted to see the avowed Jack Mormon as one who retains the ethnic dimension of the Mormon identity while forfeiting the religious.

27. Barth, "Introduction," p. 14.

28. The original report, a commendable effort, was written by C. Locke Marshall.

29. Raymond Breton, "Institutional completeness of ethnic communities and the personal relations of immigrants," *American Journal of Sociology*, Vol. 70 (September 1964), pp. 193-205.

30. Besides such analogies, the Indian at the blackboard might well have recognized that the interests of Mormons and Bloods sometimes conflict.

31. My approach contrasts with that of Thomas O'Dea. While O'Dea grounds his most elaborate discussion of Mormon "near-ethnicity" in the dichotomy of church and people, just as I do, he nevertheless employs a cultural rather than a sociopolitical approach to ethnicity and ethnic boundaries. See Thomas F. O'Dea, "The Mormons: Church and People," in *Plural Society in the Southwest*, ed., E.M. Spicer and R.H. Thompson (Albuquerque: University of New Mexico Press, 1972). Specifically, O'Dea discerns the "elements" of "quasi-ethnicity" in "cultural content," "historical experience," "self-image" and the idea of a "sacred homeland." Ibid., pp. 150-55. Of course, the last three of these four elements might well be construed as constituents of the first, "cultural content." Then again, in considering "ethnic relations in the American Southwest," O'Dea seeks the "vital features of a system of mutual valuation" in which Mormons are participants. Ibid., p.119. Here, his concern is with ethnic attitudes—yet another constituent of culture—rather than with the processes of ethnic interaction.

32. Keith Parry, "Joseph Smith and the Indians: The clash of sacred histories," *Dialogue: A Journal of Mormon Thought*, Vol. 18 (Winter 1985), pp. 65-80.

33. MacMurray and Cunningham describe how conflict with gentiles "helped create the ethnic and religious boundaries" of the Mormon community in the

nineteenth century. Val D. MacMurray and Perry H. Cunningham, "Mormons and Gentiles: A Study in Conflict and Persistence," in *Ethnic Conflicts and Power: A Cross-National Perspective*, ed., E.D. Gelfand and R.D. Leen (New York: John Wiley, 1973), p. 205.

34. Keith Parry, "Blood Indians and 'Mormon' Public Schools: A Case Study of Ethnicity and Integrated Education," in *Education, Change, and Society: A Sociology of Canadian Education*, ed., R.A. Carlton, L.A. Colley and N.J. MacKinnon (Toronto: Gage, 1977).

35. Keith Parry, "Confrontation at Cardston: Trouble on the Mormon-Indian Boundary," in *Anthropological Perspectives on Mormons*, ed., John L. Sorenson and Mark P. Leone (Urbana: University of Illinois Press, forthcoming).

36. Keith Parry, "Hunting and gathering in the federal purse: Ethnic competition for resources in southwestern Alberta," typescript. To the Mormon reader, this topic and those that precede it might seem dismal. Though boundary studies permit Mormons to identify and respond to real problems, such studies must often appear to be pessimistic since ethnic boundaries are, by their nature, points of value disjuncture, of information failure, of conflicting interests and so on. Viewed from the cultural standpoint, on the other hand, ethnicity will usually assume a more positive aspect, as, for instance, in the study of the missionary experience on which I am now working.

INDEX